REALISM IN ROMANTIC JAPAN

THE MACMILLAN COMPANY
NEW YORK · BOSTON · CHICAGO · DALLAS
ATLANTA · SAN FRANCISCO

MACMILLAN & CO., Limited
LONDON · BOMBAY · CALCUTTA
MELBOURNE

THE MACMILLAN COMPANY
OF CANADA, Limited
TORONTO

HOLY MOUNTAIN, FUJIYAMA

REALISM IN ROMANTIC JAPAN

BY

MIRIAM BEARD

NEW YORK

THE MACMILLAN COMPANY

1930

FOREWORD

THE stream of Japanese life is rapid and an observer wishing to keep pace with its flow must rely less on libraries than on newspapers. The sources for this book, beside personal experience, have been chiefly the columns, rich in colorful and otherwise unobtainable material, carried during the past ten years by the English edition of the *Osaka Mainichi—Tokyo Nichi Nichi* and *The Japan Advertiser*. Grateful acknowledgment is here made particularly of the articles in the latter, signed "Santaro," and by that good judge of the Eastern and the Western worlds, Dr. S. Washio.

MIRIAM BEARD.

CONTENTS

PART I

THE GREAT BRONZE FACE

CHAPTER | PAGE

I. A Touch of the Exotic 3

II. Opinions, Please 16

III. The First Timers 26

IV. The Color of Life 44

V. The Great Bronze Face 66

VI. Eternal Change 80

PART II

"UKIYO"—THIS FLEETING WORLD

VII. Tokyo City—A Colossal Personality . . . 93

VIII. Human Molds 110

IX. The Social Web 132

X. Struggle behind Screens 145

XI. New Woman and Modern Man 169

XII. Geisha, Moga, and Modern Morals . . . 207

XIII. Arts and the Public 231

XIV. The Mind Makers 264

XV. Campus and Café 288

XVI. Buddhist Modernism 307

XVII. The Proud Peasants 330

XVIII. The Upthrust of Masses 361

XIX. Competition for Power 381

XX. Crimson Canopy and Paper Banners . . . 407

XXI. Gentlemen of the Opposition 429

CONTENTS

PART III

IN THE TWILIGHT OF THE GOOD OLD DAYS

CHAPTER		PAGE
XXII.	Grandparents	451
XXIII.	Where Problem Play Yields to Pageantry	466
XXIV.	From "Forgetting Windows"	486
XXV.	The Lotus and the Dynamo	502

LIST OF ILLUSTRATIONS

Holy Mountain, Fujiyama . . . . *Frontispiece*

Facing
Page

Old Costume and New Technology 46

A Champion Wrestler Casting out the Devil in a Bean-throwing Rite 50

The Great Buddha at Kamakura 68

Girls on the Ginza Buying Santa Claus 100

A Boy of the People 112

Women Driving Piles 182

In the Wake of the 1923 Earthquake 186

Royal Princesses Watching Girl Students Demonstrate the Ancient Women's Art of Self-defense 192

Geisha Celebrating the Erection of a Bridge in Tokyo . . 212

Princess Tokugawa 222

The Younger School of Writers Holding a Demonstration against Critics 232

Scene from a Modern Problem Play 232

Prince and Princess Chichibu at the Imperial Art Salon in Ueno Park 236

A Knight in an Old Play of Loyalty and Sacrifice . . . 252

The Classic Drama is a Refuge from Realism 260

An Actor Portraying a Romantic Ideal of Womanhood . . 260

Shinto Priests with Ancient Implements Performing Rites at the Sacred Rice Fields 340

The Minister of Agriculture and Forestry Visiting the Sacred Rice Fields 346

Priests of Meiji Shrine Dedicating Poems Written in Memory of the Late Emperor 346

An Arrest during the Votes for Men Campaign 364

Water Gypsies 374

A Day Nursery in Tokyo 378

Preparing a Poster for a Political Rally 382

Facing
Page

A Glimpse into Marquis Okuma's Home 388

Prince I. Tokugawa at the Opening of the Japan Red Cross
Society's Museum 412

Prince Saionji, Last of the Genro 424

Blind Man's Buff Knows No East or West 430

A Sacred Dancer in the Temple Grounds 436

An Old Feudal Castle 488

To Japanese Eyes, a Very Elaborate Interior Arrangement . 492

A Carving of Kwannon, Goddess of Mercy, at Nara . . . 504

The Sacred Deer at Nara 508

PART I

THE GREAT BRONZE FACE

CHAPTER I

A TOUCH OF THE EXOTIC

"BUDDHAS, madam? We carry them in all sizes and styles, to suit every purse. With halo—or without?" The enthusiastic young salesperson had paused, with stretched-out arm, before a counter richly heaped with the gilded and dragon-bedizened spoil of a dozen Far Eastern realms.

"A little bit of that Oriental atmosphere!" she exulted. "A snappy new note in home decoration! It would accent, madam, any nook in the library." Finding doubt on my face, perhaps, she flashed upon me the super-smile of a graduate in go-getting and chanted that last and best refrain from the sales-liturgy of New York shops: "Useful, of course, but it's good to have a touch of the exotic!"

The statuette beneath her hand was plainly what, anywhere west of Suez, is known to-day as a "curio." An image of the Hindu Redeemer had modishly been remodeled into a lamp. Out of the holy neck sprouted a rod, bursting at the top into a giant, crimson cabbage of silk, a shade fringed with long tassels that swept about the Buddha's sacred ears. Through the very body of the "Light of Asia" passed a cord, filling the two bulbs above his head with the more blinding glare of American electricity. So transformed, he was labeled no longer God, saint, savior, even devil, but mere "oddity."

Yet I recognized him. He had been no more serene on that windy day at Kamakura by the sea, when I had stood before monster petals of the lotus-flower, his throne. His

3

eyes were tranquil, as they had then been, two narrow mirrors of eternity, seeming to say: "Even so unmoved I sat in India, long ago, beneath the Nyagrodha Tree, when the blind dragon, Muchilinda, came to worship me, and the Four Heavenly Kings and Brahma bowed before my feet, while about my snail-capped head circled the five sad-colored birds. With an equal calm, my good bazaar-woman, I wait here beneath the unhallowed bloom of your lampshade. Seize this poor body of mine; hawk it for a trifle or a trinket. Dreams are not grasped by fingers, nor can a price buy me, the Buddha."

"Only fancy him in a boudoir!" exclaimed the young woman. "Indeed, he'd look smart anywhere!"

"But all day," I objected, "I have looked for something American. I want a simple gift for sending to Japan, to a Japanese woman. She's a Buddhist, immensely devout, and she'd hardly be the one to own this lamp. Haven't you some small article I could send her, very attractive—typically American?"

The sales expert looked depressed. "So you wouldn't want this brass tea-tray, with such an unusual design, the Chinese god of war? Fearfully chic. No? How about this gay little cigarette box, made out of a real mediæval hymn book? Or this luncheon cloth, cut from a genuine Russian peasant's holiday shirt? Or some Danish pewter? Or a bit of Paris glass? . . . American you say? . . . Why, my dee-ur, *we* don't carry those *Colonial* goods. All *our* things are *imported!*"

Empty-handed, as I had left so many shops that day, I walked out upon Fifth Avenue again. For untold hours I had searched down streets of the world's most sumptuous shopping quarter in vain. In all the spectacular display of more-than-Babylonian New York, I had failed to find, before the dropping of dusk, a single, simple, fitting present—all-American—for an Oriental.

The gifts, to be sure, placed in our care on parting from Yokohama, had been for the most part modest; a pair of painted chopsticks, a small paper fan, a cardboard box with delicate pattern, a wooden tray. One girl had brought a curiously shaped dried gourd from the vine above her verandah and given it to me, ceremonially in two hands, with a radiant smile. A woman had entrusted to my mother, as a token of friendship, a previous belonging of her dead son, a doll of classic workmanship—all she possessed after the havoc wrought by an earthquake. Among all these objects, not one was presented without dignity; moreover, not one could be called ugly. A country innkeeper had offered a towel, as a souvenir, such as coolies bind about their heads, but so artistic was it that, in this country, it might be sold as an "arty little dresser-scarf." There was also a cheap crockery bowl, from which a rickshaw man might eat his rice—it was so tasteful that many an American housewife could happily have employed it for a "mantel ornament." These were simple things, yet I had discovered no return for them here, as characteristic of national feeling as they.

In the days of that old sea dog, Commodore Perry, three-quarters of a century ago, the matter was not so perplexing. To the Land of the Gods, in 1853, as presents from our Young Republic, he bore, among other articles, the following: 60 ball cartridges, 2 telegraph instruments, 1 locomotive and tender, 100 gallons of whisky, 4 volumes Audubon's *Birds of America,* 8 baskets of Irish potatoes, 1 box zinc plates, and 1 barrel of whisky (especially to H. I. M. the Emperor). Deeply touched by this tribute, the Emperor and other officials shipped in return to the Government of the

United States: a gold-lacquered writing desk, a gold-lacquered bookcase, a censer of bronze supporting a silver flower, conch shell goblets, porcelain cups, flowered note paper, fine scarlet crêpe and white pongee, together with twenty parasols of various patterns.

Since the days of the historic interchange, the Young Republic has had seven decades of craft schools, museums, study endowments, community singing, little theaters, industrial art campaigns, world fairs. It was natural for me to suppose, in the lapse of such time, that American hands had produced more exquisite objects to supplement the selection of the Commodore.

Colonial ware in the shops I therefore passed by, as well as Indian baskets and blankets, for rush-bottomed chairs, pewter pots, hooked rugs, plates with revolutionary caricatures were for the most part fashioned on European models, and the more original forms to a Japanese woman would appear only sturdy curiosities. The wilderness they represent, moreover, no longer exists. I sought, rather, some small object—neither wholly primitive nor wholly "inspired" by laborious hours in a museum—so little influenced by Europe or Asia that it could convey an American "essence."

Instead, I found everywhere, in shape of fabric or vase, not America but the Orient from its highest to its most tawdry aspects. Elephant-headed deities of India were displayed as book-ends; the Chinese Goddess of Mercy as a paper weight. I saw Korean bridal chests made over into radio cabinets, and Tibetan idols, advertised as a "Little bit of the magic East," combined with a handy ash-receiver. I found skirts of defunct Manchu government officials ready to be draped across the piano to "enrich the atmosphere" of American homes. Each of these pieces was proclaimed so "alluringly suggestive of mysterious Asia" that one would

infer the possessor of a well-stocked parlor would have no
need to travel.

European influence was entwined with Oriental. As I
walked up the Avenue between rows of shops, each a warehouse of alien cultures, the windows gleamed on either side,
displaying treasure of lacquer, pottery, damask, leather, teak
representing the lives and dreams of nations from the Sung
Dynasty in China down to ultra-impressionistic Vienna,
civilizations entombed or yet in the making. A pageant of
time was unrolled behind those miles of limpid plate glass:
statuettes torn from Spanish churches, sacristy cupboards and
tapestries from French castle walls, velvet armchairs stamped
with the crests of proud Italian nobility, portraits of English
gentlewomen, scrolls from the shrines of Mongolian gods,
jewels from the necks of mummies, mirrors of Hindu queens,
cotton jackets of Japanese errand boys, rugs of Peshawar,
Cubist fancies of modern Paris.

But where was America? I felt as aloof, as foreign here
on the pavement of Manhattan, as on any of the world's
great merchandising boulevards, from the Rue de la Paix
to the Shanghai Bund, from Tokyo's Ginza to Unter den
Linden and Bond Street. Even at home, as surely as beyond
the Atlantic or Pacific, I was still globetrotting. Strange cultures overlapped around me, in layers more numerous than
the stories of New York's highest skyscraper. Was there no
bric-a-brac I could buy without recalling a Tartar prince,
no tweed garment without a reminiscence of a Scottish
clansman's plaid? Had I returned, indeed, at all from
travel? Or must an American remain in spirit forever
abroad?

A curious sense of isolation possessed me. I could not
look at the fragments of European civilization, whether the
stucco cherubim or Renaissance candelabra, as any more, or

any less, a part of the American scene than the Oriental. I
felt both Orient and Occident were far away, their harmonies oddly clashing with the rhythm of this third sphere
of ours which deserves, from circumstances of its discovery,
a new name—the *Accident*. I realized what had haunted me
during all my months of travel—I was, geographically, an
Accidental.

Europe and Asia, enemies as they are, I had seen as parts
of the same thing, as neighbors on the same gigantic land-
block, even though standing back to back in mutual dis-
trust. In much of their spirit, their history, their suffering,
their dreaming, and elaborate edifices of thought, they bear
a closer resemblance to each other than either bears, to-day,
to the newer continent between.

It is indeed impossible to extricate East from West in parts
of Europe, in Russia and the Balkans. In the melting pots
that boil around the Mediterranean, Greek, Goth, Persian,
Norman, Armenian, Hebrew, Gaul, Roman, Turk and Saracen have been mingling for two thousand years and more
their liturgies, alphabets, cornices and domed basilicas, philosophies, religions, illuminated manuscripts, designs of
vines and serpents, images and symbols, ecclesiastical vest-
ments and incense burners, poetry and arithmetic, spires and
frescoes. Their history can never be wholly separated, so
closely was it interwoven time and again: when Alexander
marched to India; when Roman eagles stretched over the
Tigris; when Chinese emperors rode in chariots through
Turkestan to the Caspian Sea; when Arabs swarmed across
Gibraltar; when crusading knights assailed Jerusalem; when
Napoleon faced the Sphinx. Dragon, Eagle, Crescent, Cross
have fallen, risen, succeeded one another, and the end of
the epic is not yet.

Every year, by archæological expeditions, still other meeting-grounds of East and West are being recovered from their crumbling mounds. German scientists have laid bare at Turfan and other ruined cities in Turkestan the astonishing culture-centers that served, centuries ago, to bring Greek and Persian ideas into contact with Chinese and Hindu; centers from which the roaming tribes carried designs and handicraft models into northern Germany. The links, so long missing, between the Serpent of the Vikings and the dragons of Old China, between the pointed roofs of Japanese pagodas and German Gothic guildhalls, between the key-pattern on Tibetan scrolls and Greek vases are gradually being forged again by students such as Josef Strzygowski. British spadesmen are bringing to light, in the Indus Valley, cities like Mohenjo-daro, flourishing 3,500 years before Christ, until now unknown to history. We are invited to imagine a broad range of high civilizations that once formed a gorgeous span between Egypt and India, with branches reaching out perhaps to China, the South Seas and Japan. We are only beginning, in this decade, to wonder what *is* East and what *is* West.

A Continental man, therefore, who journeys East to-day, is really not altogether outside his own world, as he may suppose. He finds, in the Orient, other nations accustomed like his own to take life at a leisurely pace, to appreciate the tragic more than the happy ending, to consider wine a legal drink, to exalt art as an adult occupation, to sleep with the windows shut, worry over the proximity of Russia, and belong to the League of Nations. The European greets, in Asia, castles, palaces, shrines and monasteries as familiar friends; whether in Italy or China, Germany or Cambodia, he encounters crumbling remnants of antiquity. There is a certain kinship about them all; in pyramids, avenues of sphinxes, bishops' castles, forlorn columns crowned with

papyrus-flowers, elephants or acanthus leaves; in mauso-
leums, arches of triumph, ziggurats, marabouts, stupas, rock
tombs, aqueducts, chapels, mosques, minarets, pagodas, or
campaniles, aged fortresses of Soochow or Avignon, Osaka
or the Rhine Valley.

The European sees mediæval handicrafts to compare with
those still lingering at home; historic dramas that in high
solemnity recall his own Racine or Shakespeare; reminders
of aristocracy and a scholar caste; roads marked with wayside images; crowded populations in which relics of folk
costumes, local dialects, or myths about pixies or badgers
survive in glaring contrast to the deep unrest of the onward-
grinding machine age. He follows the footsteps of Saint
Nichiren as of Martin Luther; of General Yoritomo as of
the Duke of Wellington; of empire-builders like Genghiz
Khan; of Akhbar as of Napoleon; of Yuei Kui-fei as of
Cleopatra. It is hard to say, of Asia and Europe, which more
mirrors the other!

The American, however, as he bustles through the ports
of Kobe or Canton, races from Vladivostock to Bombay,
steams up the Red Sea to Cairo and on to Athens, Mar-
seilles, Paris and London, is surprised at all that gigantic
panorama and most of all by its sheer novelty. He marvels
at sacred dances, thrones, crown jewels, walled cities and
meek women—things of which, in his home town, it may be,
he has only heard through Chautauqua. If he hails from
some smart suburb, where every domicile differs in style
from its neighbors, Dutch elbowing Italian Renaissance,
Louis XIV facing Stratford-on-Avon, the very uniformity
of the architecture amazes him. How strangely British the
British cottages seem! And the Japanese how ineffably
Japanese! He wonders tentatively how it would feel to be
surrounded by fellow citizens all of his own race; how he

would like to have, not fragments of fifty civilizations, but the close-fitting shell of a single national culture.

There is, unquestionably, such a thing as a purely Accidental point of view. We of the third sphere are unable to look at Europe or at Asia as they may survey each other. Wherever we go, across Pacific or Atlantic, we meet, not similarity so much as "the bizarre." Things astonish us, when we travel, that surprise nobody else. With an inquisitive awe that the European cannot duplicate, we gaze upon our first castle; the gray, ruined battlements like a coronet on some high cliff's brow are to us hardly reality, certainly not a memory, but more like a nursery dream. We watch a geisha dance; with her almond eyes and butterfly hands she symbolizes to us, as never to her countryman, "the subtle East."

Often the American pours out his humble or effusive admiration over scenes the foreigners scorn as banal, as Lafcadio Hearn frequently did; or before objects they may regard with semi-religious veneration, he bursts into such unseemly mirth as that of Mark Twain, our typical traveler, in his national tourist-epic, "Innocents Abroad." The American is capable of making a symbol for romance out of a common pair of chopsticks; again, he may think of a Korean angel only as a convenient match holder. The Accidental cannot wholly conform to standards of elder worlds; he is too profuse in his reverence, too loud in his hilarity, too remote in his age and experience.

But it is perhaps this very aloofness that gives travel, to simple Baedeker-carriers of America, its inimitable zest. This great gulf in civilizations assures us that the age of exploration has no end. If we may no longer find, like rovers of the past, hidden empires, uncharted rivers and unknown tribes, if we move on a way routed by guidebooks and checked by chambers of commerce, if all the "principal points," the tombs and museums, are marked on our pocket maps—even so, for us the era of adventure is very much alive. No agent, no tourist bureau has yet forever fixed for us the greatest "sights" of our time: the personalities of changing cities, modern nations and the thousand-branched flowering trees of their civilizations; alien hemispheres and the manner of their mingling. The epoch of physical discovery may have closed in human history; the epoch of synthesis in universal civilization has but dawned.

More and more European writers are proclaiming this modern rôle of travel. Count Keyserling has broken fresh roads for the globe-trotter, with the wide generalizations of his philosophical "Diary." Paul Valéry recognizes that "The day of the completed world is dawning. . . . And henceforth there will be an ever more bitter conflict between the habits, emotions and affections contracted in the course of anterior history and strengthened by immemorial heredity, by culture." Others, debating "What is the European mind?" "What has Asia to offer us?" "What will be America's meaning in the world?" pronounce judgment on continents and hemispheres as they pass.

The tourist, then, is no longer to be just a seer of sights; he is an adventurer among civilizations. He ceases to be a merely passive admirer of antiquity; he becomes a speculator on the future, watching the upward rush of masses in Japan, India and China, the drama of nationalism in Afghanistan or Turkey, the revolt of modern women in the societies of Peking, Constantinople, Cairo, Bombay and Tokyo, the comedy of youth, flapping in "Oxford Bags" along the Ginza, jazzing in Shanghai, dieting for slim lines in Egypt. For him the pageant of civilization manifests itself in shop-windows or in parliaments, on street corners, in temples and

bazaars, in market places of Holland or the tropic shores of
the Formosan Island, in the Javanese puppet-dances as in
Broadway farces. It is a spectacle which knows no curtain.

One of the supreme contrasts to American civilization on
the globe is Japan. In that, more than in her "quaintness"
or "oddity" lies her worth to us, as tourists. She presents a
powerful opposite to all we have seen or thought before.
Her civilization rests on a foundation which is the antithesis
to our own. The American way of living is a synthesis of
European cultures, modified by vast natural resources and
fabulously increasing wealth; it is the speediest, most flamboyant, most democratically comfortable. Japan's peculiar
culture edifice, on the other hand, is a composite of Asiatic
elements; it is supported by the most restricted natural resources behind any of the leading Powers; it is the most
exquisitively severe, the most delicately restrained, the most
generally sensitive that the world now knows.

When the American returns from a sojourn in Japan he
looks at his native land as if reborn. Everything from political conventions down to the custom of eating with knives
and forks seems to require a revaluation. Europe, on his
next visit, also assumes strange aspects; he can neither survey
fortress strongholds of Germany's princes of the church nor
the thatch roofs of Devonshire homes nor visit Italian opera
without awareness in the back of his mind of Oriental counterparts or contrasts he has seen in villages, temples, castles,
cities. He is haunted by remembrance. New weights are
added to his private scales of judgment.

Comparison—with all its pleasurable pain—obsessed me
as I walked slowly home up the Avenue, turning at last into
Broadway just as the electricity began to sparkle in the twilight. Wheeling streams of luminosity flashed from search-
towers above my head. Tall brooms of light swept the sky

clear of stars. Broad fans of radiance wavered before the pale features of that Victorian damsel, the moon. Cloud-reaching precipices climbed, terrace on terrace, to right and left, and on their high brink, crowned with blazing admonition, I read: "Try our Non-Slip Garters!" "Use Our Type-writers!" "Whizz, The American Automobile!" and "Bingo, the Great American Pencil Sharpener!"

Spurts, fountains, bonfires of electric ecstasy shaped the names of all-Yankee creations. Lightning of red and green urged upon me nickel plumbing, fast cars, breakfast foods, patent can-openers, downy mattresses, soft drinks. I saw here the traces of many peerless, native productions: wheat-cakes; bathtubs; jazz, the only music that laughs; the highest buildings, the swiftest subways, the quickest lunches; the most sophisticatedly humorous movies. And I paused . . . what would I among these select as a fragment of this most mechanical civilization to send to the most sensitive? What could I detach as a symbol from New York to ship, as a gift, to Tokyo?

In Tokyo the moon rides high and triumphant, as yet unsuccessfully challenged by the electricians. Even the clang of tramcars dies away in the ancient silence of the night. Far off in a garden of the city, when this evening comes, per-haps, someone will be writing a poem on a fan, comparing the lunar luster to that of new snow. Someone may be sing-ing behind a lattice in throaty quavers, to a three-stringed lute, a song of love. "Crow not, cocks! Make no stir, ravens! Let no rustle break the spell of moonlight, flooding my bamboo balcony with peace."

Festive lanterns will be lighted here and there along old-fashioned lanes. Swinging together in the easy rhythm of a summer breeze, they will form two gold lines to lead the wayfarer deeper into the dark maze of the city's labyrinth.

Above him, as he strolls, he will see the light gleaming suddenly within paper windows. Like broad squares, of rosy or silver tissue, they stand out from the dusk. Against them, as on a screen, the gesturing shadows move. Phantom people are rising, kneeling. Now the giant mound of a woman's head, coiled high with hair, looms as a distant thundercloud. Now a sleeve shudders to the ground like a black waterfall. Forever, seemingly, in motion, the apparitions are wavering, stooping, enlarging, withdrawing. Among their thousand nightly shapes in Old Tokyo I have numbered many a grotesque but never a coarse contour. Each window held a cinema-succession of pictures, here sharp, there blurred, but all flawless in linear rhythm. Each shadow was in essence Japanese, the vivid projection of a spirit that in America has no counterpart. It is an experience worth seeking five thousand miles from our own Pacific shores.

CHAPTER II

OPINIONS, PLEASE

"AND what have you come to observe?" Thus, in the chill break of day in the guise of an alert representative of the Tokyo press, mysterious Asia extends her welcoming hand.

Do not look over the railing, traveler! Out yonder the fog is streaming away in white banners. And there come the fisher-junks from the mainland, cutting their way through green water and the glint of rainbows, unfurling as they drift their slow sails of madder brown. One now turns toward you its bold, high-beaked prow; three sailors stand upon it with folded arms and the proud look of successful pirates. Come, come, traveler! This will not help you to formulate any "opinions having a vital bearing on issues of the day."

And this you must do. Perhaps you have been brought up with the idea that the whole duty of the traveler is merely to travel. Perhaps you thought you were coming to Asia, not to inspect the progress of feminism but to see a woman— O just any woman!—wearing a kimono; and maybe you were on the point of rushing off, not to study the traction situation, but to ride the nearest rickshaw. Crush down these innocent thoughts, traveler. You are four centuries too late.

Batteries of ogling cameras face the missionaries and the merchants alike. Eager and agile young men, armed with fountain pens and pertinent questions, dart around, begging them to straighten their hats and grin, to give some "views" on the Christian prospects, the volume of sales of kerosene, the matter of Philippine independence, skylines, and what is thought of Japanese immigration.

"Are you interested in our woman movement?" asks one inquisitor, with the shrewd and quick glance that distinguishes the professional reporter of either hemisphere. "Will you collect data on our labor problems?" "What is your outlook on music and disarmament?" "How do you like Yokohama, as you see it now?"

No use to pretend that your purpose is frivolous; that you have little, if any, knowledge about the rising East. Asia has long stretched out her splendors passively to *be* traveled, to *be* discovered by the Westerner. But at last Japan rises up, stop-watch in hand, and confronts the would-be explorer. "Come now, Mr. Balboa, what do you visit us for? Have you some impressions of Progress in the Pacific? What do you think of the future of transportation? For mercy's sake, Mr. Balboa, are you going to stand like a statue, perfectly mum, on a peak in Darien forever?"

A narrow plank is the shaky bridge between the two hemispheres. And no traveler, without a new and deep excitement, can go down it, step by step, and set foot firmly on the Orient. Above him the red, rayless morning sun bursts through white mist, as though on a giant Japanese flag. On the pier he recognizes rickshaw men, squatting in the tilted shafts of their carriages, reading hieroglyphic newspapers or smoking brass-headed pipes. And then the chaos of an alien world engulfs him. As he speeds up the crowded streets of Yokohama by auto or by coolie the fantasies of his dreams whirl by on either side: women with flapping sleeves, dragon-curved roofs, lanterns and signboards splashed with gorgeous characters of Asia's calligraphy, balconies hung with airing garments, flaunting acrid rose and arsenic green, ocher and crimson and blinding purple—the brilliant colors of the true Orient indeed.

Like a mad shuttle the vehicle weaves between the hiero-glyph-emblazoned telegraph poles in the middle of the avenue, dodging bicycles and rickshaws and mothers with babies bouncing on their backs. From the sunlight it shoots into a hollow, dark cavern of a station, whispering with the soft *susurrus* of Japanese speech and echoing to the clop, clip, clickity-clack of countless wooden shoes—a thousand pieces of chalk squealing on a giant blackboard the first bars of the great symphony, the Song of the Wooden Shoes on Modern Pavements.

The train to Tokyo is an ordinary train; but even Alice-in-Wonderland had no stranger companions than its passengers. A gentleman sits across the way, wearing a brown silk kimono, a Western straw hat and patent-leather shoes. Beside him, a bundle of cerise robes, cuddles a bright-eyed baby. An ancient woman, whose face might denote a hundred years of melancholy experience, slips off her sandals, and, kneeling on the seat, lunches with chopsticks on rice, pickles, and tiny white fish with blue eyes. And yonder sits a maiden in dark blue robes, with waves of glossy, black hair piled, pompadour-fashion, above her thickly white-powdered face; from a folded silk kerchief she takes out a movie magazine.

Outside the window, the scenery rushes by. The peak roof of a temple is gone before the eye really recognizes it; a white gate; a factory with a tall chimney marked in cabalistic characters like Cleopatra's obelisk. Trainmen announce the stations alternately with little boys calling Eskimo pies. *"Hinagashi Kanagawa-a-aa!"* one cries. *"Isu-curemu!"* the other shouts. *"Shinagaw-a-aaa!" "Ise-curemu! Isu-curemu!"*

After the pier Tokyo Station is the second official stage in the progress of Japanese hospitality. It is here that the

fourth largest capital city in the world receives her foreign
guests. Every season they come in larger throngs: delegates
from California to business conferences; baseball heroes
from Chicago; medical specialists attending a congress on
tropic diseases; the artists, dancers, musicians and lecturers
of Europe; the new ambassadors; the scholars of India and
China; more than 5,000 American globe-trotters every year.

On the day we arrived, there were many committees of
reception. Japanese Christians had come to welcome the missionaries. Branches of commercial clubs took charge of the
business men. The air was thick with the clicking of camera
shutters and the boom of flashlight powder. One committee
was headed by our host, then Mayor of Tokyo, Viscount
Shimpei Goto, very much that day the figure of a European
statesman, in frock coat and black-ribboned spectacles. With
him were friends, some in light Western palm-beach suits
and straw hats; others in suave black silks, stamped with
heraldic crests. It was Viscount Goto who, years before, had
supervised the designing and building of the Tokyo Station,
that dramatic Oriental point of arrival and departure, where
great pageants of humanity have been staged.

Chinese abbots, for instance, yellow-robed and greeted as
"Reverend" like so many Christian divines, came here as
delegates to a Buddhist conference. They were met at the
platform by other reverend Japanese, presented with the
Buddhist Year Book, and taken on tours to leading temples
and to an exhibit of sacred relics at the Imperial Museum.
Red flags, two years later, blossomed before the station.
The Soviet labor chiefs came marching out, singing, to be
received with orations. A thousand policemen battled to hold
in leash the swaying, milling crowd of Japanese working-
men who struggled to welcome the visitors. And again,
in 1922, the American Ambassador, Cyrus Woods, after the

earthquake, left at this point for home. Emotional throngs filled the plaza until no room was left to walk or move; in solid masses they stood weeping, answering the tears that stood in the Ambassador's eyes, as he departed from the people in whose tragedy he had shared.

For all her guests—and they are as diverse as those of any metropolis on earth—Tokyo has her popular outbursts and her rituals of hospitality. Many of the ceremonies she has adopted from the West: limousines, flowers, and frock-coated welcomers; salutes of guns; the entwined flags of the visiting nation and the Sun; dinner parties at select hotels with addresses and handclapping; theater and monument viewing; symbolic gifts; unveilings; lectures, movies, interviews; siren whistles from tugboats in the harbor; exhibitions in medical colleges, labor schools, art academies; presentations of university degrees or royal honors. You can mention few rites that are absent from the long program of modern international entertainment which Tokyo supplies no less than New York, London or Paris. Much, however, of her courtesy is purely her own: chrysanthemum parties in the Imperial Palace grounds for visiting officials; geisha dances for the business man; tea ceremonies for his wife and daughter; rounds of temples and shops for the tourist; festivals and celebrations for all. Japan is very rapidly developing that class of persons who specialize in international reception. Men and women are giving up the traditional reticence toward strangers, entertaining them in their homes as guests, acting as guides, chairmen, or after-dinner speakers on amity among nations. The whole complicated modern machinery of good-will fostering between countries is there in motion.

But Tokyo Station has yet another significance, for it is here that Orientals, in full possession of their ports, harbors, and railroads, welcome the aliens of the other hemisphere as equals no less than with the pomp and panoply of their accustomed ceremony.

Western ceremony, did I say? I was very wrong. Where did we of America get our basic forms of reception and ceremony? From European courts. And where did Europe acquire her technique of display? To a great extent, from old Constantinople, under the Byzantine emperors, in the days of her Greek-Oriental magnificence. Wondering barbarians of Europe came to the Golden Horn, saw the "Streets draped with rich stuffs, candelabra burning on every balcony, wreaths of laurel, torches and flowers" in honor of triumphing generals; they watched the games at the Hippodrome, the liturgies of priests, the processions with flags. And they went back to their Northern forests with the mechanics of ceremonial stamped on their rude minds; on this basis developed the pomp of France and of all Europe after the Crusades. It is part of the humor of history that we of America have learned largely from the East our public behavior; how to extend the glad hand to Queen Marie of Rumania, how to decorate the halls when Rotarians foregather, how to inaugurate Presidents or celebrate the Fourth of July.

When we go to Japan to-day, we are returning to the hemisphere that taught our uncouth ancestors their manners, the fundamentals of their public life. If we find that Japan has "borrowed" from us certain ceremonies, let us remember, with sufficient humility, that we learned a generous measure of them ourselves at the gates of Great Byzantium, in the days when Greeks, Armenians, Persians, French and German knights made obeisance before the jeweled throne of the "Emperor of the East."

By rickshaw or by automobile, at the enchanting time of dusk, it is customary to take guests for a spin in the streets.

And between the fragmentary visions that they catch and the explanations of their hosts, their first "impressions" of Japan present a composite picture something like this: Silver castle on a wall. Swoop, swoop under a scarlet gate. Old man walking majestically, arms folded on breast, right in the way—he wears a union suit with a pink sash. Have you heard about the new branch of the Rotary Club here? Lantern waving, waving, nearer, nearer, why, it's on a bicycle handle! You really must visit our Radio Exposition tomorrow. A moon-shaped bridge. Tombs reeling in a common bed of moss. And what a grayness, what pale mist, and silhouettes in deeper grays and blacks! A gnarled treebole. A woman with flapping sleeves. Parasols like dark moons; Sumida River, overhung with balconies, aflare with the red light from barge lanterns. A samisen, complaining in the distance. This is our Ginza, our Fifth Avenue! Plate glass windows; wax dolls, fiercely mustachioed, posing in latest-fashion business suits. Limousines. Teapots on roofs. Banana stalls. Paper books. White-robed figures, statues of Grecian quietness, on distant balconies. Narrow lanes. Narrower and narrower. What do you think of our city now?

Above the roofs stands out the green shape of a temple-like structure. On the pinnacle, a Cubist angel is poised for flight, two stone wings spiring upward—and, quaint horror, it has no face!

This, the traveler is informed, is the Imperial Hotel, where he is to live. In the heart of the city it stands. Not far from it rise the glittering, electric-shining skyscrapers and theaters of the "modern" Marunouchi district. Before it stretches Hibiya Park, where chrysanthemum shows, riots and labor manifestations are held; and to the right the ancient moat and gray walls, castle crowned, of the Imperial

Forbidden Palace. The hotel then stands, neatly, between two worlds, Eastern and Western, old and new.

Lights trickle through the pillars in its walls. Fountain and pools and gardens surround it. Balconies heap and rise, Aztec or Chaldean in appearance ornamented with what seem to be pale, petrified tennis balls. Great searchlights wheel and swerve at night, casting an artificial moonshine on the gardens. In sum, it is the mixture of the two worlds between which it stands as meeting-place; it is a dream of the Orient created by an American architect, Frank Lloyd Wright—a dream in which both the Oriental and the Occidental feel deliciously out of their elements.

The spacious lobby inside is the gathering point of all the community, foreign and Japanese, tourist and established resident. It is a low-hung cavern in which spiralling staircases lead to strange little porches, where urns pour upward subdued light. There are fireplaces big as caves. The rugs are patterned with rings of concentric colors. The chairs are problems in Euclid. Electric stands hold both the lights and the heating wires before which, in winter, the inhabitants must sit closely, turning from time to time to broil the other side.

Maids in green kimono—a color startling to the Japanese who do not make their garments of either green or yellow— scutter hither and yon with a soft "Hai!" in response to hands clapped in the autocratic manner. Boys in bright green suits with brass buttons carry messages.

Foreigners fresh from the ships fill the lobby, looking all the more huge and excited because the ceiling is so low. They buttonhole one another wildly. "A rickshaw—with a lantern!" "What do you really think of the Japanese?" "I've bought a kimono already!" "George, *have* you seen the bathtubs? In little stone squares, and you come out *just* like a pink waffle, honestly."

Around the walls, sunk deep in armchairs, like spectators in opera-boxes, sit morose individuals recognizable at once as old residents by their air of detachment, of bored amusement, and the insouciance with which they beat their hands for another whisky-tansan. From time to time they smile amiably on the newcomers and say: "Yes! And how do you find the Japanese? Better note down your impressions while they are sharp!"

Smaller in stature and gayer in costume, the Japanese trail through the agitated crowd, in troops and trains, quietly gazing and staring. Octogenarians in black silks. Women, whose high pillow-like sashes, embossed in chrysanthemums of gold thread, give them a humped-over look. They move at a slow, lingering pace, and stare and stare as they go, obviously also gathering "opinions."

"They have come to see you foreigners eat beefsteak," a neighbor declares; "see you walk around the room in your dusty shoes, look at your clothes, hear jazz!"

Jazz! The same delirious strains that accompany the ships all the way over the Pacific, drift out from the great hall, blazing with light and hung with huge stone wings like those of Assyrian bulls. And in this gay arena, large-jointed foreigners caper about with tiny Japanese ladies, who two-step with agility in their straw sandals, their long sleeves waving. Tall and blond Englishmen dance with Spaniards; a German waltzes, in an archaic hop-hop style, with a Chinese girl in a stiffly embroidered skirt and jacket and tremendous pearls. It is like a casino on the Riviera—but still more cosmopolitan.

Above, in the gallery, fans of gold and silver and gray flutter in the hands of the Japanese who are standing there with eyes that shine, perhaps with dismay and perhaps with laughter or envy. Who knows? They beam down on the jiggling, jouncing, skipping, ta-ra-ra-ing performers beneath. And around them idle other observers—foreigners watching the Japanese watch the dancers of all races. Reporters busily take down any available or startling "observations on the scene" for the benefit of a vast, news-hungry audience of several million daily readers, who long to know "what an Italian prima donna thinks of Japan," and, even more, "what a Japanese wrestler says about foreign social entertainment."

It has all the fascination, this hotel, of a huge amphitheater in which every one is both actor and audience, representing his own nation and surveying all the others. And it provides for the show a suitably exotic background: peacock tinted roofs; walls stuccoed with a golden sand; tableware patterned in astronomical rings; a concert hall and theater decorated with cubistic statues of stone, suggesting headless goblins. It is a superbly impressionist picture, designed for impression-seekers from all parts of the habitable world. From the five continents and the seven seas they come—to stare at one another.

CHAPTER III

THE FIRST TIMERS

"AND just what are impressions, after all?" The baffled traveler, overwhelmed during the ensuing two weeks by the mighty flood of Asian life, begins to wonder. "At what stage does impression turn into judgment?"

Every day I had done a score of things "for the first time." The thrill of "something never done before" was offered at every turn. I slept on a floor with a bean bag for a pillow; attempted to play "Go," a chess game as interesting as Chinese Ma Jongg; heard multitudes of school children, at an open-air concert, sing that saddest and least martial of national anthems, "The Kimigayo"; failed to eat spaghetti with chopsticks; saw a Buddhist festival, homes, department stores; made the acquaintance of countless objects—bronze lanterns, gods of good luck and lacquered shoes—and of numberless individuals—bankers and schoolgirls, municipal officials and poets, labor leaders, diplomats, rickshaw men, shopkeepers, and *grandes dames*.

I had made my first Oriental genuflection. Kneeling, I touched my forehead to the smooth floor, with a cautious lookout to see whether hostess had finished her bow—for the younger or less important person, in Japan, must not be the first to raise the head. And already the strange world of Oriental manners was beginning to seem natural. The bow became as friendly as the hand-shake, and I felt graciousness, as well as formality, in the gestures and nods and kneelings all about me.

With a delight worth going around the world to experience I had entered under the wide, curving eaves of an Oriental home. The new scale of proportion that is gained from sitting on the floor, looking up to things, instead of down, began to appeal to me. Gradually the miniature gardens with diminutive trees and ponds or family treasures such as small doll-like images no longer looked so "dwarfed." They even appeared normal, especially after I was told that some of the finest objects were purposely created microscopic because, as the Japanese devoted to Zen philosophy claim, "there exists no object too tiny to mirror perfectly the Buddha."

And I heard my first lyrical song. A woman, bent over an ivory-inlaid harp, struck a shivering chord. Opening her small mouth she sent forth a series of disconnected, quaveringly throaty complaints. Again she set the strings to humming. Suddenly she had finished. I was inclined to congratulate myself on my "Occidental imperturbability."

But the second time it was different. I did not wish to laugh; the tenth, the fifteenth time, rhythm and melody seemed to pierce my consciousness and then emotion. Vague new concepts of music unfolded. I grew aware of melancholy sweetness in folk ballads such as the fisherman's "Yalu River Song," of the lithe, graceful charm in strange dance rhythms, and of a certain eerie sorrow in the crying of bamboo flutes. And at last, the sound of a humming koto-string could set my blood vibrating with fore-knowledge of the pleasure in store.

If, at each repetition of a bowing, a chopstick meal, a song or a garden, my impressions were different—"how" I asked myself, "am I ever to know what I think of these things"? Should I live a hundred years before I have the right to speak my mind on any thing? If I shudder at a song the first time, and love it the last—at which stage have I the right to describe my sensations? What *are* impressions? Are they worth anything?

Certainly, travel is more than the seeing of sights; it is a change that goes on, deep and permanent, in the ideas of living. History is handled no longer as a mere chronicle of dates but as a progression from one stage to a succeeding. So travel is no mere heaping up of episodes but an evolution. It is of constant development and not of fixed judgment that I dare to write: of the steady submersion of the ego in a stream of life.

There are phases in this process. The earliest is a sense of bewilderment in the number and variety of scenes, gorgeous, comical, or amazing, that the East presents. It seems that two weeks in Tokyo are like a ten-minute trip through an overcrowded museum. You must rush, staring and crying out, through rooms and corridors, without a pause. The feet grow heavy as basalt rocks; the optic nerves, bruised by a thousand images, refuse to register; and the mind, seeking in vain some balance in all the maze, turns round and round on itself like a kaleidoscope or a pin-wheel.

There is no connection between the things one sees on any given afternoon. A crow perched on a red temple gate. The posturing of dancers, stamping little feet in time to drums. The laughter of schoolgirls as they run over a curving bridge, purple sleeves and black hair flying. Weazened old rickshaw men looking like a colony of mushrooms under straw hats. Chopsticks. Paper festival flowers. The gilded lotus stalks of funeral carts. Ox-wains. Union suits striped red and green. Dusk, silence and the woodland cry of marriage flutes. Bicycles.

Turn by turn, the funny and the romantic compete; the saxophone and the samisen, the runabout and the rickshaw.

A stone image of a wayside divinity sits among coins scattered by the pious; on the same block, an office window displays dynamos. In a dark cave of a shop, apprentice boys are squatting, carving away their eyes and souls over crystal dragons half an inch high; yonder is heard the thumping of enormous Japanese typewriters, and the rolling of trucks full of latest editions of the evening newspapers.

Bazaars offer their procession of colors and designs; in a street full of splendors, you may select strips of gorgeous cloth, patterned with fans, drums and butterflies, or an ultra-modern affair—green giraffes standing in a yellow trolley-car track. Thus does recent invention combine with the ancient Japanese spirit of drollery.

In the morning you may visit the office of the Young Men's Buddhist Association, the ultra-modern Y.M.B.A. of Tokyo; in the afternoon, walking down a long lane of wooden walls, suddenly turn a corner and come upon a shrine and a sacred dance 1,000 years old. Fascinated children stand around; on an upraised stage, hugely padded figures in robes of angelic white, gold gauze or blood-dark red, wearing gilded masks in the shape of agony, are stamping and gesturing. And music, whining and throbbing, lifts above the beating of drums. Later, coming home at five o'clock, you may be caught in the rush hour. Clogged and kimonoed stenographers, business men and shopping housewives cling and cluster on the trolley cars until they resemble trundling human beehives.

Impressions! The word becomes inane. The great problem in Japan is to avoid as many as possible. For a few cool, dark hours at night, it seems like Nirvana to creep upstairs into bed under a white dome of a mosquito-net. Yet, even as they close, on tired eyelids the brush of the mind paints flashing pictures in which Buddhist gods, stenographers, stone lions and lanterns, kindergartens and reporters all mingle in senseless confusion. And then the bed rocks.

The weary sight-avoider opens his eyes. What new impression is this, that disturbs even the quiet pauses of the night? Suddenly he remembers that, the evening before, an old resident, a very gentle creature, had remarked: "Yes, it's been so sultry lately. We do need an earthquake to clear the air. Perhaps we'll have one to-night."

The sensation of living on a new planet—that is the second stage. "Home," "America," recede from the mind, seem farther and farther away. Nearer and nearer draw the problems and the drama of all Asia: Siam, Ceylon, Borneo, Turkestan, Afghanistan, Korea, China, and Russia the Colossus. One has a feeling of mighty and impending forces, just across the China Sea; stronger grows the sense of belonging to a new hemisphere, with a different scale of proportion, other conceptions of culture, life, family, religion, handwriting, dancing and playing. Strange senses of beauty and humor, never used before, are set alive.

Even Europe, to an American, means this in a far milder degree. Though it enrich his horizon by a better understanding of the mediæval, yet it is only family history—the story of his own ancestors or the national characteristics of his fellow citizens' ancestors; moreover, so much of Europe, the people, the literature, the habits, are familiar already— they form the groundwork of American traditions. In the Orient, nothing can be taken for granted; everything must be examined afresh, from philosophy down to paper doors. It is a true spiritual transplantation.

In the matter of beauty, for instance, the loveliness of Japan is not what is expected; it is neither the "gorgeous" East, nor the "quaint, pretty-pretty" little island. Japan is a great group of islands, in area approximately as large as

Italy, and its feudal castles and palaces breathe of power and severe grandeur. But Japan is also an unexpectedly simple place; the temples are not on every corner nor are many of them miracles of color; there are not many ornaments, high lights of splendor, in the cities; nor is the people's costume, except the youths', radiant.

One must learn, if one is to see the beauty in Japan, to like an extraordinarily restrained and delicate loveliness. One must learn to admire the subdued, cameo faces of noble-women and their dark, discreetly embroidered robes; the arrangement of just three branches of flowers at once in a room; plain, satin-sleek wood, in tones of gray and fawn; pure porcelains of moon-green without hint of design; the rôle of symbols in gesturing, in pictures, in all daily life.

A quiet charm lies in the very landscape. This may be embodied in a group of bright-clad babies, flying dragon kites, on the stone steps washed clean and shining of some forest temple; or in Shinto shrines, austere erections of plain wood and white paper. It may appear in a fleeting glimpse of purple Fujiyama, looming suddenly at the end of a tele-graph-pole-encumbered avenue; or in vistas of the rippling sea, dotted with white triangles of sails, framed by the gnarled branch of an ancient pine tree.

I had to learn to see beauty in vignettes, in half-tones; to grow into an amateur of dusk and mist, shadows at night, the grayness of fog, the pearliness of afternoon light. Even the songs are minor, and low; not to be judged by standards of the brass band.

Rain, the steel-blue, wind-blown stripes of the Hiroshige prints, calls for a special appreciation. The smaller streets become a sea of mud, a wilderness of people, hopping, plunging and striding along on wooden shoes. Umbrellas of yellow paper, by the hundreds, glow and roll, some like

cartwheels, some like gigantic mushrooms, some like miniature moons.

Wind, too, has its particular qualities. It drives the long
sleeves of little girls in fluttering purple strips like scrolls;
it tears carnival flowers from the door-tops and sends them
eddying in the lanes. And snow, the wet, thick snow of
Japan, muffles the gateposts, lanterns, and houses and turns
them into white, silent camels.

A beauty harder to enjoy is that of Japanese handwriting.
Without a little study of it, it is impossible to guess at the
mental processes of the people. One must imagine what it
means to live in a world of pictures, instead of sound; what
it signifies, when you think of a word, for instance "horse-
power," mentally to *see* an inky picture of a horse with four
splashes for feet, others for tail and turned head—united to
the character, power, a sword. One must fancy what new,
sensuous glory there can be in the writing of the human
hand, realizing that nearly all Japanese, even the rickshaw
men—for Japan is ninety per cent literate—have in their
minds two or three thousand pictures, each of a peculiar
grace. They have drawn with a brush in school "winter"
with its fine inky icicles, "many" with its fluttering strokes,
"fire," "flowers," "tea," "bamboo," each with its differing
flare. Without some study of writing, the street panorama of
Japan—the characters splashed on every lantern, banner, balcony, signboard, and coolie's coat—loses much of its
cultural import.

Other things must penetrate the senses. Ritual and symbol—in antithesis to American wilfulness—rule every action.
No woman can wear a pattern of cherry-blossoms in the
autumn; she must not hang a picture of one in her home at
the wrong season. The smallest gesture, the tying of a
string, has its right and its wrong mode.

Nor must beauty be missed in humorous settings where incongruity often tends to dull the mind. At state parties can be seen official gentlemen in frock coats, who have left their congress boots with their cylinder hats at the door, and who parade around in woolen socks. Comic? Surely! Yet the hands of these same gentlemen are the thin, nervous, expressive hands of the East and they unfold appreciatively for their guest scrolls of ancient paintings, yellowing silks with masterpieces of dragons and waterfalls.

To an American, there is something exceedingly amusing about the dignity of things feudal. When he witnesses on the stage a mediæval princeling in scarlet satin pantaloons nine feet long, he giggles; there will always be for him something artificial about the stateliest of ceremonies, the most supremely expressive of antique statuary. But he finds amusement as well in modern sights: in a western-style gentleman on a train removing his plus-fours that he may not spoil the creases as he doubles up on the seat, or hanging up in a Ginza soda-palace, beside his hat and cane, his collar and necktie.

Yet the jokes are not all on the Japanese. The sense of one's own Western absurdity expands. As I strode, big-footed, a female Gulliver, along the streets of Tokyo, I felt indescribably out of scale. My clothes seemed coarse and plain, their somber hues harsh against the radiance of flower-garden textiles; and my eye, finally accustomed to the high pitch of Oriental colors, began to find Occidental tones flat, off-key, obvious. The West has not learned how to mingle pink, vermilion, ocher and grass-green in one harmonious whole; it timidly makes most of its garments of one or two solid colors. The East knows no such inhibitions; its children wear, without being "noisily" dressed, every shade of a dozen rainbows in one swirling scheme. As lacking in complexity as his costume are the brusque manners of a democratic American.

The whole code of life is different in the Orient; nothing seems easy to do. You sit upon the floor as neatly as an untrained elephant. You spill the stuffed fish which in an unguarded moment you have undertaken to eat with novel implements. Or you find yourself committing unpardonable breaches of etiquette, such as taking a piece of cake when your hostess first asks you, instead of waiting for the third humble request. You walk through the doorway into the dining room at the first invitation almost as though you might be hungry, instead of hanging back, reluctant, until a modest host repeatedly invites you to share an "unworthy meal."

Your first tea-ceremony is half comedy, half tragedy. To a delicate little house, at the scented hour of twilight, you move in slow procession through a bamboo grove, carrying a lantern on a lacquered stick. And then, kneeling, you essay to imitate the disciplined manners of the hostess. But your own huge paw engulfs the cup and you make a vulgar clank when you set it down. A despair seizes you—as it does at your first garden party, when the host puts a brush into your hand and bids you paint a picture for him or write your favorite poem on a jar.

Luckily, no one expresses surprise at your errors. The story is told of an American who, at a tea-ceremony, broke a rare bowl, a family treasure five centuries old and flawless. Its owner, without a quiver, bowed and softly said: "Yes, yes, It always happens so to that antique cup."

Of this courteous consideration, I was most aware at my first private dinner party, a tiny picnic on a verandah at night. The gourd-vine hung its globes above, and the cicadas were crying in the garden. The supper was a be-

wildering series of pretty things, little bits of greenery in
porcelain dishes, soups of delicious fragrance served in
hot conch shells, all offered with careful, balanced grace.
Then . . . triumphantly, in tripped the hostess with an
enormous beefsteak, set the steaming carcass before me, and
beside it the steel implements, dagger and pronged spear,
with which to rend the flesh—for she wished to make happy
this carnivorous animal, her Western guest. You laugh,
reader? Would you go to all the trouble of serving choice
whale blubber for an Eskimo friend?

For one who consorts largely with that portion of the
populace known as "The Honorable Inner Chamber,"
queerer standards arise. At great dinners of state one meets
some of these ladies of the old school, their hair wound in
glistening coils, their robes precisely folded, their hands
thin and motionless on their laps, their feet withdrawn from
view, their faces still and eyes downcast—and you! Oh, how
you rattle on! You cannot keep your hands quiet, though
they are far too large to wave; your eyes roll in what must
seem to them uttermost abandon. And you will not control
your tongue—that dreadful feminine American tongue. It
works by itself.

All at once a third period breaks. It becomes suddenly
possible to be, not merely a spectator at a strange show, but
a participator. Oriental life catches up the visitor in its
swift currents; and he finds that, after all, it *is* possible to
feel at ease behind the closed gates.

Things, evidently, are happening which are more familiar,
more interesting than they are baffling or mysterious. The
headlines, shouted by bell-ringing newspaperwomen, when
translated, are quite intelligible. "Viscount Goto addresses
Boy Scouts! Mayor of Yokohama in Fist-Fight! Woman
Joins Political Club!" And, in a daily reading of *The Japan*

Advertiser with its translated editorials of the Japanese press, the public problems become reasonably clear. The *Osaka Mainichi* is discussing the new budget of the state. *Tokyo Nichi Nichi* decries Mr. Hearst's mania for frightening his people. *Yomiuri* insists that no railroad train be allowed to desecrate a cherry-blossom park by the Sumida. *Tokyo Asahi* is excited about peers in politics. *Kokumin* is wrought up about married women school teachers.

Things happen just across the street. Hibiya Park and the grounds before the Imperial Palace are the center of popular demonstrations: firemen's festivals or May Day demonstrations of 15,000 persons. There took place in 1918 the rice riots; and later, the manhood suffrage parades; open-air theatricals for the relief of earthquake victims; celebrations of Buddha's birthday, now as popular as Christmas; political meetings; movies to educate Japan's newly enfranchised millions.

The Imperial Hotel itself is a focus of activities. The strike meetings of the giant wrestlers are held here; and the halls are filled with these burly men in silk gowns, their long hair knotted in antique style. Or up-to-date geisha arrive to study foreign dancing. Or some famous European, such as Einstein, is welcomed by countless wreaths of roses and armies of eager students. A wedding in "high society" is performed at the Little Shrine around the Corner so to speak; after which the corridors are thronged with frock-coated gentlemen and ladies in ceremonial black silks crossed by golden sashes "worth a thousand dollars apiece."

Something is always occurring in Tokyo that an alien can understand: lectures in some of the numberless halls, theatrical experiments, political or labor conventions, exhibitions of modern art or ancient handicrafts. And to all these things, the interested foreigner has access. Rather than mystery, it is the overwhelming aggregation of facts that dismay the stranger in Asia.

For three major points about Japan have been too little emphasized. First, it is the Far Eastern country that can best be known. It publishes exhaustive statistics of its life, incomes, forests, industries, labor and woman movements, universities, and every phase of growth. China, in spite of the labors of foreign missionaries, business men, and engineers who have piled up impressive statistics, is still largely guesswork; no one knows even the exact population or death rate. But in Japan it is possible to secure vast masses of information—so much that it seems like an avalanche. Various societies pour it out in bulletins; English editions of newspapers are filled with clippings, translated articles, poems, editorials. And every person who calls has some new data to give—on the soap business maybe, or the personalities of actors and actresses, or the prospects of the next premiership, or the question of disarmament.

The second major fact is that much of the dim past of Asia is still visible in Japan as nowhere else. Relics of Chinese history, in music, art, drama, Noh dance and tea ceremony, that have long ago vanished from the "Republic," are preserved in Japan; even the purest and highest forms of Buddhist spiritualism may be found, though Buddhism has disappeared from India, its native heath, swallowed up in Hinduism. Out of the ten great schools of Northern Buddhism, five have gone from China; they are all alive in Japan. Stranger yet is the indubitable fact that in drama and sculpture are preserved the Greek-Hindu traditions which came across the continent of Asia in the centuries just before and after Christ. To ignore Japanese civilization, is, in effect, to neglect some of the living essence of Greek, Indian and Chinese cultures.

The third fact is that the Japanese are happy to guide an interested traveler who knows what he wants to see or study. Nor need he be "misled by propaganda" either, if he remembers that what a reactionary official will not disclose a liberal will shout, and that one must always balance opinions. No other Oriental people are so able and so eager to introduce a stranger to their life. The Japanese will lead one to relics in temples of every age; scrolls in libraries; and works in museums. They will interpret dramas that were old when Queen Elizabeth was young, played by actors trained in the traditions of Shakespeare's contemporaries. They will open feudal castles and modern labor schools. They will show costumes of the Wars of the Chrysanthemums or of the Reformation Days, ancient books of textiles or gateway patterns, fairy tales, documents. It is hard to tell which is harder to assimilate: the revelation of New Japan, with its masses of statistics, or that of Old Japan, with its treasures of history. But if one wants time and freedom to think he can go about alone in perfect safety, everywhere; participate, more than in other places, in the customs of the native people; enter libraries at will, attend meetings and exhibits, walk in all sections of the city or in country regions, attend Parliamentary sessions or dances in private homes. Japan is indeed a gateway to Asia.

Sheer novelty preoccupied me during the first weeks. I reveled in surprises; I feasted upon oddities. Elated wonder was called up by the most miscellaneous novelties: peaked roofs, slant eyes, volcanic landscapes, petrified crabs, archery and juggling, singing insects, Lilliputian trees and toadstool lanterns, the thumping of hour-glass drums or the rolling of festival carts laden with fan-dancers, images and paper banners, through the village streets on sacred days.

The whole delight of the tourist, as I then believed, lay in just this gusto for new sights, in a ravenous curiosity that is forever fed, yet never sated. Heartily I agreed with that long-dead English traveler, Tom Coryatt, who, in 1680, after a tour of Italy, set down as the chief sights worthy a tourist's eye:

> Stone tombs, great gates and manners of the people,
> Besides the height of many a tower and steeple,
> Snails, butterflies, black sheep, black hogs, and storks,
> And the neat use of eating meat with forks.

Chopsticks amused me quite as much as forks appealed to the stout Tom. I took the same omnivorous interest in whatever appeared next: in the flap-winged cranes, long-tailed peacocks, mortuary monuments, the habits of bowing and kneeling, or the length of the streams. But I could draw up no plan for the future, conceive no meaning in what was revealed. I could not see my way clear into the months ahead.

Obviously this fiesta could not go on interminably. Novelty, like poor lacquer, in time rubs off. The most curious customs, the oddest habits, grow natural after a while. Did not the wild English of three centuries ago become accustomed themselves, at length, to the "neat use of forks?" And then, after astonishment pales, what looms beyond?

The easiest solution is to leave a country the moment enthusiasm flags. As soon as a fresh sensation on every corner of Nippon is no longer achieved, it is possible to rush on to fresh ports, untried marvels, collecting more and more photographs—of pickled babies in a Chinese apothecary shop, ragged armies with parasols and rifles, hordes bathing at Benares, capering devil-dancers in Tibet, or the Himalayas at dawn. One may go on and on, until the circle of the world is closed. But what of him who remains in a country, long after he ceases to marvel? What is there in travel, beyond endless vistas of amazement? I had not paused to discover until my first ship-day came.

The arrival and departure of ships creates a rhythm in the life of Tokyo. Particularly in the Imperial Hotel, one is conscious of a change in atmosphere periodically, as the "Empress of Asia" steams away with a crowd of acquaintances, or the "Resolute" anchors with the new host of sight-starved tourists. The tempo of departure and arrival beats in the very air.

Comparatively few people stay for long in Japan. The average time limit of the four thousand yearly round-the-world tourists is from six to ten days—not more. They have time for a dash in the streets, a meal at a geisha house, and then they hop along to the next port. The business men who visit the country are always in motion, always just going to Kyushu, off for a tour in the South Seas, or freshly arrived from Russia with a batch of "inside news." Even the Japanese embark and disembark on the ships in a similar stream. They are going abroad to Oregon for a lumber conference, to study in France, to inspect colonial prosperity in Korea, to investigate traffic conditions in New York. Reception and farewell mark all the seasons.

Unused to this ever-recurring cycle of ship-days, I came down one morning to the lobby, and found it noisy with the collecting of luggage. Shipmates who had crossed the Pacific were leaving with their purchased curios and involuntary impressions. Each had a different set of objects to carry home, and each a different judgment of Japan.

The biscuit salesman hurried up to say "Sayonara!" It is pretty clear, he intimated, that the Japanese are poor business men. They took two weeks of his time, putting him off with geisha parties. They served tea to him in their offices. "Would you believe it?" Tea—in pale blue thimble-size cups—tea to him, the most hustling go-getter either side of the Alleghenies! And then at the end, they refused to buy his biscuits. Their customers had their own biscuits, they said. Simpletons! In America, we'd rustle out the advertising and in no time we'd *teach* the public to eat new biscuits or any darn things we chose. No, Japan may be quaint, but she is backward and inefficient.

The traveling salesman for a brake-lining concern took a more cheerful view. What an up-and-coming daisy of a country! "Full of Yankee pep, these Japs." Of course, they wasted a lot of his time, with tea and geishas and all like that. He felt sure enough foolish sitting on the floor. But oh boy! what a cargo of brake-linings they bought! On the whole, he believed, the outlook remains bright for this jolly little nation.

An elderly gentlewoman had found Japan quite too sweet for words; a lady-in-waiting had been gracious to her, and she carried away the most darling gifts, silver boxes, fans and a doll. A missionary, nearby, was more skeptical; he had met no courtiers but the starving peasants in the South and the half-imprisoned girls in the cotton mills. One lady had seen Fujiyama "quite near"; another had watched the black smoke of Osaka chimneys. Some one else "just loved" old Japan and couldn't see why it must "copy the West"; her friend was charmed at its progress, casting off those futile feudal ways and getting "better roads." This person adored the geisha; that person denounced immorality. Some had seen but two cities; others had visited twenty places. And off they went, with a tremendous crunching of rickshaw wheels on the gravel road—off to fresh sensations in India, China, the Philippines—and then, home.

Left behind in the lobby, I instinctively sank back into one of those deep armchairs along the wall which belong to old residents. An old resident—though he may have resided just two weeks in the East—feels profoundly set apart from a "griffin," or newcomer. He wears a relaxed expression. He feels that he has been inoculated against virulent surprise.

But on the very heels of the departing tourists, swept into the lobby a fresh wave of griffins, from the giant liner riding at anchor in Yokohama. There were dozens of flappers, scores of elderly aunts and uncles, platoons of widows, gift-trotters, retired editors and congressmen seeing the universe. And their cries of amazement were precisely what had been our own. Big, awkward, voluble, they poked about the hotel. "What, Susan, do look at that girl in the kimono! How odd!" "If you clap your hands, the waiter will come!" "I declare, I'm wild about rickshaw riding already! And have you seen the little fan I bought in the station? Too quaint, with Fujiyama hand-painted on it!" "Is this hotel Cubistic? How perfectly weird! Harry, *have* you seen the bathtubs? They are all in tiny stone squares like waffle-irons, honestly!"

I sank deeper into my leather retreat. I was shocked to hear these good people expressing thrills at mere fans, kimono, clogs. Good heavens, what a regiment of raucous aliens they seemed! How spendthrift they were with "odd" or "quaint"! Was it possible that only two weeks before I too showered those adjectives; knew that amazement? Now, already, my eyes were dulled to novelty, and in some indescribable way, I felt no longer wholly alien.

Emotion was lowering a veil before me; impressions were becoming less sharp. A Buddhist temple portal was no more a queer, distorted welter of dragons in my mind. Richly clustering associations with legends, with music and ritual, with personalities of by-gone evangelists like Nichiren, or saints like Shinran, were all creating native atmosphere. I saw the temple through this mental mist, quite as I have looked at Gothic cathedrals in France, through a haze made up of sentiments, dreams and chants or half-remembered pictures of saints on parchment scrolls. People as well as buildings ceased to seem curiosities, as I learned to know their hobbies, families, careers, unhappiness and hope. No, I was not so perpetually startled now—far more absorbed. Perhaps I had ceased to observe, so clearly and directly; but then I had unexpectedly begun to sympathize.

CHAPTER IV

THE COLOR OF LIFE

A WARM-TONED atmosphere envelops Japanese living and thinking. It differs from our own "intellectual climate" as widely as the wet skies of Holland from the windy thinness of Rocky Mountain air. Very commonly, we suggest the fact by saying that life in the East is more "colorful" than in the West.

More varied it certainly is. A racial psychology, in part more archaic and in part more highly sophisticated than that of the average modern American, holds him in the fascination of its range. He finds persons among the populace of Japan entertaining a devotion to the "horse-head" Kwannon, recalling those men of old Greece who adored a horse-headed Demeter. He encounters primitive superstitions about fox-spirits circulating, exactly as they did in Athens where a citizen who "slew the wolf might give it a sumptuous funeral, probably to avoid a feud with the wolf's blood relatives."

Yet, side by side with these mentalities running back to the dawn of society flourish the large numbers of skeptical, worldly-wise and very penetrating minds, trained in the teachings of those Hindu sages who were expounding the sublime oneness of man and the universe some two thousand years before our Good Grey Poet startled Boston with the cry: "Walt Whitman am I, a Kosmos, of mighty Manhattan the son!"

44

The mental meteorology contains high lights and shadows unfamiliar to us, gusts of unknown sensations and lulls of a curious apathy. Obedient to the feudal warrior ethics, stricter than the modern code of honor, a ship-captain commits suicide, holding himself responsible for the lost lives of his men; or a nobleman, involved in a bank crash, resigns fortune and title. Delight in nature, keener than ours, summons crowds from Tokyo, by the tens of thousands, to cherry-flower resorts in Spring, where they spread red picnic-mats, pin verses on the boughs, and dance all day. A graduating class in a school of stenography makes Shinto votive offerings to the spirits of broken typewriter keys. Vehement young men with curved ancestral swords in their hands break into a ballroom to stop "vulgar foreign fox-trotting." Feminists rally round the battle slogan: "The Sun is Female!" Skilled carpenters refuse to build a suburban villa unless a *Heigushi* is raised, a pole hung with paper prayers, dyed cloth, a fan and a woman's looking-glass and comb. Taxicabs carry Buddhist tablets as anti-accident talismans. Workmen laying sewer pipes can hardly be persuaded to stretch them in straight lines, so insistent is their hereditary love for the more artistic curve. "Part of the eternal magic of the East," is the phrase with which the indolent are wont to dismiss all such phenomena. But the energetic are not satisfied with that. What are the causes of this magic? they inquire. Is the apparently deeper "color" in Japanese life merely the rosy hue on the foreigner's own spectacles? Or is it apparent to the Orientals themselves, to poor as well as wealthy? May the toiling straw-coated farmer be as conscious of it as the knight's daughter practicing the harp on her balcony? Is it as palpable to-day as formerly, in the fairy-tale eras, when a ruler might indulge his utmost fancy: order a hill spread with white silk to imitate cool snow in summer or command a bridge of candy, an arched span of pure sugar, flung across a garden pond for his court ladies to tiptoe over?

Enchantment exists in Japan, I firmly believe, and, since it depends not on superficial signs like kimono or parasols but on the minds and hearts of the race, it will remain a long time. Westernization has not yet slain it; indeed, Japan has shown an astonishing power of assimilating foreign ways to her own spirit. Certain buildings, though of concrete, show in contour a strong Oriental taste; paintings, though on canvas instead of silk, betray a distinctly national feeling; ancient dramas flourish incorporated into the movies. While superstitions are fading of course, the religion of Buddhism itself is vital and growing to meet changing needs. Modern steel bridges are erected, but inaugurated by fan-dancing and lantern processions. A petroleum company may start a gasoline station, after Shinto rites in a striped silk pavilion have dedicated it. We need not fear that Japan will immediately succumb to machine-age uniformity.

The "color" of her life is maintained by a strong emotional character. Her people have kept much of the mediæval gusto for pageantry and pilgrimage, incense-burning and ballad-singing. Frankly and merrily, like Italians or South Germans, they indulge their genius for fiestas. They bring their traditional zest to modern sports, swarming on baseball grounds as about the wrestling ring. Throngs waited for the opening of Tokyo's first subway, embarking at dawn with babies and lunch baskets to cruise about all day in beatific enjoyment and at its close write poems on the happy innovation. They have not put on a blasé spirit with Western habiliments.

Yet this emotionalism has its darker side. As in all ancient countries, a brooding shadow of fear and sorrow hangs over

OLD COSTUME AND NEW TECHNOLOGY

the human heart. Asia and Europe both are haunted by a consciousness of the tragedy of existence; they retain the painful memories of a long and troubled historical past, centuries of battles, defiant dreams, faith and despair; both feel the pressure of civilizations now grown too old, too complex, too crowded. In the case of Japan, the shadow is deepened by keen economic distress.

Leisure for reverie, gay or sombre, does much to enrich life. And Japan is not yet congested with the ticking of clocks and watches. The slow-booming Buddhist bell does little to measure the passage of time; the Western urge for hustle does not yet diminish the capacity for long calls and longer entertainments. Efforts to rouse the nation to a "time sense" by a "Watch the Clock Day" have not quickened the common "walks of life" into a run. The people's pace in work or in play is, as indeed in much of Europe, more deliberate than an American's. Only one man, the jokers say, and he an actor, takes pains to keep time accurately. He makes it his hobby to call up radio announcers and correct their versions of the hour.

The evidence of antiquity, obviously, is another chief cause of Japan's unique disposition. Visible everywhere are the ruins and monuments that immortalize historic deeds, indicating the spot where the boy warriors of the White Tiger Band fell upon their swords rather than yield; where a dragon-god gave a hammer to an emperor; where Hideyoshi dreamed of conquest; where a dying duke penned a poem. Story-telling names are born by localities, such as "Hobgoblins' Conference Valley" or "Bridge of Three Laughters."

But much of this antique heritage is invisible. Ancestral spirits, invoked by candles and countless moss-capped memorial lanterns, hover as phantoms in the air. Traditions linger to rule conduct and naturally it is hard to weigh their influence for all possible degrees of skepticism exist. Some people will refuse to buy a straw snake for warding off lightning; yet they purchase annually a rooted strawberry tomato plant to "prevent children from growing peevish." Others deny the efficacy of simple bean-throwing against evil spirits; while they continue to make the offering of "diamond-shaped cakes and red rice pies" to their little daughters' dolls, in the spirit with which we honor Santa Claus.

I am far from blind to the fact that it has become the mode to deny this "color" to the Orient and in particular to Japan. Fashion urges us to de-bunk nations as well as their heroes. Tired of blowing bubbles of romance for generations about Asia, the West begins to prick them suddenly with indignant pen points. We recognize with our critical spectacles the famine and corruption in "placid" mammoth China; the disease under the mystic veils of India; the rags protruding through Persia's poetry; the cruelty in necromantic Tibet; the grim monotony of industrial machinery in "flowery" Nippon. But one of our chief errors has been a too vague expectancy. When we use the word "Orient" we must know what section of the globe is implied—Near or Far East at least. Brought up on the Arabian Nights, Omar Khayyam and Chu Chin Chow, the Bible stories and sundry detective fiction, we paint the whole East in terms of Asia Minor. The very name "Orient" summons to our vision pomp and blare, glass bangles and veils, raw colors and considerable tinsel, thrumming of gourd-drums and convolutions of dusky dancing-girls, all little sisters to the serpent. Our minds are stocked with names and images from "Bible Lands"; our histories frequently treat merely Turkey, Egypt and Palestine as the "Orient."

When we use the much abused adjective "Eastern" we may mean only the traceried walls of the Saracen, the harem-gardens of Persia, the pyramids of Egypt, the Arab's domed mosques. We may be thinking of bazaars in Bagdad or Cairo, of Damascus, Samarcand or Ctesiphon, the crumbled pride of Babylon and Nineveh, or Thebes, or the Alhambra. We may use the word as a synonym for the dazzling extravagance that accompanies power, forgetting that, in such a sense, New York is one of the world's most "Oriental" cities to-day. This is poor preparation for Japan.

Another good reason for many of our misconceptions is the fact that we forget there is a barbarian and a classic East. The greater part of all Asia has been overrun by nomad tribes of Central Asia, by the Golden Horde, Tamurlane, Genghiz Khan, the Arabs, the Seljuk Turks, the Kurds, the Manchus and Khitan Tartars. Spreading their savage splendors, tribal music and legends, love of bright hues and heavy jewelry—the "new-rich" taste of the barbaric conqueror—they have trampled much of classic Asia under their horses' hoofs. Japan is one of the few corners of that hemisphere to escape invasion; it was her peculiar good fortune that the Mongol armada was shattered on her shores by "divine winds" and valor such as dispersed Spain's navy on the coasts of Elizabethan England.

It is the classicism of Japan which one learns to value—that severely good taste and sober charm, such as ancient India, old Hellas, or antique China must have possessed. Her theater is not half so gaudily sensual as a Broadway extravaganza; its moral atmosphere would have suited our Pilgrim forefathers. Moderation is the essence of her art; her painters would make a single pine cone symbolize a forest; her poets condense their dreams into thirty-seven syllables. Her courtesans are more demure in manner than

many a fashionable London sub-deb. Her music, compared
to the blare of a jazz band, is but a low, melancholy thread
of song.

Japan is a living museum in which we may divine what
China must have been before the Northern invaders subdued her to their mood. China's greatest painter, Wu
Taotzu, for instance, is known to us chiefly through copies
now in Japan. No building in China "earlier than the eleventh
century A.D. is known to be extant to-day"; yet Japan has a
surviving temple founded in 586 A.D. The musical dramas
now heard in Peking were probably "introduced from Central Asia in the wake of the Mongol conquerors"; but in
Tokyo we may listen to music much older, more nearly like
that Confucius recommended for the education of a gentleman. Moreover, Chinese motion pictures made in Shanghai
often show, as a background for their historical plots, a life
startlingly akin to that of contemporary Japan but far removed from that flourishing in China. In a certain cinema
house on Pell Street, New York, the shadows of an antique
Cathay are occasionally revived—people who wear kimono,
soft and flowing as the Nipponese; houses of the frail design of Japan's country villas, with open verandahs, the
simplest ornaments, screens in quiet patterns and nobly
proportioned vases. The inhabitants kneel on the floor
as do the Japanese. In short, the age is resurrected in
which China taught Japan the fundamentals of her civilization.

Not only does classicism strive with modernism in the East,
but so, too, does puritanism with love of display. The same
conflict in tastes which has raged throughout the Western
world, between Roundhead and Cavalier, New England
divine and Southern fox-hunting squire, Boston and Coney
Island, has always divided the Oriental peoples. Like the rest

A CHAMPION WRESTLER CASTING OUT THE DEVIL IN A BEAN-THROWING RITE

of humanity, they are torn between ideals of frugality and luxury, repression and expansion, high thinking and fast living.

If one comes to Japan expecting to see a "luxurious Orient" he will be impressed, instead, by this conflict which greets one everywhere in the Empire. The scarlet and ivory peony-gates in Nikko are like a glaring foil to the bare wood and thatch of a lowly hermit's hut in some remote ravine. The "moral pantomime" of the Noh, presented by aristocratic amateurs, is the complete antithesis to the "Pageant of Paris," presented by Osaka "Follies" girls. The Zen scholar looks at life with a faintly ironic skepticism; he ignores gods, prayers, ritual or doctrine. But the follower of Shingon re-quires litanies, perfumed water, haloed images of the Merci-ful Goddess, rosaries and dancing. This eternal duel of standards has been fought in monasteries, palaces, camps and cities of the nation for a thousand years.

Certainly there are at least two Americas, one of the re-former and another of the cabaret-devotees. Greece contained together the mystic frenzy of the wine-god's followers and the calm of the Apollo-worshipers. Christianity has in-cluded both the majesty of the Catholic Church and the simplicity of the Quaker sect. Mohammedanism has covered alike the puritanic Wahabi and the carousing Barmecide sultan. So it is no wonder that there should exist in Japan, side by side, the *"buke"* and the *"kuge"* factions; the rugged habits of the warrior and peasant and the luxury of the merchants and nobles.

Two cities, Tokyo and Osaka, embody this dualism. In Tokyo, the social tone is still largely given by a governing class which preserves much of the outlook of the samurai age. Feudal knights who ruled the nation for the three centuries developed their own ideals, exalting martial virtues, thrift, temperance, loyalty. They disciplined their bodies with fencing, their manners by the tea ceremony, and their minds in Zen philosophy. Abhorring display, they would not visit a popular temple or theater; the penalty for entering a geisha house was severe under the laws, and the stigma of engaging in trade was indelible.

The proud daughter of a samurai, wife of a deceased artist, found her home enveloped by the great Tokyo fire of 1923. She had a moment in which to save something from her burning house. Should it be a sketch of her late husband to preserve as a memorial or, as a crass materialist might have done, to sell for a little food? No, instinctively, as became the child of a knight, she rescued only a cheap photograph of the Empress. It is this spirit that the descendants of ruling and fighting men still uphold as the supreme expression of nobility of soul.

Stern tastes then are found among many persons of the upper strata of Tokyo. The tea house of an "elegant" is a simple structure, a meager assemblage of straw and bamboo, without hint of carving or gilding. In essence, it is a rarified peasant's cottage. Warrior and peasant in Japan were, in Spartan simplicity, more akin to each other than to court-noble or merchant. The wielders of power adopted, from choice, the tastes that were forced, from necessity, on the toiling masses of farmers. And it is neither among the older aristocracy nor among the rural people that one can hope to observe that celebrated "Oriental luxury."

In Osaka, however, a splendor built on commerce flourishes with increasing vigor. The merchant princes are more and more open-handed with largesse, bequests to charity or art; above all lavish on private enjoyment, automobiles, presents, parties, and the theater. Women of Osaka are noted for the bright hues of their kimono and the liberal use of rouge. In Osaka the irrepressible bourgeois are now ruling the place.

Merchants have for the past three centuries wielded a growing influence on Japan's standards. During the "age of peace" they were outshining the nobility in Tokyo with finery, golden doll furniture, costly pipe ornaments; they developed a theater and a tea-house system to please themselves. But this "Vanity Fair" of old Tokyo, as it has been called, is steadily being transferred to Osaka. And as formerly puritanic samurai strove to suppress the carnival spirit of the merchant, so to-day Tokyo competes with Osaka for supremacy over a nation's ideals.

Obviously, therefore, opinions must forever clash about the "sorcery" of the Orient. It cannot be explained in a word; it exists in innumerable forms. There is an enchantment peculiar to the Far as well as the Near East. Asia draws us to her with a barbaric magic and a classic; a primitive and a sophisticated; a martial and a mercantile.

Americans, we constantly hear, are "materialistic" and devoted to "mere things." The rest of the world, it is assumed, is somehow above this worldliness, grown spiritual, protected by its texture of culture. I believe that the exact reverse is true. Asia and Europe are "civilized" precisely because they have a keener sense of "mere things," a better evaluation of sheer materials than most Americans. They care more for mundane objects, investing them with poetic tradition, legend and association. They are the connoisseurs in "things," such as damask and oak, linen, lace and cloisonné. The creation of such cults is, with us, just beginning.

European women, for instance, retain much of the ancient feeling for goods that we have lost. The *Hausfrau* knows her silver, her quality of dress goods, her embroidery. Both French and German men are proud of expert discrimination

in fish, sauces, tobaccos, wine and breads. They talk about
them more. The farmer, as well as the bourgeois, appre-
ciates his goods intensively—has he not, in crowded regions,
carried the very soil of his vineyards uphill? He knows every
tree, every plot of grass, every tiny stream in his neighborhood. In the forests of Europe every twig is carried away for
use, every spare limb lopped off. The feeling of the people
for flax, oak, pottery is not yet sunken under a flood of mail-
order goods of machine production. Out of this atmosphere,
this sharpened appreciation of material values, this tactile
sense, this sensory background, comes European "culture,"
in part.

And Asia in many ways has a finer and more sensitive feeling than Europe for "mere things." The Japanese are exceptionally responsive to the most delicate phenomena of
nature: the shapes of leaves, globes of dew, the pointed
shadows of birds, the cones of mountains and the triangles
of sails on the horizon. Even the cotton kimono, worn and
old, is, in design, compared to cheap Western fabrics, actually
distinguished. Many a kitchen-maid's apron of Tokyo could
serve as "cushion cover" in the West; the errand boy's jacket
is worn by fashionables at Palm Beach. Poor city dwellers
keep a potted tree or a bowl of goldfish to satisfy their
æsthetic nature; the chrysanthemum shows are thronged by
rickshaw men and simple housewives, all floral worshipers.

I do not mean that the Japanese are more sensitive than
we to everything in life. They have far to go, for instance, in
the humanitarian treatment of animals or care of lepers. Yet
this division in sensibilities is not strange. Large sections of
London in Elizabeth's day were insanitary wallows; her
citizens were less appreciative of paved streets than they were
of the gleaming words of Kit Marlowe. Much of Europe,
a little while ago, thought more of architecture than of

peace. Many an American is more appealed to by bathtubs than by clean politics.

What Japan does signify is an older society with a clearer perception of art. It seemed to me that I had never known the meaning of color, until the day I watched, on the Tokyo stage, an armored warrior dancing—flash of green and silver against a pine tree trunk. I had never before grasped the serene contrast of old ivory against black lacquer; of scarlet brocade on new straw mats. I became conscious of so many materials and surfaces: pineapple silk, scarlet crêpe, blue cotton, tiles damp with rain. I understood the fondness of a people for paper—in which they have tutored the West— of a hundred kinds, pebbled, film-thin or cream-thick. I observed subtlety in fawn or amber hues, such as we have only recently introduced into our clothes. I began to notice the lines made by gestures: the hands of a tea-master as he proffers the bowl; the slope of a lady's head as she bows; the crisp lines of kimono sleeves falling exactly as in prints. Just as rural England gave me a new feeling for homely things like pewter, hedges, vine-clasped stones; just as in Germany I learned the beauty of weathered oak-carving, of gorse in bloom; so Japan meant to me an enormous increase in appreciation of objects—a new spiritual-materialism.

This direct, clear grasp of life, which has been the property of ancient peoples, is rapidly losing its force. It has departed from craftsmen of Italy and Armenia; and from the rug makers of Central Asia. The machine age is destroying their once close contact with the earth, creating a new type of materialism. What we see in Japan is one of the old wellsprings of beauty, once widespread over the world, but everywhere drying up.

To make much of little—that is one of the secrets of Japanese civilization. Life has been mellowed by attaching to its every phase from the cradle to the coffin some legend, sentiment, verse, proverb, or symbolic gesture. As in all very old countries the visible world is surrounded with an invisible aura of precious associations.

Certainly, it does enrich life if everything seen suggests a dozen others, no matter how irrelevant. If you buy rouge, to know it is more efficacious bought on the Day of the Ox. If you see a crab, to recall the Heike family who, after the battle of Dan-no-ura, flung themselves into the sea and became crabs. If you hear the number four, to think of "the four elements, earth, water, fire, wind," or "the four troubles, birth, old age, sickness, death." Nearly every mountain has its genius of the place. The humblest as well as the highest is related to the divine. Many were formerly so sacred that no woman's foot might be set upon their peaks, but to-day it is said that only one is denied to ᵗʰe feminist climber.

The Japanese spirit has enveloped the smallest objects with a reverence that has enhanced them all. The connoisseur of cricket-singing knows the difference between a bell or pine insect and the music of the grasshopper. He invests the little creature with the dignity of ceremony; annually, crowds of cage-carriers fill the gardens in Tokyo, walking at dusk along lantern-lit avenues to the open, grassy levels where the insects may be freed. Their song, it is said, is in praise of the "Seven Flowers of Autumn."

Nor is passage of time just a series of calendar dates; it is a religious procession. There are days set apart for running through the streets in penance; days for purchasing badger images, fireworks, a new sash or a broom. The most auspicious time for repairing the house is in December when master and wife, children and servants join in dusting paper walls, mending and polishing, taking out art objects from storerooms for an annual inspection. At this period the scholars go around, hoping to catch a glimpse of the treas-ures of the past unwrapped in the art collectors' homes. Temples are as full of bustle as private residences.

Tradesman's day is a sample of the curious but inexpensive inventions which add to the joy of existence. In shopkeepers' homes a "mimic bargain sale" is held before the statue of the God of Riches and the family in jest auction off to one another all the household possessions.

On other days, it is lucky to make a lantern parade; or for girls to buy new scarves for their heads and join in the circle-dancing, singing *"Yoiyana! Yoiyana!"* as long as breath holds out. There is a great ingenuity and a wide choice; you may commemorate, if you like, the meeting of the Sky Prin-cess and the Herdsman Star and admire the firmament; at others times, there will be kite flying, banner raising, flower shows, a season of wrestling, for eating *mochi,* for putting iris leaves into the bathwater. You may go out in boats in the month of shell hunting; or make mushroom searching an excuse for a holiday.

"A great waste of a nation's wealth," the statesmen call all this, instancing the fact that week-enders in the maple sea-son spend as much as $200,000 on excursions out of Tokyo alone; indeed, lawmakers of ancient days, 1200 years ago, were trying to abolish many of these customs. To-day women complain against them for they no longer desire to spend their hours in cooking, cleaning and sewing to prepare for celebrations, while skepticism holds back youth from some traditional rites. So the love of a good time, inherent in the Japanese nature, is gradually seeking novel channels.

However, the playfulness, which lends the race much of its attraction, has often been described in a too delicate fashion. In fact, the more we learn through translated novels and historic biographies to know the people, the more certain we become that the "color of life" is with them a full-blooded and no anæmic hue. Nor is the happiness which they find in song and festival peculiar to this people; once it was the property of the human race at large.

Novels of a Rabelaisian flavor written a century or two ago, if rather shocking to many modern Japanese, reveal the earlier urges which still impel the race. They introduce us to a rough, sturdy, roystering element that thrives on jokes, laughs loud, drinks deep, and enjoys high animal fun. This older society resembles to an amazing degree the England described in Defoe, Smollet and Fielding, the France of Pantagruel, or the Spain of Gil Blas. Rogues wander in search of adventure. They get into scrapes in every village. Women force them to buy a ladder they don't need; the whole town jeers as they tramp off with the load, trip up and bang one another with the burden. They get entrapped in marriage mix-ups; there is a fight; the trouble is suddenly solved by the death of the wife in childbirth; soon the corpse is in the coffin, knives are sheathed and the mourning goes on merrily as at a typical Irish "Wake."

A vivid panorama, this former Japanese society must have presented. A jovial duke might kidnap a farmer, frighten him senseless with specters and leave him to waken on the morrow, a purse of gold in his fist. Crowds, apt for a fight or a frolic, swarmed around mediæval castles. In country-sides, alive with pagan—that is, pre-Buddhist—memories, festivals took place like those of ancient Greece. When the harvest moon shone bright, the hills would be noisy with drums and flutes. Out of the shadows of the trees would steal figures, men in women's kimono, girls with masks, bacchantes; all would stamp and circle, clapping and singing about the rice gathering, during the night, faster and faster, more and more close to the elemental forces of nature, as the Moon-god rose.

Such a vigorous joy in life also animated mediæval Italy, Spain, England, and Germany. It was not so "dainty" and "exquisite" anywhere as it was full-flavored and filled with primeval gusto. In twentieth-century Japan as throughout the world, such festival delight and gayety is being crushed out by machines, by movies, radio, efficiency, class struggle, the sense of time. But enough is left to give us some vision of an order that is passing.

Pain and grief, almost intolerably strong, are as responsible for Asia's beauty as her love of play. And conscious as I was in Japan of a joy perhaps more sunny than ours, nearer to a natural and more "golden age," I was also moved by an imminent sorrow, deeper-lying than Occidental forms. An emotional tension in the people was apparent on their stage and in their art; there was the presence of immemorial "tragic tradition."

The grand manner in tragedy is fading from the earth, with the ancient simple gayety, and the Japanese are one of the few peoples among whom this instinct yet lives. Europeans are losing it rapidly; Germans lament the turning away of bourgeois taste from the Wagnerian hero and the Goethian Faust to mere "good-humored comedy." England gives Hamlet in modern dress more for a curiosity than to meet a popular craving. We are not beholding great successors to the classic tragediennes, stately and imposing, such as Mrs. Siddons, Modjeska, La Duse, the Bernhardt. Certainly in America we thirst for the "happy ending," revolt with a shudder from "those gloomy Russians," and nourish no more the arts of declaiming, or posing in Byronic melancholy.

But in Japan a kind of stark Elizabethan tragedy survives.

No people are more demonstrative at the theater or the cinema than those supposedly "impassive Orientals." No people are more keenly alive to the "honorable horror," as Elizabethans used to say, of tragedy in the novel; more in love with light melancholy; more sympathetic with lofty grief.

This emotional surcharge in the atmosphere has many causes, beside the economic. True enough, the bitter struggle for life is probably the chief contributing factor. But there are others: the emphasis of many Buddhist sects on the vanity of the days; the accumulated burden of a civilization too venerable; a lack of diverse outlets for emotion; and the memory, which can only slowly fade, of a racial past in which, as with the Greeks, sorrow was held to be one of the noblest emotions and tragedy the highest expression of art.

Pessimism and unhappiness are widely spread, in aristocratic as in humbler circles, among young men and women no less than among their elders. The natural and simple way they had of showing their feelings astonished one who had come to Japan with assurance of observing a secretive Eastern nature. Never have I seen girls weep so unaffectedly as little misses on a railway platform when teacher left on a journey; never have I seen audiences at a play draw out so many kerchiefs, with one accord, and hold them to streaming eyes. Equally usual is the sight of men looking at a landscape with undisguised tears, for all beautiful things to a Buddhist are melancholy because transitory. Japanese feudalism did not develop quite the same "strong, silent man" tradition as England; it was no disgrace for the haughtiest knight to cry at a poem.

Young men would often confide their longing to escape the burdens of life in cities such as Nagoya and Osaka, the oppression of the family system, the struggle after graduation from college to find a foothold in society in an "old man's country." They dreamed of hiding away in the green forests of Nara, in monasteries, spending the rest of their years in meditation. Women, sincerely and simply, explained their deep desire for Nirvana, for the cessation of strife, that formed the dark undercurrent of their minds. They were weary of the efforts to fit into a family scheme; to marry according to reason instead of inclination. They wished to retire to some country estate and "farm"; but in Japan land is not cheap, and retiring to rural regions is no inexpensive project.

Others, of the educated, scholarly type, told me bitterly of the lack of joy in their youth. They had missed, they declared, the high vitality and good spirits of a natural childhood. The dead weight of classic education, of Spartan discipline, and the rigid demands of the upper-class etiquette had cramped their souls. They longed to make up in play, in tennis or in golf, in hiking and swimming, for their lost freedom. So sport has meant this release to Japan—it is not a meaningless "imitation" of the West according to current opinion. It finds its keenest response among city dwellers, long denied physical, carefree pleasure. The festivals were, after all, too much ceremonial, too little exercise.

The classes whose position was insecure and whose earning power was barely sufficient for existence felt the tragic character of life, obviously, far more. And they had the sympathy of intellectuals, who were sometimes deeply oppressed by the peculiar problems that confront Oriental labor. But I also met rich men's children who were pessimists, for they wanted to take some share in humanitarian movements without knowing where or how to begin. There were disheartened radicals; persons with earthquake fear;

stragglers for achievement in all kinds of fields, business, the arts, or politics, battling amid the harsh competition. I knew parents who had retired from activity in despair at the way the world seemed to be going; young people whose dream was to follow the world.

From such sources was derived some appreciation of Japanese literature, so permeated with reverie and mood. I began to see why many short stories end on an undecided note: "She stood, hesitant. From across the trembling lake came the cry of a water-bird." Or, "They looked at each other, sadly. They scarcely stirred. The cherry petals drifted all around them." Or, "Overcome with sorrow, he knew not why, he leaned from his balcony. How frail was the beauty of the Spring!"

Much of this melancholy that in the West recalls only Byron and an outmoded temperament lives on naturally and inevitably in Japan. There it does not seem at all overdrawn, or a pose. It is not affectation when novelists describe women in terms of saddened moods. Such an one, they say, is a "woman of autumn," and her pallid face is best to be seen "among the chirping of autumn insects under the soft glow of a lamp." Another is full of disturbing grief, reminding you of a temple bell, tragically ringing in a dark ravine. One, young and bright of eye, recalls "the faint, purple dawn of a May morning, soon to pass." These typical examples, selected by a writer in the *Woman and Life Monthly,* could be duplicated endlessly.

It is comparatively easy for an American to comprehend material woes. He understands when friends complain of a lack of opportunity or lost chances for love, work or play. But an inhabitant of the United States does not suffer, as do so many Japanese, simply from excess of civilization.

Culture is older in their country than in most parts of

northern Europe. The oldest temple is more venerable than
the most time-mellowed cathedral of England, as Dr. Scherer
has pointed out. Precedent and legend, manners and ethics,
derived from India, Persia, Korea, the Tartars, Java, the
Loochoo Islands, perhaps Madagascar, have accumulated
layer on layer. The result is exactly what has happened in
all elder countries; civilization, so heaped up, so codified, so
traditional, has become a dead weight on the people. They
are enchained by etiquette. Culture consists essentially in
controlling impulses. So we may witness a mother over-
guarding her little girl at play, tucking in her kimono at
every move, and so proving how inadequate and difficult the
garment is for babies to romp about in. One has only to
see the restriction in the smile, in the posture of the hand
receiving a gift, above all in that sublimely complex art of
restraint, the tea-ceremony, to know what accumulated
formality is like. Two thousand years ahead the United
States may be held down too; we may become less high-
pitched in our laughter, more conscious of decorum and
propriety, proceeding on that long road toward a cultured
state. Perhaps Americans are divining the future, as well as
the past, when they sojourn among the Japanese.

The crowding of massed peoples, no less than the piling
on of observances, makes the burden heavy. The overfull
countries of Asia must have intricate codes of behavior or
they could not be inhabited; men could not endure their
own kind were not legends and ceremonies present to soften
association. Life in the human ant hills of China is made
bearable only by the rituals, the family-shrine that dignifies
the lowest mud hut, the yearly festivals. Life in the great
cities and the narrow villages of Japan is also made possible
by a careful manual of behavior, the customs of bowing, the
good manners of the most humble. It is all necessary, how-

ever hard. And we, in America, are entering the same path: our wide spaces, decade by decade, closing in; our huge metropolises, our stadiums, our motor roads, gradually evolv-' ing new rites, formulas and social practices, unknown to our anarchic forebears.

The peculiar thing about Japan is not that she has had sorrow, repressions of body and mind, but that they should have found such outlets in poetry, drama and all the other arts. She is distinguished, not by grief, but by her use of it. Europe's suffering throughout its history has expressed itself in the tremendous symphonies of Beethoven, the paintings of Spanish martyrs, aspiring cathedrals, thunderous melo- dramas, mass uprisings; she has poured out her energies and blood in crusades, gigantic wars, voyages of discovery, at last soaring by aeroplane into the impossible. But the suffering of Japan was compelled to find another avenue of escape.

She endured a longer period of peace, under the Shogunate, than any other power of the earth, not excepting the United States; her inquiring spirit was held back by the isolation policy; her energies were dammed up by a strong govern- ment. Warrior tempers were disciplined, during these gen- erations of unmitigated peace, by stoical restraint. Denied expansion, her people turned in upon themselves, discover- ing the minutiæ of life; perfecting carvings, the size of a pea, for a tobacco-pipe; lavishing their love of fancy on intricate tiny ivories, dwarfed trees, miniature gardens. A cramping and a codifying went on. They developed the drama which has the most subtle expression in the world— the very antithesis of the European classic declamation school. Their art, manners and psychology in many respects diverged widely from Europe's, and bear even less kinship with America's.

The emotion of Japan also marks her from the rest

of Asia, for the simple reason that her woes have not been so great. In the darkest eras of her middle ages, she was spared many of the calamities that overwhelmed her neighbors. She has now a comparatively higher standard of living, even for the poor. Piracy, plagues, famines are avoided by governmental action. The blind are by braille texts enabled to read and vote. Horrors frequent in the ports of Asia, such as crawling cripples and the dying in the streets, are rarely, if ever seen. Customs like foot-binding or widow-burning she has not had to overcome. In so far as Japan agonizes less, so is the "color" of her life softer in its harmonies.

The traveler must move, therefore, among a people joyous and sensitive, baffled, repressed, struggling, wondering, grieving, controlling. Poking about bazaar streets in pursuit of curiosities will not suffice; he must seek perception, ever expanding, of mood and emotion. It is only the "sights," fans and rickshaws that grow commonplace to the visitor—human curiosities, never.

CHAPTER V

THE GREAT BRONZE FACE

"MYSTERY," forms the staple allurement of advertisers seeking to boost tourist traffic in the East. Promising the eager globe-trotter a close contact with the "inscrutable" Orient, they invite him to visit bazaars, temples and tea houses. Sedulously they avoid boring him with things that he might understand, such as gatherings of boy scouts, presentations of "Robin Hood" by schoolgirls, banquets of merchants, parades of striking street-car conductors, congresses of women temperance advocates. But in the very search for mystery its essence may be missed.

The singular charm of mystery in Japan is its will-o'-the-wisp character. Never can one predict its presence. Mockingly it flickers from a chance phrase in a friend's discourse, flashes in the smile of an *onnagata,* appears in full daylight in the shape of a stone fox, seated on a tiny throne beside a skyscraper business house. The deeper delight of a visitor to the island is in the discovery of a fantastic quality of mind or soul which—while it does not prevent the Japanese from doing business, running drug stores or municipal campaigns —remains exotic to the Westerner. Nor need one ever fear that this "mystery" will altogether diminish, as one approaches it intimately for, indeed, the East is quite as incomprehensible to the average Easterner as to an outlander.

Take the simple matter of Buddha's ears. I had noticed with surprise the curiously elongated ears on the statues of the Redeemer everywhere. One day a Japanese friend pointed out to me that his own were unusually large, much like Buddha's. "Yes," he happily said, "large ears with us are a sign of wisdom and prosperity, a mark of beauty." "Queer!" I thought, "O enigmatic East!" It was not until long afterward a plausible explanation was discovered in the important work on Buddhist art in India by the German scholar, Albert Grünwedel. It seems that the inhabitants of early India, especially those of rank, were in the habit of weighting the lobes of their ears with silver ornaments, as is yet done among some tribes of Africa. Early statues show the ornaments clearly; later ones, as the practice diminished, retain only the exaggerated length of lobe; so China and Japan, not realizing this origin, wove poetic fictions about the curious ears of Buddha.

Listen to the liturgy which is used in Buddhist temples. The ancient language of Buddhism is comprehensible now in India itself only to scholars. The masses of Japan have never seen a Pali text, have never heard expounded from a pulpit the higher and more esoteric meanings of Buddhism. Just as the Turks have been good Mohammedans, though largely unable to read the Arabic in which their Koran is written; just as the mediæval Europeans could in the main not appreciate the Latin of the Church service or read the New Testament in Greek—so, to this day, the finer secrets of Buddhism are sealed to the larger part of its faithful flocks. Indeed, no one man could master in a lifetime the entire range of Buddhist literature collected in the archives of Japan, the widest collection in the world; only recently have Japanese scholars started the enormous work of systematizing and publishing their treasures. The whole world's knowledge of Buddhism is yet imperfect; though it will be immensely increased, no doubt, in the near future.

Look into the great bronze face of Buddha. Walk through the pine groves of Kamakura to the flower-throne. Glance up, above the enormous shoulders, to the metal lips that curl in ambiguous smile, into the eyes that look out upon the Pacific waters, beyond which lie the Americas. This is the face that we of the West—not forgetting Kipling—have chosen to hymn as the very embodiment of Eastern enigma, the molten essence of mystery.

It is, in fact, chiefly a Greek face. Neither India, China nor Japan is wholly responsible for its creation. In all the Orient there survives, if indeed one was ever made, no authentic portrait of the Buddha created during his lifetime or for several generations after his death.

Ancient India was not so interested in the human figure as in abstract thought and ornamentation. The personality of her savior took form, then, in that upper, northern corner of the Punjab nearest to Persia and the West, and the chisels of Greek workmen, as well as native, are thought to have carved divinity from the rock. The Greeks contributed some of the symbols of deity, together with features and gestures, to India—for example, Jove's thunderbolt and the halo, originally the sun-god's rays. And they did more than lend their art to Buddha's service; the propagation of the faith went on under those Grecian kings who, after the death of the world-conqueror, Alexander, ruled wide portions of India. Menandros, while bringing Indian territory into sub-jection, became an eager convert to the Eastern faith. When the Indo-Scythians swept down from the north, themselves worshiping many Greek and Persian gods, they ended the rule but not the influence of Hellenism.

In my tourist innocence, I had not reckoned on greeting the Sun-god in Japan. I was ignorant of the fact that the Budd-hist, like the Christian, owes to Greek sculptures so much of

THE GREAT BUDDHA AT KAMAKURA

his church art; that Athens has contributed so essential an element to all civilization, manifesting itself in the ancient temples of Japan as well as in the farthest churches of Ireland; in Tibet as well as in Armenia. Nor had I realized how long this interplay of the East and West lasted; that for seven centuries, at least, a cultural interchange occurred. "Adventure-romances appeared," in the Alexandrian age, declares Grünwedel, "which, through foreign names, adventurous portrayals and exotic material, sought to surpass reality. Grecian ideals and tales went over into the Buddhist texts; Indian comparisons, fables and tales into Western literature." The stream of thought flowing out from the East is said to have percolated into the teachings of gentle St. Francis of Assisi whose parents, some tell us, were Cathari, that is "strongly tinged with Oriental Manichaeism." The influence, poured from Greek fountains, entered Hindu mentality and was carried several centuries later into China, which is so heavily indebted to India for painting, sculpture, drama, delight in calligraphy and systems of abstract thought. Borrowing in turn from her neighbor, China, Japan has preserved in very pure form this Northern-Indian art and inspiration.

So it is Apollo into whose eyes you gaze on the seashore of Kamakura. True, the Greeks would hardly have recognized him either. He is not marble but bronze; not standing in athletic, muscular vigor, but seated in contemplation on a lotus-blossom. His gigantic face has grown perhaps more sensitive, more thinly chiseled, more subtle. On his forehead is a small ornament, the "third eye," the inner mystic eye of the spirit, which the Sun-god lacked. The tightly curled hair is called by legend a "cap of snails." His hands hold no bow and arrow; they are posed in symbolic, esoteric meaning. But none the less, he is monumental proof that the

East and West *have* met—centuries, indeed millenniums, before the Civil Service sent Kipling's parents to India. Moreover, they are never wholly to be separated, one from another, again. *That* is the true mystery! Which is East? Which is West?

It is by comparison, then, as well as by receptivity, that one learns to understand a little of things Japanese. It is insufficient to rest contentedly before the Buddhas, saying, "How spiritual!" or to practice tea-ceremony and flower arrangement. That makes for sympathy, indeed, and perhaps for a refinement of feeling. But that stops short of understanding. The proof is that the Japanese, who can do all these things, fail to comprehend themselves. They do not pretend to. They have been unable to reach any conclusive answers to such simple foreign questions as "Who are the Japanese?" "What makes them Japanese?"

This is naturally a blow to the traveler. Nowadays, he is expected to bring back to the folks at home, not merely chopsticks and a "fancy dress costume," but decided opinions too. He must answer, readily, such inquiries as "Have the Japanese a sense of humor? Are they friendly to us? Did you find them as intelligent as the Chinese? Aren't they all incomprehensible, and don't they all look alike? A polite people, are they not?" The modern souvenir is no longer just an object; it is a view on the soul of a nation, perhaps picked up secondhand and at a great bargain.

It is best, however, not to ask the Japanese for a few useful replies. They are yet too acutely aware of all there is to learn about themselves; they know what abysses remain to be explored, what layers of mystery obscure their racial past, what problems combine to vex the future.

On one occasion, for example, in Tokyo, you may hear an astute politician complain that there is no way to predict the response of the "rural vote"; he can only guess what will be the next move of the millions he has recently helped to enfranchise. On another, you may meet a historian who has been incapable, after profound research, of establishing the racial identity of the Japanese; or an artist who is still incompetent to determine which original contributions Japan has made to art; or a philosopher who is seeking, and so far vainly, the "national soul." And from conversation with such men, the impression that one chiefly carries away is the size of the task of learning about the Japanese, to say nothing of the East as a whole.

The combined work of Eastern and Western scholars and of the new Orientalist societies in Tokyo, tracing back the connection of Japan with Asia, has only lifted a few veils before misty antiquity, where lie the roots of present-day Japanese culture. Even the history of Japan has largely been a chronicle of church and state, courtiers, warriors, priests and artists. There is yet to be created a synthesis of all that can be known about the common people—their folklore, dancing, rituals and games, peasant uprisings, the evolution of their dietary, costume, ideas of love, private property, and God, comparable with the story of Western peoples. Not only does much about the peasants and artisans of hundreds of years ago remain to be studied; the modern proletarian worker, a creation of the past few years, presents new problems for examination. The idea, however, of studying "the people" is revolutionary in Japan, as it was in the West a generation ago. Social service, as we understand it, is just about ten years old; sociological interest in the shadows of the "underworld" a generation old. And though the people have statistical surveys and informatory pamphlets and books on social questions, this is a mere start toward self-revelation.

Certain conditions hamper research, such as lack of financial support and the paucity of libraries, those expensive luxuries of the mind. In fact, much of the Oriental art is best seen abroad, in Boston, for example, where the collection was assembled at a time when the Japanese had not learned to safeguard "national treasures." Or the collections are in the temples or private hands, rather inaccessible. Besides financial or physical obstacles, there are circumstances which hamper free inquiry: notably the police supervision of "dangerous thoughts," study societies, and books. For many Oriental minds, furthermore, trained on classical themes and mediæval chronicles, it is hard suddenly to take on the modern mode of looking at things, to accept the rationalist interpretations of the supernatural. The Japanese are just beginning to study their family papers, diaries and letters as source material and a small amount of such documentary history is available to scholars at this time.

The wisest among the Orientals are therefore often the most cautious in generalizing. They feel as much hesitation in stating "how the geisha system works" as a sage in America about the effects of prohibition. Where the sagacious falter, the ignorant are often utterly baffling in their silence.

It is a common fallacy to suppose that one may find the heart of Asia by asking any Easterner for its key. Many persons fancy that any Japanese gentleman encountered in America, any wistful soul carrying a camera and riding in a "rubberneck" wagon can tell you what the Japanese *really* think about the immigration law or whether they have a sense of humor. But it may be that he can tell you only how it feels to run an electric-light plant in Karafuto or some such place, and how bad the subway rush is at five o'clock, and that he likes comic strips. He may know no more about the soul of his country than a hectic tourist from Peoria, busy "doing" Paris, understands America.

To estimate the value of a Japanese opinion one must first inquire about many other things: what social stratum the holder comes from, how much he has traveled, what university he may have attended, who his mother-in-law is, what his religious beliefs may be. He must be taken as a fallible human being with a limited range of experience.

Charming Miss Wisteria, your neighbor at the state dinner party, may seem as she sits there, drooping correctly with downcast gentle eyes and softly falling robes of gray and twilight blue, the very epitome of the poetic East and able to interpret it to you. But she has probably done little traveling in her country and knows nothing of its people at large. She may know less about Osaka than a Park Avenue débutante may know about the Passaic strike. Less—because in Japan, social service and uplift are not yet young ladies' pastimes.

Nor may the studious-looking young man yonder, with the spectacles and university cap, be a better authority on his own people. Maybe he has never seen them either. "Slumming" in Tokyo, as once in Little Old New York, is a terrifying novelty. In 1922 a party of university students went on a tour of the wretched quarters for a daring experiment. They were met by the irate poor with a shower of insults and pebbles. Sight-seeing is a positive adventure. When Burton Holmes showed Japanese ladies of high degree in New York City his pictures of a Yoshiwara procession, they declared this could not be their beloved Nippon. They had never visited a geisha-house; far less joined in the agitations for social reform of the more radical sisters of their race.

More puzzling to the foreigner than the people who

plainly know little about the nation as a whole are the people who feel they know a great deal. The trouble here is that they flatly contradict one another. One evening you may be kneeling in the residence of, let us say, a distinguished man of letters, listening to the conversation of a novelist, a social reformer, a government official, a woman journalist, a university professor. And what do you hear? At least six points of view, passionately or poignantly expressed, varying from plaintive to sardonic, from ardent to the severely scholastic. And the conclusions?

"The Japanese aristocracy is but a thin upper crust, and not covering a pie, either, but a volcano. Beneath are the people, those imponderable masses—a maze of primitive passions, tinged red with bolshevism, forever forced upward by the steady pressure of population and hunger, financial disorders, and tragedies of earthquake or fire. The result? One day, through a fissure, the masses will burst out. A revolution will come of appalling terror! You will see!"

"Red lava? Nonsense. Lotus eaters. Nothing stirs up the Japanese people, apathetic, content with the old furrow, changeless. Their minds can never be adapted to Western forms of thought; nor can they afford Westernization. I am right. Nothing will happen. Farmers and labor men will reject a common policy; leadership and the instinct of teamwork are lacking. The upper classes will go on herding the masses like sheep into conventional pens. Nothing will happen in the changeless East."

Hardly a question asked in such a group will elicit an unanimous response. Ask about the influence of Buddhism on the Japanese mind. One will reply that the negative emphasis of so many sects of that religion has greatly divided the Eastern from the Western mentality. Another will break in, maintaining that Japan, far more influenced by Buddhism

than by the teachings of Confucius, is therefore much closer
to Western modes of thought than China. Ask whether the
Japanese are more merry or melancholy in disposition. This
friend will quickly answer that in the earliest times, before
feudal warfare set in, the Japanese loved brilliant hues and
were radiantly happy. His fellow will object—the Shinto
ritual, expressing the native feeling, is sternly severe,
puritanic.

"Who are these newly enfranchised eight millions?" you
may inquire. "Full of brains and shrewd sense," is the quick
answer. "Was not Hideyoshi, the crafty peasant, one of the
world's great strategists, whose castle ruins still stand in
Osaka in memory of his magnificence and his astuteness?"
"Nonsense," cries a listener; "the Japanese are essentially
inefficient!" "On the contrary, look at the wastefulness of
America, and then see how brilliantly the Japanese have
managed their scanty resources." "The Japanese are different from all peoples in the world." "No, no, they are
just like anybody else, given the same environment." The
Japanese, you hear, are witty, without wit, childish, brilliant, full of the East's peculiar wisdom, mentally incompetent, artistic, devoid of artistic sense; they will one day
rule all Asia; they will be lucky to keep out of the bankruptcy court; they are anæmic; basically they are vigorous.

As you return home in your rickshaw, down the lantern-
lit alleys, you ponder over what you have heard. What is an
errant foreigner to make of this panorama? One thing, at
least, is evident: as all this controversy goes on, the East is
attempting to solve its own mystery. Intelligent Japanese
are more and more insistent that they must learn something
about themselves. Toward this search for national self-
analysis they have been pushed for three generations, by
many forces.

Politically and economically, it is more than ever necessary. How shall a modern politician appeal to his voters if he does not take into account their needs, their moods, their reactions? He must predict, somehow, the moves of millions. How shall the modern capitalist compete with the efficient, machine workmanship of the West, unless he takes up "personnel management"; studies the psychology of his working forces and their adaptability to machines, their relative ability, their manner of living, their health?

The publisher must learn what is the "news reaction" of his everwidening public. The advertiser, according to Dr. Washio, taking up the word "taishu" or "the great masses" sells by the new slogan of "service to taishu"; he aims direct for the tastes of democracy, previously analyzed.

All those who hope to command the votes, the markets or the allegiance of the multitude must come closer to the people, learn their psychology, speak to them in their own terms. Buddhist churchmen now study the adaptation of their organization to social demands. Labor men, realizing that a class movement can only be financed in Japan by arousing the ardent support of millions, are organizing in farming, factory and mining regions; they are educating and training new leaders by small, local campaigns and self-governing councils; they are showing the people how to discuss their own problems, urging them to become vocal and explain what they think and want. Japanese desirous for peace in the Pacific realize that popular enthusiasm must be awakened, in labor circles as among business men. Feminists in search of rights for their sex know that middle-class initiative is not enough; working women must enroll, if the movement is to have success. Every group, whatever its aim, must make the grand gesture of an appeal to the people.

Deeply affected by the intellectual currents of the age, literary men and women carry on the synthetic process. Turning away from conventional romances of mediæval knighterrantry, they look with a new scientific interest at the plain folk. Some, in the footsteps of Zola, study the shadows of slum life. Some frame merry tales of the "Modern Girl" and installment fiction on the order of "Confessions of a House-maid." One group proposes to create a "proletarian literature," rousing the people to class-consciousness. Another devotes its activities to political stories. Great quarrels go on among the literati about the psychology of Mr. So-and-So's heroines—is it "correct"?—as concern with their own "complexes" and behavior deepens and spreads. The further cheap literature runs, the wider becomes the audience looking, with the help of authors, into its own mind and soul.

Artists increase this introspection. Branching out from the ancient themes and methods, they are trying honestly, if not always with success, to portray modern conditions. In the new mood, they examine factory towns and fishermen's villages, with realistic eyes. In Salon exhibitions, they attempt to show the public that miners and market-girls may be as worth beholding as waterfalls by moonlight or dragons in a storm.

Foreign lectures in Japan undeniably lead to more self-searching. Just as critics of young America, such as Dickens, with their harsh disapproval of New World manners, first produced resentment, then investigation, so the English, Hindu, Chinese, or American visitors to Japan exercise a powerful influence. They may arouse anger, embarrassed misery, stanch defense; then movements for constructive reform. If there is in Japan, what lingers in the America of to-day, a somewhat morbid sensitiveness to the remarks of critics from abroad, that must be set down to this growing consciousness of self.

Self-examination is indeed the spirit of the age. Nations, as well as individuals, are delving into the past, seeking the origins of their present "psychic conditions." They are trying to "integrate their personalities" and find out why they "behave like human beings." Certainly Japan is not alone in her soul-searching. Equally in transition are Germany and the United States; they feel less "fixed" in a permanent state of culture than England, France or Spain; they share an anxiety about the powers inherent in their democratized masses. All three countries are wondering how to employ and educate large populations and what will be the ultimate effect of industrialism upon the national mind and spirit. Within the three, a prodigious amount of mental energy is devoted to "vindicating" or merely to discovering a "national essence" or a "soul." Probably the most brilliant results have been attained in metaphysical Germany; but these results, however dazzling in technique, are as contradictory to one another as the opinions of Japanese scholars about their own race.

A country honeycombed with agitation and a life made vivid by unending clash and controversy—that is what the traveler finds in Japan to-day. Black Dragon Societies conflict with communists. Students are rounded up for "dangerous thoughts"; high-school girls go on strike. Professors, banished for radical teachings, conduct quiet study groups in economics and politics among their friends. Campaigns, noisy with radio speeches, stir up clouds of scandal and send the popular temperature up to the boiling point. Protests are carried to the very throne of the Emperor. Solemn tomes discuss the origin of race. Congresses and mass meetings, proclamations and parades quicken public life; while in private, under innumerable dragon-roofed houses, behind uncounted paper screens, arguments take place about "taishu" and disputations over the future and destiny.

Such a society asks of the traveler more than passive wonder. It demands active response to its problems and undertakings and would draw him into the search for a key to national riddles.

CHAPTER VI

ETERNAL CHANGE

WHILE expecting to find in the East three qualities, "color," "mystery" and "change," I had supposed that the last of this great triad was mainly a modern feature; that some time during the past century or so the immutable Orient had suddenly adopted from the West the impulse to alter or develop her "ancient ways." The whole Orient was thought of as incredibly venerable and its ideas and customs as petrified from time immemorial. And there was not the slightest suspicion that change is no more of a novelty in the one quarter of the globe than in the other; that in fact "change" is one of the most permanent elements in "eternal Asia."

With the crudeness of a newcomer I had sharply separated everything the eyes discovered into violent contrasts of new and old, or modern and ancient, if not Eastern and Western. Thus the half-tones which are as present in Japanese life as in our own had been missed. But what was even worse was the charge to "importation" of many objects and matters which are really Eastern in origin. For instance, the notion of prohibiting intoxicating liquors, which I fancied a recent alien derivative, was in vogue in Japan as early as the thirteenth century. On the other hand, the geisha system, instinctively judged to be millenniums in age, is hardly older than the voyage of the "Mayflower," nor is the observance of Buddha's birthday as a general holiday more antediluvian than Queen Victoria.

Tourists, it may be admitted, have excuses for their attitude. One walks along the Ginza, counting padlocked cafés; attends the opening exercises of the first woman's law school in Asia; watches modern youth courting in ice-cream parlors or buying "hot dogs" at seaside resorts. In bamboo-forested valleys down the newly constructed highways, he observes ox-carts yielding place to a motorcycle ridden by a boy in speckled kimono and goggles, with a girl in the sidecar, her kimono sleeves fluttering and her pompadour tied up in a knitted sport scarf. He meets government officials, encouraging postal savings among the populace and trying to keep juveniles out of Wild West cinemas; scientists endeavoring to increase the consumption of milk and eggs; business men urging nationalization of electric power; women campaigning for a child health program.

Impressive seems the "swift march of modernization." In homes, his friends entertain him with phonograph records of ultra-modern German music which Japanese buy, it is said, in greater quantities than the Germans themselves. Turning to the radio set, placed upon the floor, his kneeling host asks him whether he might prefer a baritone solo, "Hymn in Praise of Visiting American Aviators," broadcast from Station JOAK, a lecture on "Confucius," or one on "Canned Goods." In modern skyscraper offices, cooled by electric fans, he visits newspaper magnates or bean cake kings, dictating letters to haughty stenographers, bob-haired, with plucked eye-brows, who pause now and then to powder their noses. In the country regions, he finds peasants no longer so willing as their fathers to posture with flutes in the "good old dances" to frighten insects from their fields; they prefer to bicycle miles to a political rally and wait seven hours, or more if need be, for a speaker on the "rights of the farmer." Rural or urban, the Japanese audiences he sees in cinema halls are displaying a growing interest in the present or the future; more and more they prefer an up-to-date comedy, say "Subway *Sankichi,*" or a prophecy, such as "Earth Rotates," to the tragedies of mediæval knights. And one learns that the Japanese film studios are turning out more features every year than any country in the world, topping the production of the United States itself by two hundred a twelve-month.

So glaring is the "new" that beside it the characteristically Japanese ways and manners seem very queer and old. Only gradually did I suspect that many Japanese customs presumed to be ancient are comparatively modern and indeed are just gaining popular favor. The celebration of Buddha's birthday, in fact, is the attempt of the reinvigorated Buddhist Church to compete with the growing popularity of Christmas. The pretty pastime of battledore and shuttlecock, in which young girls in the holiday attire engage about New Year's time, filling the streets with the swaying of their bright sleeves, the flash of painted paddles and flying feathers, became a widespread, thoroughgoing national pastime only after the 1780s; these girls are therefore carrying out a tradition not really more hoary with age than our youngsters' Fourth of July firecrackers. Some of the most distinctive Japanese festivals and games are in truth fairly recent revivals rather than continuous customs. The girls' doll festival, fencing, Noh dancing, for instance, had passed into a decline in Japan during the Victorian age; they might easily have died out altogether but for the victory over China in the Sino-Japanese War of 1894-1895. Apparently, the rising national spirit, after the triumph, found satisfaction in infusing new life into decadent racial customs—a rejuvenation which may be compared to the American thirst for Colonial "antiques" following the World War. More and more as modernization goes on they find their own past "picturesque" and delightful. They like New Year rice cakes and collect old tobacco pipes much as we enjoy Thanksgiving turkey or spinning wheels.

Foreigners almost invariably consider the geisha as an integral part of mediæval Japan, perhaps indeed as a most typical feature of ancient life. In truth, it would almost be as correct so to romance about London's Gaiety Girls. The mincing charmers seen in the Cherry Blossom Dance at Kyoto or in Tokyo tea houses first developed their peculiar organization after the great fire and earthquake in Tokyo in the latter half of the seventeenth century. Citizens of the ruined metropolis, after that disaster, were compelled to eat in restaurants until their wrecked homes could be rebuilt. Little shops sprang up to serve them with bean broth and boiled rice. Orphaned and impoverished girls found employment as waitresses. Gradually entertainment was added to dining, and the geisha thus became associated with restaurants and public amusement. Long after the city was reconstructed, the tea houses therefore retained their popularity. Indeed, with regard to morality, the situation suggests analogies with that following the recent catastrophe in 1923. But few foreigners have emphasized their similarity or the fact that the geisha system, as it exists to-day, was the product, not of "the Japanese soul," but of disaster and chaos, while the thinkers, as it rose, were loud in their complaints of "dying morality."

Like the rest of the world, Japan has been in a more or less continual state of transition. From the very dawn of history, she has been developing, destroying, rebuilding her religions, dietary, government, family organization, methods of farming, costume, manners, military tactics and community life. She has not been "awakened" from a "deep sleep" as the conventional globe-trotter invariably says; had there been

no Perry, the rising of commercial classes and the increasing
financial woes of feudal lords would probably have led
to a social clash. Defending trade, in the ranks of Restoration armies, says Dr. Washio, the clerks in Osaka merchant
houses marched against feudalism. With or without Western influence her civilization would have been to-day in a
Taoistic state of flux and flow.

There were never fifty years in her history that could
really be called "stagnant." True, the people at the time
may have been unaware of change; but looking back, scholars
can trace in the quietest periods the seeds of decay sown in
one governing class, the budding power of another, falling
clans, and emerging classes. It is now clear that Japanese
history consists of great cycles, like our own, of struggle,
attainment, enjoyment, decay, relapse and then rebirth.

Modern historians no longer divide western history into
the former water-tight compartments. Even in the case of
France, sharp lines between "ancient" and "modern" are
difficult to draw; the French Revolution only sealed processes
begun generations before. Blue blood was already thinned
and feudal economy was already doomed. What cannot be
done any more in European history must also cease to be
done in Oriental history.

Not even religion has been absolutely fixed and settled
in doctrine anywhere. Equally with Christianity, Buddhism
has known periods of flowering in ritual and art, periods of
revolt and revival of more primitive simplicity. Reformers
would rise, preaching a new dogma; hierarchies of priests
would seize power, turning enthusiasm of the people to
profit; then a fresh reformer would be called forth, to de-
nounce the old and proclaim a novel formula of salvation.
Certain of the Japanese preached marriage for the clergy;
some, celibacy. In times of civil-war carnage, the gentle

would teach mercy, love of nature, and retirement to the hermitage. In times of peace and prosperity others, conscious of national power, would demand a national religion, truly Japanese, instead of alien. Always, the rhythmic laws of human life have applied to Japan as well as to the West.

No less than the modern generation, the mediæval people were eager for changes. In truth, Japan has had a remarkable succession of reformers, planners, and inventors of social schemes. There were attempts to put through prohibition as early as 1200 A.D. Many princes tried to restrain luxury by stern sumptuary laws; to force a return to frugality and morality. Nichiren was as fierce in reforming zeal as the Italian Savonarola. Hideyoshi was as farseeing in his outlook and thorough in his program as a Napoleon or a Bismarck. Seekers for knowledge in the dark days of isolation paid for their learning of Dutch medicine and astronomy with their heads as unhesitatingly as in these times of internationalism Dr. Hideyo Noguchi gave his life in the cause of scientific research for a yellow-fever cure.

Skepticism, beside strength and zeal, is an inheritance in Japan. Eighteenth century natives were already, on their own accord, beginning to point out the impossibility of many fables then passing as "history." Perhaps because they were conscious that so much of their culture was "borrowed," the keener minds were forever seeking some true "national essence"; were always in an agony of acceptance or denial over each innovation. They found no peace and rest of soul, those mediæval men and women of "quaint old Japan." Great ladies, caught in war tragedies, were hunting solace in Buddhist nunneries or in good works, founding orphan asylums and other charities long before they appeared generally in Europe. Ambitious men were ever dreaming of the ascent to power; statesmen were pondering the problems of maintaining peace and possessions; cloistered monks were going through the soul-searchings of Christian novitiates, trying to discover the import of life. In their straw and metal armor, with keen-bladed swords in their hands—finer than those made by European armorers, by the way—the mediæval knights, in the manner of our own forefathers, were fighting out destinies of class and kin. Thus "modern changes" are but new revolutions of a wheel that has never stood still.

Usually, we assume at least that conscious will was confined in old Japan to a blue-blooded aristocracy, headed by a Mikado, who created the social system, while below toiled the "masses," blind and inarticulate. We forget that the facts deliciously contradict this fancy. Surely if he hears our talk about "aristocratic Japan," the spirit of that plebeian little upstart, Captain Hideyoshi, must indulge in shouts of ironical glee. A simple peasant's son it was who brought to long-suffering Japan her first genuine unification, her most enduring and most glorious peace, and wove for her the stout fabric of feudalism that held the nation together until Perry came. None of the aristocracy achieved these three giant tasks, for they, flesh of a flesh with typical feudal noblemen in Europe, cared more for splitting heads than using them in thought; they had carried the havoc of civil warfare throughout the country for generations without let. Like a very embodiment of angered popular will, rose Hideyoshi to confront the self-seeking nobility and crush their power, survey their lands and levy taxes. A delightful sense of humor this ugly little Captain must have had, for he compelled the warriors, leaving their swords behind, to come before him and practice tea-ceremony in his presence. He made fine arts more fashionable than warfare, this "common" Japanese, and, surely with an inward chuckle, would reward the fiercest of fighting dukes, for his good behavior, with a rare tea bowl! Wise and practical, as well as witty, he surrounded the rebellious noblemen with loyal retainers, enmeshing them in a national whole, until the feudal web he wove was strong enough to stand the test of centuries.

By law, example and custom, he created the nation which his successors developed. Even more clever, in one respect, was Hideyoshi than that other "common little upstart" of Europe, who operated two centuries later—Napoleon Bonaparte. The Japanese nation-maker was contented with actual power and cared not who had the name. He raised no covetous eyes toward the imperial throne.

In the bewildering panorama of modernity, as throughout the past, there is accordingly direction, purpose, continuity. No merely aimless, blind "imitation" is responsible for the vivid and curious manifestations of the present. Will and desire have called into being what exists in Japan: railroad engines puffing at the foot of Mount Fuji; cement villas rising above bamboo groves; cafés where saxophone and samisen sound in alternation; election days opened by the united roar of factory whistles and temple bells; forests of industrial smokestacks growing by mediæval battlegrounds; new religions and philosophies; innovations in architecture and diet, labor and flower arrangement, agriculture and costume, music and marketing; relations with the whole world by radio, international business or Pan-Pacific parleys.

The Western spirit in its Japanese incarnations escapes being drab or dull, because the natives are not so much imitating as adapting to their own needs and ends. In music, for example, contact with the West has served to stimulate their racial inspiration. The orchestra idea they have applied to their peculiar instruments; and I have heard some twenty samisen, usually played solo, strummed to-

gether as an accompaniment to a purely Japanese musical
comedy. Importations have not supplanted the old so much
as they have revived it. Concerts of Beethoven in Tokyo
have drawn huge audiences of appreciative listeners; but
the venerable songs of the Noh opera are also finding more
general interest. Handsomer Noh theaters are built; people
seem eager to hear the old and compare it with the new.

Weddings in the "new style" at Tokyo may be taken as
an illustration of the combining ability of the Japanese.
Young people wish a modern, picturesque and interesting
form of ceremony; nothing sufficient is provided by the
ancient formulas and they do not want just to take Western
contraptions, such as the veil and the bouquet, so ugly in
their eyes. In collaboration, therefore, hotel managers and
Shinto priests have worked out a modified form of tying the
knot. A complete equipment is provided by one hotel in
Tokyo for managing the "up-to-date" ceremony efficiently
and artistically. There are beauty parlors in which the bride
and her friends acquire the magnificent, sleek coiffures essential to formality and don the specially embroidered robes.
A Shinto shrine is located in a room nearby, where guests
assemble, kneel, and listen to a liturgy read by the priests
and accompanied by ancient music on the flute. Then, instead of a stiff wedding procession, ingenuity has devised a
unique arrangement; two golden screens are drawn aside,
noiselessly, disclosing bride and groom already kneeling near
the altar. Guests listen to the prayer and the plighting of
troth, after which young girls, arrayed in scarlet and white
kimono, bring them ceremonial wine. At the conclusion of
the simple but charming ceremony, the party moves into an
adjoining room for photographs; then the banquet hall
downstairs is opened for refreshments. Finally, the guests
may adjourn, through a convenient passage, into the Imperial

Theater to witness a play, while bride and groom take a
taxi to the railroad station, ready for a trip to some temple
town in the mountains, probably sacred Nikko.

In the more profound social and economic development
of Japan, the same process of selection and adaptation can
be seen. True, it may all be termed "imitation" in a larger
sense. But those who use the word with a flavor of scorn
usually forget how enormous is the bulk of Western borrowing, not only from the East, through Arabs, Egyptians and
Jews, but from one Western nation by another. France
learned embroidery, silk, glass and silver manufacture, and
indeed the greater part of her staple industries, from Italy—
Italy which was long a filter for the Eastern arts. Spain owed
"most of her industrial and agricultural arts" to Arabs in
her midst. Germany, following France, took the path to
industry; the development of watch-making, metal-founding,
the manufacture of paper, carpets, wool and silk goods, she
owed largely to expelled Huguenot craftsmen who settled
within her borders; most of her vegetables and orchard trees
were imported from France. Until the eighteenth century
"all the arts practiced in England were of Continental origin," brought by fugitive Flemish and French artisans. And
after England developed modern industry, her methods were
copied by her neighbors on the Continent as assiduously and
as closely as the Japanese ever borrowed from the West.
When Germany was trying to introduce modern industry,
she invited English factory foremen and operatives to teach
her, precisely as the Japanese called in American, German,
Dutch, French and English instructors. All nations have
imitated; yet none has ever turned into a complete and exact
replica of another. Japan, in the light of world experience,
is no exception, either in her ability to borrow, or her will to
remain individual.

Least of all have Americans a right to speak condescendingly of imitation. We are all pupils of heirs; there is no wholly original nation on earth to-day, in Orient or Occident, owing nothing spiritual or ethical, industrial or artistic to outside influences. We may only talk of change in a relative sense, mindful of the way we are all caught in the process.

So the phenomena of this age in Japan, moral, intellectual, legal, cultural, economic or religious are part of an international reweaving of life. What is going on there is not sheer innovation but an effort to master and direct it. And of course it is idle to predict results. It is impossible to know whether, in Orient or Occident, humanity will prove itself capable, physically or mentally, of controlling its evolution; fate may intend, in both hemispheres, not an ultimate Utopia, but the wreck of mankind. At any rate the development in Japan has this significance: it is a phase of the common world struggle of our times between humanity and destiny.

PART II

"UKIYO"—THIS FLEETING WORLD

CHAPTER VII

TOKYO CITY—A COLOSSAL PERSONALITY

GREAT cities are looms of change. Rolling from their restless shuttles come the living tissues of society, the blended weaves of culture, idea-patterns, subtle webs of law and ritual and art. Throughout Asia, as in Europe, civilization has been chiefly an urban fabrication.

Endlessly altering, they are yet eternal. As Mother Rome survives her Cæsars, so Peking outlives her Mongol and Manchu conquerors. Few of the civic colossi have disappeared wholly from the earth, leaving behind no columns, wells, tombs or pottery shards. Asia is strewn with their ruins, hidden in jungles like Angkor-Vat, buried under soft mounds as at Japanese Nara, or left bleaching on hilltops as along the Chinese Yangtse. Even spirit, like stone bodies, endures; Canton in China has been plebeian and a "rebel" for nearly a thousand years, while, for a still longer space, Japan's Kyoto has remained aristocratic. They are more than populations, the cities. Transcending in personality all their living inhabitants, summing up the memory of their millions dead, cities reach into the future. With every generation, as life under capitalism grows more urban, as fresh multitudes crowd into metropolitan labyrinths, they swell in vigor and importance. To-day, in either hemisphere, the globetrotter irresistibly is drawn from town to town, boulevard to bazaar, until he scarcely has eyes which see the countryside.

Wonderfully akin, rather than curiously opposed, are

93

Asian and Western cities. In significance, type, and historic rôle, they have been far more similar than in their skylines, variously commanded by pagoda or mosque, spire or dome. East or West, they have been creators and transmitters of high cultures, market places where law and commercial ethics expanded while the arts and learning found patrons. Centers of intellect and government, they have been makers of the cosmopolitan mind. More persistent than racial or national patriotism is the pride of the townsman. Older by several thousand years than the distinction between East and West is the deep cleavage between rural and urban man. The gods of the tent-dweller and those of Sodom and Gomorrah were in conflict long before Christ and Buddha walked and taught.

Cities are perhaps more international than the minds of the folk who build them. Certainly world types exist, determined rather by destiny and occupation than by race and continent. The same black smoke unravels in the skies above industrial Pittsburgh, Essen, Manchester and Nagoya. Two defiant merchant cities, long resistant to feudal lords, are on opposite curves of the world—German Hamburg and Japanese Osaka. Two of the mellowest seats of empire are separated by half a globe—Rome and Peking, the "Eternal" City and the "Forbidden." In sunny, drowsy oblivion lie Würzburg among the vineyards, Avignon below bleak white ruins, and walled, canal-threaded Soochow. Cities are youthful, new-created like Angora, undergoing remodeling like Belgrade and Madrid, or experimenting prodigiously in leadership like Berlin and Moscow. Others are haunted by ghosts of a regal past, notably Vienna, Constantinople, Hangchow and Venice. Many towns such as Kyoto, Potsdam and Versailles, remain courtly in atmosphere, though their palaces, erected for lords and ladies, may now delight gaping democracies. The flavor of Italian Florence and of Japanese Tokyo was determined by luxurious merchants no less than by prodigal nobility, and to this day they mingle a commercial with a regal air. It appears then that "hostile" Orient and Occident may well fraternize in and through their kindred cities.

Tokyo, first among power-centers of Asia, can least be described by a single word—"Oriental" or "Westernized." No adjective can compass so colossal and complex a personality or produce a mental image of this city built both of bamboo and marble, flooded alike with Chicago winds and Neapolitan sunshine, overlooked in the daytime by warehouses and on clear evenings by a purple giant, Fujiyama. No one hemisphere can claim this metropolis, with temples of Buddhism entered through gilt-crusted gates and temples of commerce approached through Corinthian columns; with toymakers suggesting those of Nürnberg and a palace modeled on Buckingham; concert-halls and canals crowded with water gypsies; slums and Luna Parks; clatter from subway turnstiles and from wooden shoes.

In size Tokyo is breathtakingly great. While within its legal boundaries only approximately two million people live, the vast urban district within the commuting range embraces a population of more than five millions. Every day, moreover, this aggregation enlarges: roads expand, skyscrapers rear blunt heads, new electric handwriting blinks in the evening sky. The legal municipality lags behind the actual speed of building, but Tokyo already looks forward to dredging the harbor and achieving a world port, to incorporating Yokohama and becoming a human bulk forty miles square.

Streams of human energy, gathering volume in the hinterland, tend to overflow here. Miners in dark Kiushu, farmers on Southern plains, and spinners in barracks at the foot of

Fujiyama look toward Tokyo, the seat of government, for legislative relief. Artists, singers, actors, seekers after place in universities or publishing houses, "climbers" into society or diplomacy—all hope to find patronage and opportunity in the capital of the nation. Those who organize revolt against the social order or wish a good berth within it; those who struggle for a higher life or long to enjoy this one are drawn toward the major city of the Empire. Thus the swollen floods of ambition and strife, as well as calmer currents of artistic and intellectual effort, make Tokyo their objective.

Power unparalleled in Asia is symbolized in architecture along the avenues. Wealth and journalism, fashion and labor, religion and the navy have set up their citadels. Here are international banks within the inevitable Parthenons; brick offices owned by merchant clans, masters of steamships and mines; solemn edifices, surrounded by solemn statues of statesmen, housing various departments of government; shops where modes in kimono or sashes have their "first showings"; public halls in which striking waitresses or agitating bus-conductors may air their grievances. In suburban regions loom the private palaces where elder statesmen, meditating on rear verandahs, determine peace or war and thus shape destiny for East and West. Down many lanes may be heard the roar of presses, rushing editions of twenty newspapers and a hundred periodicals. A "Wall Street" rumbles with limousines carrying silk-hatted stockbrokers to their offices. Ramifications from all these streets and buildings stretch out over the world, touching the entire Orient and affecting the fate of Europe and America.

Many of these urban manifestations are in startling contrast, if not in violent conflict. Thus, the numerous churches and sects are measured against one another in Tokyo's monasteries, religious colleges or convention halls. Buddhism as a vital force to-day has headquarters rather in Japan than in the motherland of India; here it most vigorously confronts Christianity and invites the rival to defend itself.

Youth and age make their opposing stands in the city. Old people, jealous lovers of "Yedo," are trying consciously and actively to maintain the life, dances and festivals, music and manners of the past; they are the more eager reactionaries because the youth movement is most clamorous in their midst. Students, ever the radicals, flock in thousands to Tokyo, the Orient's greatest scholarly and literary Bohemia. "Modern girls," to the delight of the novelists if to the despair of the moralists, are most abundant in the city's offices and cafés—a striking after-earthquake phenomenon.

A dozen types of drama strive for favor in this unique capital. Audiences totalling four million a year divide their patronage among ancient dramas, handed down possibly from Greece and certainly from early India; the highly artistic plays of mediæval Japan; Chinese opera of the Manchu era sung by famous Peking stars; Hindu legends refashioned and fan-posturing; modern Japanese comedies of detectives and harassed husbands; "problem-plays" of peasants; and the eternal triangles. None of the world's great theatrical centers can show more intensely interested and serious audiences, as wide a range of dramatic fare, or productions of more genuine power.

Two great political kingdoms—of Asia's most successful democracy and of the world's oldest imperial dynasty—here guard their neighboring strongholds. In Parliament and from numberless public forums, politicians address themselves to twelve million voters; radio stations and journals at once transmit orations to woodcutters in the "Alps" and fishermen on lonely islands. But in the very heart of the lecturing and campaigning region, out of tranquil moats, soar the gray walls of the Castle belonging to a descendant of the Sun Goddess now reigning as a constitutional monarch.

Like Honolulu or Geneva, Tokyo has become one of those spots marked on the globe as a "convention center." For the whole nation the city forms a rallying point; no federation, whether of girl guides or trade unions, temperance advocates or social workers, could complete the year without some procession, petition, or "monster mass meeting" in Tokyo. Huge hotels and auditoriums, clubhouses and university buildings have already held distinguished medical, business and religious conferences of international significance. Clash of problems, tendencies, aims and abilities is the very life of the place. A tourist, therefore, must not rely upon the streets alone for his knowledge and judgment of the city.

How much of any metropolis, indeed, may be known from the street? As a rule, neither the heights nor the depths. The home in Asia, as in Europe, among middle and upper classes, is still part shrine, part fortress surrounded by hedge or wall; it generally lacks that American domestic grandstand, the front porch. No casual wayfarer may penetrate beyond the "spirit screen" into a well-to-do Chinese or Japanese abode. Nor can he watch "society" as openly as among people who habitually entertain at hotels or resorts. If to know the upper crust of Japan requires friends, to learn the underworld calls for an informed and experienced guide. The tourist ordinarily does not see, behind the shop displays, apprentice children toiling in dark cells or, off the broad boulevards, the narrow lanes where shrinking poverty hides away, withdrawn as in Parisian alleys or crooked streets of London or tenement New York.

What then of Tokyo can be seen by all visitors? Crowds, above all, shuffling along in search of bargains or diversion, gathering at civic meetings or at temple festivals. But among the first sights is that celebrated avenue in Japan called the Ginza. It has become famous for its shops, some low-balconied and hung with gilded signs, others rising to skyscraper dimensions; for its restaurants, graded in style from native to Victorian, Cubist and plain cafeteria; for its problems of traffic and wayward youth; for the night life created by hundreds of hawkers' stalls exhibiting their assortments of wares: dwarf trees and crimson, chewable seaweed, goldfish and love-charms. Chiefly, however, the Ginza is considered the symbol of modernity as New York's Fifth Avenue is of spending and Broadway is of jazz. Running through the heart of the "new city," it is connected with streets in which industrial progress piles up its warehouses, office-buildings, banks and giant newspaper plants.

The traffic along the Ginza, wheeled and human, is both appalling and suggestive. It is evident that the richshawman is doomed; motor cars outnumber rickshaws by several thousands, while bicycles outnumber the two together by tens of thousands. This sudden excess of modern vehicles has produced the tremendous problem known only too well to the West. The street is congested with taxis; tramcars are clogged with passengers; motor-busses push between ox carts and auto trucks; and sprinkling wagons squirt water along the sidewalks, last refuge of the hunted pedestrian.

As the Ginza is the natives' own, so are the city parks. No sign warning the local inhabitants to keep away from such preserves shocks and frightens the tourist with an omen of racial revolt. The foreigner may roam as freely but no more freely in Tokyo than her citizens. And one of their charms which repays a visit to the parks is the evident delight of the people in all such breathing spots. Hibiya Park offers the crowds of Tokyo municipal movies, band concerts, parades of firemen showing off their equipment, play grounds and dance pavilions, exhibitions of landscape models and flowering plants. In summer it has caves cooled by electricity, artificial fireflies hidden in foliage and a glass "Dragon Palace" for the children. Other popular resorts provide a Luna Park complete with merry-go-rounds, a cinema-house quarter, zoölogical and botanical gardens, art galleries, athletic fields, commercial and "cultural" collections.

There are still magnificent art collections in Tokyo, notwithstanding the heavy losses by fire in 1923. These are being sheltered in fireproof buildings and consequently rendered safer for public inspection. The Imperial Family has broken precedent by exhibiting some of its treasures from time to time, though of course many of the rarest and finest heirlooms remain secreted or in out-of-the-way places where special privileges alone pave the way to a viewing.

In about twenty-five civic libraries a foreigner may select from excellent card catalogues books and documents in English, French or German if his Sanscrit and Mandarin are rusty. He may bend over his reading table with kimonoed students in the freest sort of international quest for knowledge. One of these libraries is devoted solely to the drama, especially Asiatic drama, and is therefore a peculiar attraction.

The visitor may also find innumerable bureaus and agencies where he can study native social enterprises. There are employment offices, night schools for workers, kindergartens, day nurseries, welfare centers, and labor schools, and accompanied by guides one may see the background against which such services operate. The social unfortunates are largely hidden in Tokyo. Not there, as in India and China, do

GIRLS ON THE GINZA BUYING SANTA CLAUS

beggars, lepers, smallpox sufferers, mutilated children and paralytics encumber the highways and wail in temple grounds. Gigantic as the problems of the Japanese are, hopeless as they sometimes seem to those who are trying to solve them, they are at least coped with by workers in profound earnestness. Clinics and asylums are provided by local means if occasional foreign gifts supplement this relief. The nation in Asia which first adopted Western finance and armament has also been first to foresee its civic future and plan far ahead its road-systems, central markets, water-reservoirs, and other features of general welfare.

Radiating in all directions from the heart of the city, ruled by business, amusement, religion, politics and social work, run the thousand quiet little lanes where the emphasis is not change but continuity of life and custom. Children form the chief color in this sector. They peep from balconies, wearing costumes as gay as the bed quilts airing in the sun. A wee gentleman bowed to me one day so low and long that I feared for his balance but of course from the street below I returned his courtesy as best I could. Little boys bob up and down in the thoroughfares in the universal game of hop-scotch or sit with their brushes sketching under the eyes of a teacher, amid the mazes of small bridges which span the narrow Sumida River and the canals, making of the scene an Eastern Venice. Midgets of girls, with dolls on their backs, play at being grown-ups. Little mothers, big enough to exchange the dolls for the heavy babies, dance in circles despite their burdens. Wherever a shrine or a temple offers an open space, it becomes a playground and refuge from the automobiles which come, rolling like thirsty juggernauts, down the cramped lanes.

Quite indistinguishable seems one lane from the rest. Nor

does one shop-dwelling look different from another special-
izing in the same ware. And apparently habits are as uniform
as the living-selling quarters. All day the quiet craftsmen
and their round-faced sons are seen kneeling patiently at
their tasks of carving or painting or offering customers tea
while the wives and daughters sit close by, sewing, hushing
the infants, or setting out rice bowls and chopsticks. And
I knew that when I came back at dusk, I should find them
resting in a regular way, the apprentices playing nimble
games with ball and fan, women visiting and chatting, old
men bowed over "Go" tables, accompanying each master
move of the game with whiffs from long, brass-headed pipes.
Monotonous, but endeared like the refrain of a folksong,
evening would return to the little streets of Tokyo as I
strolled along them. Lamps were lighted on barges and in
the windows of houses leaning above the canals; from restaurants poured out a warm smell of fish and strange soups.
Aimless and amiable groups would scuffle and flap to and
fro on their pattens, or stop to buy goldfish and a dwarf
tree, over which they would later sit in reverie at home,
achieving a voyage in miniature: the goldfish bowl transformed into a cool, country lake; the tiny tree into a romantic
forest. For most of the populace, however, it seemed a sufficient climax of the day merely to watch the moon climb
above the house tops and drag a narrow wake across a
sea of dark tile. Far from defeating the night by auto horns
and electric blare, the greater part of the citizens of Tokyo
yield to its influence at an early hour. Only the night watchman, clapping his wooden sticks, continues on his rounds
when the noodle man retires. Recumbent under flowered
quilts, in the recesses of the now cave-like shops, these simple
folk surrender to the reign of those two almost outgrown
urban phenomena: twilight and sleep.

In these peaceable humdrum quarters, one begins to real-ize how small a portion of Tokyo's inhabitants are aggres-sively modern or passionately conservative. Only a minority out of the millions can pretend to support the "old régime" by patronizing the arts. Only another minority can proclaim itself "emancipated" and uphold Ibsen, Picasso and the jungle throb of saxophone and traps. It takes more time and money than the average citizen possesses to belong to either the old or the new Japan, to practice either "bushido" or free verse. And thus, while slumber overmasters the enormous dark-ened bulk of Tokyo, there is but a small core, at the center blazing with electricity, noisy with loud speakers and trom-bones, where "amusement" is interpreted as activity, rather than tranquillity.

"Down town" is a conception new to Japan. In the good old days there was little difference between shopping and residential districts. Most articles were standardized and simple and easily supplied by the nearest artisan. It is with-in the past two or three generations that the great division has come between the centralized, powerful and essentially commercial region of the Ginza and the sections where the well-to-do live.

During the last half of the nineteenth century people moved reluctantly into the two-story brick buildings being built along the Ginza, protesting that, as they were not a "carnivorous race" like the Europeans, they would soon become pale and anæmic, living in stuffy houses. But electric trams began to run in the days of the Russo-Japanese War and real estate "booms" commenced. Department stores started to compete with one another, the clothing and furnishing business tended to segregate, and the price of land soared with the help of speculators. Next, above the gilded signs and low balconies pushed the heads of five-, six- and eight-story structures. And at last the march "up town," so characteristic of American cities, was begun. This movement, city planning now accelerates.

For the democracy of the down-town district must be exchanged the exclusiveness of gates and fences in the middle and upper-class residential sections of Tokyo. At first a solace is found by an American in the beauty of the gates and the inimitable individuality of the fences which betray a most astonishing diversity of bamboo patterns and shapes. Yet there are areas where a monotonous sameness rules even in these matters, counterpart of the bourgeois life which reigns in other sections of the world. Behind the uniform gentility of these surroundings, the small irritations and temperate joys of the middle-class families take refuge. Back of the gates and fences dwell the respectable, peaceable "average readers" of the newspapers—he who studies the cartoons, aspires to a radio, hangs a framed picture of "The Cherubim" on his wall with just that innocent pleasure experienced by his fellow American putting up a cheap print of cherry blossoms or placing a green lacquer cabinet in the corner. There is the same interest in the high cost of living, the same shudder at flaming youth and bolshevism, the same befogged discussions of politics and foreign affairs, troubles with the cook and "static" interfering with the radio.

This bungalow-dwelling bourgeois quarter might seem to an American suburbanite rather too meager in its display to deserve the comparison. It is rather too artistic, on the other hand, to be so dismissed. The spirit of Tokyo—which I accept as a mocking fox sprite—may with a twinkle, at the least expected point, swing suddenly a gate and disclose a great garden in which banks of shrubbery half conceal a laughing stone god, a moss-lipped lantern, and a wide pool with blooming lotuses on its surface. Only a second to peep, however, and the gate closes tightly on the dream.

Around the precincts of Shiba Park, with its altars and graves, stand the houses of great lords in the Buddhist Church, their gates more richly ornamented than those of common citizens and far outshining in most respects the castles surviving from feudal times. Here Buddhist Fathers meet for consultation; entertain visiting delegations from Hangchow, City of Heaven; organize campaigns among the voters; and discuss the remodeling of the social policy of the sect. They have charming shelter, choice gardens, ponds full of red and silver carp that swarm to the call of an acolyte; and once in a while through an open gate one may see a priest moving sedately, hands folded in wide sleeves, chin buried on breast, in meditation.

While the Ginza may be classified conveniently as "modern" and Shiba Park as "old Japan," the large territory adjacent, devoted to castles, government houses and diplomatic residences, is an agglomeration of many influences. There are palaces, here and there, in various styles, belonging to members of the reigning family. One resembles a pleasant English country mansion with tennis courts and shadowed lawns. Another, where the autumn garden party is held, is an imposing replica, in shining white, of the British Buckingham. The one romantic site is Chiyoda Castle, dominating the center of the city. Its venerable walls, suavely curved at the corners like a samurai's blade, rise from broad moats; over the ramparts lean the long arms of twisted pine trees, writhing and seeming to reach, Tantalus fashion, to cool their fever in the still waters below. High above the trees stand out the guard houses, black and white, severe as Puritan versions of pagodas.

This martial severity, rather than the fabled opulence,

characterizes all the old castle dwellings of Tokyo. Here
and there a gate, an ancient wall, a garden of pines com-
memorates the home where some feudal lord was compelled
to live, under the watchful eye of the Shogun. In Japanese
books are to be found the pictures and complete records of
these dwellings, showing clearly the types of architecture
permitted to each lord, apportioned in grandeur according to
his income in bushels of rice.

Even had a lord desired to live in luxury like a Medici,
he might not display his splendors to the street. His gate
might be just so broad, with exactly so many iron-bossed
panels and black-latticed loopholes for his fierce-eyed sentries.
His wall might be built only in a simple, stern manner, its
beams of dark wood embedded in gray or white plaster,
topped by glossy tiles. Nothing could be further from the
tourist's customary dream of "that gorgeous East." Behind
the grim barrier, his lady must live, left behind as hostage
for good behavior when he traveled to the provinces, to
while away her days with harp-playing and poetry. She could
not hope to look over the wall, upon the outside world, for
only the highest pine trees in the garden might do that. No
doubt, she envied sometimes their tall victory over con-
finement.

Mingled with relics of the past and also clustered near
the moat are the homes of foreign legations and embassies,
marked by national shields on their gates. Government buildings are not far away, adorned by the heavy statues of
admirals and frock-coated statesmen, their Victorianism in-
destructible either by fire or an awful convulsion of nature.
With a stark, almost terrible simplicity, on Kudan Hill,
above the city, stands a monster *torii* of iron commemorating
the soldier dead of the Russo-Japanese War.

Around the hotels, clubs, government buildings, palaces,

legations and private homes of this region about Chiyoda
Castle has grown up a social life rare in the Orient. Here
the "natives" have never been unwelcome intruders, as in
the "foreign settlements" of China, ostracized by hotels and
shut away from parks and *bunds* by imported police. They
meet the foreigner on a basis of social, as well as business,
equality, and it has had a noticeably improving effect on the
bearing and manner of the foreigner. In response to this
situation, highly diversified circles of Japanese society have
risen, each capable at least of entertaining its kind, aristocrats consorting with aristocrats, money greeting money,
diplomats, artists, priests, writers, and musicians on the
receiving line for their colleagues.

Only a native connoisseur of the city, of course, can unfold
to a traveler the inner life of Tokyo. Behind the modest fence
of polished wood, may lie concealed a spacious mansion and
rare landscape garden, in which a master hand has regulated
the very tune played by the waterfalls. Back of a bleak expanse may lurk a restaurant known only to Tokyo nobility,
whose cook-proprietor, a true non-commercial artist, will
never be persuaded to serve more than five guests at a meal.

But if one is lucky and patient he will be taken behind
the scenes, where he will hear among other things explanations of just what the "Yedo spirit" was which modern
Tokyo scorns. There are people as devoted to its memory
and relics as Westerners are to old London and old Paris;
they are busy collecting diaries and letters, and compiling in
leisure hours histories of its various quarters and streets; in
fact, an enormous Japanese story of Tokyo now awaits trans-
lation. Moreover, a large group of people believe the "Yedo
spirit" must not be allowed to die and have banded themselves together for its preservation; some five hundred
tattooed men, with an eighty-year old veteran fireman as

president, formed the "Children of Yedo" society, which meets regularly to sing the famous songs and to pass resolutions against invasions by Western taste.

As nearly as I could understand from the descriptions of elderly people who proclaimed themselves children of Yedo, the city's celebrated spirit must have been the brand of mediæval Florence. It was a temper both fierce and gay, generously hospitable and often carelessly cruel, adapted to fashion, wit, revelry and song. It was in brief a blend, produced in the Japanese as in the Italian town, by combining spendthrift noblemen and their roving soldier bands with canny and display-loving merchants and their retainer craftsmen.

Noblemen's courtyards, in the Yedo days, were alive with music and military drill. Near the castles, in dark mazes of lanes, huddled the "wasps' nests" of adventurers, resembling the Italian condottieri, whose swords and stabbing knives were at the service of the wealthy lords. Nor were these the only gallant fighters in town; amateur groups of citizens formed in every quarter to protect their homes alike from raids and from the "scarlet flower of Yedo," as they stoically called the constantly ravaging fire. Whenever wind would sweep the flames in gorgeous horror through the city of paper and straw, citizen and warrior together would sing the *kiyari* and run with bamboo ladders, buckets, and insignia to the rescue.

There was wit in the city as well as reckless courage. Many an entertainer, renowned for his sallies, took the precaution of shaving his head like a tea priest, so that no one dared to take offense at his bold tongue. Feasting sometimes for many days on end made glad the great inns; before the earthquake the Shinagawa district still preserved such abodes of revelry. Numbers of big mansions with heavily carved roofs and fluttering curtains before the wide doorways were pointed out, where, in bygone days, friends accompanying a traveler to the outskirts of the city would entertain him for a week with dancing and wine, before they let him go.

A great deal of practical, public spirit had early manifested itself among the merchants, if not the warriors. Grown rich on the wealth brought from the provinces to be spent in Yedo by a score of splendid lords, they had money to lavish, not on theaters or festivals alone, but on public works beside. United into a feudal mutual-aid society for relief in times of calamity, it was very easy for them to transfer their funds in modern times to a Western-style chamber of commerce. The government had built a vast waterworks system for the city, bringing water in bamboo pipes for twenty-seven miles. Tradespeople, even beggars and outcasts, had also their guilds, markets, societies and officers—in short, a civic attitude.

Pageantry of caparisoned horses and purple umbrellas, insolent grand seigneurs and wretched beggars and dogs, wandering minstrels, friars with alms bowls, courtesans in flamboyant robes, bishop princes with their armed retinues, ladies escorted in palanquins, artists watching the *Ukiyo* or "Fleeting World," with a half-loving and half-satirical eye, moralists denouncing the new fads in music, apprentice boys dancing on their half-yearly festival day—the past of Tokyo was in reality quite as akin to mediæval and renaissance Italian and French cities, as the future of Tokyo is, to-day, bound up with the future of Western capitals.

CHAPTER VIII

HUMAN MOLDS

PERHAPS it is unnecessary at this point to emphasize the obvious fact of the extreme diversity among the Japanese in face, dress, gesture, breeding, mind and temperament. But Americans, resentful enough when lumped together by confident European visitors, are often inclined to view others, especially Asiatics, in the same hasty way.

Cartoonists are responsible in large measure for shaping our minds. As they train us, day after day, to look for John Bull, Uncle Sam, Marianne, Fritz, Italy with the cock-feathered helmet, the Chinese Laundryman and the Japanese Tin Soldier, we easily fall victim to a personification of peoples as a whole. Probably because our world tactics have so recently and vastly widened, we tend to oversimplify races. Too many of us who no longer think we know the exact expression, length of beard, costume and age of Jehovah in a distant Heaven, are still anthropomorphic in our concepts of distant peoples.

Not very far afield need a tourist go to find variety in the Japanese humanity. It was demonstrated to me every day by the procession on the street beneath my window. I would be roused at early morning by a high clear song of three words, *"Yo-o-o, Ya-ay, Yi-bam!"* chanted over and over, hour after hour, a chorus of women's voices, until I might have fancied some ship passing with female sailors raising ᴠ ditty of the sea. But in fact each woman was holding a

110

rope, while together the group hauled and swayed, lifting a heavy iron weight on a bamboo frame and letting it fall, booming, on the top of a sinking post. Female pile-drivers were these, laying in an ancient way foundations for a new, highly modern sewer system.

To the tune of this sweet, if monotonous, refrain, and against the dark backdrop of a temple courtyard across the way, trailed during the morning a long file of passersby. A commonplace crowd enough, positively dull to a Japanese, but in my startled eyes it had all the piquancy of a pageant:

A geisha, tinsel flowers in her hair, with powdered hands holding a drum, riding in a rickshaw.

Two farmers, bent double with exertion, harnessed to a cart, dragging a heavy load of fertilizer out to a farm.

A limousine, equipped with straw flaps over the wheels to keep mud from spattering the lacy gowns of foreign-dressed Japanese ladies.

Boys on bicycles; boys on stilts.

Man in kimono with military cap and wooden shoes.

Man in kimono with silk skirt and square-toed boots.

Man in union suit.

Man in union suit with mushroom hat.

Man in Prince Albert coat and high hat and brown boots.

Two little boys in speckled kimono riding an American toy footpedal automobile.

Man in kimono pushing a baby-carriage made out of a soap box on wheels.

Joyous little girl in fluttering robes in the colors of all lovely things—chrysanthemum, autumn leaves and ocean spray.

Two solemn old men in rustling garments of black, straw-sandaled, leading by the hand a big-eyed urchin, clad in a black velvet Lord Fauntleroy suit.

Three coolies in blue tights and blue cotton coats having white characters on the back, advertising a well-known plumbing shop.

A venerable, whiskered man who might, except for his fedora hat, serve as a model for that Chinese sage in the paintings who lives in the wilderness and rides on a wild stag.

In his costume or mode of conveyance, each of the passing personages explained who he was, and what his class or occupation. Not merely a group of "Japanese in native costume," walked the street but a series of highly individualized human beings one by one. Yonder kimono, for example, the initiated can say, is too brightly splashed with color to admit its wearer to good society; she rides in a rickshaw because the higher geisha, no less than actors and doctors, to uphold professional dignity, thus mark themselves off from the tramping throngs. That meek lady trudging behind her husband's back must be about forty years of age, judging by the brevity of her sleeves, and fairly poor, judging by the pattern of her sash, which is a full year out of date. The happy little girl wears on her back the stiff, pillow-like brocade bow, so bulkily tied that every one knows she has a very "Victorian" mamma; her companion's sash is lighter, betraying a more radical parentage. Unmistakably, the gentleman in ceremonial black, with a well-known crest on his sleeves indicating sword-bearing ancestors, is on his way to make a call. Just behind him, a man is plainly *en route* to business, for he wears a serviceable bourgeois kimono of brown silk. And the timid, tottering peasant in the rear is surely a visitor from a distant province—only observe his white hair, long and woman-like, drawn up to a neat knot on the top of his head!

The eye is popularly supposed to make the race look uniform. But though I have seen the slanting, perfectly curved almond shape of the prints, I have also heard Japanese themselves remarking on the rarity of this beauty. Though there were eyes so fine and narrow that they might have been painted with a delicate brush, they were by no means universal. Many wide-opened eyes can I also recall, glowing and round as the most resplendent Italian orbs; pop-eyes;

A BOY OF THE PEOPLE

dull, glazed eyes; eyes clouded with too much study; eyes sparkling with mischief; eyes that were friendly and kindly and humorous; others that snapped with satirical fire.

At any large gathering in Tokyo, the range of types, not only physical but temperamental, is striking. Seated at the same banquet table or clustered about the ballroom will be jolly souls, plump as the deity of fortune, and anæmic but aristocratic-looking persons with long, thinly chiseled features. Some will be fragile, sharp and shrewd; others, tall, muscular, intensely vital, with rubicund cheeks and a bluff manner; a few will be worn and listless; winsome young girls will offset vivacious boys with heavy manes of hair, left long like Bohemian artists; dull, shy, even frightened folk will appear beside talkative, boisterous, aggressive "hustlers." Very plain are the evidences of many racial mixtures; unknown as are the true origin and number of peoples mingled in the modern nation, their variety is evident. There are high-cheek-boned Mongolian faces and low ones, reminiscent of Malaysian or Southern Chinese; while almost Caucasian features may be blended with these. The racial layers, reminders of conquering and conquered tribes—manifold, indeed, as the heritage of modern Americans—have been strikingly overlaid with social strata produced by culture, class, profession or province. A man, for example, indicates his station very clearly to a Japanese fellow-citizen by his laughter; and he betrays his local origin by small differences in speech, such as the pronunciation of *Arigato* as *Aringato*.

Indeed, the Japanese are keenly conscious of differences among themselves. They are moved by the slight suggestion of a "womanish cut" in a man's kimono, indicating the sway of classic taste. A great deal of ancient local patriotism has survived, left over from the long centuries when every region could boast some speciality, be it a kind of cake, a marriage custom, a curious ritual, nimble craftsman hands, or remarkable length of hair of its women. Very strong still is the hereditary antagonism of North and South, of agricultural, ruling regions against industrial, commercial aspirants. No longer, to be sure, would a Tokyo citizen entitle a descriptive book about Osaka, "Travels in the Land of Pigs," but he may retain a kind of nervous condescension about his Southern neighbors which is heartily reciprocated. Even between one university and another there is deep-rooted animosity; Oxford is not more supercilious about the University of Manchester than the Imperial University, which produces government officials, about Waseda, whence spring the journalistic antagonists of government policies.

It is possible, then, to separate persons into groups according to clan, college, family, city, wealth. But within the group each individual stands, after all, alone. One may carry in his mental baggage more poetry and legend than his fellows; another more sport and humor; a third, painting and philosophy; a fourth, practical common sense about business. I have known colorless people, merry people, and lazy, shrewish, coldly keen, mystic, rebellious, haughty and gentle folk. Some I met who, like the novelist Arishima, a follower of Tolstoian doctrines, were motivated by high general principles; I also knew others whom no general ideas, but a bitter-tempered mother-in-law, commanded.

Not only did each Japanese seem different from his fellows, if perhaps only on minor points; he also seemed to conflict with himself. I might discover one of these creatures of mood, on Tuesday, in uproarious gayety; on Wednesday, plunged in gloom, despairing of the "future of Asia"; on Thursday, at a tea party, very shy and uncommunicative; on Friday, at his home, confidential and eager to relate "the story of my life." In short, friends appeared to be variable, as well as various.

Eccentric people, faddists and hobby riders, abound in Tokyo, especially in the literary world but also in politics. One spends his leisure outside office hours in collecting ivory badgers; another draws gigantic plans for a garden city of his dreams; a third has a mild, happy mania for rare pebbles suitable for walks, or indulges in blueprints of buildings which will express "the souls of East and West." Nor is it merely among aristocrats that hobbies are cherished; among the new crop of politicians, raised by "the people" are many pronounced "characters." There is a peasant who is devoted to the drama, for instance, and, when not leading embattled farmers, writes and directs village problem plays, often producing them in the teeth of police opposition. There are diet cranks, camera fiends, baseball fans, men who adore China as some Americans worship England, men who are fanatic nationalists, men who withdraw from active life to steep themselves in philosophy.

Consequently Japanese civilization, like Western, is a great light that requires a thousand facets for its reflection. No one human being can catch all, or most, of the broad beam. The rural politician is ignorant of tea ceremony; the native Mary Pickford is far from a trained mystic; the aristocrat is indifferent to remote village customs; the artist may know as little of ancient, racial, commercial development as the merchant knows of Buddhist sutras. It would be possible to meet hundreds of men and women without acquiring an idea of the many-sidedness of their culture.

To use the words, "the Japanese," is perilous; to generalize about the race still more so. Not even peasants fit into a common mold, for some grow rice and breed silkworms in the hot, fertile south, while others grow wheat in the cold

north at Hokkaido or cut trees in the "Alps"; there are superstitious folk in the hinterlands who have not seen a railroad
train and there are landlords who have introduced electric
power and large-scale machinery. There is an ever-decreas-
ing number of small proprietors toiling on the steep flanks of
terraced hills in the most intensive agricultural activities, it
is said, in the world; there are radical tenant-peasants, organized in unions, engaged in striking, voting and acting as
rural representatives of the community; there are rustic
youths and maidens who have no thought but escape to the
city and the bright lights of the Ginza.

To speak of "the geisha" is similarly difficult; so many
kinds exist. Some of these gilded ladies wear Western sport
clothes and get their pictures, as ice-skaters, into the journals.
Others dress in modern kimono; yet others in costumes of
two hundred years ago. Many only dance; a few, the "intellectual companions" of statesmen, "converse." Large troupes
appear as professional actresses in Tokyo's geisha theater;
a minority in Osaka, the tired business man's town, may be
seen scantily draped in "living statuary groups," dancing in
"American Indian" feather scenes, in "Pageants of Paris,"
or "Glorifying the Japanese Girl."

Presumably one could classify "the Priests" but here,
again, types are diverse. Shinto priests, holding hereditary
office, may be powerful, worldly churchmen. Nuns are often
engaged in social work or leading reform societies. Jolly
Friar Tucks, rotund and palaverous, may wear Panama hats,
eat flesh and make merry with the geisha. Ragged wretches
live precariously from daily coppers of the superstitious
poor. Exquisite ascetics, trained in the highest spiritual and
philosophic discipline known to the East, sit in lonely meditation in forests. Many Buddhists are busy with philanthropy
or hymnology; others only with doctrines. The thousands

of Christian native workers are divided into several sects. Occasionally new creeds are launched; to add to the confusion a branch of Shinto, preached by a peasant woman, remarkably resembles in some of its tenets Christian Science.

"The workers" is a term no more precise. Among the herded population of great cities or industrial settlements, some four and a half million persons are laboring in mines and factories under conditions sometimes suggestive of those in England a century ago. Millions more are producing in mediæval handicraft shops under conditions akin to those of France four centuries ago. The psychology of the two classes is distinct, like their problems.

Usually, when we refer to the "Japanese," we mean a very thin upper crust, a few thousands separated from the multitude. Yet the higher classes are diversified beyond the millions below. Among the aristocrats, members of really old families are enrolled beside the descendants of lately ennobled commoners. Covered by the title, "Prince," are scions of the blood royal and of ambitious but plebeian statesmen. Moreover, the distinction often drawn between "common merchants" and "proud samurai" is largely a delusion since, thanks to the hustle and shrewdness of those samurai in the past, feudal clans of yesterday have become millionaire clans to-day, not at all ashamed of wealth extracted from canned crab, bean cakes, mines or power plants.

The "white collar" class includes within its ranks a few hundred thousand government officials, teachers, administrators, army and navy men, and workers in business offices, journalism, law and medicine. Yet their outlook is less uniform than their salary average. They include all brands of opinion, from Fascist members of the Black Dragons to surreptitious Socialists, Communists and ultra-conservative scholars of the classics, writers of Chinese poems and modern lyrics, playwrights, founders of experimental colonies, women reformers, jazzing flappers, farmer leaders, sentimental humanitarians, temperance advocates, militarists and liberals.

To be sure, definite and recognizable types are to be found among the Japanese. But an astonishing number of these seemed to me not so national as they are international. Resemblances of class and occupation create human molds that set at defiance the barriers of race.

An artist in Kyoto who limns pine-tree pictures with black ink on pineapple-silk screens is of course different from a painter in New York who splashes huge canvases with oil in Cubist ecstasies. But the two have at least as much in common—a sensitiveness to form and a pride in mastery of medium—as either has, let us say, to a trolley-car conductor of his own nation.

Religious reverence, if it be profound and genuine, regardless of its object, makes a spiritualized human being; the finest type of Christian preacher and the most sincere teacher of the best—and it is the rarest—school of Buddhism, possess certainly an affinity deeper than either bears to a war profiteer.

A scholarly man, similarly, belongs to the world rather than to a country. It scarcely matters whether he has studied Latin or Pali, old French chronicles or early Chinese ballads, Anglo-Saxon land tenure or Japanese village law; it does not even matter if he has devoted himself to things so idle as the Black Magic of Taoistic formulæ or the hair-splitting of Hindu or early European monks. The very mode of life produces a caste that is recognizable from Heidelberg to Bombay. Scientists, pundits or philosophers of the earth form a supra-national stratum of their own and no doubt always did—Plato, Buddha and Confucius were almost contemporaries.

Courtesy, too, speaks an international language. A great

lady of China or Japan has the same fundamental instincts as great ladies of any time or land. Wishing to make her guest feel at ease, she welcomes, smiling; she introduces her very discreetly behaved *jeune fille* of a daughter; perhaps she provides a little informal music or a glimpse of her garden. Not for her are the timidities that may assail the bourgeoisie; she is poised, distant but gracious, and faintly amused.

The brisk business man is also a world product. Traders, lunching in Japan's scores of chambers of commerce or going to cotton spinners' conventions in England or lumber meetings at Seattle, have experiences and ideas matching those of their Rotary brethren everywhere. The "self-made man," the reckless gambler, the imperialist, the wealthy philanthropist or collector of art are but universal phenomena in a Japanese setting. Young women who bob their hair and devote themselves earnestly to the Charleston, become quite as much "flapper" as German, French or American sisters. Nor can a man turn fiery Methodist or plunge into Salvation Army work in the slums of Kobe, without learning to react according to his religious impulse as much as his race.

Within very broad lines, therefore, it is possible to feel thoroughly at ease in Japan and to find circles corresponding fairly closely to those familiar at home. But hopeful travelers who want to find all the rest of the world exactly like themselves or totally unlike themselves are doomed to disappointment; the Japanese can no more than other sections of humanity be classified with botanical accuracy.

Aristocrats, for example, may have a long European training, yet beneath their foreign acquisitions native traditions may be their guiding star. Yonder tall French elegant, suavely discoursing on the last Salon exhibition, may be wholly Con-

fucian in his attitude toward women. This English-looking
count with the Oxford accent and the irreproachable tailor-
ing may spend his spare time on the ritual of Shingon or the
history of the Turkish flower code. The bureaucrats with
their formality, together with doctors, engineers, architects,
metaphysicians and technical experts have been largely fashioned in Germany. And yet—red tape or gold medals may
be only additions after all and the fundamental fact about
the men may be their feudal loyalty to group or clan.

On the other hand, folk who may seem at a glance wholly
Japanese may actually be radically Europeanized. Army and
navy officers, elaborately decorated and medaled, in glittering
uniforms with feathered hats, are fairly faithful counterparts
of their colleagues on the Continent. Parliamentary members,
in general, resemble those of European countries more than
the medley at Washington.

It is not easy, always, to disentangle the Europeanized
from the Americanized Japanese. You may sit and cheer on
the baseball bleachers with Keio University boys just as
loudly as you might in Missouri. But afterward, in the evening, when you chat in a student restaurant with these same
boys, you may find their minds influenced by French and
Russian novels and their temper a mingling of gloominess
and nervous enthusiasm that is Asiatic-European rather than
Missourian. Outward appearances often are deceptive masks.

Another very curious element enters into foreign judgment of the Japanese people. We ourselves are no longer
so rigid in our notions of beauty, religion or class. We
approach the modern Asiatics with an appreciation that
would have been unthinkable to our grandparents. In contrast with our own Parisian frocks, the kimono seems not
shocking but, if anything, a little prim; so our ideas about
sandals and revealed ankles have changed. The sleek, silk-

clad lady of the East, her costume composed of rich tones and simple lines and her face so pale, thin, arch-eyebrowed and ineffably blasé, seems nearer to our present ideal of fashionable charm than the Western daguerreotypes of the "naughty nineties." Unquestionably, the Victorian women who went to Japan with pinched waists, furbelowed skirts, tight boots, Merry Widow hats atop mounds of false pompadour, would find the women of their own races to-day about as "heathen," "immodest" and "alien" as they then thought the Japanese. I know that numbers of missionaries, returned after long years in the Orient, have suffered this reaction.

Westerners are often conscious of being imperfectly adapted to the modern age, even though they have had a longer preparation than the East. It is possible for a woman in Japan to shelter a telephone in her cupboard and in her heart the precepts of marriage of a mediæval churchman— but does not an Occidental woman miraculously combine ancient ideas of war, chivalry and a classical education with new opinions on dancing, taxation, the rights of married teachers, censorship and wallpaper? Like the Japanese who this day throws beans on his floor to drive out evil and to-morrow attends a lecture on "the rational life," foreigners are capable of eating hot-cross buns on Good Friday and scoffing on Easter. The Western world offers a plethora of contrasts as striking as those offered by Japan. Germany can show the Wilhelminic headdress beside the boyish bob, the Cubist apartment house elbowing the Rococco beer palace, the Passion Play and the futuristic movie. New York's skyscrapers dwarf the cathedral spires, just as warehouses in Tokyo overshadow the temple roof; the brownstone-front residence and the gaudy cinema palace look quite as quaint together as a modest Japanese dwelling in the lee of an electric-lighted Ginza. Neither the West nor the

Japanese can pretend to furnish homes or brains with sub-lime consistency.

We are, in short, as hard to classify and judge as the Easterners. No longer does Europe possess in their pristine perfection the celebrated favorites of fiction: nobleman and courtier, country squire and rustic bumpkin, the short-sighted and long-bearded professor, humble creatures "in trade," the ferociously mustachioed musketeer, the lady bountiful or the perfect butler. Economic cataclysm and armed revolution have cracked and up-ended the strata of society; while in America the machine has raised and crushed millions to a level even more uniform. It is this world process which is affecting Japan. The glory of romantic types—knight, peas-ant, courtesan, fine lady, artisan, sage—is waning. The nation as a whole is becoming fluid, as dialect gives way to common speech, local festivals to country-wide celebrations and village gossip to national news; as noblemen enter busi-ness and merchants marry noblewomen, outcasts confer with government officials, princes play golf and farmers play politics. It will be long years before the human fluid of this society is solidified into rigid molds.

In the very expressions of faces, reactions to the world process can be observed. There are Japanese who do not allow their spiritual questioning, ambition, enthusiasm or revolt to disturb what they feel to be "correct" in appear-ance and manner. Thus, women may be heard reading, in public, expert reports on child welfare, with downcast eyes and the hushed voices inculcated by ancient moralists. Others are unable to maintain tradition at a high pitch; they come to private parties wearing that ceremonial mask of solemnity which is as inevitable in their good society as the conventionalized grin of an American hostess. But before long, as each launches on a favorite topic, discussing photography, juggling, children's diseases or the prospects for the cocoa business, the masks begin to slip. Soon dark eyes are shining, the smile and the outright laugh break through the classic restraint and now and then a young girl giggles so merrily that she must perforce hide her blushing face behind a magenta-colored sleeve.

Certain individuals have gone far in discarding formality. I have seen women, returned from Paris with something of the French vivacity, roll their eyes, shrug a shoulder expressively and actually gesticulate. The men companions never having been abroad, were patently scandalized, suspicious and yet a little, oh a very little bit, delighted. The young generation, capturing all too well the Western spirit, tends to become rather forward, breezy and effusive. And the modern dramas permit actors to wave arms, wring hands, shout and weep; while Nora in "The Doll's House" has a chance to do something surely never achieved by Japanese woman in the past—she slams the door. This action, much as its symbolic meaning shocked our own grandmothers, has positively stunned Japanese audiences by the vulgarity of its noise.

Men of affairs to-day have less and less leisure for ceremony and some of the more daring refuse to make New Year calls. Women who support themselves by teaching, nursing or social work have neither patience nor money to dress themselves like puppets. Their unpowdered faces show clearly the lines of suffering and sympathy; they speak frankly and simply about problems they encounter; their well-worn kimono have no hint of formal "chic" and their sashes are tied so hastily before they run after the morning tramcar that they hesitate to remove their covering silk coats. Feudal discipline with its stoic dictates has already much relaxed; no one can predict just what, once it has more generally loosened, the Japanese faces and hands may yet express.

Abundant emotion there is sure to be and evoked by many things that ,ordinarily leave a Westerner tongue-tied or mildly interested. Sights of nature—cherry petals about to fall, birds in autumn flight—stir in the cultivated Japanese tears of sadness. As Buddhists, reminded of the swift passing of all life and beauty, they stand with glistening eyes, while the Occidental at their side cheerfully remarks: "How picturesque!" It is not considered unmanly in Japan to display grief over a poem where an average American would merely be embarrassed. And if a Japanese may be reticent about his wife, he yields to no one in frank admiration for his mother.

I did not find people "impassive" or "inscrutable," once I grew accustomed to their manifestations of excitement which are often much slighter than our own. A well-brought-up Japanese brightens genially where we might indulge in a laugh; and his displeasure—or hers—may be read, if not in a frown, then in an almost imperceptible stiffening of the posture and a freezing of the expression in eyes and mouth. The depths of feeling that underlie this enforced formality of behavior, however, often disclose themselves in forms intelligible to the bluntest Westerner. Two self-controlled, cultured individuals, whom we learned to know in Tokyo, the celebrated novelist, Arishima, and a beautiful woman journalist, Madame Hatano, found apparently no solution to the problems of their lives but voluntary death together. Yet when we saw Arishima for the last time, he was as gently calm as ever, talking about Whitman whose poems he had translated and about Tolstoy whose theories he had applied, surrendering a large part of his lands to his tenants. Quietly remarking that he intended soon to abandon also his large mansion in Tokyo and move into a "smaller home," he bowed and disappeared. So Madame Hatano, on our last evening together, was rationally tranquil and composed.

Human beauty to the conservative Japanese, as to all classic peoples, involves this element of calm. Where the bars are let down for the free play of emotion, the early ideals are threatened. But the barriers are breaking as they gave way in the West.

A Tokyo magazine devoted to the drama and the motion picture is an excellent illustration, for it represents two ages in conflict. One side of the cover displays a theatrical idol; the reverse, a film star. The one portrays a Japanese actress of the old school; mournful, languid, she hardly lifts her heavy-lidded eyes; dark tragedy haunts her soul, although her body wears the gorgeous raiment of the courtesan. Turn to the other side then and behold a Hollywood show girl of the cinema! Her blue eyes roll, her laughing red mouth discloses a full set of bright teeth, her hair is a defiant disorder of yellow curls. She is bold, "full of pep," and clad in a red bathing suit. Back to back, these twin portraits summarize the two ideals in competition: that of the classic world where beauty meant restraint, and that of the jazz age where it consists of fun and animation.

But laughter, either in East or West, is a comparatively modern ingredient of beauty. Early Dutch masters, it is true, admitted a few roguish damsels and a "laughing cavalier" to canvas; however, it is only recently, and above all in America, that cinemas, billboards, magazine covers and advertisements have made the broad grin a requisite. In other times, grief was the highest emotion to be immortalized, in sorrowing Niobe, haggard Mater Dolorosa or agonizing martyr. As for the Renaissance, it was above all a divine calm that hallowed the ideal. The Mona Lisa's smile is a ghost.

Astonishingly in harmony on this point were Orient and Occident. Sphinx, Mother of Buddha, Hindu Mermaid, Persian lady in her flower garden, Chinese court favorite under the plum blossoms, Mexican and African goddesses, Greek nymph or caryatid, gentle Italian madonnas, wistful Griseldas of mediæval legend, heroic Brunhildas in "symbolic groups," pallid Victorian maidens—they were no less placid than the queens, *Kwannons,* poetesses and dancing girls admired by Japanese artists.

For the first time, then, a sharp break has come to Japanese dreams. The national ideal of a beautiful woman has indeed often been modified. At one era, she was round, short, healthy and red-cheeked. Later she became an unearthly pale, tall, swaying human willow of the prints. Now, she may be animated. She must, in fact, show her teeth!

What is happening is no less than the slow, half-conscious universal evolution in concepts of beauty and character. As men begin to need commercial and professional ethics instead of a knightly code; as modern audiences, grown squeamish, shrink from the tragic scenes that delighted their ancestors; as young people muse on romantic love more than on filial piety; as women in spinning mills learn to forsake traditions of obedience for combinations in defense of rights; as statesmen, appealing to the populace, develop "democratic personalities" and "pleasing voices" for the microphone—the Japanese find themselves without a definite, perfectly adapted pattern for their evolving behavior. Old models are outworn; those for the future have yet to be fashioned.

Fortunately for common understanding, the ideals of the fading past in Japan may be appreciated as facts and do not have to depend solely on theories. There are living men and women who represent the heights attained by feudal society. They are examples of a supreme adaptation, each to a fixed niche in a settled order; they have achieved self-mastery, which is nobility, and resignation if not profound contentment. Three men, in particular, come to mind, having a likeness of kind with mediæval Europeans, no doubt, and yet subtly of Asia—three human molds unknown to the new society of America formed in the eighteenth century. One was an abbot; the second a rickshaw coolie; the third a Southern knight.

An ethereal kindliness and detachment distinguished the Buddhist Abbot. He had lived to a great age within the confines of his temple grounds. He had been "cloistered," however, within nature rather than away from it in a dark stone building in the manner of multitudes of European monks. The walls of his frail cottage were open to the glory of springtime bamboo, autumn foliage and the cicada songs of summer. Instead of retreating from the splendors of the natural world, he had moved near to them. Kinship with flowers, birds and animals was his creed and he tried to win from them a message instead of preaching to them in the fashion of a St. Francis of Assisi.

An old temple park formed his home. It had neither plan nor symmetry. Mere time, it seemed, had designed those avenues of cryptomeria as it had persuaded the tombs to lean comfortably in billowing folds of rich moss. The roofs of the buildings were thatched and drooping, so that from a distance they resembled monstrous brown porcupines waiting in a dim and dripping wood. There was a pool, shining without a ripple, forming a mirror for the twisted stumps of aged wisteria and the lotus-shapes of bronze bells.

Nevertheless nature was not the sole companion. The Abbot's retreat was not to a primitive wilderness; he was surrounded by the relics of a refined civilization. Within his temple archives were treasures of Japan's noblest art epochs; each room possessed a masterpiece on screen or scroll, of bamboo leaves in a breeze, of blossom fêtes, dragon dances, pheasants lurking under long grasses, or a wild bird seeking its nest through mist. Statuary was set within shrines depicting no Savior in agony for mankind, but a serene and passive divinity whose unperturbed face crowned a kindred loveliness of floating scarves, curling clouds and lotus-petals.

The Abbot of this sanctuary looked as though its tranquillity had passed into his very being. His eyes were bright and his smile perfect in its utter serenity. It was the face of one who had conquered ambition: the desire for heaven, the lust for worldly wealth or ascetic mortification. He had apparently found Nirvana to be no more nor less than Nature and her sublimation in art.

America has had "other worldly" divines but in a more positive sense—men who were eagerly humanitarian or apostolic, sympathetically benign or "wrestling" with the powers of darkness. The finest European monk's face I remember to have seen in the galleries of Rome was the replica of a Savonarola, ecstatic and ordeal-hollowed. But the Buddhist Abbot was as far from passionate yearning toward divinity or acute concern with interpretation of doctrine as he was from an impulse to preach or reform. His achievement was essentially an equilibrium.

It may be conceded that there are few persons like the Lord Abbott in Japan. Not of his ilk were the wretched, holy "medicine men" who wandered among the poorer quarters of the cities; nor the energetic Buddhist social worker, eager to adopt everything from new pedagogic methods for his kindergarten to the foreign art of "shake-hands." But in the Lord Abbott I thought I saw a high model peculiar to his faith; and I know that such high peaks in any faith are rare.

The *kuruma*-man who used to sit outside our door was less handsome than the Lord Abbot. He was wrinkled and bent and very old—few of the younger men are taking up the rapidly abandoned rickshaw trade. But something made him akin to the High Priest. He, too, had a philosophy in his face.

On a northern farm he had spent his youth. Under the former régime his parents were forced to surrender half their produce as taxes, lest perchance they should save a little coin and grow "independent and rebellious." He and they lived the lives of animals in toil, hunger and exposure to bitter cold. He was innocent; he believed firmly in badger-spirits ever since, one dark night, a badger robbed him. He had nothing that an American farmer would call ambition—it could never occur to him to covet a Ford or a radio.

For all his plain and rough background, his expression was both soft and confident. Though he had toiled, it was after all in consciousness of a definite place in society—the peasant in old Japan was above the merchant in social esteem, if beneath him in wealth. He had suffered greatly, but felt a certain stoic compensation. He had labored, but not without a chivalric code.

One black night near New Year's time, I was riding in his carriage. A tipsy reveler, one of those frequent at that season, made a murmured remark concerning the strange passenger which she of course did not understand. At once, the rickshaw man stopped, severely ordered me to remain seated and set upon the insulter with threats and jabs of the fist. A large crowd gathered, acted as general umpire, and decided in favor of the *kuruma*-man. The insulter slunk away.

Very stately and solemn the *kuruma*-man stepped within his shafts and bore me home, the honor of his passenger preserved.

They are not all subtle, the workers and farmers of Japan. Far from it are the burly chaps in flowered quilts who come to roar with mediæval mirth at the slapstick marionette shows in temple fairs. But on many of the old people, I have seen written this peculiar consciousness, this ancient dignity rooted in the soil. Very sad are their faces sometimes, for they have known the awful devastations of earthquake, fire and typhoon much too well; but they are spared restlessness, as no prospect of change or sudden fortune unfolds for them. Worn by the life struggle on a three-acre holding, hopeless of relief, they yet have contrived to accept life and death, not stolidly but with a certain noble pride.

Having a definite groove in society and a code in life makes akin the Lord Abbot and the rickshaw-puller. In spirit, too, both are brothers of the southern knight who, in a small provincial town, had been our host.

Art, instead of sport, had formed his education. He showed no trace of the easy, lounging air of an English squire; he did not need the pose, for he was never stiff in manner. Equally far was he removed from a polished Continental correctness. In one personality and without effort, he combined innate dignity and cordiality.

His robes were the symbols of his class standing. The lines of his crested black sleeves, the folds of his wide silk skirt, the small crisp fan in his sash—these were all severe and plain. His hands were those of an artist—hands that were seeing, rather than touching, so fine was their perception of pottery texture, brush strokes, fabric and flower forms. His face no one could forget.

It was a curious blend of the stern and the kind. It seemed

to reflect a mind in which harsh, military traditions were softened with poetry and legend. A haughty gentleman, no doubt he was, rigorous in his ideas of what became his class and family; he might be an uncomfortable man to have for a superior. But he was as strict with himself as he could be with others; no matter how early he woke, were it three in the morning, he refused to admit the weakness of lying awake on his couch; so he would rise and stand until dawn when the hour of prayer arrived.

A polished pride was his, finished with good breeding. It was as though he had looked out on the world as on a completed masterpiece, requiring an æsthetic appreciation. In conventional scrolls a landscape, however wild and rugged, is always softened by some haze of fog, rain or twilight; and it seemed that this courtly gentleman of the old South had gazed on life as on such a scene, discreetly veiled in poetic mirth.

His son, be it hastily observed, had been educated at Princeton, where fog is fog, and football is football, and twilight is just the time to hop in the motor and "step on it." His face is not the duplicate of his father's. And indeed that change meets the visitor at every turn. Old types are vanishing; new are growing, in conformity to the transformation of society. It has become difficult to say how permanently the Japanese may be Japanese, or how unalterably American is the American. Perhaps there are only social, not racial, types after all.

CHAPTER IX

THE SOCIAL WEB

To the visible curiosities of Japan—costumes, faces, poses and manners of the people—the mind quickly becomes adjusted and therefore dulled. Touchable objects like sandals and sashes, urns and mats, moon windows and wine tubs recede into the commonplaces of every day. But the same thing does not apply to the intangible curios of the Island Empire; namely her concepts. It would take a lifetime to exhaust the variations in those invisible marvels: her ideas of love and friendship, harmony and fun, the state, class and family, business, law, paradise and Utopia, hell and sin, music and hospitality. No fabric from her looms, including the pale gauze worn by angels in Noh theaters, is so unique as the richly and tautly woven web of her society. No pattern stamped on tea cup or scented fan is so characteristic of her brain and heart as the social design imposed by her statesmen, artists, merchants and philosophers upon her very life.

Far more colorful, moreover, than the merely material objects surrounding a Japanese person are the human relationships that bind him to society, and the reactions these bonds produce in his mind. It does not really matter, for instance, whether a man wears a sack suit instead of a kimono, if he has pledged himself by ancient ceremonies to his employer—if, before joining a shoe button factory, by way of illustration, he has drunk a cup of wine blessed by a Shinto priest and containing a drop of his business chief's blood, mingled in sign of good faith. It certainly is not important whether a house is lighted by electric bulbs or tasseled lanterns, if over the inmates tyrannizes a mother-in-law. Far more vital than the fact the Taro family has bought a radio in place of a harp, is the fact that all members by common consent "tune in" on a mediæval ballad. However much the signs of "foreignization" may destroy the "picturesque," it is embedded in the social system which remains highly Japanese.

We too often contrast "feudal" with "modern," as though the two were incompatible. Japan is living witness to the fact that they can merge; that people may ride on subways, play baseball, work in spinning mills, study scientific agriculture, build skyscrapers, navigate the seas, demand votes for women, and yet retain withal, in their relations to one another, ancient sentiments and customs. Loyalty, for instance, such as bound feudal folk to their lord, is not destroyed by industrialization; it may only change its form. Indeed, a modern state, such as the Japanese now have, demands more rather than less fealty; engineers who watch great civic waterworks and railways, firemen, public health officers and telegraph operators must render the government quite as constant a service as ever armoured samurai to his prince. The most technically developed country on earth, the United States, is the very one which has created the "religion of service," calling its government officials "public servants," and emphasizing "coöperation" in industry and "loyalty among employees." In becoming Westernized, therefore, Japan does not have to drop wholly her feudal ideals, as many suppose, but rather to extend and utilize them. She does not even have to give up the proud name of *samurai,* or knight, for it comes, we are told, merely from the humble verb, *samuro,* to serve.

All kinds of mediæval group sentiments, clustering around

family, clan and community, survive in Japan. Her craftsmen and actors, the same as her bankers, belong to hereditary "families," often with a centuries-old prestige; the local
spirit is alive in politics; her people tend to work in groups
rather than as individuals. Modernization is not eliminating
these divergencies; it is but transforming them. The United
States, under a democratic form of government, shelters
countless antagonistic groups; leagues of manufacturers or
farmers, "rings" of politicians, and such semi-feudal organizations as Tammany Hall, together with social and religious
bodies, clubs and associations. In fact, modern life, while
differentiating people, tends to produce more groupings than
ancient social orders; its conflicts, for instance between
Knights of Columbus and Ku Klux Klan, are quite as irreconcilable as those which divided two feudal principalities.
The local and caste feeling bred of monarchy persists in
Republican Germany. And it is to be expected that the
Japanese should be still strongly marked by local and group
lines as they were under the Shogunate. Indeed, it is evident the longer one lives among them, that mere stage prop-
erties need not alter the drama; that "Hamlet" can very
well be played in modern dress.

More and more conscious every day of this all-enshroud-
ing social web and caught myself within its folds by ties
of friendship, I began to think of the Japanese, less as isolated individuals, and more as parts of a national whole.
Gradually I realized how complex and how diverse were the
filaments that linked a man or woman to the national life-
fabric: the threads of clan, family, guild, club, corporation or
social, political and religious affiliations. Often these threads
got tangled, or pulled the individual in opposite ways, fealty
to the state drawing against loyalty to the family, religion
drawing against business, various codes of ancient and mod-

ern ethics in conflict. I understood what inner confusion resulted in the minds and hearts of my friends from these contesting claims. To take but a simple humorous example: the people were recently urged to join a "Swat the Fly" campaign by eager advocates of public health, while at the same time Buddhist fathers, alarmed by this cruel slogan so contrary to their faith, begged the populace rather to observe a "Save a Fly" day!

Very personal and direct are most of the ties that bind a Japanese to his fellow men. Personality counts heavily as with us; in politics it largely outweighs programs and often in the literary world overshadows talent. The populace is devoted to idols, forever discovering new ones, falling at the feet of Einstein to-day, to-morrow wearing "airplane head-dresses" in honor of an aviator, the day after buying kerchiefs printed with the face of an actor. Decidedly gregarious, the people work well in organizations and like to play in crowds; the corporation is the normal expression of their business spirit and the festival of their recreational moods. So far are they from resembling those "elusive" and "inhuman" creatures called "Oriental" by our Western writers of cheap fiction and lurid drama, that it would be truer to say that they are fond of gossip and *Gemütlichkeit* like southern Germans, group-minded and hero-worshiping like Americans, conscious of "family" like the British landed gentry, as willing to "stick together" for mutual benefit as the Irish refugees abroad.

No Japanese gets much chance to be elusive. Even a very rich woman is involved in the family system, watched over closely by elders and with the responsibility of a household in her care; she has few hours "off" her domestic job. Neither is the rich man free. His home, if he be a figure of importance, begins to fill with ceremonial callers soon after dawn. If he is a politician of the elder type, he must act as benevolent "little father" toward his followers, advising them on marriage, trips or intimate personal problems. If a banker, he is probably head of a family clan, finding openings for country cousins, making matches with other business families, perhaps securing some bright boy to adopt into the house. Whatever he does is in consultation with a club, committee or "society for the advancement" of something or other.

How strikingly the private affairs of men and women may be involved with public life—how personal even the government may be—is illustrated by the story of a certain athletic carnival. The Home Office and the Education Ministry had a quarrel; one claimed that students should join the exhibition, because sport is so good for health, and the other insisted that they should be prohibited, on the ground that sport interferes with brain work. Immense excitement was stirred up everywhere; students went on strike; newspapers were filled with protests. What resulted? In characteristic fashion, the situation was reported cleared when Miss Iwahara, sister of a representative of the Home Office, became engaged to Mr. Naito of the Education Ministry.

A thousand small but time-consuming obligations prevent that cold efficiency which in other places has tended to gather indigent relatives into charitable institutions and throw upon the public responsibilities which once were private everywhere. There is less abstract talk of "social science" and more concrete scratching of coins to pay board bills for afflicted great-aunts, uncles financially ruined by a typhoon, orphaned cousins of fishermen drowned at sea, or widowed sisters with six children. Partly because the population is so large and partly because the Island Empire is especially subject to natural disasters, the Japanese has "his nose to the

grindstone" in stern reality. Storms, earthquakes, fire bank-
ruptcies, added to the ordinary infirmities of mankind,
scarcely give a breadwinner and his housewife a moment's
chance to play at being "inhuman." A man pays the priests
who call at the door for alms, gives gifts to teachers in the
Confucian manner, makes New Year calls upon his landlord if he is a farmer, or bestows presents on his business
superior if he is in an office. In many ways, he regards all
this with more joy than sorrow. At least, his writers tell
him, husband and wife spend more time together than in any
highly industrial Western country. In the tens of thousands
of home-shops, no less than in the peasant communities, man,
woman and children work side by side. Factories and offices
have not broken up that intimacy to such an extent as in the
United States. They do not keep husband and wife apart all
day and prevent them, as a native once described it, from
"running in and out of the house to look at each other."

A major problem, it seemed to me, was belonging to this
kind of society without being "swamped" by it. Escape even
for a little while from its demands is rare in a country where
money is comparatively scarce for travel, sport, holidays,
even for books. The Buddhist Church is not so wealthy that
it can offer generous refuge in its monasteries and nunneries.
The average young couple can hardly find capital enough to
start a separate home. As in Europe, land is too expensive
and overpopulated and taxes too high for them to retire
to the country, "picking up" some deserted farmhouse and a
few acres to till. It is chiefly by scaling mountains that men
can flee from the crowds and venture into the wilderness.

And yet a few individuals succeed in eluding the manifold
pressures of society. I know several persons who, on some
chrysanthemum farm in a quiet valley of the South, or in
some forest retreat, or even behind the thick black gates of

an old house within city limits, live aloof from the surging multitudes. In their detachment, there is a humorous serenity that seemed to me unique. Such people are generally members of the Zen sect, and humor forms the very root of its philosophy—the only system apparently which insists on a smile as the first essential to understanding and conduct. The true Zennist founds his life upon the following incident from the story of Buddha:

One day the Lord Buddha, seated among his disciples, took in his hand a flower. As he gazed upon it, a wonderful, mystic smile curved his lips. His pupils, surprised and puzzled, knew not what he meant. But one, his favorite, looked up to him and, in the selfsame manner, smiled. Master and pupil, in silence, communed. And the Lord Buddha explained that some of the profoundest truths, even about the simplest flower, defy communication by word or deed, and can only be transmitted through the transcendental smile of supreme sympathy.

Aloof as they were, these friends did not seem morbid, gruesome, or abnormal. Humor saved them, combined with a worship of nature. The landscape of Japan, so gracious even in its wilderness, is an ideal surrounding for a poet-hermit; and the houses invite rather than exclude the sun and air. The retiring Zennists remain genial and poised, because they do not repress emotions within dark cells or peer too far into the depths of their own souls. They give themselves outwardly to nature, trying to feel kinship with birds, deer and fish, trying to unfold toward trees, hills, waterfalls and the rare flowering plants. Instead of an occasional visit to a gallery, a lecture or a conversation on art, they practice it as a daily discipline. They find an art in everything to be studied: the bow, the acts of common courtesy, fencing, flower arrangement, singing, landscape gardening and handwriting. Instead of hating man and this material world, like a passionate mediæval mystic, they try to look at both with a smile as near Buddha's as possible. How far they succeed I do not know; but that their Zennist serenity is worth making a pilgrimage to see, I can bear testimony. One feels none of the shuddering that is caused by the apparition of ascetics in India. Truth, as they see it, must be reached alone but with effort. They kneel in meditation upon some metaphysical problem until, unaided, they discover an answer. If they fail, they may remain thinking, without help, for the rest of their lives on that particular question; they cannot be tutored into heaven. Truth, when they do attain it, is to them neither creed, formula nor ritual. Zennism promises no salvation in the hereafter; it is but a way of living, a discipline of body and attitude of mind; it assures the disciple that, through its synthesis of art, humor and self-control, he will attain knowledge so profound that, like the Buddha's, it can be expressed only in a smile.

The young people of both sexes, however, are less and less able to find in Zennism their channel of escape. It is not inner peace they seek so much as actual physical escape from social restraint. They want, not harmony and poise, but vivid joy. Unfortunately, the modern opportunities for this sort of freedom, especially automobiles, require money—a flexible and wealthy society. And if the young Japanese can no longer take flight along the same paths as their forefathers, they also find closed to them most of the new. Those who will not or cannot flee from society but accept responsibility instead are in still another quandary. It is no longer so easy to belong to a system that is in a constant state of flux, the forms of feudal allegiance altering, the ties of family and clan giving way. Even patriotism ceases to be quite the same in quality; for the worship of ancestors loses something of its hold upon the most loyal family member with every shift of domicile. Reverence for the Imperial Household, while always profound, is affected by the increasing democratization of the Household itself. Recently, a private in the army and striking workers in a Soya bean sauce factory attempted to present petitions directly to the Throne, defying all historical custom. No more, in any station in society, rich or poor, common or noble, may a man or woman feel utterly secure and settled in a niche for all time.

"To what shall we belong, the old or new?" more persons ask themselves. And if they choose the new, then they must be prepared for a stern and slow combat, working up inch by inch in this "old man's country" where, as in Europe, high posts are seldom attained by men of thirty. They must face the possibility of ultimate defeat in a land where a swelling population with a rising standard of living has been unable to solve its food—far less its luxury—problem.

It is because they so often face their problems intensely, indeed with agony, that in the course of countless discussions around the *hibachi* in private homes or over the tea cups in cafés, one finally comes to comprehend the social web in its personal aspects. If society is to be radically changed, sweeping laws will prove inadequate. Difficult and genuine recombinations among individuals, young and old, of diverse types and temperaments, must be made and it is plain that life is already resolving itself into a perpetual series of just such adaptations.

Though the Freudian jargon about "attuning the individual to his environment" is but slowly penetrating Japanese literature, the problem is real, and sensitive natures are overwrought by the struggle to attain better relations with the family, the opposite sex, the group, friends and the crowd; with the society of the nation; with Asia; and even with the wide world. Frequently the cultured thinkers seemed less concerned with the attempt to secure or maintain a comfortable place for themselves in the local scene than with the fitting of the nation into the greater "society of nations." They looked on life as a world-flux, in which they and their race were but a movement. Instead of following Confucius, who taught stability, they admired Laotse, who believed in eternal change and declared that the happy man is he who is at home in constant motion like "a fish in moving water."

But the direction of change involves fraternizing along new lines first of all, whereas the Japanese have been trained to meet one another primarily on a family and caste basis. Age and rank have subdued every gathering of the upper classes to the metes and bounds of their rigid formalities. The mature man in his dark robes, arms folded within ample sleeves, is all too sure of his superior status in society and if the aged woman has the similar advantage of respect and its corollary, dignity, which relieves her of the necessity of being coy or brash to win recognition, she, too, is apt to be satisfied with the mere number of her years. The presence of the titled requires an elaborate ritual of ceremonial bowing and deference, regardless of their public worth or private genius. In the United States either a man or a woman, by sheer force of personality, may win attention in a company of "social betters" but Japan resembles certain countries of Europe in her mechanically arranged relations defined by titles, rank, honorifics, and age.

If formality is a cohesive force, it is at the same time a deadening weight on conversation. That particular cement still awaits successful creation in this Island Empire. Certainly its courtiers in distant times had a rather easy kind of association: men and women exchanged and interchanged epigrams in verse, hunted and danced together, and enjoyed an extraordinary freedom in love-making and marriage. But the great retainers of the later ages, influenced by martial repression, have been better trained for silence or monologues than for that curious inter-firing of questions and answers which other races, perhaps following Socrates, name "conversation" and which the French particularly claim as their fine art. However, it has been nowhere the rule, outside Japan, for men and women of the upper classes to meet as social equals, neither sex nor title predominating in importance, for the free and interesting communication of ideas as such.

The Japanese at least are beginning to see that solving all such problems depends on clearing up great public issues. Marriage cannot be discussed independently of the family system; the family system is not to be altered without a new economic life; a new economic life inevitably is bound up with world markets. Everything they touch is but one ripple in the ever-widening circle of international affairs. So their talk, as it develops from year to year, enlarges to meet the universal currents.

Actions speak even louder than words. Women who "free" themselves from marital control pass as wage-earners under impersonal but probably more stringent business regulations. Men who defy their elders succumb to industry. The more the Japanese remove themselves from the influence of parents, ancestral spirits, clan kinsmen, local gods, the more profoundly subject they become to the power of city, class, state, party, federation, and the nation. The peasant family, wading in the rice-paddies, or tending mulberry trees, may neglect to bow and tremble as a knight rides by; but it may default on the mortgage when silk shares fall on a stock exchange thousands of miles away. The little apprentice boy at the loom may cease to fear his master's anger; but he may be out of work when a rival shop is founded in the land across the Yellow Sea.

The point is not that the Japanese are growing freer and freer in their relationships; by all their efforts they are not merely breaking down some antiquated feudal society. They are really enmeshing themselves deeper by words and actions within the international web. East and West humanity is all united in a single fabric; the more it shakes off the ties of family, class, village or national patriotism, the more surely bound it is by international relations. "Freedom" as an Absolute is an unrealizable aim; if our ancestors could proclaim liberation of the individual, we, their descendants, can only urge closer and closer coöperation on a more gigantic scale. Our speech thus has an effect which reaches far beyond "expressing the personality"; it gathers us into world communities.

Enlargement is the key to what is happening. For every fragment of the social web that is cut away, a new and greater segment must be woven. Family ties dissolve in civic life; but trade unions, boy scout clubs, political societies, chambers of commerce form ceaselessly. Clans weaken; but federations of clubs grow strong. Old merchant guilds relax claims; but the Business Man's Party arises. Village patriotism fades; but farmers unite over the national area. Blood kinship means less; a common cause means more.

A vivid paradox is thus offered by Japan, Russia and the United States. These three countries lead the world in the number of divorces, and in collective action. Americans are less family-minded than Europeans, and more crowd-minded; owing to our standardization, our communications, we think in larger terms, geographically and socially. Russians have the same break-down of the more intimate family life, and the same building up of great social groups. Also in Japan, the third "new" nation, these striking contrasts are found. People press into the courts with family disputes, and yet they seem perfectly able to agree by the multitude, in Girls' Associations, in Social Harmony Societies, in Rotary Clubs and nationally organized movements.

With Americans, Russians, and Japanese the change is an apparently irresistible process. There is no choice. The Japanese are as impelled toward change as they are to follow the earth's daily rotation on its axis.

CHAPTER X

STRUGGLE BEHIND SCREENS

HOUSES in Japan keep pace with their inmates in manifesting both variety and the process of a remorseless transformation. Naturally, those that have fallen under a foreign spell represent every form of enchantment, ranging from late Victorian and Louis XVI to ultra-modernistic, as well as every degree, some containing but a single room and others consisting of a complete mansion in the alien manner. But the purely native homes also indicate a distinct scale of artistic taste, wealth and social status, passing by gradual steps from gold-corridored mediæval palaces and garden-enfolded estates of noblemen or merchants on to suburban villas, small town dwellings, farm compounds and the fragile shelters of the slums.

To an American there is a lively and peculiar fascination in the genuine Japanese dwelling. For what is best in modern domestic decoration—plain surfaces, pure line, lacquer and natural woods, delicacy of tint and restraint of ornament—is not only akin to, but actually profoundly affected by ancient Japanese taste. Our Victorianism was disturbed, through Whistler and Sargent, by Japanese æsthetic tradition; we leaned toward "nocturnes" and "symphonies in blue" and had our portraits posed before screens instead of the reputable plush curtains. Early Greenwich Village bohemians groped clumsily in the same direction as they *batiked* butterflies or gourd vines, arranged fans, green vases, flower branches or other "color accents" behind their

145

sitters, etched pine cones and experimented with the "exotic" and the "Japanesey." In Europe the influence has been partly direct, descending from their own masters, such as Vermeer, whose plain, bright interiors are thought to show the results of the prints imported from Japan, and in part transmitted from America by the genius of Frank Lloyd Wright. This inspiration has been close to the very root of the creative movement in modern Europe and is so avowed by its artists. Toward the Japanese in spirit and often in actual design veer the efforts of Germany, Austria and France to achieve a "new art" for the "machine age" with low-set furniture, plain woods, mottled and tinted wallpapers, screens, dull-finished picture frames, high lights of pottery and lacquer, sturdy line and wide spaces. Our feminine costumes no less than our book covers, textiles, wallpapers, pottery and woodwork and often our gardens are inescapably "Orientalized."

A strange experience, then, it is to journey to the true fountain of this most recent decorative trend. And odd is it to find these Japanese principles, filtered through American channels, tinged by contact with European sources, brought back again to Japan as "modern art" and there accepted as such with enthusiasm. Despite transformations, it appeals to the instincts of native artists and is now entering, in the land of its origin, upon a period of development. Some of the Japanese think this may afford the solution to their great æsthetic problem: the harmonizing of the classic and the mechanistic ages.

A great inconsistency, indeed, is presented by the Japanese home. In affinity with the temper of the modern age, it is yet the very least adapted, from a purely practical point of view, to modern life. Unsurpassed for sheer, sophisticated elegance, it is also unmatched for discomforts and actual danger. No other great nation is confronted with this peculiar problem: an abode almost devoid of furniture, not to be walked upon with shoes, lacking ovens or stoves big enough for a scientific diet, having insufficient privacy between rooms or facility for the new kinds of entertaining, and alarmingly inflammable. Moreover, no detail about this domicile may be changed without affecting the scheme of the whole: chairs and tables destroy the artistic proportions and the illusion of space; a heating system calls for a cellar and, beside, spoils the woods, warps the paper and splits the lacquer; the introduction of meat brings in a strange new series of dishes and kitchen ware. The manners and dress of the people, so carefully adjusted to the old, must radically alter to fit the new order. And finally a shift in diet, if general, would mean a revolution in agriculture, as a shift in architecture would mean a sudden demand for coal or other very expensive fuels. Thus a revolution in private households would threaten the delicate balance of the national economy.

Home and change are words entwined in a unique way among the Japanese. To the Chinese, accustomed to clay walls and heavy furniture, the "new home" means largely a break in family relationships. With Western countries, it may mean a different scheme of decoration, labor-saving appliances, various scientific and artistic additions. Only in Japan does it imply a rebuilding of the entire edifice, a remodeling of its inhabitants and a reorganization of the national production. But to make this clear an intimate picture of the home as it exists must be given.

Sheer light forms the glory of a Japanese dwelling. How different from our dark walls, coarsely pasted with heavy designs or painted in solid tones are these spacious stretches of luminous paper, flooded from without until the whole house glows like the interior of a giant, pale lantern! No pattern is to be found along their surfaces except that cast by the whimsical hand of nature. Shadows, soft and gray, quivering and indistinct, repeat the shapes of branch or vine outside, of bamboo-stalk or trumpet-flower, of furry pine or cluster of bulging gourds.

The effect of the rooms is exceedingly varied and rich, though it is attained by means very much more normal and quiet than those the "modern artists" employ. Papers are utilized to bring out pleasing contrasts, rough slate-blue touching smooth white. Fragments of wood are introduced in their choicest natural tones, umber and sand, or darkened by age through the gamut of the wine tints so that the slightest artificial touch of lacquer comes as a shock. It is in details the connoisseur shows his mastery: in the irregular placing of shelves, the framework which holds them, the division of wall into panelling and the marking of screens into sections by a most delicate sense of geometrical forms.

The Japanese are not afraid of ornament, however, and they can employ it boldly. They are not always, as too many of their Western imitators are, finicky, anæmic, fond of doll-like proportions and the too-too-cute. Huge and magnificent, on the contrary, are many of the treasures displayed in the grander homes. I have seen in the *tokonoma,* or niche of honor, a scroll on which a life-size maple tree was bursting into autumnal flame; I remember another depicting a dragon wreathed in a cloud of fumes; and on another, a life-size tiger roaring through a forest of bamboo. The color radiating from the paintings is echoed by the objects on the shelves of the *tokonoma,* in crystal or jade or ivory statuettes, inlaid boxes, or baskets holding sheaves of autumn grasses.

A living warmth is reflected by the furnishings of such a room. A cupboard, tucked away in a recess, opens its gilt-dotted door to disclose the special treasures of the host: his figurines or ink-boxes or collection of bronzes. Furniture, though meager in quantity, is nevertheless impressive. A great low table, little more than a foot high, but fully six feet long and very broad, may be utilized; it is made of the most ponderous woods, ebony or teak, and carved and polished until it gleams like a rectangular pool of black water. Instead of chairs, large cushions of the finest gold-threaded silks are spread about and convenient elbow pillows, pink and cerise and tasseled, are available. Beside each kneeling guest, in cold weather, appears a brazier of porcelain or perhaps formed from a polished and hollowed section of a tree; these big bowls, half-filled with the finest sand, have lumps of hot charcoal embedded in them, and each contains a pair of long golden chopsticks for stirring up the glow.

A room like this is not so bare as most of those seen in tea houses or geisha pavilions by tourists. It may contain several objects, including the ivory and pearl harp of the lady of the house and, in the corner, a single immense screen, perhaps representing masked dancers, a spider-demon and a knight with sky-blue pantaloons. Over the door is set a piece of colored carving known as the *rama,* a strip of latticework in the shape of tossing waves or intercleaving vines and birds. Vivid light pours in upon the whole chamber, leaving scarcely a shadowy corner, and so everything is caught and enhanced by it—painted screen, flamboyant scroll, big bowls, heavy brocades, and the burnished shelves with their freight of silver and cloisonné. On a fine day two sides of the room may be flung wide open to the garden, the finer part of which is in the rear. If it is dreary weather, one may look out only through the frame of a window curved like a crescent, a bell or a circle. No "wee, Japanesey miniature" is this broad stretch of territory, yielding vistas of rivulet or shrubbery, bronze statuary and tea cottages half concealed in foliage. At twilight one may be led along the stepping stones with lanterns, pausing to learn the name of story-telling points, the "Water-God Shrine," the "Jewel-Shaped Peak," the "Bridge of the Eight Crow Cries at Sunset," the "Coast of the Early Dawn," the "Hamlet for Meditating on the Moon," "Boat-Shaped Hill" or "Beach of a Thousand Years."

Each part of the garden represents in symbol some scene famous in literature or legend. Here a dying hero is commemorated; yonder queerly shaped stone suggests an island in the Inland Sea. Thus a walk in the garden is a tour through the centuries of Japanese romance.

Every time the visitor calls, the decorative keynote of the rooms has been modified. The house, like the garden, seems to follow the rhythm of the seasons and its mistress wears robes with harmonizing patterns. The few treasures in the small *tokonoma* are retired every few days and fresh ones brought forth, so that to know a Japanese home of an aristocrat one must see it again and again and watch the gradual progress of the year imparted from every screen and shelf.

The *tokonoma,* as the garden, requires considerable insight into art and custom for its proper appreciation. To admire it sufficiently, one must know just what animal statues may be shown with certain flowers, that a bamboo may accompany a tiger but a maple tree only a deer; one may then recognize the skill of the hostess in adapting her resources to the conventions.

In reality, this recess, so governed by laws of propriety, is a shrine. The objects placed there are symbols rather than "ornaments" and the flowers are arranged, never for their own sake, but as honor offerings accompanying the picture. Yet the high seriousness of the Japanese about their treasures is not peculiar to their race. It was true of other classic peoples, viewing art with a purpose, using it to honor or to represent, and not as aimless "beautification" to "brighten up" an idle spot.

A Buddhist may use the *tokonoma* for religious purposes, placing there an image with incense jar and lotus blooms. A Shintoist, like a Methodist, discards the "idol" and lays on his shelf only a mirror and some evergreen leaves. But the *tokonoma* may also serve worldly ends; a politician may hang a scroll with his leader's favorite saying, such as the celebrated, strong and sure calligraphy of Viscount Goto, or a motto left by some hero, such as Admiral Togo. A person who in the West would be merely an "autograph fiend" has in the East full credit for his hobby; his *tokonoma* scroll and the screen before his low doorway may be filled with magnificently splashed signatures and "sentiments" of the famous. There are auctions in Tokyo where these may be bought and often at fabulous prices.

A wealthy Japanese must have in his private vaults many sets of religious, seasonal or festival scrolls combined with appropriate vases, statues, tea pots and brocades. Impossible for him are the strange medleys "picked up" by Western "art lovers," and exhibited helter-skelter in museum fashion. He must own at least one series of landscape paintings, a fresh scroll for every month; or perhaps a set of twelve zodiacal animals to be shown in rotation. To be sure, they need not be all by the same hand; he may include a single dragon picture, costing half a million yen, in a more commonplace series. But he may not display his treasure, however extraordinary, more than the alloted period. A scroll, even as an evening dress, is suitable only at certain times and on specific occasions; only a boor would wear a tuxedo to breakfast or hang a plum-blossom scroll when a painting of a crow on a dead tree would be *de rigueur*. He will need, moreover, several pictures and outfits for festivals—The Doll or Boys' Celebration, New Year, weddings—and for honored guests. Nor is his expense and responsibility ended there; for if he is a "new-rich" and his wife uneducated, it will be necessary to summon a professional arranger every week or so to choose the display. Consequently, the interior decorator in Japan must not simply "do" a mansion; he must keep "doing" it the year round.

To one who watches the slow pageant of the year within such a household, there comes a new revelation of the meaning in the word "home." In the West we try to give our dwellings some center, either by the couch or by the fireplace, with its crackling logs, sentimentally known as the "hearth." But we rarely achieve such a superb focus as the Japanese and Chinese get with their sacred alcove and family altar. We have been unconscious of the whole year's turning, revolving about that intimate shrine.

Thus it was always with considerable awe that I would come calling in winter through a garden encumbered with wet, heavy Japanese snow, filled with the white hush of overburdened boughs and sparkling heaps of drift. With bows and salutations entering the house, I would invariably find the great scroll in the *tokonoma* also representing a winter scene—perhaps, a white heron standing in snow with a white moon rising through mist and an appropriate poem dashed in ink along the edge. The porcelain tea service would show designs of wintry landscape; the screens before the doors would bear paintings of bamboo stripped by wind and left shivering and leafless; the cushion stuffs would be patterned with evergreen. The lady of the house would wear a heavily padded kimono faintly embroidered with silver snow. House and inmates would be one with nature outside.

Again I have come to such a home on the occasion of a
Buddhist funeral in the family, discovering the whole
dwelling transformed into a sanctuary. White-robed women
gathered, smiling—for Buddhists must not dishonor the
dead by tears and lamentations. Now every *tokonoma* was
hung with ancient, time-dimmed paintings of the Buddhist
pantheon, figures of the Merciful Kwannon, of aureoled
saints and hermit-sages fingering Indian rosaries. In the very
inmost chamber, on a high altar, a fire was smoldering in
a vessel and each visitor, as he passed, added a touch of incense; then calmly and with a bow departed from the simple
but august ceremony.

The house of the lower bourgeois is like the mansion of
the millionaire in general outline. It, too, is ruled by the
ideal of selective harmony, by similar principles of taste. But
of course it is several shades less elaborate. The scroll in the
corner is tinier, though sure to be charming still, perhaps showing a cock with a fanciful tail instead of a tiger or
a bird on a bough in the place of a forest. The tea pottery
perhaps is not from the hands of a celebrated maker, each
piece a miracle in moon-green or iris blue; but nevertheless it has its touch of seasonable imagination—a blossom spray or a fallen pine cone. Though reduced in size
and equipment, the home remains unified and gravely
refined.

Down to the humblest shelter, by imperceptible degrees,
restraint percolates as a matter of taste. In some cottages
only a single scroll is possessed but that is in good form,
probably representing "Fujiyama—the one symbol appropriate the whole year round." I have been in homes of
village officials where the solitary painting consisted of a
finely written poem never to be outdated or outmoded. I
have been in lowly huts where the tea pot was the sole

object of art but it was soberly brushed with a few ink strokes depicting a fisherman's skiff and a rippling wave.

Even the city slums are spared that dismal ugliness which adds to the gloom of the poor in Liverpool or New York, which marks the shanties of Chicago and the alleys of the London Limehouse district. They arouse sympathy because they are so pitiably inadequate and bare, more than horror at squalor and chaos. What is elegant simplicity in the mansion becomes stark emptiness in the slum.

The Japanese ragpicker—among the poorest of the poor— owns nothing that could actually be considered ugly, a positive offense against culture. Nor can his house, two or three mats in size, be called a gloomy brick prison; it is merely a too hopelessly fragile matchbox. Its walls are repaired not with creamy squares of paper but with hieroglyphic advertisements and pages of daily journals. For furniture it holds a cracked brazier with a lump of charcoal; a few fragments of pottery, broken but good in design; a sleeping quilt which, though thin against the bitter cold and probably rented for the week, is yet finely flowered. The kimono of the poor woman, frayed and dangerously insufficient for winter weather, is of a cut similar to the robe of a countess and of an ancient pattern conceived by a loving draughtsman.

A Spartan restraint binds upper and lower homes together. As in the most lavish dwellings I never saw the vulgar ostentation frequent in the West, walls covered with poor design, vases crammed with flowers and tables strewn with bric-a-brac, so the poor quarters looked to me more shiveringly bleak than ours. In the municipal asylum of Osaka, for instance, the tiny cells where old men were housed were very clean and neat and contained exactly nothing—for sleeping quilt and bowls were put away in a cupboard during the daytime—except a sheet of inscribed paper on the walls, in lieu of scroll. One, I recollect, bore upon it the single character, like an epic in one word, "Patience."

Linked together, then, in so complete a unity, from the restrained elegance of the merchant's villa to the forced bareness of the laborer's hut—how is this native scheme of things in Japan to be altered? Must and will it be altered on any scale?

The answer partly depends upon whether one considers civilization more a material or a spiritual product. The Japanese themselves disagree and among them may be found mystics who emphasize soul and scientists who stress economics. What created Japanese taste? Did scarcity of flowers bring out the floral arrangement art, or was it Zen philosophy? Do people wear their most vivid patterns as the hidden lining of their silk coats because they are naturally discreet or because stern feudal laws forbade merchants to flaunt in public their finery? Is Japan what she is because poor in material resources or because enriched in spiritual values?

However one may look at the issue, this fact seemed to me clear. Precisely because they are so strictly adapted to practical purposes, the artistic ideals of Japan make their appeal; there is about them not a trace of baroque extravagance or sentimental Victorianism. They achieve what we are learning to seek: direct, strong simplicity.

Certainly, the Japanese have built their civilization out of the fewest possible objects. They have eliminated more than other great nations. With a handful of sticks, tiny bundles of straw for thatch and matting, small rolls of paper and a little writing ink, they have put together a domicile for the people at large that is more than habitable; it is poetic. Their dinner is also the most artistic arrangement possible for simple and cheap articles, meager vegetables and bits of fish, eel and rice. The furniture is of minimum size and convenience; beds roll up in the daytime; screens in a moment can create several rooms out of one; the braziers are the plainest and yet handsomest method of warming. The *tokonoma* is the least complicated and most perfect device for displaying possessions to advantage. The garden is a dream; from a shrub, a lantern, three stones and a flap of moss arises a mood which, as the painters say, suggests "the sweet solitude of landscape in clouded moonlight with a half-gloom between the trees."

Even the bath is exceedingly efficient, giving the utmost comfort and cleanliness for the smallest amount of fuel. And the critic who condemns the Japanese family for not having a great tub of hot water for each member just ignores coal cost and similar realistic factors. He forgets, too, that fifty years ago Americans scarcely dared step into any bath without a doctor's prescription and that a bowl of cold water and sponge still suffice for the average Englishman.

Household conduct partakes of the same practical refinement. Sprawling postures are incompatible with floor life; hence the people are trained to sit bolt upright, fold their feet neatly, keep their robes in order, and make small and delicate gestures. Were not every object accurately placed, rolled, folded or passed from hand to hand, all would be chaos and strife.

Given such a society based on such economics the problem of adopting Western civilization or changing old ways is not an abstract one but a very definite, if difficult, affair.

Unquestionably, irresistible currents are sweeping the nation as a whole toward modernity. Enervation is overtaking the race as it has overtaken the Western peoples in this industrialized era; they shrink from hardships habitual to their forebears. Boys no longer wish to fence barefoot in the snow at dawn, or sit motionless at learned lectures, without lifting a finger so much as to brush a mosquito. Nobody suffers discipline so willingly nowadays; children can hardly be procured as apprentices and geisha no more like to sing in harsh weather until their voices are broken by repeated colds to an admired "tone." Nobody accepts scorn from superiors quite so happily; even tradesmen must be called *"san,"* or "honorable," by gentlewomen. Contemporary crowds would be horrified at the public executions of criminals, once taken for granted as in the England of Defoe. Common folk now wear socks in winter, formerly a luxury of nobles and courtesans.

Rising standards have been general; people consume more rice per capita than their grandfathers did; millions more, and in remote towns, thanks to electricity, may read at night; and literacy in Japan, as everywhere, results in restlessness. One step leads irrevocably to another. Electric wires render a wooden house more dangerous than before; the growth of cities brings the need for public marketing; automobiles make safe playgrounds essential; the country must be made more attractive to hold its own against the cities. Under increasing economic competition the people want to acquire "pep" like Americans, by better diet, athletics, and recreation. Above all, the expansion of the population must be provided for by some comprehensive reform, either in agricultural methods, such as grazing sheep on the hills and teaching people to enjoy mutton, raising more wheat and making them eat bread, or heightening industrial efficiency which requires in turn better fed and sheltered workers.

While statesmen and economists struggle with the problem of starting some national program of industrialization or improved dietetics, and while they debate ways of paying

for it, the very wealthy Japanese are easily and quietly revo-
lutionizing their own habits. If they wish to entertain more,
or be more comfortable, they simply hire an architect and
build a complete foreign mansion, send their children abroad
to learn the appropriate behavior or hire tutors to teach
them how to acquire it on the spot.

Impeccable were such of these homes as I saw; and their
owners appeared wholly at ease in the new environment.
One nobleman had built a great English country place,
faithfully reproduced from the ivy that clambered over stone
walls to the velvety lawn, from the baronial hall with its
oil paintings to the Japanese servants who not only wore the
livery of English butlers but had somehow absorbed the
exact, suavely bland expression of their British prototypes.
Another estate held a French *château,* where in a boudoir of
rose, gilt and crystal, on brocaded sofas, sat *jeunes filles,*
some in kimono and others in Paris frocks, discussing the
poems of Paul Claudel. Yet another home was German
from cellar to pointed roof and of course provided with a
music room; while a fourth was a purely American domicile,
with low bookcases and wide fireplace, roomy couches and a
sunparlor looking out on a court where vigorous girls were
laughing and playing tennis.

Equally at home in both worlds were many business men
and high government officials. With remarkable versatility
they and their wives and daughters could handle Eastern or
Western etiquette; they maintained both native and foreign
wings in the same dwelling. Like a Chinese statesman in
Peking, they would ask when inviting us whether we preferred an Eastern or a Western dinner, for they kept up two
kitchens simultaneously. Usually the "foreign" was French
in cuisine, served with French wines and decorated with
flowers arranged in the imported manner.

The Imperial Household lends countenance to this amphibious existence, so to speak. The private rooms of the Emperor and Empress in their palace are remodeled in "strictly foreign" style. "The rooms for their two infant daughters" were planned, according to report, in "semi-foreign style." Prince Chichibu before his marriage erected a special mansion along wholly Western lines.

It is in more modest circles, naturally, that the hot debate over the new home occurs. Thousands of business and professional men who spend the day in "down-town" offices at night return to kimono and cushion; tens of thousands of university and high-school boys and girls who wear foreign dress to classes, sit on benches or chairs, and practice athletics find kneeling on the floor at home positively painful; multitudes of mothers who want a more modern hygienic bringing-up for their children cannot without sacrifice and struggle pay for much improvement. So among these people the keenest and frankest arguments over "civilization," "modernism" and "the domestic revolution" are heard.

Some solve their difficulty by moving to the new suburban "garden cities" and renting a concrete "foreign-style" house. A few semi-Japanese apartments have been recently erected in Tokyo with provision for community laundry and cooking. Many persons add various articles to their residences regardless of æsthetic principles; they hide a telephone behind a screen, put a lantern around the electric bulbs, conceal a phonograph near the *tokonoma,* spread a rug over the chilly matting, or boldly install a wicker chair or two and a desk in spite of the fact that they do look like mastodons in the low-ceilinged room.

"The foreign-style parlor," a single room attached to the Japanese abode like a trailer to a motor-car, is the solution preferred by a considerable number of persons. Business men

may entertain customers here; daughter may practice on the
piano and learn foreign etiquette in the right surroundings;
son may sit at a desk for his studies. Sometimes the whole
family prefers this wing, while only grandmother remains
faithful to the former apartments. Thus a very strange dual
life is led. It seemed natural enough, however, once I grew
used to it, to sleep in a purely Japanese chamber on a bed
spread on the floor, under a green silk mosquito net draped
from the ceiling like a tent, and about me the small dressing
table, three feet high, low chests of drawers and a miniature
lamp; then to come down for breakfast in the morning to a
high-ceiling, opaque-walled room, filled with huge Western
furnishings, and partake of a twin meal, with a choice of
Japanese bean soup and foreign cereals, green tea or black
coffee. Before long, I decided that to live with one culture
alone was distinctly monotonous.

In no two cases did I see the same nation and era represented by these rooms. Some had reached the stage of
Cubism; some were in the college pennant and souvenir
pillow times; a few, reminding me of some of my Chinese
friends' homes in Peking, had adopted English chintzes and
Axminster rugs. Others were frankly Victorian with tin-
kling chandelier, enormous carpet and engravings handed
down from the "age of sentiment." These last were such as
linger in great areas of the United States and conservative
circles of England, France and Germany. Rather from traditional homes of the Continent than from America, however, was the custom derived of separating sexes by tables
after dinner, ladies grouped about one lace-covered barrier
and gentlemen at a discreet distance around a second, discussing politics.

Dissatisfied as so many remained, in spite of their importations, uneasily suspecting that these rooms were more prac-

tical than harmonious with the rest of their quarters, the "modern art" wave reached Japan just in time. The Imperial Hotel, the first attempt to combine the cultures of two hemispheres on a grand scale, in the beginning alarmed both the Japanese and the foreigners by its sheer novelty; but gradually other hotels and theaters, applying the idea in other ways, caught the fancy of the public. With the help of "modernism," still so flavored by its Eastern origin, many Japanese feel that they can retain the best of their civilization, using their own textiles for draperies and upholstery, their own unvarnished woods for furniture, their straw rugs, the *tokonoma,* heirlooms of screens and bronzes, their own wallpaper. And against such a background, toned like the more ancient homes, the national costume does not look so strange; nor do the lacquer dishes and chopsticks seem out of place. With a new self-respect, artists and architects have gone to work with fresh courage; and in this case, at least, the fusion of East and West, the mutual contribution dreamed by the mystics, appears possible.

Time, courage and money, more than the average bourgeois possesses, are required for this slow process of amalgamation. And most of the men and women of this class are yet in a stage of mere restless complaining or timid experiment. Frequently, mothers have said to me with a sigh: "For our children, there will be some answer. Not for us." Others shook their heads and exclaimed: "We must educate! We must educate first!" And I have heard a wise old woman in the corner interject "Yes! And begin with the boy babies!"

"Why do you do it?" I used to ask my acquaintances when they dropped in for tea. "Why do you want to give up your Japanese houses? They must be so easy to take care of and so informal to live in. Why do you wish to change the

kimono? Nothing looks more comfortable." And then I
would find myself confronted by a wholesale indictment of
native domesticity, to which each woman contributed her
favorite argument.

From my window I had perhaps seen these women
approaching down the rainy street, and thought with pleasure how like the prints were their slim, swaying figures in
the distance. As they hurried along, dragging their wooden
sandals, their soaked skirts clung and flapped and their long
sleeves unscrolled in the wind. They clutched at the scarves
about their necks and tried to shelter their bare heads behind
big paper umbrellas. To an outlander, the picture was
gratifying.

With plaints, however, they entered our quarters. Their
wet feet were cold. The wind had sought all the loose edges
of sleeves and chilled them. The drenched skirts of their
robes would be hours a-drying. And before I could reassure
them that, anyway, they had looked like the dream of an
artist, they declared emphatically and unpoetically that,
above all things, they detested having chilblains.

At home, too, apparently, they were always shiveringly
conscious of winter cold. To keep warm, they knelt close to
the brazier, huddling above a glow that scarcely heated
finger-tips and gave out beside a noxious gas. All vitality,
they insisted, went into the effort of fighting chill; and the
day-long shrinking toward the fire was not without a cramping effect upon the mind. When I suggested a furnace, knowing that these particular friends could well afford it, they
objected that Japanese houses had no cellars; when I men-
tioned stoves, they answered: "Heat warps delicate wood
and lacquer. It has been tried again and again, always dis-
astrously. Furniture unglues, cups chip, beams split, paper
rolls up, family treasures wrinkle and crack."

Winter, I murmured, would soon be over, and what could

be jollier than a light Japanese dwelling in warm weather? "Ah," they sighed; "when the walls are open, flying insects dash in, beating against the paper screens and lanterns. Reading at night is almost impossible and even sitting up is no pleasure." My enthusiasm for the picnic-character of the home was not wholly dampened—"surely, they had the lightest housekeeping of any women in the civilized world?"

"It takes the whole day," they protested. "Our furniture is so low, we must forever be bending and stooping. The woodwork which you like because it seems so plain acquires that satin sheen only through years of daily rubbing with slightly oily bath water. The paper walls you admire must be dusted with patters; our houses must be 'patted' clean every day for we cannot wash them, as you do windows, at long intervals. The mattings to be spotless for stockinged feet must be incessantly scrubbed; before parties we shine every bit of it three times. And those bed quilts—what an arduous labor to be forever rolling them away and hauling them out! Those sliding doors! They cannot be pushed open, like yours. One must kneel, and with three fingers, just so, press them noiselessly along the grooves. And the decorations in the domicile! They are never finished, as in Western houses, but must be attended to regularly, put up in boxes correctly labeled and tied with brocade cords; the scrolls must be carefully rolled; and not even a great master of flower arrangement can achieve a correct design in a moment. We have no time for social life."

"But you all have servants," I exclaimed, bewildered; "three or four at least, instead of just one or two as you might in the West."

"Slow and inefficient!" they wailed, as housewives all over the world have a habit of doing. "They never get through the daily tasks. And besides, so much of our housekeeping must, according to all tradition, be done by us. We are taught to look on it as a ritual, each act with a flawless and precise formula; we alone can tend the *tokonoma,* take care of the finest pottery. Our mothers would never understand if we left all that undone."

Their grievance against conditions extended to architecture and the planning of room space. Designed in the manner of all homes in mediæval Europe and Asia for a regular, close community life, in which women expected no "relief" from the presence of children, never had to hurry through the daily ritual of housekeeping in order to "go out somewhere," and in which, moreover, social life was very simple, consisting chiefly of occasional group and family festivals—for all that, the Japanese home was adapted. To-day, it lacks exactly those elements modern Europeans and Americans have learned to add: privacy, opportunity to entertain, facility for preparing a varied and carefully chosen diet. Specifically, these women wanted three new rooms: a nursery, a living room, and a revised kitchen. To the first and last of these, the West itself has but recently given much thought; and the second was, until our day, considered necessary only for gentry.

Children can make more noise and mischief in a Japanese house, unquestionably, than in any other. They can punch holes in paper walls, reach and upset anything left on the low tables and shelves and whenever they shriek it can be heard through thin partitions by the neighborhood. Watching them is an engrossing occupation; women have acquired the habit of wearing the babies on their backs, even indoors, to hush them, and they often spoil the older ones by ceaseless attention.

Contemporary men and women require more quiet and privacy than their ancestors. The official, the writer, or the business man, who brings home his papers for evening work, is distracted by countless noises and interruptions. Through flimsy walls is transmitted every cough, every flap of the duster, closing of a shutter, cry of a tradesman or patter of wooden shoes on stepping stones. The babies bounce in and find it very easy to clamber over a crouching father and spill the ink on the foot-high desk. Of such "incidents" are modern Japanese stage comedies made.

But it is about as hard for members of the family to entertain friends as to find solitude. Japan has lacked the concept of the home as a social center; men go out when they want a gay time, usually to geisha houses. When husband and wife celebrate together, they also go off to theaters, or at least to temple bazaars, on excursions to the country or seashore.

For their children, if not for themselves, these Japanese women wanted a different atmosphere at home. They wished their boys and girls to meet friends naturally, to see a little of the world before marrying and then to marry from choice, if also according to family guidance. More and more the wealthier mothers were feeling the competition of foreign hotels, where sons wanted to dance; and of modernized schools, where daughters became accustomed to associating with strangers, to play-acting and speech-making. They wanted to make their homes a rival of public institutions by giving parties—though very cautious, Japanese parties, of course, with *koto* music and perfume games and a revival of circle dances, such as mediæval lords and ladies delighted in.

For their offspring likewise they wanted higher furniture. School boys and girls, now compelled to study most of the day, grow stooped and hollow-chested from bending over low desks. Lung trouble among students is all too common. Yet Western chairs and tables are not only big and awkward

in a Japanese house; they cost a breath-taking amount compared with the small, fragmentary native possessions.

So, too, in fact, does a new-style kitchen cost too much.
The darkest, dampest, smallest room in a Japanese house is
usually the culinary quarter. The charcoal stove is primitive
and requires skillful handling. Hours every day go into cooking rice to the proper damp, tepid consistency, and in preparing meals. When a guest comes, there must be countless
courses, each more carefully and artistically arranged than is
customary elsewhere. Not light either is the labor of serving
in the dining room, stopping, kneeling, bowing, carrying
lacquer tray after tray, making all the deft and prescribed
motions.

The diet which can be prepared with this equipment is insufficient for their children, so the women declared. It
lacks the energy-producing nutriment for strong life, especially for youth busy with athletics and strained by heavy
study programs. Japanese food, moreover, though perhaps
the best to look at in the world, is not the most easily di-
gestible. And one must eat very large quantities of rice to
get an equivalent of the food value of meats.

"Yet," they said, "if we introduce a few articles of foreign
diet, it means a whole series of changes—stoves, baking
apparatus, knives and forks, big plates and all your cumber-
some fixtures. These are expensive, and so are the ingredients of Western dishes. Some of us can afford to buy
milk for our babies, instead of nursing them for two or
three years in the ancient way, but if millions of mothers follow our example, where is Japan to pasture herds of cows?
And if we all want more meat, where shall beef and mutton
be procured? Enlarging Japanese diet brings us back to the
question of peasant life."

Foreign dress, similarly, they thought of chiefly for the

younger generation or for their husbands. The head of the house, forced to keep up two wardrobes, one foreign for the office and one native for home and ceremonial use, is obliged to consume nearly half of the family's clothes budget. A woman belonging to the very high income class of $1,000 a year might expect to have some $50 a year for her own clothing and thus be compelled to buy the cheapest sort of European apparel, which is sure to look badly. But wives were already sewing foreign clothes for their small daughters, according to directions published in newspapers; and usually they themselves had one European outfit for hiking in summer.

"Our daughters," they continued, "no longer look quite well in Japanese kimono. They stand very straight now, instead of drooping slightly; they are athletic and tall and after they have worn comfortable dresses to school they find the tight sash oppressive; their walk is impeded by sandals after they have tried shoes; and they have less time and patience to spend on kimono. Once dressed in Western clothes, attire can be forgotten; but the kimono is disarranged by even slight motions of walking or housekeeping and must be adjusted again and again. Moreover, really fine Japanese kimono, handpainted and of exclusive design on the best quality of crêpe with richly embroidered sashes, are every bit as costly as fashionable European dress."

"Our children will wear the new clothes, at least for the street," they used to say. And in Tokyo two contrasting generations are a common sight: a small, bent grandmother in native kimono, and beside her a strapping big girl, red-cheeked and athletic, wearing serge skirt, red sweater, orange tam o'shanter, big black boots, striding along at the rate of one step to grandmother's three. Exercise and better nutrition are unquestionably having their effect on size and figure.

Statistics show the gradual improvement, most noticeable in towns, and more marked in the case of girls than of boys. At girls' schools I was often asked to stand back to back for measuring purposes and was frequently matched in height by tall Japanese girls. They are no longer quite so lithe and willowy, and look just a little strange—to other Japanese— in kimono, quite as a Vassar hockey star would be rather a bouncer if put into her grandmother's furbelows.

"For the children"—this was always the refrain. I felt that the "new woman" in Japan, the woman who is planning to alter civilization at its very source, the home, could not be separated from her children. She was thinking and dreaming for them, rather than for "rights" for herself, which she regarded as still so far away. "My daughter may vote," "My daughter may dance," "My daughter will marry from choice," seemed to be their partly wistful, partly patient attitude.

Moreover I failed to separate the "new woman" from the modern man. Few women apparently could think of the future as it might affect their sex without also thinking of men. Men in all ranks of Japanese society are battling for a living against bitter competition. The middle classes are overcrowded quite as much as the laboring. To succeed in the keen game of survival men must exact equal sacrifice from the women, must insist on cheap living, the toil of housekeeping, the careful spending. They are to be regarded, and are so regarded by the more thoughtful women, not as tyrants from choice, but as victims of grim necessity. The women I met, who were meditating the most thorough-going reconstruction of home life, knew also that it could not be attained by campaigning or demanding as in the case of a more prosperous America. It could be won only by a transformation in the national economy.

CHAPTER XI

NEW WOMAN AND MODERN MAN

Buying for a Japanese home is very generally done by the woman. Rooted in the past as he may be, the man, like the conservative European, unhesitatingly entrusts to the housewife the budget of the family. Expecting trained skill, he relies on her to stretch his usually meager salary to the limit. And as consumer and public, therefore, rather than as rebel or agitator, the middleclass Japanese woman takes significant place in the national life.

The thousands of darkly clad, plain women with a few yen tucked in a purse at the girdle who go out every day in the great cities to purchase soya bean sauce and cotton stockings, lacquer trays and flannel underwear, are apt to be overlooked by the impetuous sensation seeker. If there is nothing bizarre in their appearance however, there is something portentous in the fact that they, instead of men, form the milling throngs in the department stores, fill the thoroughfares as they "window-shop" for spring patterns, or stand spellbound before stalls of magazines with bright "pretty girl covers." It is just such regular folk who hold the power to convert or to destroy Japanese culture at its root—the home. The housewife with the parcel of groceries is not so picturesque as the geisha with the fan or so striking as the feminist with the banner, but, innocently, or with conscious determination, she is in fact active in modifying standards of behavior, health, costume, decorative art, recreations, edu-

169

cation and human relationships. So when we say "Japan" must guard its ancient taste, or "Japan" must progress in living conditions, in reality we mean this demure being, whose sleeves bulge with purchases, must do these things.

Silent, passive and unorganized as are the bulk of urban middle-class housewives, they already form a distinct "public." To their fancies the larger shopkeepers cater in displays of tinsel and novelty goods, offer conveniences in the shape of escalators and nurseries; for their eyes the advertisers flaunt pictures on billboards or in newspapers of grandma or daughter testing a new dentifrice or radio; to their newly aroused self-consciousness the makers of luxury wares appeal, suggesting marcel waves and new rouges and creams. Their extra spending money makes them increasing patrons of the arts and letters; a Japanese authority goes so far as to declare that "the majority of the reading public in Japan are women" and that the magazines selling most highly are women's magazines. From surveys of periodicals made through the aid of a translator, I discovered how strenuously competition strives for woman's favor, with such topics as home and children, marriage and morals, cooking and dancing, with sensational confessions of beautiful sinners, of interviews with personages involved in marital scandals. Operating on the presumption that women as a class are "low-brow," some of the cheaper sheets became so gross that women themselves organized to demand censorship. But theater managers and cinema producers, as well as editors and novelists, look to feminine Japan for audience; to suit their taste the "love interest," long weak in Oriental plays, is being touched up and the war-loyalty theme more neglected. That this emphasis meets hearty approval is shown by women's own plays. But limits are recognized. A dramatist's portrayal of a "Japanese Cleopatra" was so amorous that it was banned by the police. Such ceaseless activities are having a far-reaching effect on the nation's standards, ideals and mentality.

In this growing feminization of society, Japan shows clearly its unity with the modern West. It is a process observable all over the world. To German women, for example, Werner Sombart, in his monumental history of capitalism, attributes a trend in furniture styles away from the solid and massive, for which they have little feeling, toward qualities instinctively preferred—lightness, variety, novelty. What is happening in America needs no comment. Further industrialized than her Asiatic neighbors and with a higher standard of living, Japan approaches more nearly Occidental conditions. As craftsmen lose their power to dictate modes and as capitalists expand large-scale production, more depends upon the discrimination of the bourgeois woman buyer. She is the chooser among the mass of wares; the general level of national discrimination cannot be far above her own.

Oddly, it is most of all with the United States that Japan may be compared in respect to the rôle of women. In both countries, living standards and particularly home environment are discussed with animation—in our case because we are freer from ancient traditions and in the case of Japan because she is trying to throw them overboard—and the result is that both must start to build afresh on cleared ground. The two nations, moreover, isolated as they are, can afford to be somewhat more concerned with home and women than their neighbors of Asia, occupied by revolution and famine, or of Europe, engrossed in politics and finance. Indeed, it is only the comparative poverty of Japan that prevents its women from filling the enviable positions of Americans across the seas.

Newspapers have been quick to reflect this feminine trend. The white light of popularity they are always willing to play upon any promising newcomer: the beauty parlor owner who invents a winged headdress "to encourage our aviators"; the noble nun who heads a culture improvement society; the wife who wins high alimony for cruelty by a mother-in-law; the college girl who enters the Japanese Hollywood; the Osaka school child who visits her parents on vacation by airplane; or the clerk in the Ford Company who is first of her sex to climb Fuji's snow-mantled height in winter. Nor are editors content to mirror; they initiate. Much of the momentum of the woman's movement is due to editors organizing mass meetings in auditoriums of newspaper buildings; they have spoken themselves on "problems of women" and the feminine character; they have been promoters of women's societies. Very well, too, they know how to arouse the men's sympathies by well-timed symposia on "Is womanly woman passing?" and by editorials giving "100 recipes for a happy married life," ranging from "If husband is a samisen lover, it may not agree with his wife, who is a soprano," to "If you must quarrel, start it at once and make it a good one." Significant is the fact that in Japan and the United States, as hardly elsewhere in the world, visiting foreigners are greeted at the top of gangplanks by the breathless query: "What do you think of our women?"

More than innovating buyer and public audience, however, is the woman of the middle and upper classes. Contradictory as it may seem, she is the conserver of her country's older civilization. More and more, Japanese men, pursuing the same course as the men of the West, tend to leave this function of guardianship in the women's hands. And to-day the Japanese woman plays a vital rôle in the national evolution because she is no longer merely the most decorative object ever produced by Japanese culture—she is also that culture's last custodian.

For one thing she retains the color in costume with the variety and mobility once common to the clothing of both sexes. The man tends to become drab and standardized in the garments of the industrial age; though he still wears the kimono a great deal, it is generally of dismal propriety shorn of elaboration. The male is busier to-day. Men of the upper classes no longer are luxuriously idle courtiers or warriors in reserve and even the nobles feel the necessity of entering government service or business. As they take these steps they lose interest in and facility for the arts that suited another day. So women now arrange the flowers; steadily they preëmpt the tea ceremony, originally a masculine accomplishment and, while I have watched surviving tea masters at their craft, I have more often heard men laughingly declare that the ceremony bored them and they "had no time" for it though, in the same breath, they commended the proficiency of wife and daughter. Another former prerogative of the men, the Noh dancing, is being studied by women of aristocratic circles. While sons prepare at commercial high schools for business careers or study law and engineering at college, daughters more often remain alone in their training for domesticity and æsthetics. Unmistakably a part of this late division of labor is due to the common world tendency to let the sentiment and tradition of the past accumulate in women's hands, while men of the corresponding social class take to machines, business, or politics. But the Japanese women are peculiarly fitted to conserve—more so than their sex in the rest of Asia, in India or China, for in those countries the women have not been so carefully educated and drilled in the arts; they are not equally literate and disciplined, and formal studies are chiefly in foreign schools, where instead of native art modern stenography is emphasized. Indeed, Rabindranath Tagore, in 1929, selected a Japanese girl to teach the fine arts to Indian women at his school.

The unique culture of which the Japanese woman is now the repository gives her a special interest for the world. We can hardly witness anywhere to-day, even among Latin races, the spectacle she presents of femininity still so sophisticatedly ornamental, still associated with the cult of flowers, music and poetry—and still a bit tinged with mystery. Art for her is an aura of leisure rather than a subject for casual debate in Monday Clubs. The emotional atmosphere enveloping the upper class of Japan is something that reminds us of our own past, of mediæval courts, of the romantic era of sentiment, and a little, too, of Queen Victoria. As a fine lady, the Japanese woman preserves traditions that everywhere else, in a democratized world, are passing into oblivion. As a *jeune fille* of good family, she demonstrates to the era of flapperdom the flower-like quality of girlhood in the vanished "age of innocence." Even as geisha, she retains so much of æstheticism that the most puritanic Westerner feels his conscience lightened for making a tour of the red-light districts of Kyoto or Tokyo. Geisha, of course, are not the representatives of so high a taste as the ladies. The geisha twang the samisen, but the ladies pluck the koto; it is the difference between the banjo and the harp. The geisha dance figurative episodes of simple stories, Urashima—the Rip Van Winkle; the lady dances the stern martial epic of the Noh. The geisha make crude jests; the lady writes classic poetry on gilded and tinted oblongs of paper. The geisha wear the colors of the rainbow in their robes; the lady dresses in severe hues, but her quiet sash is worth the whole of their wardrobe both in design and monetary value.

What the geisha do represent is the age of selfish pleasure—the *hetairæ* of ancient Greece. They are reminders of
the centuries when the Japanese men had time to while away
endless hours at boating parties with guitars on the moonlit
Sumida waters; in interminable dances and tedious games; in
balladry; in gardening; in long and delicate feasts. They
belong to the time when woman was the center of many arts,
and herself combined them all in the fine art of pleasing.

But the geisha are to-day more than that; they are not
anachronisms solely. They are the most daring element in
society, as well as the conserving. Very rapidly they are putting the past behind them. In some quarters, strict edicts are
necessary to keep them in ancient attire. They are consciously
and valiantly trying to compete with the *moga,* or modern
girl, and they are aware that the age of leisure is over, that
they must now present novelty no less than training; many
accordingly wear short skirts, have bobbed hair, read the sensational novels, talk about Russia and patter about jazz,
patronize the cinema, and take up fads, such as winter sports
or swimming. And thus they retain a certain degree of their
old power as arbiters of public taste. They are in the lime-
light; their pictures appear in the press in every strange costume introducing every novelty and their "stunts" are broadcast. No less than the former *demi-monde* in France, they
are experimenters and, if they are successful, their acquisitions are passed on to the reputables by degrees. In this way,
both as heirs of tradition and as initiators, the geisha have
a real share in Japanese culture and development.

But the relative force of the geisha is overemphasized,
largely because the public knows more about her than about
the lady. Most of the Japanese have never seen a great
matron in her home and have no idea what she represents in
terms of national power. Thousands of the men have no

higher ideal than that offered by the geisha; she is to them all that is poetic, entertaining and brilliant in womankind. As such the geisha is of genuine importance in social concepts. Yet the lady has also her place at the apex of society. She is not seen so much at the theater or opera, her toilettes are not copied to the same extent, society reporters do not jot down her doings as is customary with her kind in the West, nor is there any longer the sort of court life which makes her the topic in the tenements. The lady is isolated, alone, relatively, and that is the reason for her survival in so archaic a form, no doubt. She is the recluse, the amateur, and therefore preserves traditions better.

Very different from the hard sprightliness of the geisha are the manners and gestures of the lady. She is economical of motion, if not of time; there is nothing superfluous or hurried in her bearing. For every action in her life, there exists a perfect formula. When she rises from her knees, it is in one long, flawless curve. She pushes back a door noiselessly, sleeve drawn back, fingers correctly posed. To watch her tie a package with a string, smooth a silk painting on an ivory roller, open a fan, lift a cup or stir embers in a brazier is to observe a performance of almost priestly precision.

Constantly she reminded me of pictures; I was always recognizing some painted prototype as I watched the movement of her sleeve or the angle of her wrist on a harp. It was not surprising that she should suggest the past, for she is in fact a model created by her ancestors. In act after act she serves the dead; it is not housework she performs but house-ritual.

Memory will be eternal of one who like a tall shadow, without noise, moved about her room. She knelt silently, folding carefully her dark-blue, severely cut robes and tucking together her white-socked feet as formally as her slim hands. Her hospitable feelings toward a visitor were manifested by a soft gleam in the dark eyes, a touch on the knee, or a fluttering laugh—but that emphatic sugariness known as "graciousness" in the Occident was utterly absent. For the most part, she was silent. Her long, thin face, poised on the drooping neck, was undisturbed by expression. She seemed suspended in a kind of cataleptic trance. Encountering such a personage was at first a defeatist experience. But understanding grew with friendship. Certainly I did not find her "repressed" or "old-fashioned" as travel-writers so frequently describe her. She seemed curiously free—free from the overwhelming American obligation of vivacity. She did not seem afraid to move; only that movements were as frumpy as frills on a gown. She did not seem afraid to speak; only that her channels of being were deep and quiet, and that what she knew was seldom in the shape of words.

For one thing, she knew how to live beautifully. The art of keeping in perfect order the perfect house was hers. She was not educated in the sense that the word is used at Vassar; she did not know the formula for hydrochloric acid, the date of the battle of Waterloo, or the score of the last hockey game. But she was skilled in the art of selection among family treasures; in pouring scenery with vari-colored sands on lacquer plates; in singing the rare and sophisticated arias of the Noh. She knew the meaning of fan positions, patterns in silks and styles in painting, the difference between the thin blue of Hirado porcelain and the rich purple of the Kutari. In her mind was a wealth of historic allusion and poetic comprehension; she could derive hours of pleasure from the simplest verse: "O wilderness! Cicada's cry enters into your rocks!" Her education had made her, not learned, but sensitive to many lovely things.

The lady, too, had had more experience of life than one might guess from her gentle demeanor. True, she had never smoked a cigarette, driven a motorcycle, worn breeches, pounded with a gavel, or danced at a night resort. But in her way she had seen surging life. Fire, the "Red Flower of Yedo," had burst above her home more than once; she had seen men dying, women pulled from under tottering timbers. She had nursed sufferers from typhoon and flood. She had learned the mastery of emotions otherwise devastating as a fire. With steely fortitude she sat in the rocking cradle of earthquakes; serenely, she had attended the funeral of her own child. She had accepted a great deal of personal unhappiness, of loveless marriage, of family repression, of financial misfortune, with a resignation that was neither docile nor grim, but decidedly stately. She was not, as a feminist might think her, "sheltered."

Chatter, however, about any of these things was far from her notion of propriety. She could tell you, if you asked; she could confide with a quiet simplicity many intimate thoughts. But it no more occurred to her to take the initiative or "converse" than to wave her hands or fox trot. Both were foreign innovations. Like all Japanese of the old school, she faced bravely that greatest of American terrors—silence.

Silence! I had scarcely suspected the meaning of the word until I visited in her home. It was not that she or her friends were heavy or dull. No, the silence was dignified, or pensive; akin to a dream. And in such noiseless hours, by mute intuition, people often reveal a great deal of themselves—things that are covered up elsewhere under a stream of talk about weather, Airedales, sex, and golf. Kneeling side by side, these women seemed almost listening to one another's personalities.

How shall one evaluate the lady in Japan? It is wrong to dismiss her as a doll, in the light way of casual observers; for she is a highly complicated being, certainly as complex in her feelings and training as, let us say, the Chairwoman of the Pocahontas Ladies' Tuesday Club in "our own town." Neither can she be admired as a flower, exquisite and without blemish; she has never really known what we call "happiness," and her life has been one protracted self-mastery. What we may at least say is that she represents a marvelous example of femininity skillfully molded, mind and body, to fit specific social circumstances.

The geisha hands on the heritage of the cults of pleasure. The great lady preserves the tradition of cultured responsibility. And what of middle-class women? Of those who are respectable, in contrast with the prostitute, but less æsthetically reared than the lady?

They, too, preserve elements of old ideals: housewifery, the sanctity of the home, the genteel maternity. Quite as in the Victorian and Wilhelminic periods in England and Germany, where the wife made a little "castle" of the home and an altar of housekeeping, the Japanese middle-class woman carries on her domestic rituals, her habits of thrift and self-sacrifice. She supports the fairy tales and recipes for festal days, just as German women still bake special cakes for Christmas which once were dedicated to heathen goddesses of the hearth. She prepares food to send in paper ships down the river at the Feast of the Dead, just as to-day in Bavaria food in the shape of ships is made for All Souls' Day. And the Japanese women practice many a curious, ancient form of religion; for every lunar change, they drop a bit of egg in a bowl of soup to represent "the moon in water" or prepare the "half-moon in the sky" with mushrooms, sweet potato and white fish sausage.

Such customs the native writers calls "dainty playthings of mothers and daughters," for most men are delighted and proud that their women retain the ideal of womanliness which we would express as "ladylike," but they more generally, I think, phrase as "beautiful sentiment." The genteel woman in Japan has her tabus in keeping with her social position, but they are distinctive: she must not display teeth in laughing or eat meat or cross her knees. She may smoke her old silver pipe but it was my impression that she seldom indulges in wine. She makes men feel grandly superior and they naturally enjoy that. With all the flourish of a Southern Senator at Washington once making an anti-suffrage speech, a member of the Japanese Diet can still refer to "female grace" threatened by the ballot.

Sentiment is part of this universal respectability in every land. Women must have tender fancies, love ballads, nature, mushroom hunting and goldfish breeding. Painfully the older women tremble, blush and giggle in the presence of the men. More attractive in their dismay are the maidens, but they present none the less a genuine spectacle of nerves. In James Fenimore Cooper's day it was considered a social necessity for females to swoon; so in this respect the Japanese women are luckier than their Western sisters of the age of sentiment. No one quite demands that they faint.

It is a mistake, of course, to press analogies too closely. The conservative women in Japan present a different problem from their own kind in distant countries. For one thing they are not consolidated by the Church to the extent that this was accomplished in large parts of France and southern Germany. Buddhists have only recently awakened to the desirability of winning the active allegiance of the sex by the agency of the Y.W.B.A., the social work club, or the charity bazaar. Consequently, political parties can less securely reckon on their opinions if an opportunity comes for them to vote.

Yet woman at large is a stimulating force in Japan, not a merely passive weight. There is in her character a vein of strength and even a gallant audacity which has been brought to light by the demands of war, earthquake suffering, the changing standards of living and the spread of industry. She has been acted upon by these forces and has herself developed ideas, initiative and courage to shape events. She has shown potentialities of growth. Together with man she is determined to help direct the national destiny instead of floating blindly down the stream of events.

Although the determined leadership in "movements" has belonged largely to the rebellious middle-class women who had time, education, money and social backing for their reforms, a combative spirit has manifested itself elsewhere, too, among mill operatives and farmers' wives, underworld adventuresses, school children, and *moshi-moshi,* or telephone girls as well as among noblewomen, playwrights, and business women.

Indeed, the variety that exists among Japanese women cannot too often be stressed. Contemporaneously live women toiling at the mouth of coal mines and girls flying æroplanes in a Japan-Korea 1000 meter altitude test. There are broad-faced, coarse-handed, island fisher-girls and anæmic, nerve-tortured urban exquisites. One principal of a girls' school summons Shinto priests to perform a "soul-quieting ceremony" over her restless charges; while another, wishing to stir up her girls, calls in instructors in modern literature and barefoot dancing. The widest differences are apparent in physique: from the lean, aquiline, Kyoto type and the heavy beauty with dead-white face and enormous eyes, to the dark, squat figure suggestive of Malaysian origin. They also differ in training from the most animalic of women who take hardly more than an instinctive care of their young to the scholar and the mystic. They differ in disposition from the flapper to the nun, the victim to the virago, the naïvely blushing schoolgirl to the boldly bald writer of "confession stories." Some are dolls; others artists. Some are barely conscious, still living on a submerged, intuitive plane of existence; while others sweep world horizons with wide-open eyes.

Not even a single phrase describes the courageous sort. It is a decided error to divide the sex into the "subjected" and the "emancipated." For the subjected range from the hungry laborer of the rice paddies to the tutored lady-in-waiting at court; while the emancipated are also in all ranks of society. There is the "publicity hound" who thirsts for notoriety at any price; the sheer adventuress; the muscular sport enthusiast who sees no further than her hop, skip and jump; the shy creature who works toward a goal, mole-like, underground; the radical agitator facing jail; and the iron-willed crusading moralist.

Frank, naïve, reckless, emotional types abound, seeking the most extreme escapes from conventions, if devoid of constructive ideals. Far from the timid creature of tradition are these free-loving, free-living, often dangerous, devil-may-care adventuresses. Remote from the foreigner's notion of "progressive, rights-conscious woman," they are not feminists but passionately and often primitively feminine. Such was the noted lady who made a name and fortune by going as servant to households of politicians and writing up all she witnessed and heard in so unshrinking and gaudy a style for the newspapers that she created the season's scandal of Tokyo; a proclaimed free lover, she ran off with a handsome novelist to idle grandly on the French Riviera until, on

WOMEN DRIVING PILES

the verge of bankruptcy, a mysterious bullet ended her life. Many such have their day in Japan's literary circles and it must be said that, as far as willingness to share private scandals with public curiosity goes, no women of the world are more ready than some of the Japanese.

There is another characteristic species of daring woman—she whom a single idea lifts for a time out of terrified conventionality. Such was the fifty-six-year-old peasant woman who, attending her first public meeting, addressed an enthusiastic throng on the woes of her farming district; she was so abashed by her own boldness in speaking loudly to a crowd and so startled at the salvos of applause, that she swooned then and there upon the platform. Such also were the young pupils of a large high school in Tokyo who held a mass meeting attended by nearly a thousand men and women, at which they rendered fiery speeches on love and marriage; these were unfortunate "Year of the Horse" girls, born under that zodiacal sign occurring once in sixty years, which condemns victims by ancient superstition to celibacy. Rare is the man who will break the tabu; the few noblemen who have defied the legend are celebrated for their independence; and as a rule, thousands of these "Horse" girls, facing certain single life, crowd into medical schools, social work and business positions. Only girls early weighted with so tragic a destiny would have ventured to plead in public for a release from tabus.

Yet it is the martyr who is most conspicuous in Japan where she still receives almost mediæval admiration. This type of woman does not initiate or lead, but knows how to die, ceremonially, first placing upside down the scrolls and paintings in the niches, turning topsy-turvy all the screens, placing white paper prayers here and there, shutting up the household gods that they may not see, and robing herself in white before the act. There is indeed in the country a great amount of this quiet morbidity, perhaps more than existed in England in the time of Richardson. I have met women and young girls who confess that they think of death cheerfully, but are helpless to think of life so blithely. They yearn for martyrdom.

Desperation may turn outward as well as in, however, and appear in strange places. A frail, elderly, respectable, modestly robed little woman it was who rushed toward the Emperor with a suffrage petition, crying out: "A request! A request!" expecting and receiving jail for the sacrilege. Far different was a young wife of a Korean conspirator who plotted against Imperial lives—a girl of the slums, bob-haired, pretty, who had picked up a bare livelihood in low restaurants of Tokyo and had spent her free time reading Tolstoi and "playing with Communists." Enormous popular interest followed the trial, the condemning of the pair to life imprisonment, and the dramatic suicide of the girl in her cell.

Finally there is a highly evolved, mentally fearless woman, who breaks through her own inhibitions and her country's traditions, not for a moment or for an impulse, but permanently and through seasoned conviction. Of this species have been the social workers and agitators for several decades, particularly the early advocates of temperance. Of the same sort were the matrons who recently went among the mining districts, taking pictures and exhibiting lantern slides as they lectured on the labor conditions, whose propaganda helped influence the Government to end the labor of women and children underground. Such as they were the women who formed a Federation of Societies after the 1923 earthquake and whose relief work was later taken over by municipal authorities. Kindred spirits have been the writers on problems of peasant and factory girls; the educators, notably Mme. Y. Yoshioka who established the first medical school for girls and Mme. Sumi Ōye who gave her own fortune to found a domestic-science school; the numbers who have dedicated lives, toil and often private means to public welfare, more often quietly than noisily, for the past fifty years.

This devotion and discipline, this nervous force and mental seeking, this emotional richness and spiritual creativeness appear in countless ways among the race. Bursting through surface conventionality a hundred seemingly unrelated, sporadic "movements," societies, agitations, individual and organized efforts take form. But these are not actually so unrelated as they seem; they are all steps in an irresistible social progression.

Fundamentally what seems vital to the average middle-class woman—to her who has long borne the title of "Okusama," or "Honorable Back Room"—are immediate and intimate concerns: marriage, "culture," economy, comfort, hygiene, child health. But it has taken time to convince her that she cannot obtain what she wants by remaining in the honorable back room. She has been told that she must organize and plead for them with lawmakers and the community. Surrendering some of her genteel training and "beautiful sentiment," she has begun to do so.

In a remarkably short time, it has grown thoroughly respectable to organize at least for the furtherance of domestic and patriotic ends. No less a personage than the sister of Prince Konoye, Abbess of a 1300-year-old Buddhist nunnery at Nara, who resembles in her stiff silks and snowy, neatly folded headkerchief a Christian nun, was the eminent sponsor of a "self-culture" group and of relief work among women prisoners, charity being a Buddhist tradition. Other

notables have accepted positions as patrons of the Matri-
monial Aid Society which presented tableaux of wedding
rites through the centuries beginning with the legendary
first marriage of god to goddess and coming down to propaganda for "modern economy." The League of Women's
Societies held an Economy Exhibit at Osaka showing how to
get fifteen wedding kimono for $200, and how to live hap-
pily ever afterward in a two-room house, one furnished in
Japanese, the other in foreign style. Numberless are the
small "culture" groups in principal cities, meeting for lectures on foreign sewing, hairdressing or pouring tea. More
serious than among Occidentals indeed is the public concern
over marriage and domesticity; for where in the West do we
find a girls' school, as at Tokyo, founding a "chair on marriage," proposing a "marriage consultation office for graduates," and the solemnization of weddings within the school?
And if they do not yet attend meetings, the tens of thousands
of "white collar" men's wives and daughters, in small towns
as well as cities, read about them in thoroughly "reputable"
magazines, very much on the order of our own Ladies' Home
Journal, dealing with "home life in foreign countries," "how
to powder," "knitting for the children," "history of our New
Year rice cake customs," or "What duty do the gods command?" varied by short stories on "Constancy of a Woman,"
and moral essays such as "Don't judge people by their
exteriors."

Equally within the orthodox sphere of interests now lie
questions of food and costume reform. Zealously, young
girls study home economics and women learn to sew strange
clothes for the children and make their own light garments
for summer. The Government acknowledges their endeavors
by sending a woman expert to study abroad and report on
Western dress. A great deal of experimentation goes on;

IN THE WAKE OF THE 1923 EARTHQUAKE

some are creating robes reminiscent of the ancient Japanese garb before the kimono was imported from China; others transform the kimono by brighter colors, lighter sashes, and innovations that strike the conservative Japanese as positively indecent. In food the change is equally noticeable—a great increase in the milk and meat consumption of city-dwellers statistically demonstrable—until Tokyo has been forced to develop sanitary control and pasteurization stations like any Western city. As a collateral come modified manners; and the topics considered by groups grow bolder; a gathering of men and women recently argued nothing less than this: "Why should not women have a good time while men freely do so?"

Yes, organization—provided the aim is feminine and correct—with every year becomes more accepted as a phase of Japanese behaviorism. The Government itself sponsors the Japan Young Women's Association, federating some fourteen thousand "maidens' societies" over the country, whose aims are "to lead the girls of Japan in the right path and avoid the temptation of becoming so-called 'modern girls.' " It is permissible to organize to develop graces, to urge others to become "good wives and wise mothers." Ladies of the very highest society, wives of officials and a Viscountess or so have gathered together to promote a "save a sen a day" movement among the nation's women, in order to reduce the foreign debt. Glittering titles have hallowed the Japanese Women's Overseas Association, constructed on an English model, to help emigrants abroad; the President was even selected from among the Princesses of the Blood. Red Cross work was inaugurated by society as early as the Russo-Japanese War. To the East as well as the West, patriotic activity and humanitarianism now seem proper for the most honorable back room.

But if organization is highly proper for young women in patriotic leagues and their mothers in culture groups; if discussion of possible innovations in domestic comfort and convenience are permissible, a dangerous precedent has been set. Nothing can then prevent a larger and larger number of women from using their organized power as a weapon and enlarging the discussion of community affairs.

The pressure of local politics upon the home in one case was met by the indignant protest of housewives who besieged the offices of the Tokyo gas company with complaints at the high prices and then proceeded to the Home Office to lodge the same with that branch of the Imperial Government. "Our cries from the kitchen must be listened to and accepted!" the little band declared. Women of a Tokyo suburb in another case campaigned against the threatened establishment of a geisha quarter in the neighborhood. Similar occurrences in other places helped to enlist the housewives in reform movements and partisanship.

Peculiarly a problem of Okusama's, rather than her humbler sister's, is the geisha; for the well-to-do man, instead of the poor one, supports the whole elaborate system. Frequently it is mandatory, since business is customarily transacted, with feasting, at the tea house, just as in New York the firm must take the out-of-town buyer to the "Follies"; the hundreds of yen spent in a night on skilled dancers and rare dishes of lobster and octopus must be charged up to the firm's "overhead," unless taken out of the family's immediate income. With the geisha question is joined that of liquor, for "saké," or rice wine, is consumed at the tea houses in large quantities. The matter of entertainment is an elaborate structure that stands or falls as one. Hence the Woman's Temperance Society has aimed at the regulation of liquor and geisha together, as parts of the same thing. Still, more, therefore, than in the West, temperance has become involved with moral issues.

Yet they are not fanatics, the leaders of Japanese women's enterprises; nor are they wholly blinded by moral indignation. Many of them know that to abolish the geisha system means expensive provision for training, re-education, and support of the out-of-work girls; some in fact urge the amelioration of economic conditions first. And likewise it is not total abstinence of liquor most of them demand but regulation, especially as far as minors are concerned.

On both issues they have had definite successes. Geisha, in 1929, for the first time were excluded from the official Coronation ceremonies. The freeing of girls held against their will has proceeded so far that the segregated geisha problem has caught in its dragnet the question of the "private geisha" who lives alone and eludes the police and the reformer. To the alcohol debate, the Government itself has turned a hearing ear.

Alarmed, indeed, was the Federation of Saké Manufacturers in 1928; so nervous that it announced a "Let's drink day." This followed the proclamation of a "No Saké Day" in memory of the earthquake disaster by the People's Temperance Society, supported by other special organizations of students, women, Christians and Buddhists, numbering some two hundred thousand. The reformers held an evening procession, in which women joined the men who marched, six thousand strong, carrying square, inscribed lanterns through the dusk and singing the prohibition anthem: "Who Can Forget the Nation's Peril?" Wringing protesting hands, the distillers complained that saké is sacred—is it not used in high rites by the Buddhist Church? "Saké is reverence!" they cried. Women should not forget their "beautiful sentiment" so brashly. Moreover, since the breweries and distilleries paid some hundred million yen a year in taxes, it ill befitted the Home Office to sponsor a day of aridity. In short, the universal wet wail was raised.

Little by little, as she takes interest in such movements, Okusama sees that the possession of the ballot is inseparable from their solution. The W. C. T. U. has a political division urging woman suffrage; and significantly prominent at the first women's political meeting, May 10, 1923, were social workers and temperance advocates. The web of politics entangles the most reluctant reformer at last.

Year by year the acknowledgment of politics as the means to women's ends grows wider and more powerful. In 1922, the first woman demanded the right to join a political party; a bright young country girl, a social worker in Tokyo municipality, to the panic of the politicians, declared her wish to support the party of her principles. A year later a political meeting of women was broken up by rowdies—that familiar aspect of early suffrage struggles in the United States. A couple of years afterwards, behold, the delegates were coming, five hundred strong, from all over the country to campaign at the capital; they were seen rushing about the city in motor cars distributing handbills and marching with flags to the gallery of the Diet where they cheered—shades of "beautiful sentiment!"—cheered the introduction of their measures for the ballot and higher education. Within another two years, they were making house to house calls, holding meetings at private homes and in auditoriums, besieging parliamentarians, publishing a monthly, called "Woman Suffrage." Soon they were working together with the prohibitionists in the campaign season, their methods duplicated by the latter. Fifty bold men had by this time joined their organization as paying members. Then political parties began jockeying for feminine support, some promising education, and the Seiyukai, the actual ballot.

With every prospect of local suffrage soon and eventually the realization of universal voting, women began to understand that they needed more education—knowledge of things which no girls' domestic science or fine-arts school had taught them. Thus the Tokyo Girls' Law College was opened in 1928, by the Women's League for Political Rights, to give instruction in jurisprudence and economics.

Education is indeed the one movement supported with whole-hearted enthusiasm. Only a minority in Japan, as was true during the suffrage campaign in America, wishes the ballot or will take any steps to get it. But on the question of higher education less timidity is shown among "respectables" and more energy among enthusiasts.

Education the Japanese women have, far more universally than any of their Oriental sisters. But in general their schools are inferior to men's in standing, in the courses offered, and in their faculties; mostly, too, they are of a narrowly domestic nature offering little training for business, civic or professional careers. Out of the seventy Government institutions for higher learning in Japan, only four have admitted women; two of these are for teachers, one is a music, and the other an art school. Some Imperial universities have admitted women to study, yet only one gives them a degree and in the country districts, especially, there is the need for more instruction.

So women teachers began to organize in 1923. They conducted a fiery agitation soon afterward when a high school principal replaced a woman instructor by a man. The Young Men's Buddhist Association opened its hall to the agitators; and alumnæ gathered to demand "progressive" principals for all girls' high schools and better education for women in general. This program of course the Tokyo Federation of Women's Organizations endorsed.

Some women are discussing coeducation tentatively; feminine students of at least three universities are campaigning, calling on Diet members, broadcasting appeals to girl students throughout the land. Rural experts join the educational agitators, declaring that "rural unrest" can be allayed only by providing "better wives" for farmers, more schools and lectures for adults. And recently, political parties, the Seiyukai and some proletarian groups, adopted the principle of extended education in their platforms. Thus rapidly have women's interests become campaign material.

Now, as a matter of fact, the slogan, "education for women," is bandied about as a cure-all for Japan. Many rely upon it to rejuvenate the nation, create a stronger and healthier race, lift the mental and economic level as a whole. But others look beyond a fetish to the application of trained and rationalized tastes. Once women learn to use Western domestic devices, such doubters inquire, how are those to be paid for in the average home? If they learn professions, how are they to find room for their talents in a field already grimly overcrowded with men?

Women are becoming convinced that the demands for "rights," however obviously due them and however gladly granted, are but half the issue of sex development. There must be a national income sufficient to pay for the elevation of the womanhood *en masse*. This is a thing which has been lacking in most of Europe, so naturally the query arises as to how the humble silkworm can spin enough thread of itself to emancipate both sexes in the nation. The women are facing the bluntest realities when they ask one another: Must we remain ultra-thrifty, drudging housewives or go

Wide World Photos

ROYAL PRINCESSES WATCHING GIRL STUDENTS DEMONSTRATE THE ANCIENT WOMEN'S ART OF
SELF-DEFENSE

into factories and offices as the cheapest unskilled labor? Is there no way out of the dilemma?

Wherever she begins then to interest herself in modern life, whether in kindergartening, shorter hours for spinners, the geisha system, or higher education, Okusama winds up at the ultimate question: Who is to pay for campaigning? Who is to pay for putting into practice what a law allows?

Certainly a very large degree of success is possible to the women in Japan—enough to tempt them on. Individuals already win high compensation as actresses, beauty experts, or physicians who go about in their own motor-cars practicing among the wealthy. In business the bars may be pushed aside; one woman is president of one of the largest country newspapers and a philanthropist; another, a spinster of eighty-four, recently left an accumulated fortune of nearly a million dollars to charity; a third had the distinction of helping to precipitate a bank crash. Magazines offer a livelihood to many writers; social workers and policewomen slip into government service. So has a measure of victory attended efforts to raise the status of working women; underground work in mines was prohibited in 1928, and the hours of spinners were shortened. Moreover organization among laboring women has gone steadily forward; the Kwanto Labor Federation established in 1924 a special women's section, with its own magazine.

None of this can blind the eye, however, to the fact that women have yet, as in so much of Europe, achieved only an illusory "freedom." They are still for the most part the unskilled: the cheap labor in Japan as in other places is largely employed in textile mills. They buy "economic independence" mainly in remote regions, away from cities, in factories too small to be regulated by the Government at the present time; they are overworked, underpaid—seventy per cent of Japan's laboring women are said to receive some fifty cents a day—and hard to organize. Less than one per cent of more than eight hundred thousand working women belong to any organization.

But they are thus quiescent because, harsh as their lot is, to most of the workers it is an actual relief from poverty on the farm. The peasant woman, overburdened with family, working in the fields as well as in extra-seasonal occupations indoors, such as basket-weaving, leads so severe, so isolated and so exhausting a life that young girls turn to the mills and the city offices as a refuge. There is said to result a dearth of women on farms; complaints arise that willing, trained peasant wives are scarce enough to form an additional reason for the boys' exodus to town.

Among the farm girls who have sought the cities, some have fared well. The cities offer thousands of women positions as typists, nurses, clerks, bookkeepers, salesgirls, telephone operators and teachers but the average wage is barely $20 a month. They occasionally gain high recognition, it is true; four girls were sent to Peking as typists accompanying delegates to a conference in China; they are learning to work in the man's world, to be self-supporting in the modern fashion, to achieve more personal independence. But skilled professions open slowly. Competition is ferocious in its strength.

It is then not because Japanese women are "subjected" and "unawakened" that they arouse intense sympathy and keep in the center of the stage. It is because the leaders among them are all too clearly awake; because they look steadily at the future and cry, in the words of a woman writer: "Civilization is the sweet wine made for the rich!"

The more honor therefore accrues to the race that produced the brave personality of Baroness Ishimoto who dared to raise the vital issue for men and women alike—for the whole nation's welfare in fact—namely birth control. An instigator of Margaret Sanger's visit to Japan and a labor sympathizer who spent several years among the miners, she endured for a long time an extreme aloofness from other women propagandists able to work for popular objectives but less competent to look far and frankly to ultimate conclusions. More fearlessly than masculine politicians she has claimed that birth control rather than emigration is the key to Japan's destiny. Lately Baroness Ishimoto has seen powerful recruits accept her revolutionary creed. Silent noninterference has been the attitude of the Government toward the spread of such information among the population and in the upper classes a tacit approval of the principle is now widespread. Agitation for birth control among working families was launched by the Osaka Federation of Labor in 1922 on the ground that large families inevitably force submission on the part of employees. In Tokyo the "reform mayor," Mr. Horikiri, opened a clinic in 1929 for the dissemination of information on the subject among the poor of the city who could furnish proof that they needed it. As far as Hokkaido the news circulated and thence came inquiries and appeals for similar aid, although the mayor was compelled to confine the work of the clinic to the poor of Tokyo.

The age of marriage is already rising: for the girl, from 18 to 20 and for the men, from 25 to 30. No longer is it quite so inevitable for a man to saddle himself with a throng of dependents, out of Confucian considerations, the moment he graduates from college. The girl now may expect a year or two of study in a high school before wedlock. Frank discussion goes on in periodicals over marriage and the family system. People are remembering that after all the old

knights of Japan would have regarded themselves de-
meaned had their families comprised more than three or
four children.

One by one, men of science, economists, agricultural and
other experts have come before the public with outspoken
declarations that only by birth control can Japan face the
future. And finally a Government committee assembled to
consider economic problems discussed the grave question of
limitation of population and thereby won for itself a place
among enlightened nations as Baroness Ishimoto won for
herself a place within the nation.

Japan's social problems, her growing population and its
increasing demands, are part of the world's problem. Inevitably therefore women who take up the national study have
been brought out from the "honorable back room" not
merely into public but also into international affairs. New
and important relations are arising between the women of
Japan and the rest of the world, just as the men make contacts, sportsmen, scientists or Rotarians, diplomats or economists, associating with their kind. Girls compete at Olympic
games and grown-ups at international peace parleys. Individuals naturally paved the way for elected delegates. A
veteran newspaper correspondent, Miss Takenaka, was sent
to China by the press to follow the trail of women revolutionists and report on their military education. An archæ-
ologist and anthropoligist, Mme. K. Torii, journeyed with
her husband through Mongolia, wrote a book herself on
"Eastern Mongolia," and collaborated with him in a work
on the "Stone Age in China." Returned travelers lecture,
one sort vehemently denouncing the "shallow, painted womanhood in the West," its indelicate dancing and Epicurean
view of life; others urging the Japanese to grow bolder that
they may discuss on equal terms with the brazen females

across the Pacific. Visitors to Japan from the ends of the earth add to the international connections; parties of American business women stopped off in their journey round the world; a woman consul was appointed to Japan in 1922 by the Armenian Republic; educators, social workers, suffragists, and journalists make Yokohama their port of call in surveys of the globe.

Consequently Japanese women are not thinking nowadays —as once they did—solely about the Occidental women. They are conscious of their sex as a whole—of women beginning to vote in parts of India, of militants with guns in Canton, of Burmese suffragists, of Persians waiting on the prime minister, of Moscow feminists, of Turkish rebels, of Palestinians objecting to orthodox rabbinical courts.

With all the women of the earth they are now measuring themselves. Legally, the Japanese woman is emancipated far beyond what an outlander might suspect; thirty years ago, polygamy was abolished, widespread education granted, the right of consent to marriage obtained, more control over property acquired, protection from desertion by the husband extended, and the right to engage in business established. But as far as sheer personal forcefulness goes, by and large she is not yet a match for the Chinese woman, her closest neighbor. Only a half-century behind Americans in "rights," she is a full century in psychology. And she knows that what she needs is more social life, more association with others— in short, more companionship. She has had secret strength, quiet determination; now she needs a more open development.

It is thus that Japanese wives realize the importance of working with men, of meeting them in public, of achieving a community practice in which free discussion is possible. No merely frivolous aim, then, is the cry for "social life."

It is the atmosphere which men and women must create together.

Woman as consumer, as conservator, as initiator and finally as companion of man, is a prime factor in Japan's evolution. And the truth is being recognized to an increasing degree; men begin to seek the coöperation of women in their schemes, whether radical or conservative; they begin to favor comradeship in public life and in the home. Man works through and with woman; not, as we are too often taught to think, always as master over her.

Indeed, we have thought too much of the Japanese woman as an isolated figure—a doll posed against a silver screen or a defiant feminist on a platform. In reality, the "new woman" is inseparable from that other phenomenon, "modern man," who has been urging and positively leading her forward. Neither can the conservative woman be isolated from the conservative man. Both sexes, everywhere, are fascinated and antagonized by each other.

It is absurd to write as though woman was a weak victim struggling to break from an ogre; more real to describe both men and women as struggling side by side, now aiding and now persecuting one another, against a mutual master— civilization. They are caught in a common mesh of destiny. Japanese man is as interested in Japanese woman as is the stranger from abroad; he thinks about her almost excessively. He may deride her, but he forgets her never. He is constantly soliciting the foreigner's views about her and the observer's opinion often reacts on his own.

In fact, the Japanese man evokes sympathy as a direct outcome of interest in his mate. She lives up to the picture we have of her in advance. But he is all too often caricatured as the inhumanly arrogant, indifferent "Oriental tyrant." Arrogant he can be, a tyrant on occasion, but indif-

ferent? Not noticeably. The very man in the street is growing accustomed to walking beside his wife and even
escorting her by the arm; it is "high-hat" to show a little
attention. But whether he does or not, he is less emancipated
than he looks. He may appear to be sublimely aloof, as he
strides along, arms folded, eyes on the horizon, with scarce
a glance at the meek creature trotting two paces behind. But
to take him at his face value is a mistake; from all that I
have gathered in conversations or by evidence of literature
and art, it seems, he spends an amount of his leisure on
this theoretically inferior being which is altogether inor-
dinate. If he is not passing the hours of reverie trying to
decide between the "old-fashioned girl" and the "moga" as
an ideal mate; if he is not lavishing time and patrimony on
courtesans; if he is not caught in the toils of some free-
living, literary adventuress; if he is not surreptitiously reading women's magazines, gaping at cinema-romances, flirting
with a stenographer in the office, sending money to Hokkaido for the relief of a widowed great-aunt, defying papa
to interfere with his marriage choice, then, you may be sure,
he will weep from sheer devotion and reverence when you
refer to his aged mother.

He is only too happy, as I soon discovered, to talk about
woman in general. He is glad to have a chance to say: "Ask
my wife to wear foreign clothes; it is cheaper," or "I ask my
wife to cook Japanese diet; it is more healthful," or "Women
should not eat beefsteak; it destroys their charm," or "We
will never succumb to woman's influence like Americans,"
or "You see, our women don't talk so much." Strangely
familiar are the words I have heard repeated in Europe from
alarmed burghers, distressed at the prospect of an American
feminine invasion of their own prerogatives.

A man, if eminent, is glad to write for a symposium on

what he thinks of his wife: "My wife has saved and scrimped that I may buy books and study. I am grateful." Or: "My wife is womanly. Therefore I appreciate her."

He surveys woman with a jealously observant mind. He is acutely conscious of her appearance. Novelists describe with keen perception the modern creature, the boldly slanting eye, the perfume, the free manner; "almost one would have taken her for a geisha." The schoolboy wonders whether he will ever meet the emancipated girl in very truth just as the schoolgirl muses on whether the chivalrous movie-hero will ever encounter her in real life. The gentleman of the old school frowns because his wife wears sleeves shorter than she ought "at her age too!" The atmosphere is charged with this tense absorption in sex.

Despite his occasional hauteur, the "Oriental tyrant" is largely ruled by women. He is as emotionally entangled with sex as the Latin races. And there are a variety of reasons for his bondage. For instance upper-class men have fewer opportunities to cast woman from the mind than Americans now have with their sports and business enterprises, for in Japan recreation usually involves the tea houses and both business and politics revolve about the eternal and expensive geisha entertainment. At the other social extreme the millions of peasants and poor craftsmen spend more hours at home toiling with their wives and children in shops and rice paddies whereas our mode of agriculture entails a greater division of labor while our artisans are largely industrialized factory workers. Moreover there is little individualized public life in Japan as yet; most of the festivals are arranged for the family as a unit. Since the family is so tightly knit, the claim of women relatives is indubitably imperative—the younger ones for support and attention and the elders for Confucian politeness and reverence at least.

The man who has no family obligations is rare. Anchorites are not very numerous in Japan.

Yet another reason for men's absorption in women is the change going on in concepts of love and life—a movement so profound that the man finds it impossible to take women and their ways for granted. *He* still worries over what *She* will do next. And he still has a chance—or thinks he has—to influence this change. At any rate he has an amazingly wide range of types to choose from for his bride. In the Cabell fashion a man beyond the Pacific may dream of the girl of romance, enchanted. But the upper-class Japanese really has a chance to marry one. Both theoretically and actually he may select a mediæval wife robed in flowing grace and possessing the traditional modesty, docility, charm, poesy, sentiment and probably the inanity of an age that is mythical elsewhere. And on the other hand he may marry a modern girl capable of fox-trotting, flying a plane, helping him in business and keeping him pleasantly enlivened by her vagaries, her broad interests and her manner. But like any other human, he wants two incompatibles miraculously amalgamated. With ingenuous frankness he admits it.

A writer in the *Kansai Bungei* said: "I should like to have for a wife a pale Kyoto girl with jet-black hair and classical beauty whose thoughts are far away from bobs and shingles. As for my head servant, I should wish for the economic but ignorant-of-toilette woman of Osaka and, lastly for a friend, I should like to have the Tokyo girl, preferably a 'modern' one with foreign dress and shingled hair (and perhaps stockingless shins) from whom I would drink my fill of youth and vitality. And when I'm tired of her company, what could be more restful than to return once more to my Kyoto wife waiting for me in the true Japanese home playing the koto or singing poems to the moonlight!" It is an elabora-

tion of the popular Count Keyserling's pronunciamento
that the man should choose an old-fashioned womanly
woman for a wife, and the "comrade" as a supplement.

Nor is this temper something recent. Throughout the
centuries, Japanese men have worshiped before the Merciful Goddess as before Buddha; they have carved and cast
female statues of the rarest grace, angels and haloed deities;
their ballads, dramas and dances celebrate the memory of
queens and peasant women, tragic and noble as the heroines
of the old Greeks—Tachibana, who was a living sacrifice for
victory as Iphigenia was in the Trojan War; the women of
the Heike clan who killed themselves rather than endure
defeat, more stern than the Trojan women who only wept,
if we believe Euripides, and wedded their conquerors. In
modern times, no people has more glowingly developed the
theme of woman than the print-makers of Tokyo. There is,
indeed, through the interminable history of the artist's preoccupation with the feminine form, no richer chapter than
theirs; with deep, poetic response to the geisha's appeal, they
mirrored every turn of head and lift of arm, fold of gray
and sea-green skirt, diverse poses, arranging plum blossoms,
playing with kittens, or "plucking the eyebrows." For all
time, their pictures stand as refutation of the current superstition about the "indifferent" Oriental man.

In the improvements in the legal status of women much
has been granted lightly. All has not been wrung from men
by vociferous feminists. The Supreme Court, in 1927, ruled
that a deserted wife "may claim damages from her husband
and from the woman who lures him away." The Ministry of
Justice in the same year was considering the admission of
women to the bar in six leading cities of Japan, especially as
lawyers in juvenile cases. And it should be remembered that
men of feudal traditions, a generation ago, gave the nation's

women rights that were, at that time in the Orient, extraordinary. As early as 1898, the Civil Code was revised to give them the right to own property and to marry without parental consent after the age of twenty-five. At the same time polygamy was abolished—a step which a man, Mr. Y. Fukuzawa, had been advocating. Earlier still, in 1872, the right of petitioning for divorce was allowed to women. In 1878, according to Mr. Suyeo Nakano, a local governor urged that propertied women, heads of families, be given the vote for prefectural assemblies. Many of the nobility of that century made special breaks with custom in the matter of marriage, some concluding liberal contracts in writing with their brides, some deliberately choosing the unfortunate "Year of the Horse" girls. The Emperor Meiji himself ordered the passage of an act permitting the Empress to be present at enthronement ceremonies. In other words, the liberals of the Japanese Reconstruction Period included women in their scheme to a degree seldom recognized.

Men are becoming eager either as conservatives to utilize the untapped strength of the woman for their own ends, or as radicals to lead them along paths to reforms. A decided struggle between the two elements has gone on for several decades, over the control of public opinion. Indeed, the Japanese no less than the American is forced in his scheme for progress or for standpattism to take the women into the reckoning. The French and the Italians can perhaps afford to discount coöperation; the Germans and the English plan to attain their ends by politics, rather than by long campaigns of education. But the Japanese know very well that laws cannot alter circumstances if the silent mass of women remain untouched, unwilling to participate.

Government authorities expect to use the known conservatism of women as a counterweight against radicalism.

Significant instances of its utilization are the appointment of policewomen to watch the "dangerous thought movement"; the sponsoring of a number of countrywide patriotic societies; the supervision by the Minister of Education of the Maidens' Societies with their 150,000 members. Tokyo Municipality's "Social Education Section" held in 1924 a series of weekly lectures on social work for women, to give them the "feeling of the community" and the idea of "social requirements." Buddhists, as well as Government agencies, now know the latent power; and men inaugurated the Young Women's Buddhist Society. "It is regrettable," said the organizer, head of Musashino Women's College, "that the Y. W. B. A. had to be promoted almost entirely by men. . . . Japanese Buddhist women have not been prepared to do active work in a movement of this kind. . . ." But the wives of the Minister of Education and the Premier were present, and plans were made for training women as leaders to replace the men as soon as possible.

With an eye to the future fully 118 members of the Diet endorsed woman suffrage in 1925 and many more since that time have accepted the idea. It is men who act as heads of the "choose your own mate" bureaus now springing up; men who are generally presidents of women's colleges and secondary schools; men who theorize and guide social practices. Nor are newspaper men behind professors, politicians and priests in their possession of opinions on women's rôle. The Society for Women's Advance, which successfully worked for the opening of more government academies to girls, was organized by both sexes, but the editor of the Osaka *Asahi* addressed the two thousand members of the Union Congress of Women's Associations in 1922 and sponsored in fact the entire meeting; the topics taken up were education, marriage, inheritance and legal reforms. The managing editor of the paper deprecated the "taking of babies to public meetings, the incessant and careless feeding of babies, the unkindly attitude of mothers when asked questions by their children, and the unlimited production of weaklings." Another editor declares that "the enhancement of women's prestige and the development of their personal character are symbols of national civilizations." Judge Hideo Yokota is conspicuous in the movement for a single standard of morals.

Perhaps the most dramatic instance of men's share in the conscious development of the sexes was the remarkable debate on birth control in 1927 when two white-haired, venerable scholars faced each other in argument—the hall packed with about a thousand men, young and old, and among them some twenty girls.

Men in social work continually urge more volunteers to help, getting along in the absence of women with extreme difficulty, trying to wash the babies, tend kindergarten, teach school, and run the charitable offices. When women do start charitable work, men are eager to recognize it officially, though sometimes they are also human in their desire to direct the work which women decide to do.

Far from wishing to give too roseate a picture of man as the friend and forwarder of women's emancipation, I still believe his desire to have woman as comrade in all things has been under-emphasized in writings about the Orient. Moreover in the past as in the present, the transmission of civilization from one country to another has been the work of both adults; the diffusion of culture from China and India to Japan was due to the patronage of empresses, noble abbesses, court ladies, who opened shrines and launched philanthropic works, studied the new poetry and fine arts, adopted novel costumes, dwellings and manners. So the introduction of Western civilization to Japan was the work of women as of men—women who opened schools for the new education, court ladies who tried on Western garb of high-heeled shoes or ostrich-plumed hats and studied waltzing and etiquette, experimenters who learned the violin or volunteered as nurses in war time. In fact in the merging of civilizations, both in the seventh and in the twentieth centuries, Japanese women and men have been similarly involved, helping and hindering each other, busy creating the new national patterns of life in unison.

CHAPTER XII

GEISHA, MOGA, AND MODERN MORALS

THE very eagerness of urban men and women to meet in public, play, discuss and coöperate for common purposes indicates that it was not a special quality of the Oriental soul that long held the sexes in Japan to separate codes of conduct so much as the accidents of history and the movement of economic forces. If they fail to have an easy public relation it is not solely because their ancestors were Japanese. Rather, it arises from the fact that most of them lived in remote villages or isolated castles, cut off by high mountains and poor roads from general communication, rather than in free cities such as those of Renaissance Europe with their rich and stimulating international traffic in goods and ideas. And if we find society in Tokyo very unfamiliar it is by no means due to the slant eyes of the population but to the circumstance that their metropolis was never mistress of the seas like Venice or queen of an empire like London.

Unquestionably the strain among adults of the two sexes when they meet socially is still rather painful. Neither Japanese etiquette nor morality—scarcely the house or the language as far as that goes—is prepared for so unforeseen an emergency. Such devices for "making contacts" as the ball, fox-hunt, musicale, or sofa and picture-album have not been racial pastimes. Important differences persist even in vocabulary and handwriting; only "women and members of the lower classes" for instance are expected to prefix with

207

an honorific such words as sun, soup, money, hot water and
a funeral.

Everything conspires to create a hectic situation. Morality
teaches the "good" woman to consider the most accidental
touch on her sleeve as the audacious beginning of romance.
Formal manners compel the "correct" couple to be reserved;
a pet name or address more familiar than "you" is unthinkable for them. Yet this restraint is not permanent control;
and when boy and girl, so brought up, attempt to associate
in the modern mode, the result is apt to be, as in Spain or
Latin-America, more than comradeship; indeed a love affair.
Girl students at Nihon University, campaigning in 1928 for
co-education, however, promised to be good: "Possible immorality between younger male and female students seems
to be the outstanding reason for our rejection. . . . Girls
who aspire for a higher education are usually determined to
study and are not inclined to fall in love with boys in their
classes. . . . It is only fair that we should be given a trial."

Naturally in these conditions emotional tension is often
acute. The shyness of the girls sometimes verges on agony,
while the apparent frigidity of the young men may cover
tragically frustrated longing for happiness. Education and
the ideal mate are both luxuries; a mere change in moral
ideas cannot alter economic fact. Bitter is the suppression
behind the bland smile of youth. One may sometimes read
it in the smoldering fire of the dark eyes; and one may hear
it spoken frankly in confidential hours. This combined fear
and longing, with uncertainty and repression, create a dark
environment for all recent Japanese thought.

Certainly too the glittering figure of the geisha stands
definitely in the way of higher forms of association between
men and women of the upper classes. Most poetic of courtesans though she may be, her shadow is cast across the love

and marriage relations of other women while her ignorance
tends to retard the mental development of her masculine
patrons and admirers. Her hired subservience helps to make
"society" in Japan what it has always been throughout the
"spiritual East"—namely, a distinctly commercial propo-
sition.

Still it would be wrong to suggest that the geisha has all
the privileges. That would even be ridiculous. Japanese
wives have been rather exceptionally free among Orientals,
going about without veils or bound feet, the grand symbols
of subjection. Nor were they ever confined so strictly to
Purdah or to polygamous harems as their sex in India,
although at the courts of the emperors and the shoguns a
practical seclusion obtained. Wives of the feudal warriors
were expected to be the helpmates of fighting men, stern in
duty as they.

Of course, like peasants everywhere, the farmers of both
sexes have toiled in the fields side by side and celebrated
in the festivals together. At the other extreme of the ladder,
courtiers of both sexes in olden times knew a splendid gallantry of a flavor with that of mediæval Europe; they filled
their days with fiesta, dance and song, elaborate dressing,
the patronage of art and literature, nature-worship and the
gods.

Among these two groups a quite unmoral freedom of
association and flirtation prevailed, devoid of any hint of
daring such as the "moderns" feel. Love, without sin, if
without constancy, was the flower of the courts of Nara and
Kyoto. But between the people and the court circles there
was very slight contact. There was no middle-class Madame
de Maintenon or lower class bluestocking as in France to
hold a salon and mix minds and manners in courageous pro-
fusion. Until the present time there was lacking a variegated

bourgeoisie to cut across caste lines with the stimulating urge of urban intellectual and professional demands.

In view of such a statement it may seem contradictory to add that Japanese society is different from Western, not because it is less "feminized," for it is rather more feminine —the hetaira largely supervises the transaction of politics and business—but because it is so thoroughly commercialized. In all countries from the Near to the Far East, from the Golden Horn to the Yellow Sea, men have for centuries been accustomed to hire or purchase entertainment and adulation from classes of specially trained women variously known as ouled nail, bayadere, nautch, or sing-song girl, hetaira, kii-san, joro or geisha. This peculiar class of women, set aside from the family, to sing, dance, flatter and "converse" a tiny bit, has been definitely Eastern. They have been held to traditional forms of sensual excitation, disciplined in certain arts and required to serve ideals of beauty and charm. They have frequently been servants bound to keepers and only loaned out or sold to wealthy patrons—in that respect as in the first each a variant from the professional entertainer in the West who receives her income to-day from the public at large and, if she supplements it through an individual patron, has a freer choice of conduct and career. Until the present time, Japanese men have played women's parts upon the stage—a custom which prevailed in ancient Greece. There is yet another vital distinction between the courtesan of East and West: the former has a recognized position in society which in the West is accorded only to the wife.

But the reasons are historic. In ancient times it was a general custom for all women to serve the gods, some in continual obedience to divinity, others at stated intervals. Women, it was thought, could best tend the gods and it was said that "a man who prayed to gods must wear women's garments and give himself a woman's name." Thus religious prostitution was a regular feature of temple worship in all the classic States. Nor indeed was mediæval Europe unfamiliar with this adjunct of the ecclesiastical institution; it rose and fell in harmony more or less with the tastes of local rulers and financial circumstances. However, the Catholic church in time officially pronounced marriage a sacrament whereas in Japan the church might sanctify the amours of the *miko*—a sacred dancer—but it did not hallow weddings. Hence separate traditions and ideals flourished in the two worlds. Whatever a European male might do in private, he usually addressed his sonnets to married women and painted portraits of the lady.

In Japan, on the contrary, the geisha has had no such rival for romantic favor. It is her portrait instead of the lady's that is painted and treasured. If she no longer serves the temple, she still serves the secular devotees accustomed to temple ceremonies. At religious festivals the *miko* was wont to wave her sword and beam upon the worshipers and she received due tribute in the old adage: "On the sacred boards she is 'killing' all the men around." Moreover women with lutes and puppets were wandering over the country—precursors of the Japanese drama—before the Elizabethan age. In mediæval port towns and the halting-places along the traveled roads, "houses of freedom" were opened. So a government in the seventeenth century, anxious to build up a new capital and attract to it knights and nobles, offered an institution long in favor when it presented them with a licensed quarter. It was in its "houses of freedom" that the geisha were then trained in the arts of amusing according to the classes of patrons. In the late eighteenth century when the Shogun's capital, called Yedo, was large and prosperous,

these girls were available for public as well as private entertainment—a situation of which the rich merchants who were
now in the arena were quick to take advantage. Wives and
daughters remained away from public functions and this
hired entertainer took their place. Elaborately robed and
perfumed for such occasions, with rhinestone combs and
paper flowers in her hair, her face and the front of her neck
plastered with white chalk, she did the official receiving of
guests. She now welcomes the aviators with wreaths; she
patronises the modern drama and at performances of Ibsen
is always present, giggling and rustling in the theater aisles.
When a new bridge or electric light system is to be opened,
she comes with her sisters, in men's kimono, singing a lum-
berman's song and making the event most festive. When
round-the-world trippers wish to see the "exotic Orient," she
is the one called upon to oblige.

A brightening of costume and a lightening of feet followed this public demand. Centuries ago the courtesan was
forbidden to wear precious jewels and might deck herself
only in dark, sober blue, as if a sort of Puritan conscience
ran through the jurisprudence notwithstanding the absence
of romantic marriage. Or was the sumptuary law a start
toward family elevation? Anyway, that more classic model,
plainly dressed, mature and reasonably dignified, who
does not sing and does not dance, may still be met amid the
modern crowd if one is properly introduced. It is the more
difficult to learn of her existence however because she is apt
to be the companion of the highest men in the realm—the
diplomats and statesmen rather than the "up and coming"
commercial class. With one of these so-called "intellectual"
geisha I was fortunate enough to spend an evening. Kneeling beside her small table of rice cakes, she talked about
"proletarian novels" and the Premier's next political move

GEISHA CELEBRATING THE ERECTION OF A BRIDGE IN TOKYO

very much as an Occidental wife, sitting behind the tea urn, might discourse on H. G. Wells or the latest message from President Hoover. She was neither young nor beautiful. Her face, truly aging, was guiltless of paint or powder. Nor was her hair lacquered or elaborately dressed but her small, bright eyes were frank and shone with merriment. She held a reserved command over our small party—guests at the tea house where she lived—asking questions, speaking about the latest theatrical offerings, and discussing the future of her sisterhood on which she had decided views.

"We geisha are too much at the mercy of individual patrons," she maintained; "and all our relations are personal. It would be better for us to be like your Western geisha, who acts in cabarets, and pleases a large public, draws her salary from business men, and is free to go and come as she chooses. We have so little liberty; we see the world only through the men we meet. We are so dependent —and so tired of it."

Yet, even if she had indeed seen little of the world, she had obviously learned much about her patrons. She was shrewd, poised and brightly tactful. She glanced from one to the other of our group, neglecting no one, planting retorts and questions and laughing with quiet amusement. Twinkling at the novelist she would say: "We geisha are all reading your newest. Your heroine is a real woman, we think. And how *proletarian!*" and she would roll the adjective on her tongue with a smug relish reminding one of an American flapper using a brand-new phrase of psycho-analysis at a dinner party. To the banker she would murmur: "Do you know what new pet name we have for you? Miss Thousand Ages and I have made up one for you." And to the diplomat: "You know So-and-so? Oh, I've known him for years. Have you heard about his latest divorce? Did you know about the time he got too much wine and climbed a tree? Stayed there for hours. Miss Wisteria laughed so hard he never asked her to come again." And toward the women, she would lean intimately and plead: "Tell me, what kind of face powder do you use?" One thing about her struck me forcibly. If she was an example of what the rulers of Japan found desirable and interesting in their companions— and she had for years been the favorite of one of the nation's "Grand Old Men"—it showed that their wives might in time aspire to compete.

But the most beautiful geisha bear scant fidelity to the advertising illustrations or posters of their dances. Bland, simpering faces and cheaply flowered robes ablaze with blossoms, butterflies and dragons fail to convey the lure which the finer tea houses hold for the Japanese. Dandies expect something else of their favorites. I saw some serious, slim young beings whose only occupation appeared to be pouring wine and wearing eighteenth-century costumes. The room to which they were summoned was a quiet background for their display. Fawn tones formed the walls and the floor was a shining stretch of matting. The only ornaments were a potted dwarf tree in the *tokonoma* and a screen with a design of sea-green waves on palest gilt paper. We sat in rows, before each of us a foot-high table of glossy black lacquer, ready for the girls who came in bearing trays of hot conch-shells filled with fragrant soups.

These geisha had been especially selected for us to meet by a "gentleman of the old school" who wore on this occasion the rich blue silks of his ancestors. Each girl was tall and slender. Her hair was looped in very old-fashioned, intricate, drooping coils, such as one never sees on the streets; the coiffures were, however, unornamented, devoid of any flower or comb, and depended for effect on sheer grace of line. All were dressed in the same way, in robes of peach-colored silk, the hems heavily padded and seemingly soaked to the knees in embroidery of palest silver, of indistinct blossoms and clouds. Their sashes were tied into stiff pillows of burnished silver. Nor were the outer robes the floor-length type, but long, falling away into trains that swept the room behind them. They moved noiselessly, barefoot, in single file, like a frieze. As the evening passed they brought course after course, of stuffed fish, delicate soups, mounds of colored pickles, and tid-bits of things. They neither spoke nor smirked, and soon withdrew.

Other geisha were invited to entertain. Some were very young apprentices, with make-up on their childishly round faces—silly little gigglers who could play the drum, seemed ravenously hungry, had adenoids, and had missed going to school. They got the best cakes and candies which they begged from the guests and gobbled as fast as they could—perhaps to increase the bill. There were dancers, in florid costumes, carrying gilded fans, who postured in the rear against the screen. And always near the doorway knelt a huddled mistress, in dark clothing, with beady eyes set in a mass of sallow wrinkles. She was the chaperone, and she sat glowering like a witch, if occasionally strumming on a *biwa*.

Next came troupes of conversationalists. They wore simple, striped silks, and their splendor was in sashes. They tripped to and fro, stopping by one guest and then another, darting questions, teasing the men about their deeds or their books or their plays. They had nicknames for figures best known in their geisha world and enthusiasms and dislikes which they plainly showed. Toward some, they acted with kittenish affection, "kidding" for autographs. Toward others, perhaps overawed, they were coolly polite. From certain guests they definitely shrank. These types of girls had hard little faces and for all their arch glances and banter they were obviously ignorant little prisoners. None had had a high-school education and all their knowledge was gained from papers, installment novels, and gossip.

I was particularly amused by the freedom with which they scolded the men, berating them for imaginary faults and making fun of their looks. Apparently the Japanese males are only human; in theory they require obedience and silent respect from women, but in practice they are all too ready to pay high for a little "horseplay" and rough treatment. They roared with joy at general "wisecracks," and beamed in their turn when struck by a flying joke. They hung upon the favor of the girls, glowed when their doings—a business merger or a poem—were praised, and struggled against an inferiority complex when the geisha turned away. I have heard Japanese say that the geisha quarters are considered veritable "training grounds," where men sharpen their wits, learn intrigue and conversation. The geisha "forms" their social behavior, much as the *salonnière* of the eighteenth century in France used to receive young men sent by their papas to be "polished."

Japanese men, so it seemed to me, look for what in Western society other women have learned to give—comradeship, a blend of sympathy and challenge. Instead of wanting what luxurious Oriental potentates have been celebrated for, mere sensuous dancing, they demand humor, chatter, repartee. Some of the greatest of Japan's statesmen have not only found in the tea house the occasional companion but have married geisha girls. Notable cases were those of Prince Ito, Marquis Okuma, Prince Yamagata and ex-Premier Hara, and at once Athenian illustrations of this type of friendship are suggested.

It is clear however that the girls as a whole are incapable

of meeting any very critical requirements as far as mentality is concerned. Usually they are acquired by a house in youth and strictly trained in isolation. They have seen little of the world except second hand. They are narrow, often crude and vulgar—if their patrons have been the same. Inevitably they tend to be obsessed with the slave psychology of pleasing those on whom their living depends and are not particular about ways and means. But one thing must be said for them and I believe it has rarely been said. Their merit is supposed to lie in their being quaint, naïve, pretty dolls. But in reality it consists in their being rather alert little creatures, living by their wits, skilled in masculine psychology and able, as the victims themselves declare, to "handle men like toys." The intimate, sensational biography of O Koi-san, ex-geisha wife of the late Prince Katsura, reveals much of that side of their character: the wire-pulling, the "suggestion" of business deals, and the important introductions.

The geisha's rôle was not designed to be intellectually or morally stimulating. Yet the girls were often personalities no less than human beings and so they figure in legend and older fiction as the dream-woman which only the married "lady" in the West long symbolized. They once had their own hierarchy, at the top of which was the ranking courtesan, called the "joro," resembling the courtesans of Italy at the time of the Renaissance. A famous Italian, so we are told, used to compel men who sought her favor to do sentinel duty outside her home for three months to prove their constancy. So in Japan the courtesans, says Santaro, "never bowed before their patrons as other women did; they never permitted their patrons to be unfaithful to them, for the men found 'guilty' of tampering with courtesans other than themselves were punished with corporal punishment;

and the geisha were always 'hired entertainers' to wait on the pleasure of the courtesans."

The idealized geisha, musically talented, experienced and sympathetic, generous to the poor and haughty to the rich, has continued to exert a potent charm over Japanese letters, art and philosophy. Nevertheless to talk of the Japanese men as "despising" women or as preserving obsolete ideals is not strictly just. They may have despised, they may still despise women on principle, as mediæval Christian Church fathers did, and they may have insisted on duty and obedience within their own households, but everything was permitted in the "houses of freedom."

Accordingly among the upper classes the hearts of men in their very youth are prepared less for the wife than for the professional companion; ballads and stories, dramas and popular paintings tend to exalt the geisha above the matron or the *jeune fille*. Though the triangle appears often enough in Japanese fiction and the jealous wife or innocent village maiden are frequent characters, it is the geisha, longing for a nobleman whom by ancient law she may not wed, who is the real heroine. The fancies of the race have not been stirred by those Western types of the married, if poignant, spouses, the Helens, Guineveres, Francescas and Isoldes. Nor is the Japanese warrior hero a Launcelot or a Tristram; he has little interest in wives—even in the wives of other men. The poetry and tradition developing among the people of Europe around the Madonna and in the courts around the chivalric ideal were lacking in Japan where no knight wore a lady's sleeve on his helmet or sought to follow her into the hereafter.

This is not to say that there has been no such thing as love. That there has been. In truth perhaps the Orient has known more kinds of love than the Occident. The relation of par-

ent and child has been particularly tender. Did not the
Buddha himself return from Paradise to show his mother The
Way, more thoughtfully than Christ who appeared instead
to Mary Magdalene? Between teacher and pupil, love loyalty
reigns on according to long custom. And indeed the relation of the people to the Emperor is, in theory, love equally
with honor while in practice unquestionably the two are
blended to a high degree. The issue therefore is not one of
introducing emotion. It is a question of its direction—
whether more of it can be poured into the narrow but deep
channel of marital love. Ironically, as it happens, the Christians who emphasize family loyalty and affection represent
societies which have been breaking down the dykes of married fidelity at the very time when the "heathen" Japanese
are beginning to build them up.

What love in Japan has missed in marital sentiment it has
expressed in æstheticism. Women have been viewed as part
of the beautiful landscape, as creatures mysteriously attuned
to nature: their black hair like the night, their pale features
like the moon. Because perhaps of the open character of the
Japanese house they have been closely associated with the
garden, with trees and flowers, and perpetually portrayed
on verandahs or beside garden gates. Music, poetry and the
dance have enveloped them with a glowing light, if chivalry
has failed to crown them.

Very rapidly, notions of morality are arising and romantic
ideals are enlarging to meet changed circumstance. A short
while ago the geisha was hardly more than a chattel; originally she served a courtesan; now, she may win a breach
of promise suit against a scion of nobility beside any other
girl. A few years ago, a woman public speaker was a freak
who alarmed all proper citizens; recently, the demand for
women to practice law in Osaka was voiced and lo! not a

murmur was heard! Insensibly, men modify their self-made standards; masculine judges begin to look upon the man who deserts his wife as in some degree blameworthy. For more than forty years the W. C. T. U. had been campaigning for a "single standard" of morality without apparent effect; suddenly, in 1929, Judge Yokota handed down a revolutionary decision, condemning a man who had been unfaithful with a geisha. For the first time a geisha counted as a rival to the wife.

One may scarcely say, however, just how or when these changes occur. For example, a leading politician would at this hour be a little shamefaced to be photographed in company with a notorious geisha at a boathouse. He knows it makes better reading in the newspapers if his wife is patroness at a charity bazaar, or is pictured driving an automobile crowded with ladies, distributing handbills to aid her husband's political campaign. But why? His constituents did not ask this of him. Who transformed his taste? All that one may say is that, quite suddenly, astute folk knew that "it isn't done any more."

What makes things "done" in Japan? No easier to answer than in any other case. Public opinion grows silently and darkly underground before it thrusts a new, sprouting concept into the daylight. One cannot predict or force the issue; but he may know positively that conditions will not remain static. A new society—with different ideals of love, marriage, morals, conduct, amusement and conversation—is coming in Japan, just as woman suffrage came in America, not wholly because fanatics clamor, but because the very spirit of the times compels.

The first thing that strikes the observer is the gleefully incongruous medley of social forms, borrowed or invented, in use to-day. A public life has been summoned almost from a void. And in their eager search for excuses to know one another, the Japanese have seized upon any available means. They have utilized meetings, in the manner of lecture-mad America, beside café customs derived from leisured Europe; garden fêtes of mediæval Asiatic kings and the revelry of democratic dance halls; Western wedding breakfasts and imposing Shinto "purification" ceremonies; stately banquets with champagne, orchestras and waltzing, dignified by the presence of a dowager princess, or the rowdy informality of mob picnics at beach resorts; military reviews and charity bazaars; assemblies for school children and exclusive "little theater" showings; the blare of brass bands and the drone of Buddhist liturgies.

None of these is after all superfluous, since so many types of people, from royalty down to the humble typists, are seeking communion with their fellows, each along a separate path. The throngs of young, unmarried students in Tokyo are developing a Bohemian life of their own. Actors and literary folk have their coteries in various sections of the city. The fashionable rich are holding quiet home parties to introduce their children to other children. Business men's wives are learning how to entertain visiting Rotarians. Much more goes on than the newspapers indicate.

Royalty is now taking the lead in a sort of constructive work. The marriage of the American-educated Miss Matsudaira and the Oxford-trained Prince Chichibu has given Japan for the first time an "active" royalty in the British manner; the couple are pictured together at ceremonial inspections of factories and ships, at unveilings and cornerstone layings; the teas, receptions and dinners tendered them have brought together, as a nucleus of society, groups of nobility and business men and their wives. Instead of a mysterious and invisible divinity, the people now see the monarch making every effort to be popular and to assume a social direction. The Emperor made history by the series of banquets with which he opened his reign; he invited more than three thousand of his subjects, selected from professors, artists, and labor leaders as well as peers and diplomats. He in uniform and the Empress in a modern gown received proletarian Diet members, who arrived clutching kid gloves and silk hats. By an elaborate state ball, he set the seal of his approval on dancing. And by excluding geisha from his coronation procession, he put them for the first time outside the most reputable pale.

In other high places, the attack on the geisha system goes on. Mayor Horikiri, of Tokyo, in 1929, held his ground against aldermen who sought to cut down his salary because they were angry at his failure "to invite members of the aldermen's council to geisha parties for courtesy." Office clerks, far down the scale from officialdom, are experimenting with liberty. Suddenly, they find all sorts of amusements within their reach: cinema, radio, swimming, dancing. And all these may be enjoyed in the company of women who demand no pay by the hour. They find it amusing to escort the office stenographer and far less expensive than a geisha. Simultaneously appear just such volunteer women comrades—typists, waitresses, nurses, teachers and "beautiful girl billiard markers." The extent of this new class of "economically independent" young people may be gauged from the fact that nearly two hundred thousand salaried men and women are busy in the Marunouchi business district of Tokyo alone.

Among such salaried folk a "night life" has evolved in Tokyo within the past half-dozen years. Vaudeville troupes bring "cowboy dances" to amuse them. Luna Park offers merry-go-rounds. Pool and dance halls arise. One of the world's largest cinema houses is to be erected on the Ginza

PRINCESS TOKUGAWA, DESCENDANT OF THE SHOGUNS.
RECENTLY UNITED BY MARRIAGE TO THE IMPERIAL FAMILY

to accommodate the crowds. Already there are nearly half as many foreign restaurants as those in native style—cheap cafés which have become the ordinary man's club, and their thousands of waitresses, mostly girls in their teens, his nearest approach to companionship. The modern Tokyo-ite can pay a few coppers for a cup of tea and perhaps achieve a flirtation gratis.

The "Criminally Inclined Youth" section of the Metropolitan Police is kept continually in action, following up these developments. It attempts to wield some sort of control over cafés and the thousands of young country girls who come up to town every year. It tries to license the dance halls and their employees, to debar students in uniform, and to put a curfew on revelling hours. It arrests *moga* and *mobo*, every now and then, for suspicious behavior or unseemly attire. It investigates offices, on the ground that they are "veritable wooing quarters." But after a fight of several years, it finally admits its toleration of foreign dancing— and what is more, police begin to take fox-trot lessons "in order to understand youth." Naturally some "fall" for gayety themselves.

Just walking up and down, however, is the Tokyo-ite's chief diversion. Along the Ginza at night hundreds of boys and girls who now enjoy "being seen" and "creating a sensation" promenade in couples or groups, in splashily painted kimono or abbreviated Western garments, Harold Lloyd spectacles and college "blazers," high heels and silk stockings. This may seem on first thought of no significance whatever. But one must realize that the freedom of the streets for an unchaperoned miss of the well-to-do classes is a liberty of recent years in most countries and not everywhere granted up to date. So the opportunity to venture out for a wilful stroll is a genuine excitement and privilege.

Naturally freedom opens the possibility of license and the border line is often dim. Evidently the Japanese girl of the upper circle is not always so inherently meek as her methodic training from infancy makes her appear. It is scarcely the nature of her sex to be "cowed" any more than it is the birthright of the other. Individuals get sufficient exhilaration out of the liberty to stroll. Others set forth on the quest of adventure and may be seen in the hotels dressed in spangled frocks, their faces thickly painted, sitting with an air of superlative assurance at the tables waiting for a chance acquaintance.

These young Japanese girls have many points in common with Western flappers. Of course, they look a little theatrical to our eyes, for their hair and eyes are so intensely black and often doll-like; their paint is applied with so generous a hand and their eyebrows so arched that they are commonly called "half-past seven eyebrows." But what the two races have done is similar—they have stolen the allure of the courtesan and appropriated her rouge, bright colors and animation. And the same reaction on the public has resulted; business men attempt to discharge girls with vanity cases, forever staining the lips; police try to round them up and send them back to their homes when they seem to be street waifs, but cannot. The *moga* thrives—and the geisha trembles for her own position.

News of all this dancing, dining and strolling under the gay electric lights of Tokyo has penetrated to remote, sheltered valleys. It increases discontent among the rice paddies and the fishing nets. Whistling jazz tunes heard over the new radio, the peasant youth grows bored with ancient festivals and the cry of wooden flutes. Mentally he compares the neighbor girls with Toyko's famous *moga* and determines to travel. His sisters read about urban pleasure in women's magazines, learn to despise their wonted drudgery, and soon turn willing ears to recruiters for factories and cafés. Accordingly, Japan shares with Western countries the problem of how to keep youth on the farm; and makes attempts to create a "social life" more attractive in villages. Municipal fireworks and "home economics schools" are the starting point.

Thus it may be said that, both in the higher strata and in the low, associational forms are developing that are free from the shadow of the geisha influence. The Court no longer officially countenances the geisha. Comparatively limited groups of the rich and conservative business men and nobles are left as the patrons of the tea house where she dwells. The police have made efforts to prevent guides from making tourists believe that the Yoshiwara and the tea house are the principle sights in Japan.

Probably our generation is the last to see the geisha in her prime. The system by which she lived is withering as the police more and more assist the girls to escape the master's bondage and thus render the whole business insecure. What the reformers do not achieve, the geisha may herself, for she is often eager to be something else. In order to compete with her independent rival, the moga, she strives to modernize her own attire and mind, so much that some licensed quarters have issued strict orders that the old costumes and headdress must be preserved. Nor does the geisha want to be chaperoned like a jeune fille, while the moga wanders free; she does not enjoy being forever in debt, while the moga collects a salary and keeps it. She doesn't wish to be an anachronism, when she sees her patrons entering a new age. Hundreds have turned into waitresses, disguised in aprons. Others are trying to become free, professional entertainers on the order of overseas chorus girls, and recently a million-

dollar theater was erected in Tokyo by boathouses, chicken
and eel restaurants, in which the independent geisha became
stockholders. Annually a big spring festival is held there,
in which hundreds of such girls take part in their most richly
painted and embroidery-encrusted robes. The theater itself
is decorated in "modern Oriental" style, with walls of orange
and magenta, bowls of electric light, weird pillars and im-
pressionistic designs. And here the geisha of this type en-
deavor to capture an audience, rather than an individual
patron; they come out in troupes, carrying the loved bright
paper parasols and wide fans, under the inevitable pinkish
paper blossoms of the cherry trees, and execute the ancient
dances of their guild—the dance of the Palace under the
Sea, of the Sleepy Lion, of the Boat Festival, and of the
tea-house girl who scorned a rich samurai in favor of a poor
and humble lover.

Yet some of the geisha who remain in masters' houses are
imbued with a militant spirit of defense. When the police
of Tokushima Prefecture, urged on by reformers, endeavored
to make an inspection of a quarter, the girls went on strike.
A group of "artistes," invited to entertain the Governor, quit
the party on the stroke of eight o'clock, deserting His Excellency and his guests, and were joined in a "sympathy
strike" by hundreds of their kind. Determination won the
strike. It is no longer possible to describe the genuine geisha
merely as "dainty dolls."

Pressure of public opinion may result in defense, on the
one hand, but it also is making inroads on complacency. In
1926, two national conferences were held—one of masters of
licensed houses, and the other of police chiefs. The first was
attended by two thousand delegates from all over Japan—
among the number, thirty women keepers—to discuss the
changed situation. At the second, the police achieved a re-

form program to which they have adhered, giving more chance to the inmates to escape and more assistance to leave the trade of geisha, even if in debt to the master. All this is merely the pressure of opinion, for in 1873 the licensed system was officially abolished; geisha have since then not been legally "slaves," but only kept so by their own ignorance and the indifference of officials. It has then been a battle, not so much to rewrite laws, as to modify the attitude of official minds and to enlighten the girls themselves. The Salvation Army, the W. C. T. U., and a Japanese newspaper proprietor have been waging relentless warfare. Reporters for the paper invaded "houses" where they were assaulted in their quest for news; but the Army marched into the quarters "beating drums and singing hymns." And the victory is now decidedly on the reform side. The geisha's function in society is being usurped by the moga and her mother. She is being superseded by "respectable" women, put out of business by crusading moralists, and, to crown the scene, she is changing her very self. Her end is already in sight.

Should we lament the passing of the geisha? So strong has been her hold on the fancy of the West as well as on native emotions that the august Count Keyserling, philosophic-diarist, called her system "beautiful" and herself a keeper of the arts, a priestess of the "Holy of Holies," exclaiming: "Blessed are the people who have thus honored the geisha!" And undeniably in the more exclusive tea houses there is an atmosphere of emancipated gayety almost Grecian in its blend of license and refinement. Hardly any wonder that the innocent abroad is fascinated by the spectacle. Or that Keyserling should declare that courtesans "in Europe, thanks to our disgusting system, appear so much more degraded than in Japan."

Even liberal Japanese shudder at the thought of the possible exchange of their traditional system for one of uncontrolled license. Bathing beauties and cabaret dancers of the United States and the prowling women of the streets in great European cities generally send them home with pride to "our modest, refined Japanese girls who still know how to blush." They find the "night club" repellent, like a too vulgar profligate quarter; and I have seen them in the cafés of the sailor quarter of Hamburg in Germany, "touring" the same way Western men visit the Orient in the Yoshiwara district with a strong sense of superiority. The truly novel phenomenon of the West—the brazen, wholesale competition of woman against woman—is a thing they find equally difficult, on the whole, to comprehend.

But it is not all moral indignation that repels them; they feel that in no land is the delicate balance of social equality maintained. They object to the predominance of women in America whom they see "running" society as their husbands run railways or chain stores, aggressively and with organized "efficiency." In harmony with many Europeans, they find nothing but malignant tyranny in these loud-voiced, leisured, wealth-flaunting creatures. And their general opinion is expressed in the plea of a well-known business man on his return from the grand tour: "The Japanese women should never be petted in the name of 'ladies first' as in America. I insist on justice and humanity first instead of 'ladies first.'" Nevertheless, on the whole, European wives, domestic and conscientious, leave them about equally dissatisfied, for such women add nothing to the qualities with which they are acquainted in their own home bodies. So they acquire no design by which they wish exactly to cut and shape their national social life.

No doubt it seems crass, in the face of æsthetics, to go into monetary details. But a fact so often forgotten by the exuberant alien, as well as by many native critics, is that, even in the poetic Orient, courtesan charm and grace have to be paid for. There is lute-playing and barefooted dancing in soft lamplight. Guests recline easily on cushions and the brimming wine cups are sent around the circle. The moon seeks out in the garden vines the statue of Benten, Goddess of Love. But a single evening spent with a galaxy of delicate ladies in such a scene may very well cost the entire yearly per capita income in Japan, that is, about $112. For the ordinary mortal such "Oriental charm" is as much out of the question as is the support of a Broadway "gold-digger" by an average American. If his tastes run in the direction of a courtesan, he must try to gratify them down a sliding scale of finesse, the lowest ranges of which, such as Tokyo's Yoshiwara, Osaka's Shinmachi, or Kyoto's Shimabara, involve women not too remote in status from the slaves who were set aside for the Athenians' basest quest.

Comic poets, writers and philosophers in ancient Athens tried to call attention to the evils inherent in the diversion of wealth from family and public purposes to the private greed and profligacy of the mistresses of certain leading men. Rome found it still harder to cope with the issue. Now the same problem is being realized and discussed in the Orient. Even those who can support the most exclusive establishments and inmates come into review as anti-social characters, and in the comparisons which are being made between the menacing extravagances of two hemispheres, the most luxurious tea house is placed beside the elaborate casinos and pavilions of Biarritz, the Riviera or the Lido.

While the acceptance of the right of the rich and great to squander wealth regardless of the public reckoning is losing its sway, types of amusement are rapidly developing which rest on a different basis and which provide for the people at large recreation of amazing diversity and novelty. The Japanese people have long needed a greater variety of entertainment. Hitherto the temple festivals were the sole release of the multitudes. As in old polygamous countries, only the rich had "amusements" and those were largely concerned with courtesans and concubines. The clerk who now goes to the baseball game with the office typist is therefore not abandoning the geisha; he never knew her. The student who flirts with the waitress in a café and takes her to a movie is not lowering his artistic standards; he never hired a band of gayety girls to entertain him with lutes and laughter.

We must, then, surely conclude that the "gay white way" of the Ginza, instead of being a substitution, is in addition to the "red lantern" quarters. And the situation has strong international parallels. In two hemispheres a mighty struggle between woman and woman is being carried on. The independent, industrial wage-earner is arrayed against the prostitute. The wife secures another female as an ally if the affinity between them does somewhat require mutual vigilance. In two hemispheres thoughtful men are seeking for a new combination to settle the combat—a "new woman" who will be both domestic and amusing, both dignified and free, both wife and challenger.

If the Court, the village and the warrior's camp determined the social life of the past for all peoples—rather than the "soul of the race"—to-day the city, the factory, and the industrial and professional women are making a new social life, desirable or not, at least inevitable.

CHAPTER XIII

ARTS AND THE PUBLIC
(*Painting, Music, Cinema and Modern Drama*)

In homes and cafés we may easily watch the transformations taking place in the family and its civic surroundings as well as in social life with its evolving codes of manners and morals. But there are other struggles, other arenas that invite our interest, too. There is, for example, the ceaseless strife of Japan's intellectuals and artists to shed conventions of the past and attain a new emotional and mental freedom. Their experiments may be watched in numberless laboratories: universities, art schools and exhibitions, bookshops and newspaper offices, theaters and concert halls, film studios and religious seminaries.

A glimpse at such varied activities should comfort those who bemoan the extinction of "artistic old Japan" in this "vulgarized" commercial age and who complain that, under the corrosive influence of plebeian upstarts, money-grubbing merchants and aggressive women, the "Land of the Gods" has "lost its soul." The truth is—never in all her history was appreciation of the arts and letters more generally diffused than it is in Japan at the present time.

As in all increasingly democratic countries, a great thirst for "culture" is abroad. Ignoble folk, denied a just portion of education and enjoyment, are making up for lost centuries. A huge theater has been erected in which to show to humble throngs the Noh dances—previously only performed on noblemen's estates and before the élite. Magazines and newspapers cater to the "popular education" tendency. Cinemas and theaters, galleries, museums and libraries claim their hosts of "common" visitors. Unseen multitudes tune in on the radio for Tokiwazu music, Noh arias and Western opera. Lecturers instructing women in "foreign table etiquette" and men on the "art of the Ashikagas" are in demand even in smaller towns.

Commercial Osaka has grown as frightened as Chicago lest she be thought "Babbitty." She petitions for the establishment of a university. Not that there is the slightest need of one. Already the surplus of white-collar graduates is alarming. But the rice wholesaler and the silk manufacturer are learning, much like our own "butter-and-egg men," that a degree is the next step for their sons to take. The same process is going on in many lands: the poor climb for riches; the rich pant after culture.

Thanks to this enthusiasm, money and opportunity for leadership are offered, in sensational generosity, to the Japanese genius. On a larger scale, he may create what he wishes, instead of executing an order. Hundreds of thousands of readers wait on his words, where once a few warriors hearkened to his ballad; and if he develops a theory in art, religion or economics of which no rich lord will approve, he can appeal to his new patron—the masses. Moreover, he is finding something else in his grasp, rather more unexpected: namely, social position.

Prince Saionji, it is said, set the fashion a few years ago of inviting men of letters and actors to dine at his villa; Premier Hamaguchi, in 1929, brought together various prominent writers and bureaucrats in an unprecedented way; the present Emperor himself has made place for writers at his banquets. Millionaires now compete at auctions for paintings; the Government honors the artist by sending his

THE YOUNGER SCHOOL OF WRITERS HOLDING A DEMONSTRA-
TION AGAINST CRITICS

SCENE FROM A MODERN PROBLEM PLAY

best work to exhibitions in China, France or America. Men of ideas are ennobled and invited to lecture before the Princes and Princesses of the Blood.

In all sorts of ways, as the whole of society turns more fluid, the artist loses his feeling of belonging to a class apart. He attains a new perspective on his art by reading or attending lectures; a number of changes in classic dramas are due to the fact that several excellent actors, notably Sojuro Sawada, are not members of an ancient stage family, but college graduates. The artist is also brought into touch with social movements, as the novel, drama or painting attempt fresh themes or try propaganda. He touches political life when he begins to utter professional protest against bills limiting freedom of the press. He comes into contact with business on a novel basis when merchants subsidize art societies; I saw some important "one-man shows," for instance, in the upper story of a commercial building, whose owner combined pharmacy and patronage. Artists feel less like æsthetes, and divide into categories—classicists or modernists; they band together, no longer as traditional vagabonds, but in academies and other associations.

This is very different from the status of the artist and thinker in feudal times anywhere. Perhaps Japan was more beautiful then; her nobles played perfume games in silver pavilions; along her avenues flowed color in the raiment, banners and horse-gear of warriors; her dim Buddhist temples were stored from floor to coffered ceiling with treasures of gold, bronze and shell-dust inlay. But the creators of all this beauty were, none the less, meagerly paid, ranked low in the social scale, and were subjected to the whims of patrons or the persecution of puritanic police. Paralleling the situation in mediæval Germany, the actor was an outcast, grouped with the hangman, scavenger and animal-skinner.

The painter waited humbly in the lord's antechamber, as his fellow artist was wont to do in Italy of the *Rinascimento*. The ragged poet wandered with a roystering band of disciples from pillar to post. The story writer did not expect to be paid; he was happy if a publisher gave him a free meal. And many a proud spirit suffered from humiliation as did Utamaro, maker of prints, whose portraits of graceful courtesans are famous to-day. The Government, for what it deemed the "license" of his painting, ordered his hands tied behind his back for three days; and soon after, sickened at the disgrace, he died.

Traditionally, the Japanese artist of every creative branch is a gallant, impoverished, eccentric being whose life, as one of them put it, is "irregular and contagious." It is so contagious, indeed, that the bourgeois papa in Japan, true to his form in Western countries, forbids his daughter to marry into that circle and tries to hide away his son in a counting-house. Nor have the highest circles been accustomed to invite the artist to visit them as guest; they have considered him an entertainer-employee. Even to-day this attitude is prevalent and at box parties in the theater, when I would introduce an actress friend to a noblewoman, the latter would at first stiffen—as only a Japanese lady can stiffen—but occasionally thaw out later, under the glowing influence of the actress's charm. The position of the artist, in short, in old Japan was similar to that occupied by his distant brother in Europe and America up to a generation ago. He lived in mental isolation, priding himself on defiance. He hung around tea houses as his European colleagues about the cafés; he found the geisha amiable as the grisettes were to his French confrère. He might by good fortune acquire a noble patron but, if he had no patron, he became a vagabond. The great poet Bassho was such a wanderer and his favorite pupil, a nun, also rambled about the countryside with a train of thirty disciples. Bassho, in line with many an old European poet, such as Villon, gallantly described his impoverished state—when he had no charcoal to burn in winter, he could always warm himself with his verses! Hiroshige, the renowned print-maker, was so restless that his ambition was to dwell in a hundred houses; actually he had moved into his ninetieth-odd dwelling before he died.

Artists who are feudal in their training, tradition and status, may yet be seen in Japan. Such were the entertainers selected by many of our hosts to delight the guests in their homes. A celebrated potter would be called in to decorate and fire vases and bowls; a painter to make fans and screens; or a singer to render ballads. They would come to the party in their thickest, stiffest spreading skirts and ceremonial coats tied with formal, white tassels. They had an air of great dignity, yet were self-effacing and noiselessly unobtrusive as became retainers of an ancient nobility. A round-faced, eager-eyed apprentice boy usually lurked in the background grinding the inksticks or awaiting the summons to spread fresh pineapple silk on the floor for the master. As we knelt in a circle about a painter, "by request" he would make a moon rise above a hill or wild geese stream across a moor. A few of these painters are specialists. One would handle nothing but pine trees; in a moment he would toss a few lines of cones upon a gilded board or for hours he would elaborate an array of waving branches along the sea coast; but it would have been blasphemy in his country to suggest that he paint a bird or a bamboo. The bird or bamboo specialist could do that. And yet, withal, the code and the patronage were feudal and rigid: the painters were in every sense retainers of the few. As the stage plays indicate, they were often roughly treated by the lords in older times. Just as Isabella d'Este would menace with jail a painter who did not deliver her cupids on the dot, so an irate lord is represented in a Japanese drama as threatening a dilatory mask maker; his wrath is diverted only by the circumstance that the artist's daughter has a face more winsome than the mask.

At the Ueno Art School could be studied the exact academic training that still produces such craftsmen. The pupils, attired in kimono, knelt on mats in long, low halls and copied with minute care the superb examples from the art collection of the school—brocade-robed dancers, whirlwinds of flying sleeves and lifted fans, on panels of dull lacquer. Some were studying the processes of lacquermaking; others were sketching from natural grasses and the hues of doves; yet others were busy reproducing, with the reiterative patience characteristic of Oriental learning, a few masterly brush strokes. Whereas academic students in the West discipline themselves by copying for years from plaster casts of "antique" heads and torsos, the Easterners achieve their control by copying "classic" screens of bamboo or birds. This school develops exhibition painters, but also those humble, nameless craftsmen who turn out designs for articles of daily use. Of course, most of the craftsmen of Japan are not school graduates, but come up through the apprentice system, even more mediæval in character, which may be seen operating in Kyoto and Tokyo.

The present as well as the former status of the artist arrests attention by the analogies it brings to mind. The very machine which, round the world, "destroys the creative urge" brings boundless opportunities to the creator. Art may be perishing but never was the artist so well off. The glory of the ancient drama may be fading, yet the actor, once a wretched pariah, draws "more salary than the prime minister." Æsthetic tradition weakens, but the painter, whose

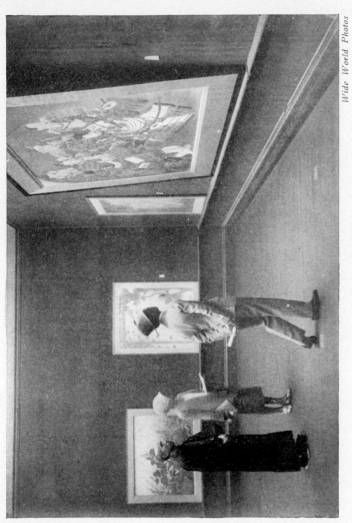

PRINCE AND PRINCESS CHICHIBU AT THE IMPERIAL ART SALON IN UENO PARK

prints formerly sold for a penny and were used to wrap
fish, now exhibits in galleries to admiring multitudes. Poetic
feeling is decadent, but the poet is well fed. Mysticism
withers, but begins to pay.

An identical problem is presented by democracy to the
Eastern and the Western artist. The Japanese observe it in
America. And Germany is a still more vivid problem because
of the very recent submersion of the scholar caste and exclusive literary circles, which took their cue from the monarchy, by a big reading public clamoring for sensation. Both
countries debate whether to yield to the multitude, to turn
disdainfully from it, or go in for "uplift" by such means as
a popular "Book Day." The same choice weighs on the
Japanese creative artist. It is so easy to cheat this mass
patron, feed out shoddy work and exploit the lower instincts
of mankind. It is far too easy to promote what Julian Benda
calls the world-wide "treason of the intellectuals." Temptations are almost irresistible; it is hard to face pressure and
offer enormous populaces what they do not vociferously
demand: sanity, sympathy, peace, and constructive enterprise.

True it is that the artist of to-day may not be capable of
satisfying the public at large with arts beloved of the few
in the past but, if he has an imaginative mind receptive to
the possibilities of democracy, he may give it an art peculiarly its own, yet stamped with genius as is all great art. If
the Japanese artist, accordingly, cannot summon from his
spirit splendid creations, worthy of his country's past, at least
the blame lies within his spirit rather than in lack of opportunity in this "vulgar age."

It is easiest for a foreigner to watch this search for a democratic art and this contest for leadership over the public,
among the painters. We may not be able to follow develop-

ments by reading Japanese books, but in art schools and exhibits our eyes tell us the story.

The Ueno Art Academy, carrying out the dualism of most things Japanese, is divided into a "native" and a "foreign" section. The two are complete contrasts in equipment, costumes of the students, methods of teaching and objects of study. In the "foreign" section I found the inspiration of those dramatically Bohemian men who promenade along the Ginza. No artist on earth, now that the French Latin Quarter has lost much of its pristine exuberance, keeps up appearances more enthusiastically then they, with their thick hair rising upright in token of independence, Van Dyke beards, broad and brilliant silk ties, bright smocks, black capes and swaggering gait. And as they drew aside the wet veils from their clay images that I might see their achievements, it was clear that they had broken with their racial traditions in similar respects. But their revolt was not from interminable discipline with Greek imaginative casts, for that idealistic treatment of the nude the race had never had. They had turned from their Chinese influences to a forthright realism shorn of all classic reticence before the imperfections of humanity. In the sculpture studio, a squat-figured girl was posing for "life" and the ungainly lines of the model were being faithfully reproduced. Yet power was not lacking in the realistic urge.

The painting studio was illuminated by futuristic blares. On easels and against the wall were studies of women reclining upon satin couches, designed for the French salon competition, sketches of bathers, portraits of fishermen or miners. And it seemed that, to the naturally vivid colors of modern Western art, had been added all the Oriental tones that flame and bite. A Gauguin painting of Tahiti, I believe, would in this room appear as sober as a dove.

The purple patches of the foreign-style students were in sharp contrast with the formal earnestness of the kimonoed craftsmen in the "native" rooms. It seemed that they were taking the same delight as Westerners not so long ago took in "shocking the bourgeoisie" by throwing down classic standards. They were revelling in portraiture, which is largely a fresh field to the Eastern painters—and indeed in this generation some first-class portraits of Japanese "grand old men," for instance Marquis Okuma, have been produced. They were enjoying the unaccustomed liberty of painting the human figure, unemphasized in the religious or courtly art of the Chinese and Japanese and first attempted by the "vulgar" print-makers. They were happy "expressing themselves" by choosing subjects of their own—instead of topics hallowed by centuries and worn down by countless predecessors to sheer symbols of tradition; they were selecting fantastic subjects such as frock-coated men in a temple courtyard, crimson cows apparently floating on perpendicular fields, and defiant little bob-haired "moga" in ostrich-plumed hats. They were daring to establish contacts with their own life and times, seeing art in the aged visages of peasants or the straining muscles of fishermen hauling in the nets. The playful freedom of youth and the mocking sacrilege of adults—Munich style—were both in evidence. So I could not but understand that quest for free expression even though a shudder ran through the marrows at the realization of what a demolition recently imported influence had caused.

Nor was it male artists alone who tried to portray sex themes. The women painters seemed especially attracted by the novelty. So of course there was a "Chinese Cleopatra" in transparent robes seated before a dressing-table mirror; she had the pose of an antique model, but the frank emphasis was wholly modern. Among the other themes handled by women were rollicking village festivals and a priestess dancer carried to a shrine in a palanquin borne by peasants.

The modernists are in close touch with painters of other countries. They display their work beside that of Chinese brethren at such showings as the one at Shanghai in 1929, held under the auspices of the Nationalist Government. They study in France in large numbers, exhibit at salons there, and are kept in communion by the French culture-exchange institute. Russia is only too ready to send to Tokyo examples of her modern art as propaganda-inter-change.

Owing to such connections in Asia and Europe, the modern artists in Japan are affected by the winds of "nationalism," "romanticism," "Orientalism" or "realism" that blow upon them from various points of the compass. Their shifting tastes are reflected in the constant formation of new circles. One group after another "goes stale" and is superseded— the story of this development being related by Bakusen Tsutsida in an article in the *Taiyo,* translated in *The Japan Advertiser.* The Imperial Fine Arts Exhibition at Ueno Park is the work of the oldest of these societies, associated with the Government; already, like England's Royal Academy, it is regarded by many as a stronghold of conservatism, tend-ing to force artists into making "prize pictures" that please the judges by strict conventionality. Not content with such an outlet, the "proletaria" group split off for exhibits of its own. In 1918 the Creative National Picture Society was formed, a group which severed connection with the Educa-tion Ministry and attempted to develop a "realistic attitude."

Perhaps the major portion of the artists wish to form a popular art on classic rather than Western lines. They try to maintain the sentiment for the traditional art of the East—if somewhat modified to accord with a modern spirit.

They are busy with exhibits and in studios, endeavoring to reshape the heritage of the past.

But the first thing they come up against, of course, is the question: what were the classic ideals? And what age represented them best? For they varied in Japan, from century to century, as widely as in Europe the Italian Primitive differed from the full-blooming art of Rubens. Thus, if there is dissension among the Western schools, there is equally bitter strife among the Japanese classicists who also re-group continually and issue defiances.

One of my chief surprises, in fact, was the multiplicity of conventional schools, each claiming that it alone represented the true path to classic perfection. This faction would go far back to the age of black-and-white painting. Others prefer the full-bodied color of a later time, supposed to be influenced by Spanish art through the seventeenth-century Jesuits. Here they carry on the secular print tradition; there they proclaim Buddhist religious art. A few would go back all the way to Indian sources. At least five societies hold exhibitions of contemporary paintings in the classic vein, and each of these has peculiar ideals and aims.

One great advantage over the Western classicists is possessed by the Orientals: thorough training and mastery of stroke. They retain an astonishing technique, which will probably endure as long as the Japanese continue to write with the brush. Since they are much nearer in spirit and training to their own past than our academicians who can do little but yearn for "pre-Raphaelite" times, the work they do is of great interest and on a high level. In the classic section of the Ueno Park annual show, one may study rows of orthodox portrayals of traditional themes: waterfalls, wildfowl, lute players, dragons bestriding storm clouds, autumn-tinted forests and snow-burdened temples. But experiments are not lacking, such as Japanese themes attempted in Western oils or modern subjects sketched with Japanese ink on silk and many modifications of the classic in gesture, hue, or composition. Personally, I liked best their black-and-white work, in pure line on silk, and felt that the colorists had lost much of that clear-eyed and unfaltering instinct of the early Japanese. But my range of acquaintance with the schools was naturally limited.

The chief split in the classical ranks seems to be between advocates of the aristocratic and of the popular arts. One school wishes to create a public demand for paintings so exclusive in treatment and subject that, even in old Japan, they would have been best appreciated by Court circles. The actual aristocrats are helping this movement by placing their treasures on public view. One of the noteworthy events of recent years was the 1927 display of some three hundred paintings and a hundred wooden sculptures chosen from the masterpieces of the past sixty years. Such an exhibit was a startling innovation, but the father of the Empress and a number of nobles and wealthy business families joined with the Imperial Museum to make this showing effective. Throngs went to see the "Hillside Homestead in the Evening" and to honor such famous names as Seiko Takeuchi and Taikwan Yokoyama. It was a sign of loyalty to customs but it was also a rupture of precedent, for never in ancient times would princes and barons have displayed their choicest treasures to the populace, any more than Marie Antoinette would have invited the poor of Paris to inspect her Petit Trianon.

The other school chooses to develop the print tradition, distinctly popular and non-aristocratic in appeal. A magnificent collection of their work was given us by Mayor Nagata of Tokyo. Plainly this was not mere imitation of the age of

Hiroshige but definitely modern. The atmosphere was less vague and mysterious; the artists' vision was strong and clear, the colors more positive, the objects more substantial. Realism, with the Western ideas of perspective and shadow and the new range of color, had entered irrevocably into their productions. Whatever loss that may imply over the best of earlier native prints, these were still so far superior to the work of the foreigners which had shaken up native discipline that the outside world may well look to the Japanese for inspiration in return. Their technical training continues to be thorough and they retain a natural vigor. Consequently their perpetuation of the habitual rises above a sentimental weakness into a forceful and genuine expression. It represents a carrying-on and not a pallid yearning backward.

A similar battle over taste and free expression is fought among the musicians in Japan. But there is only a moderate chance for compromise in this field. The fight between the Orientalists and the Westernists for the possession of the public ear and voice, as every one knows, is a war of extermination.

The natives no longer produce so much of their own music. That, it seems to me, is the chief factor in the struggle. They are losing that ancient readiness to burst into song on all occasions which once characterized peoples far and wide. As festivals, harvest rites, symbolic celebrations are given up—many by police mandate—and as trades become mechanical and efficient, the singing voice is stilled. Peasants, imbued with science, falter in their chorus to the moon; their hearts are not so simple as of yore. Miners cease to clap hands and chant in their leisure hours; fishermen are forgetting the *Oi-waki* and day laborers the old refrains. More and more music is supplied to the people by mechanical devices. Gramophone companies, radio broadcasters, cinema houses with pianos or orchestras playing "Il Trovatore" slightly off key—these now train the ears to strange sounds and harmonies.

Nevertheless the native music is perpetuated in many ways. One must by no means get the notion that it is extinct. The old-fashioned theaters, of course, have their *nagi-nata* or *joruri* singers. Buddhist priests chant in public their sonorous music which is deep-toned, grave and slow-measured like the chanting at a Catholic cathedral. Noh arias are sung and studied by aristocrats. The geisha preserves the popular ballad if she adds from time to time some new "hit," such as "Bird in a Cage." The Imperial Household is responsible for the upkeep of ancient Chinese music, probably never again to be heard in China herself—the very antithesis of that barbaric, falsetto squealing now heard in the opera at Peking and derived, scholars say, from the mimic warfare performed for amusement in the camps of Manchurian hordes. Classic Chinese music, closer to that of Confucius' time, approximates the Western musical scale, but has a clear, flute joyousness perhaps more Greek in type. Finally, on every street of Tokyo, at nightfall, one may hear the remnants of the popular taste in the cries of the vendors of bean cakes and love charms.

Modern Western music is sponsored by another set of agencies. The Tokyo Academy of Music at Ueno corresponds to the city's art school in academic importance, and its annual concert accompanies the annual painting show as a major social event. A few of the theaters, especially the Imperial, are open to visiting Russian or Italian troupes and to eminent foreign individuals. In the Imperial Hotel's theater, I heard a number of young Japanese men and women, trained in the West as pianists, singers, and violinists, perform before an attentive audience. The Imperial Theater has its own exclu-

sively feminine orchestra. A Japanese string quartet gives
the best European classic music. Phonograph records bring
the modern music into private homes. Cinema houses, finding that the delicate samisen is an inadequate accompaniment
to such films as "Busting Broncos" or "The Fightin' Kid,"
maintain large orchestras. Mr. K. Yamada, the best known
of present Japanese composers, whom we met when he was
conducting a municipal concert in Hibiya Park, heads an orchestra of thirty-five pieces at the new Hogaku-za, the huge
cinema theater of Tokyo. Some of his compositions are celebrated abroad as far as Australia and other places around
the Pacific rim. Among the people a knowledge of Western
music is furthered by the schools; at the Hibiya concert referred to, hundreds of Tokyo school children sang the
"Elektra." In many dwellings I heard the daughters of the
house play Chopin on the piano—often merely with technical
accuracy, but sometimes with imaginative feeling. And for
the humble folk, the "mouth organ" disseminates "Torea-
dor," "La Donna è Mobile" and "Yankee Doodle." A Japanese returning from America indeed expressed great scorn
at the "backward state of harmonica playing" in that be-
nighted land.

Of course, as with art, a great many persons are trying to
hold on to two sorts of taste. Radios broadcast probably
more classic Japanese music than Western, though they give
place to both. Some composers write for orchestras of
Japanese instruments; others attempt Japanese themes on
Western woodwinds. Some believe in giving up the modern
Japanese music and going back to an ancient form, with its
scale more akin to the West's. A great deal of experimentation goes on.

"Why change?" the foreigner asks the musician, following
his questions to the artist in Japan. There are at least three

answers which are common. Among these, "Because the Western is superior" seemed to me the least convincing. By a process of gradual immersion I became so devoted to some of the Japanese music and felt myself so attuned to its moods, that I think its extinction would be an irreparable loss.

One of the answers, however, that appears valid is that Western music is better suited to masses. It is the music of marching armies, of crowded open-air concerts; its crashing symphonies and enormous choirs are designed for gigantic stone cathedrals, for enormous audience-chambers. And as Japan develops such occasions, it requires appropriate music without doubt. It is significant that the "Kimigayo," that very impressive national anthem which school children often sing, was composed by a German, using Japanese material.

In addition to the requirements of expansion, the Japanese have a desire for completeness. In their old art, the best was left unsaid; just hinted at. Thus their painting was but a symbolic suggestion of a mood; their poems were but a few syllables evoking a scene, and their music was of the same sort. In *Asiatic Transactions,* a writer declares: "Perhaps the most interesting fact which a study of Japanese music reveals is that it is not a formless void, and more than this that it is built on an elaborate system of construction which, if its products were filled out with harmonies and that complicated verbosity which is the delight of Western musicians, would entitle it to a very favorable comparison with our own music." This I found an interesting parallel to Schweizer's declaration that Eastern philosophy appears less impressive to us chiefly because it lacks the verbal elaboration of our own.

Painters could not be expected forever to ignore the fact that there are shadows in the background and wrinkles in

the face. Singers wished to go beyond the small range of
grace notes permitted by a Japanese song and advance to the
full-throated, big-chested uproar that the West terms an
"aria." And this expansion of thought and throat and instrument, so to speak, is no doubt psychologically bound up with
the physical and material expansion of the nation.

The third reason for the development is implicit in the
story told us by a teacher.

He had come to Tokyo from a farm in the Southland, and
he brought a picture wrapped in his handkerchief to show us
how it looked. His thatched cottage was surrounded by a
high fence where, in spring, wisteria hung like purple waterfalls. Before the house stood an immense and slanting pine
tree. Bees, he said, made a hive in its ancient trunk; and
there was a tiny animal that lived in the bamboo forest
nearby which was fond of spending the evening on its topmost bough. Once all the villagers gathered together, suddenly shouting "Banzai!" What a great surprise they gave
the little animal! They had the merriest time and would
often afterward chuckle over the memory of that evening.

He told us of the house: the room for the honorable guest,
the room for the lesser guest, the verandah from which one
could see distant mountains; of the forest where the rabbit
and fox spirits lived; and of the wooded slope where stones
marked the graves of ancestors, lying in a peaceful community at the foot of a smiling Buddha.

When he was a little boy and went to school every morning, with what a heavy heart he would follow the winding
road! The cruel boys used to tease him, saying: "Now
would you like to go back home?" Even yet, though he has
become a citizen of Tokyo, he remembers that road, and
grows heavy with homesickness at the thought of his village,

the humming clouds of bees in the pine tree, and those great boughs flung against the sky.

His grandfather is blind. Once his renown as a singer was widespread. A wonderful man he is, who even invented a way of printing that he might write down his dreams. And such dreams as they were! Once he thought he heard an orchestra of doll instruments, *koto* and *samisen,* but all as tiny as a fairy's toys, playing softly in his sleep. Another time he heard all the great *waki*-drums of the thunder-devil beating across the sky—a fearful uproar like an earthquake. The blind man had many such dreams, some even more strange, and he kept them in writing, folded in an ancient blue scarf, together with the verses of old, old songs.

To-day there is hardly anyone left in the Empire who can play as he does the archaic two-stringed *koto* of Idzumo Shrine. The musician who dares touch it must have arranged before him the seven sanctified objects: the crystal ball, a box of incense, a jar painted with plum blossoms and other symbols. The sound of this *koto* is like two bamboo sticks rubbed together—a very deep and sacred sound.

With the grandfather lives our young visitor's father, now an aged man, too, who had sacrificed ambition to filial piety. Though his eyes turned often to the northern horizon, where freedom lay, he had stayed patiently in the shadow of the pine tree seventy years, devotedly leading his father by the hand and arranging his seven sacred objects before he sang. But this father also had dreams—which he centered on his son; away the youngest man was sent to become a literary figure in the northern capital.

He had come and succeeded. He had begun writing poems and story books for children, such as they may really understand—songs about flowers and sunshine and animals and things that they can love—nursery ditties so loved in the

West. Too long had he and his father listened to the old litanies, he said. Tedious chants they were for a little boy to hear, and overburdened with the oppressive sorrow of all things too beautiful and too long dead. Their meanings had been lost centuries ago and their rhythm was eerie and monotonous. The sound of his grandfather's two-stringed harp used to terrify him; it made him hear the voice of un-happy ghosts in the bamboo forest. Yes, he was far away, in Toyko, from the music of old Japan. And strange tunes of his ancestors are sinking quietly into oblivion at the foot of the smiling Buddha. Soon they will be forgotten.

The young man wrapped his books and picture in his handkerchief. He rose with a ceremonious bow. He would write to his father and tell him how foreigners from across the waters had listened to his simple story. His father would feel pleasure and he hoped his grandfather's spirit, too, would be glad.

More than art or music, nowadays, the motion picture has power to alter the taste of the people. In most countries of Europe and Asia, the American-made product is working a mental revolution in the face of violent protest. But Japan defies Hollywood better than most of the world. With Russia and Germany she forms the only trio of nations in which Hollywood films fail to predominate. These three have so individual an attitude to life, so much to say and so special an ability to say it that they can yet satisfy most of the native cinema-thirst. Remarkable, indeed, is this independ-ence of Japan. She produces enough classics, modern comedies, animated cartoons, news reels and travelogues to appease audiences which total not far short of two hundred million a year. To do this, she turns out a really stupendous quantity of films; she is said, in fact, actually to be "the fore-most producer of motion pictures in the world" (meaning of negatives) and to top "the United States by a wide margin" of two hundred features a year. Her output of negatives "doubles the production of all the rest of the world put together." She finds it necessary to import a mere fifteen per cent of the film footage she uses in a year—as in 1928.

More than quantity production is necessary, of course, to hold the market. Most of this mass is poorly and hastily turned out. There must be films good enough to capture the discriminating; and these are made in the studios located— ironically enough—near ancient Kyoto. The best of such films have fine points: excellent photography by the incomparable cameras made in Germany: superb pantomime developed by generations of marionette actors; a scenery rich in significant silhouettes; a fund of powerful, dramatic situations; and a natural pictorial instinct which has survived since the great days of Hiroshige.

How has Japan achieved such a position? By alertness in the beginning, just as she controlled her other industries. A shrewd business man of Osaka brought back from his travels the first machine and the first reels shown in the island. By 1901 Japan had made and exhibited her first native film. Since then she has made every effort to keep the ascendancy, by developing strings of theaters and supplying their programs, by taxing imports, and by creating a "fan" public through film magazines and "popularity polls."

Without actors and actresses able to win the hearts of the multitude, all would, however, be in vain. As it happens, the "stars" of Kyoto have followings which their American compeers might well envy; they often direct their own productions; and publicity makes their names as well known as those of politicians. Department stores exhibit bathing suits worn by the prettiest heroine and motorcycles driven by the boldest hero. In film magazines, with superb photographic reproductions, the "home life" of actors is pictured; much as in Hollywood, the stars of Kamakura or Kyoto are shown in wealthy villas or in the garden, busy fencing, picnicking, skating or gazing sentimentally at canaries. On children's battledores and adults' kerchiefs are printed the faces of favorites. Everybody knows Soganoya Gokuro, the "Japanese Charlie Chaplin" and winner of the national popularity contest; and Miss Satsuki Nobuki, who uses a vivid smile and blazing oblique eyes to mortal effect in "vampire" rôles.

Except for Miss Nobuki, male stars have been more popular than female. This is partly due to the tradition of exclusively male acting on the stage and partly to the reticence enjoined on women. Screen actresses capable of facial expression are slow in developing. Most of those I happened to see were pretty and affecting in tearful sketches but had a small range of impersonation. However, types are coming out able to portray *moga* in "apache" costumes, ingénues ruling home and fatherland. Going to the stage has grown steadily more respectable, until, in 1928, a "college girl" of "good family" dared to enter the screen work, starring an author of her sex in "The Life of a Woman."

The Japanese have a great opportunity, in view of all these offerings, to choose for themselves what they see. They do not have to surrender passively to Hollywood. And whether they decide to preserve the loved classics or to "go modern" is their own affair. They may continue to produce films about the samurai, "Tenraku," and the "Loves of Tojuro" or they may produce scenarios employing Miss Little Bamboo, three-hundred-pound geisha comedienne. They may select between "Paper Doll's Spring Whispering" or a recent success, "The Collar Button."

The Japanese are fully cognizant of the relation of the

movies to culture. Critics on newspapers and editors of film magazines debate and discuss themes and methods. Fearing the influence on juveniles of Hollywood morals, the Government has established a cinema section and endeavors to have films produced which will cultivate "in the public an appreciation of the soul of Bushido and a greater loyalty to the traditions of the nation." War between the classicists and modernists is more than imminent; it is declared.

So far the old-fashioned costume play, or "sword drama," predominates. Some sixty per cent of the productions still concern the adventures and struggles of the feudal lords and samurai. The favorite actors are those who best live up to the knightly ideals, and they are more impressive than "faked" costume plays elsewhere, because a Japanese player of this type has worn armor since childhood and wields a lance with the skill of a surgeon. Certainly the knights of King Arthur would have enjoyed its accuracy. And often the hero is an outlaw, or "ronin," brother to the "bad man" of the American wilds; he loves a geisha as his counterpart would a dance-hall girl; but the play is more concerned with feudal ethics than the other of the desert.

One of the first and most interesting results of the experimental producers is the release of more humor in the situations. To be sure a sturdy, comic, racial sense is apparent in old popular prints and cartoons, in dancing and balladry, but the dramatic outlet has been clogged. The classics are chiefly tragic; the "Kyogen" farces of feudalism contain what are probably some of the world's hoariest jokes, but they have been worn thin by a thousand years of repetition. Now the comedies of the contemporary scene create a new and uproarious delight. Commuters late for trains, "Mr. High Collar" in his foreign suit who falls into a mud pond and sits upon his fancy straw hat, the village youth outwit-

A KNIGHT IN AN OLD PLAY OF LOYALTY AND SACRIFICE

ting "smart fellows" in the big city, a woman actually dropping a trayful of dishes, when a lady is still forbidden to so
much as tinkle two little cups together at a tea party, send
audiences into gales of laughter and give the people immense
relief. What this means can best be grasped by one who has
sat with the crowds through hours of classic, armed animosity and hours more of widowed bemoaning until the
slapstick comes on. In the speed of the Wild West shows,
they feel a relaxation from their own more restricted lives,
while they get release from their conventional marriages by
watching the "flapper" heroine of the imported screens
brow-beat her parents, kidnap the hero, elude the detective
in her motor car, race an aeroplane, jazz on a table in a
cabaret, make a million dollars in no time, jump off a cliff
on horseback and dissolve in a sunset kiss—mercifully abbreviated for them by order of the Metropolitan Police.

In their merrier moods the native playwrights are inclined
to follow the Hollywood trend but, in their persistent melancholy, even the experimentalists must turn to those other
great film producers, Russia and Germany, for suggestions.
Weeping is one of the prime necessities, and profitable tap-
ping of the tear ducts is achieved by reels of incessant sob-
bing against backgrounds of moon-lit graves or summer seas,
involving suicides of young brides persecuted by mothers-in-
law, or the return of the prodigal, broken and haggard, to
"little old Gichi-fu" from his flight to temptations and luxury
in the capital. Around many of the present-day tragedies of
Japanese life, such as "earthquake insanity," powerful and
weird tales of horror and suffering are woven—perhaps in
their turn a change from the incredible restraint the people
actually manifest at such crises.

Out of their own past, as well as the present, the Japanese
are bringing new materials for the cinema. Historical plays

become more realistic; concerned less with mere brawling and more with personalities. In the period of their Restoration, so near that many men and women of those stirring days are yet alive, lies a rich treasure of incident and character. The luxurious Shoguns, surrounded by dancing women and idle knights; the fiery and shrewd statesmen who foresaw the coming of more democratic days and fought for the Constitution; the rough underworld of turbulence and misery—all these form the basis of long, rather plotless but tumultuous tales.

To sum up, so rapid is the progress of the cinema in Japan, despite the mass of commonplace celluloid turned out, that the legitimate theater faces the world situation. Can the modern drama hope to compete in popular favor with the modern film? What is the future of the playwright?

As for the "legitimate" stage, noticeably younger than the audience at an old-style theater are the patrons of the newer plays. Men in stiff-collared business suits, their leather shoes tied up in cloth bags, parade the aisles. Their wives, if not in Western dress, have at least adopted the pompadour instead of the *marumage* headdress. Their chubby children wear sailor suits of serge. Ushers in foreign black dresses and white aprons proffer the program and lead the way to the soft drink fountains. "Intellectual" geisha trail their scented robes to and fro. And crowds of young students appear, their shining eyes giving them an air of perpetually expecting something wonderful.

Not for the sake of mere novelty or imitation of the West are these hundreds assembled. They come from a genuine desire to see contemporary life on the stage. Men are here who spend their office hours handling problems of labor strikes or traffic tie-ups, for whom the troubles of feudal barons seem utterly remote. Women come to behold their

own sex on the stage instead of masculine actors in the rôles
of queens and courtesans. Unfortunately, this desire for the
dramatic finds in Japan, as in America, too few dramatists
capable of interpreting modern life in a very important
manner.

Owing to long centuries of tradition, the plays are often
stirringly acted at least and ambitiously mounted; while their
themes give valuable insight into the trends of the Japanese
mind. Among the dramas I witnessed a wide range of subjects was handled: family adjustment, religion, sex, labor
and the historic struggle for national unity. The very suggestion of such issues, of course, is a revolutionary change
to a race accustomed to the Kabuki drama, which had
action and beauty but a limited scope of subject matter.
Plot, problem, the development of character, all present
difficulties to the author in Japan.

While waiting for native masterpieces, many translations
of foreign dramas are staged by the Imperial Theater or by
more radical "little theater" groups. Ibsen has made his
Oriental bow as an "ice-breaker," accustoming audiences to
fresh trains of thought, and teaching actors a novel technique
of expression. "Ghosts" was revived with great success while
I was in Tokyo; and "Peer Gynt" was later given acclaimed
production. A book presented by Miss Ritsuko Mori, the
pioneer actress, contains pictures from scores of Imperial
Theater plays, varying from Napoleon and Madame Sans-
Gêne to Julius Cæsar and musical comedy—with all-Japanese
casts. Of course the sight of Orientals in Western plays,
either in photographs or on the stage, is decidedly queer to
our eyes. So are their portrayals of Eastern neighbors. It is
just as hard for a quiet Japanese woman to essay the part
of a voluptuous Hindu "vampire"—a drama I was lucky to
witness—as to play Katherine the Shrew in a Shakespearean

revival. But when I came back to New York, I found that American plays of the East are far less carefully costumed and acted, and possibly more absurd. The Japanese devote great pains to attain accuracy, and seldom perpetrate such frauds on the public.

Among the native plays of modern manners are light comedies on universal themes such as servants, suburban neighbors, harassed housewives and the family radio. Some attempt more scathing social satire, like the "Japanese Don Quixote," in which a samurai's son, humorously as his Spanish original, adventures in the modern world, among squawking auto horns and women haranguing on birth control from Ginza soap boxes. Others handle religious subjects. One makes daring fun with a scandalous Buddhist friar and the charming ladies behind his trap-door; a dramatization of an old legend brings in the august figure of Buddha himself; the "Priest's Dilemma" represents in philosophic dialogues the conflicting claims of flesh and spirit upon a young acolyte. Impressed by what seemed to him the false interpretation of character at the Oberammergau Passion Play, the author of the "Story of Christ" endeavored to infuse a more "Japanese virility" in place of "Western effeminacy," and he employed as one agency an earthquake during the crucifixion scene—so realistic to the audience that a high pitch of terror was attained.

Love, permitted on the ancient Kabuki stage only in discreet symbolic guise, suggested by the fan or the sleeve rather than in words, is of course a great experimental field for the new playwrights. But how far they can go in expressing outlawed themes is a question. The American, O'Neill's, play, "Desire Under the Elms," which an ambitious little theater company sought to produce in Tokyo, encountered moral opposition similar to that it received at home. A native

play, built around the historic character of the "daughter of
Shogun Idemitsu, who was wont to lure young men to her
castle and dispatch them before the dawn," was also banned.
The newspapers carried the modish headline: "Police Arrest
Vamp." In various guises, however, the forbidden topic
appears on the boards, generally culminating in the traditional suicide.

Social questions are looked at equally askance by the
police. Upton Sinclair's economic play met the same fate as
O'Neill's study in love—proscription. But little by little they
creep up. One play managed to introduce a labor strike, as
well as an independent *moga* who took sides with a worker
against her magnate fiancé. The brick chimneys of the factory smoked in the background beyond the customary garden.

Another, aptly named "Troublesome People" and called
by a reviewer "the first attempt to deal with a serious modern
social or economic problem through the medium of the
drama," delineated the pitiful plight of tenant farmers, the
attitude of the landlords and the Communist agitators and,
incidentally, "took a crack" at one element in the Buddhist
priesthood. This required, as was recognized, great courage
on the part of the author, actors and management of the
Imperial Theater—and similar tolerance on the part of the
Metropolitan Police, who passed upon it. The end was truly
Japanese: a group of landlords, inspired by a heroic priest,
voluntarily gave up their property to their tenants, which is
but a modern version of classic suicide. However, such a play
as this, produced in 1928, shows how close to the heart of
things the dramatists are leading the public.

Past issues are naturally much safer to discuss than present
ones. And so inevitably the dramatist turns toward the
events of the last generation. "Mori Yuri, Political Martyr,"
shows the reformer in various episodes of his historical

career, proposing to the samurai that sword-carrying be abolished, struggling to obtain the Constitution and, at last laid low by the hand of an assassin, hearing his dreams come true as "through the window pierce the shouts and beating of drums from a populace" to whom he had devoted his labors. Another play, by the well-known Mr. Kido Okamoto, presents the haughty knights and their clash with the humble soldiers just brought into the armies in Restoration days. The play by Baroness Kujo concerning the famous nun, Rengentsu, whose little poetry and pottery shop became the secret meeting place for revolutionists, indicates another way in which history may be handled significantly.

Frankly nationalistic, however, is a certain school of writers who would exploit the patriotic sensibilities of the people. They differ from the classic playwrights only by choosing more immediate subjects, say, Admiral Togo instead of Yorimasa. One of these brought the Battle of the Japan Sea on the stage, showing from the deck of Togo's flagship the smoke and thunder of victory and the surrender of the Russians. A second "thriller" took the Sino-Japanese War for a background, and roused the wrath of Chinese students in Tokyo for its treatment of their country. Quite on the formula of plays about American heroes who are loved by Chinese girls and rescued from villains is this drama, set on "execution grounds at Shanghai, in which the Japanese hero dies fighting a troop of Chinese soldiers, aided by his friend, the Shanghai sing-song girl, and her aged father whom he has saved from the cruelty of a Chinese official."

Gradually, as is evident, the dramatist is developing an awareness of the conflict in modern life. But he is also very near to the past, a circumstance which makes it easier for him than for fellow writers in other lands to compose "historical" plays. He has schools of actors superbly trained in voice and body to interpret any of the bygone epochs; he has the actual surviving costumes and enormous storehouses full of authentic scenery and furniture; and what is equally extraordinary, choruses drilled in antique music are available. He knows the history of the past through the ceaseless production of classics while its emotions are a part of his being. Above all he still has an audience of elderly folk to whom the Kabuki is dearer than any contemporary play; to whom the memory of the past is more golden than any event of the present. The majority of plays now performed consequently are either genuine classics or historical dramas written by living playwrights. In the latter case a tendency is apparent to remove the action from palaces to huts, from savagery to humanism.

To which side then the triumph—classical, historical or modern? That depends very largely on the actors themselves. On several occasions we were conducted "backstage" by the business manager of the Imperial Theater, Mr. Ayukawa, and thus came to know the views of popular actors of various schools of training and thought who, more than playwrights, audience or managers, are leaders of dramatic revolt. Actors are still in the strategic position in Japan. Coming as most of them do from hereditary actor families, they actually own the classical plays in person and so can forbid their performance by rivals. It is considered an act of exceeding generosity for an actor to "give" his rôle to a friend; so, when the superb Kichiemon handed over one of his hereditary parts to another, the famous dancer, Kikugoro, his deed was a matter of theater history. Many of these actors head personal stage associations and direct the productions. Most of them train their children, natural or adopted, in their parts. But recently Sadanji, the king of actors, having no son of either sort, set the precedent of training a daughter to become his successor.

So the actor-artists hold the control in the face of commercial prowess. Managers are restricted in their right-of-way. And one is prepared to find that the actors have the most positive opinions about the kinds of plays they intend to give and the kinds they intellectually prefer. The playwright who builds his plot around modern themes is fortunate if he can interest the classicists at all.

In his "green room," when we called upon him, Koshiro Matsumoto was dressing for the rôle of Benkei, the Valiant Warrior. From old charts, he was copying on his own face the authentic lines that gave his eyes a startling slant and his mouth the drooping expression of a sullen tiger. Attendants were girding on ponderous armor. And as he grew ever huger and more grotesque, his conversation about the stage and its ideals seemed more and more piquant by contrast. Finally, seeming to fill the whole room with his formidable, spiked headdress, tasseled lance and spreading sleeves, the giant smiled frightfully upon us and concluded: "The stage should interpret the age to the people. The feudal drama has ceased to grow and improve in spite of present efforts to retain its spirit. Perfect it is, but the perfect thing is the finished thing. The younger Japanese are unable to force themselves into its rigid molds; nor should they try. Certain actors themselves desire to experiment, to break the conventions, and in Western dramas they see the chance to be individuals, to have personalities no longer smothered under ten-pound headdresses and hidden beneath layers of bamboo and silk. The Japanese drama compels them to be types acting exactly as their forefathers did. They are pic-

AN ACTOR PORTRAYING A ROMANTIC
IDEAL OF WOMANHOOD

THE CLASSIC DRAMA IS A REFUGE
FROM REALISM

tures, not people." Thus he spoke, but his acting which followed was a masterpiece of tradition.

There are actors who waver between the two worlds. The excellent Kanya of the Morita family is one of these. He is equally at home as the knight's ghost in a classic vengeance drama and as the harassed husband in a modern domestic comedy. It is as though in a single evening he might play Racine and Brieux, or Shakespeare and Ibsen.

Kikugoro Onoe, one of the greatest dancers and female impersonators of Japan, is also among those who find modern plays fascinating and who lament only the dearth of good specimens. On the same program he plays the warrior, the warrior's wife, and the modern bull-dog detective. He is a mediæval lady, an old Yedo beggar, and a contemporary criminal with an astonishing versatility. But having experienced both kinds of plays, he feels a greater freedom in the new—the allure of unending possibilities. A master of the antique dance, he has tried to develop that art. Far from believing with Koshiro that the old drama is perfect, or at least finished, he would enforce evolution. One of his transformed versions of the pantomimes, the "Yasuna," was especially effective. This is a remarkable dance of a man insane with grief, who wanders by the river clasping in his arms the embroidered robe of his dead wife, now raising it for an embrace, now dragging disconsolately its purple sleeves. Kikugoro had danced it in the puppet style innumerable times, but had then modified it to suit his own fancy with freer and more human gestures, compressing the emotion and quickening the tempo. Typical of his twofold interest were his gifts to me—one a modern photograph of a part he liked best, the other a classical card on which, in the courtly manner, he had placed an imprint of his scarlet-painted eyebrows.

Completely modernized actors have also made headway upon the stage. Of these, Ennosuke Ichikawa is a leader. He gave me his views when he was heading a group at the Yuraku Theater and was making the experiment for a second time, after a lapse of ten years, of presenting Ibsen's "Ghosts." Despite the non-Scandinavian appearance of his Japanese troupe, the production had a convincing fire and aroused applause. He has effected innovations, such as combining Russian technique with classic dancing or giving old music on modern instruments. With several of his colleagues he would gladly exchange the brocade for the business suit on the boards, considering this exchange "freedom," just as American actors are apt to wish to perform in the velvets and utter the robust declamations of Shakespeare.

Stage women are even more anxious than men for the modern drama, because it offers them their only genuine careers. The men have no repressions in exhibiting an ultra-refinement of womanly grace when they play the parts of ladies, and that exaggerated delicacy which they acquire is both a mental adaptation and a product of life-long training. So a foreigner could share with the Japanese the feeling that there is something far too realistic about the average feminine appearance on the Kabuki stage in the circumstances. Since the Kabuki shares with the sublimated puppet show a quality of magnificent illusion, the intrusion of humanity and realism quickly dissipates it. Despite one or two successful Kabuki companies exclusively composed of girls who play both sexes, the classical stage is too crowded with competent men for women to find much room there. Their genuine chance for expression comes in the modern plays, where natural women are the object of the playwrights. But as though in revenge for the monopoly of the *onna-*

gata, Miss Ritsuko Mori confessed to me that it is her dream to do what Bernhardt did and play "L'Aiglon."

Beside such dramatic contests occurs the rivalry between legitimate stage and the films into which women are finding entry easier than in the theater proper and the outlet for varied talents wider and more secure.

CHAPTER XIV

THE MIND MAKERS

WRITERS on general subjects owe more to the modern age than their artistic colleagues. Painters, for instance, early obtained patronage among nobles and rich merchants and indeed, before the machine era arrived, were winning an ever larger audience. Though the best painters could never hope for an appreciation below aristocratic circles, the print-makers were able to sell their sheets to the populace. Similarly, actors and playwrights, if perforce content with a lowly status, were at least supported in a certain comfort by the commoners. Artists of these classes were thus able, under the harshest period of the feudal régime, to influence taste and emotion to a considerable degree. Writers other than play-wrights were compelled to struggle against greater odds in shaping the Japanese mind.

We may not boast that Western influence alone has at last given writers power, for they were accomplishing something even under feudalism. Toward the close of the Toku-gawa age, merchants had grown in wealth and spirit and were beginning to spend their means not on finery solely but on things of the spirit beside. They were attending lectures on morals and religion; they were patronizing book lenders for volumes too expensive to buy; and toward the opening of the nineteenth century, about two hundred years later than the print-makers, "professional writers" secured some popular interest and got pay, instead of a free meal only, in return for picaresque novels of "vulgar" life. Yet in general the hold of the aristocracy on thought was still decidedly taut. The aristocrats deemed writing a fine and highbrow art—poetry was its center—and in their eyes the poet, or writer, should be a leisured person instead of a professional. They were more willing to patronize philosophers who taught verbally or to build shrines and temples for favored religious sects. Some nobles, it is true, offered asylum to thinkers of "dangerous thoughts," aiding Christians and students of Western science in their forbidden searches for truth. And Lord Mito, one of the grandest personalities among feudal lords of any country, sheltered scholarly refugees from China, fleeing from the turmoil of the "motherland." He was one of the noble officials of the Government who encouraged learning by granting aid to schools. He himself supervised a group of seventeenth-century scholars who were put to work on a monumental history of Japan in 240 volumes compiled from archives and still valued as a great mediæval document. But the nobles kept a strict eye on results and in fact, in 1663, suppressed one supposedly disloyal history, so that all in all such opportunities for writers made up at best a restricted circle. Feudal lords were seldom so wise and generous as Mito. And if they had been, the sudden arrival of Perry's American black ships would have cut short the development of Yedo literature and sent the nation scurrying to thoughts of arms and revolution.

Against such a background the bookshops of Tokyo seem glowing symbols of the changed status of writers. Alluring resorts, as attractive to the book lover as the more famed stalls along the Seine, they cluster by the dozen about the universities and in one quarter, the Jimbocho, they stand at least three hundred strong. In these narrow booths, open to the street, even the illiterate foreigner must be charmed by the tables heaped with magazines, so gaily covered they look like peony beds; and the volumes on the shelves, though filled with mysterious calligraphy, yet yield a clue to their contents by illustrations. Juveniles are thus discernable by woodcuts of exuberant fantasy, maybe laughing leopards or tiny boys carried off by dragon kites. Modern novels are betrayed by sketches of tall, black-robed men moping under willow trees and looking dreary as heroes of a social drama these days would. The old-fashioned sword stories, substitutes for Walter Scott, are discovered by their print-like grotesques of outlaws, duellists and dying courtesans.

These bookshops are actually centers of a new age. Not only are their shelves loaded with metaphorical dynamite, ready to shatter tradition, but the very bookmakers and tenders become leaders of insubordination—victims as it were of an occupational disease. "The first factory labor dispute in Japan was started by the printers' organization," declared Seikichi Kimishima, a director of the Labor Affairs Section of the Social Work Bureau, in an interview reported in the press. "Under the circumstances it is interesting to know that the first labor dispute of store workers broke out in bookstores. This tendency is the same the world over. The reason for this is because printers read more and are more intelligent than laborers in any other kind of factories." They have to read. They have to be intelligent.

But what appears most traditional about the bookshops— the picture-writing—is undergoing a change of its own. The characters are being recombined to express more difficult and abstract thoughts; at the same time, instead of losing in its variety of borrowed Chinese characters, the Japanese language is actually being enriched to meet the requirements of a more complicated period. The very sentence structure is facing a revolution, according to Yusuke Tsurumi, one

of the experimenters with literary forms. However, what a
Japanese means by experimentation is the reverse of what
the Occident means. The West to-day, in rebellious circles,
prides itself upon the discovery of the "stream of consciousness" method in fiction, upon the vague, illusive style of a
T. S. Eliot or the unchecked meanderings of a James Joyce.
The Japanese aim, on the contrary, is toward logic and precision. Impressionism they have always had; their writing has
always been rather obscure, allusive, flowing. Centuries ago
they foreshadowed the manner of Joyce and in truth they
must exert heroic effort to write in any other way.

A beginner in the tongue very soon learns that the "verb
does not always clearly discriminate between present and
future time." Its tenses differentiate, not between to-day and
to-morrow, but between probability and certainty; hence may
arise much confusion as to the positive intentions of the
writer. Exact statements are difficult to make; the "bare
imperative," for instance, is used chiefly in military drill;
in daily life, even to inferiors, it is expressed in polite cir-
cumlocutions. The kindred idea of obligation is rendered
ordinarily in roundabout ways with a double negative. Thus
"It must be done in this way" may appear in Japanese as
"Thus if-not-do is-not." Perhaps the most interesting example
of the lack of directness is this fact, stated in H. J. Weintz's
Grammar: "The personification of inanimate objects is almost entirely unknown." The Japanese can hardly translate
such commonplace Western figures as "Time flies."

Since words and the stream of thought are changing in
Japanese literature, so, necessarily, is the idea content. Much
of the native product was as vague as the grammar and, in
keeping with the calligraphy, was distinguished for pictorial
beauty. The novelists recreated, in words, the same scenes
that the wood-block printers and dramatists chose: beautiful

women in gardens, gay life on Yedo streets, embattled warriors, ghouls. Like the classic drama, they frequently closed
with a stunning picture in place of the solution to a plot.
Sometimes they almost dispensed with action and gave place
instead to the moods flitting through a hero's mind; but
these moods were presented in the form, also, of pictures:
faith green as pines, or joy bright as maple leaves, followed
by sudden despair, black as rain clouds over Fujiyama. Dr.
Washio, who has given an important series of translations,
in *The Japan Advertiser,* of this school of fiction, calls the
stories "beautiful . . . but in the western sense, meaningless as the color prints." Such fiction is by no means obsolete
in Japan; indeed it flourishes beside the Kabuki drama, and
much of the best writing, both of novels and plays, is still
done, so some think, in standardized forms. A large public—
especially a masculine public—continues to relish the beauty
and the terror of the old romances.

But public taste is altering. The millions of feminine
readers begin to turn from fiction, in which the sword is
exalted above woman as the worthiest object of man's devotion; in which maidens as well as men are represented "falling in love" with beautiful blades and indeed coveting the
"cool, delicious death" they purvey. The newly literate
masses, lacking samurai experience, are eager for "proletarian" fare. Moreover, the circles of the critical have gone
beyond a literature so purely emotional and are creating
types more consonant with their intellectual curiosity and
social consciousness. Naturally this change costs valiant
effort, for the Japanese have had to do in three generations
what took more than three centuries for English minds,
which progressed so slowly from the mediæval legends of
"Morte d'Arthur" to fictional discussions in the vein of
Samuel Butler's "Way of All Flesh."

Only by examining the bulk of publication in the book shops does one realize how extensive and persistent inquiry and effort can be. Here are translations of important foreign books, classic and modern. Serious magazines, some published by university faculties and some as personal organs, keep the student in touch with world affairs and include such topics as cancer research or "The Economic United States of Asia." Here also are the organs in which Japanese chemists, biologists or archæologists publish their discoveries, thus joining in the universal race among scientists for priority. Here are rows of native novels, social, political, psychological, mystical. These shops are true clearing houses of international thought.

How rapidly new ideas are given general currency—that seems to me the really striking phenomenon of the Japanese literary world! They are borne to "the people" by all sorts of popularizing agencies. Publishers put out cheap pamphlet series of translations and native classics; a "family history" of Japan for general readers was advertised not long ago. Chatty magazines, some claiming a million circulation, inculcate new morals along with columns of simple gossip. Newspapers are especially vigorous leaders of the public mind; they not only print news but criticize it. The big Tokyo newspapers, said to be largely independent of party ties, are remarkably fearless and frank. They report trouble; they foment it as well. By opening their huge auditoriums to mass meetings and by lending the warm support of editors and pressmen's associations, they have actively pushed many important movements—feminism, manhood suffrage, social work. Moreover, in their pages they find place for essays and fiction of experimental schools.

Frankly for the people literature is written to-day. A large circle of writers, contending that Eastern and Western literatures have too long reflected the ideals of leisured classes, now are trying to be "mass conscious." However amateurish their early attempts, in letters or protest meetings, in these past two or three years, they have had startling success. The Osaka *Asahi,* in an editorial on social writers, calls 1928 "a memorial year in the history of our literature"; declares that "the literary world has been swept by a storm more furious than that of naturalism"; that long-established critics are now trembling before the flood, realizing that no more may writers "look on the social scene unmoved," with their hands in their sleeves and their eyes downcast.

Argument and innovation, nevertheless, are far from weak imitations of the West. Two generations ago, of course, the first impulse of writers was to copy everything, anything, from the strange hemisphere just opened to their curiosity. But their offspring soon became more suspicious; they discovered, through Tolstoi, Zola, and Ruskin that all was not well abroad and decided upon selective imitation—that is, to follow the humanitarians in praising the good and denouncing the evil aspects of Western industrial life. The present generation, having watched the Occident get a well-deserved drubbing during the Great War, has turned more skeptical. Many of its members have become mocking, satiric, and, as a countryman complains, "even unrequited affection is no longer a cause of grief. . . . Mental agony is out of fashion." They are still fascinated by science but dubious about its application. They continue to experiment with realism while knowing that the true portrayal of misery is just the first social step—by no means an end in itself.

The cry of the present doubting yet determined generation is well expressed in a poem by Baroness Takeko Kujo, Chinese scholar, a member of the nobility, and humanitarian. Since her death a few years ago a statue has been erected to her memory—one of the rare testimonials to the women of Japan. Her message contained in "Fifteen Modern Poets of Japan" is thus translated:

> I do not know
> If it be the fire of God
> Or the fire of Satan,
> But where its light leads me
> I will go.

Writing so popular and thought so wide-ranging are naturally alarming to those who fear degradation may result. Shocked at the "gutter authors" who flood the market with "confession stories" and scandalous gossip, critics urge the Government to stricter censorship. Those who dread a loss of national principles as well as taste, beg officialdom to curb radicals with "thought-control" programs. Especially are the latter frightened by the colossal bogies of Russia and China, just across the narrow channel, and by the constant rumors of smuggled gold and trunks of "red" leaflets. By women reformers, irate military men, even disgruntled professors the Government is besought to regulate literature and learning. Initiative in such matters, it is important to note, does not come always from the Court.

In proof of this assertion, the surprising case of Dr. T. Inoue may be cited. In 1927 a great hue and cry was raised against this professor, member of the House of Peers and many academies and considered one of Japan's most learned scholars. His enemies insisted upon a police investigation of his book, in which he questioned whether *one* of the three Imperial Regalia might not be a *copy* of that bestowed by the Sun Goddess. Now it is very interesting to observe that the Government, thus roused to action by private citizens, acquitted Dr. Inoue of evil-doing.

Censorship is thrust on Japanese officials by still another

force. The future leaders of Japan—judges, diplomats, educators, finance experts, and colonial governors—are selected from the mass of the nation's young men by severe competitive examinations and brought up largely in Government regulated schools and universities. Since this chosen group of youth is some day to rule the nation, their education and mental guidance are of the highest concern to the governmental authorities. Accordingly, when manifesto-making and pamphlet-circulating young "reds," popularly known as "Marx-boys," appear in this class, it seems to the rulers of the nation that the very foundations of the Empire are threatened. And, as if to augment the natural alarm, during a recent "round-up" of "radical" students, seventeen were found in one Imperial university and fourteen in another, while private, non-governmental universities could show only one dangerous youth apiece. To make yet more intelligible the attitude of Japanese officials, and at the same time to show how universal is the problem, we must remember that their own children are studying in these same institutions. It is an open secret that in at least two cases high officials have been motivated in their attitude by the knowledge that their very sons had been "infected" with what seemed to them—and would to the majority of European and American fathers—"dangerous thoughts"; were in fact members of a research society which the police sought to dissolve. What may look to us, far away, like deeds of a stern, inhuman Government, thus turn out to be the all-too-human pathetic anxieties of panic-stricken parents.

Can the mass mind be guided in its growth? Is it possible to control, either by law or propaganda, the development of national thought? The problem is set before every government and in its solution there is no East or West. The Japanese, eager to learn what Western experience had been,

not long ago sent officials to Berlin and London to confer
on such questions. But failing help from a distant hemisphere, they are drawing on their own experience in the
feudal age of the Tokugawas. The Ministry of Education,
seeking to "increase the mental stability of the nation," recently established a fund for "encouraging psychology." It
also granted a scholarship to the author of a paper characteristically entitled, "Historic Methods of Guiding National
Thought."

Proposals which might seem insane on a continent may
appear happy on an island. Islands lend themselves to Uto-
pian experiments. Though in Europe or Asia it might be
folly to forbid the smuggling of contraband ideas across
national borders, it is not so fantastic to imagine quaran-
tining insular Japan and setting up an Ellis Island for imported notions. It was once triumphantly done indeed. The
Tokugawas for almost two centuries barricaded their country
against both Asia and the West, without resorting to such
wholesale terrorization as that of the mediæval European
Inquisition. Their example, one of the most successful in
the world, naturally allures censors of the present age.

The Tokugawas were dramatic and drastic. They made
short shrift of artists: forbidding playwrights to portray contemporary history and driving them to use legends and remote historical incidents; ordering cartoonists and print-
makers never to indulge in humor at the expense of nobility
or officialdom, until they sought safer subjects like cherry
blossoms. Religion also was met by the strong hand. The
Tokugawas persecuted Christians, fearing that missionaries
were the precursors of military invasion. Nor did they spare
native faiths either; toward Shinto, which exalts the Imperial Family, they were cool, dreading to arouse loyalty for
the dethroned sovereigns. How far they went in antagonism

toward Buddhism may be judged from the reforms of 1842, which "classed Buddhist priests with prostitutes, actors, beggars, and other objectionable creatures, to be segregated in their own quarters, cut away from the society of respectable people." Nichirenism, as a most aggressive sect, they particularly suppressed. Indeed they only favored Confucianism which taught loyalty to the state.

Scholars and merchants, with reason, the Tokugawas especially disliked. Both dealt in dangerous importations; both were free agents who could not be restrained by attachment to the land, the lord, or local sentiment, in the manner of peasants and knights. Merchants were always making trouble, manipulating prices through their guilds or rice-exchanges, and trying to monopolize shipping between Osaka and Tokyo. Again and again the Tokugawas were compelled to step in, at one time abolishing the guilds and aiding lords to run their ships in competition. By law they kept merchants from displaying their "ill-gotten gains"; prohibitions were laid on smoking silver pipes, eating pickled eggs, or hanging up gaudy shop signs. The scholars were dealt with still more summarily. The study of medicine was the only branch of foreign learning recognized by the Tokugawas. Men caught smuggling books dealing with other topics were seized, and their heads, filled with dangerous ideas, were simply chopped off.

With admiration and dismay we examine the work of the Tokugawas. Certainly their aim and much of their accomplishment was excellent; they did save Japan from war, internal collapse, and from falling a prey, on the order of their neighbors, to Western spoliators. They compelled the Japanese to develop themselves, instead of relying on foreigners for all their wisdom. But were they wholly successful? Of course not. Artists slipped through the back door

of Nagasaki and learned enough about Western perspective
and methods to modify their beautiful prints; the scrolls of
the period which I saw in the Ueno Art School were eloquent
testimony to that contact.   Dramatists, though the point is
much disputed, are said to have imbibed some things about
their technique through similar channels.   Scholars, inspired
by the discovery, from dissecting a human body, that Western
medical charts were correct, started an immense "underground railway" of ideas, and banded in study groups, at the
peril of their lives, with a bravery that makes them worthy of
a high place in the world's intellectual history.   Nor could
merchants restrain their itching fingers from surreptitious
trade. And in the end, as modern research shows, the scholars
and merchants helped toward the undoing of the Tokugawas.
Funds from Osaka traders went to Restoration armies and
clerks from their counting houses marched in the ranks with
noble knights to battle.   Chafing at restraint, scholars spurred
on the forces, leading subtle intrigues against the power of
the Shogun.   Money and minds—two forces most wisely
dreaded by the Tokugawas—put an end in 1867 to the "old
régime."

Though the modern Japanese endlessly argue over this
past, none of them advocates a complete return to the Tokugawa policy.   There are many hindrances to any such pro-
posal.   Not the least is the curious fact that the martyrs made
by the Tokugawas are now lauded for their patriotism and
enshrined in the nation's pantheon of heroes.   The doctrine
fought by the Tokugawas was the sovereignty of the
Emperor; many of the scholars they persecuted were those
seeking to restore the Imperial House to actual power; and
thus the revolutionaries were ardent royalists.   This recognized paradox, which is so uniquely Japanese, prevents over-
praise of the Tokugawa censorship.

And there are other reasons why no control of thought so complete can again be exercised. Two important topics— science and religion—are practically impossible to bring again under a censor, so wide is the latitude now granted scholars in those branches. Religious discussion in Japan is indeed remarkably free. The learned compare old Buddhist sutras from a purely historical point of view, quite apart from traditional dogma and oblivious of effects on the faithful. Moreover, though there is danger that research may collide with some convictions dear to nationalist hearts, archæologists are given opportunities to unearth relics in Korea and Japan. A study of dialects and myths of the South Seas goes on, even if the results are unorthodox revelations as to the origin of the Japanese and their beliefs. And though caution is still maintained by researchers, they have managed to tread with great dexterity on quicksands.

In the field of science, one remarkable fact should be emphasized. Japan has been freer than Christian countries from antagonism to evolutionary doctrines. Buddhism itself accords in a vague way with evolution; while Shintoism offers no real opposition. And as Dr. Setaro Goto remarks, rather wistfully, in the Imperial University news *Bulletin* for 1926: "The Japanese mind must have lacking something of the pleasant feeling of the elation which a western mind brought up on the teaching of special creation would experience when converted to the doctrine of evolution."

In these times, scientific research is actively fostered by the Government. Maurice Holland in *The Industrial Transition in Japan* gives her "fourth position in the organization of industrial research among industrial nations of the world," in respect to funds, equipment, personnel, etc. Some twenty-three of her ninety laboratories are supported by the national treasury and the annual budget of one institute amounts to

$500,000. Work is carried on in fields of pottery, iron and steel, brewing, aeronautics, lacquer, tea, oil and pearl culture, and many others. "Pure" as well as applied science is fostered and, characteristically, the botanists have turned with especial zeal to classifying the cherry trees, and the zoölogists to studying the embryology of the once sacred tortoise. Japan is to-day, with some 30,000 engineers enrolled in national societies, "not dependent on imported technology"; and she has grown sufficiently independent indeed to have developed abstract scientific curiosity.

The Imperial House, though carefully aloof from all controversy, has at least shown science a certain amount of favor. The Emperor's studies and the recent invitation to a scientist to lecture before members of the Family (formerly law and finance were the only subjects allowed to speakers on Western topics) have been taken as significant.

Finally, absolute censorship is impossible because of the very complexity of the situation. It is far too late to draw such sharp lines of cleavage as the Tokugawas did. Superficial tourists to Japan may think that all is black and white: government against writers; institutions against rebellious students; nobles against plebeians. But that is far from the case. It is extremely difficult to divide Japan into classes according to comparative mental "danger"!

Take the university situation. The student body contains both active radicals and active conservatives, the two sometimes physically clashing and almost continuously in argumentative conflict. The professors are equally divergent in their views, mutually antagonistic, working at cross purposes. So are the college presidents; sometimes they appear solidly coöperative with repressive measures of the Government; but, again, they come out boldly with independent opinions. Thus, a quartet of presidents of four Imperial universities

strongly protested to the Ministry of Education during a
1928 "round-up," urging leniency for their faculties and
students. One threatened resignation. Another was reported
in the newspapers as declaring it the duty of his faculty
to study all foreign doctrines, however perilous; that anything else "obstructs the progress of learning."

If the "opposition" is so torn by conflict, even the Government itself is by no means unanimous in decision. The lower
house of Parliament, in fact, was outspokenly against the
Government in the above-mentioned round-up. On April
26, 1926, it passed a resolution, offered by Yukio Osaki,
criticizing the Government's action. The House of Peers, it
seemed, was more in favor of the repressive measures, but
here too, disunion was evident. Dr. Washio tells a story
illustrating the strife within aristocratic circles.

" 'You speak of the control of dangerous thoughts,' said
a certain peer facing Baron Tanaka (the Premier); 'but do
you think that you yourself are a good example?'. . . Baron
Tanaka felt himself humiliated. With downcast eyes, which
may be hypocrisy unbecoming to him, he replied: 'I don't
know whether I am a good example or not, but I am earnestly trying to be.' "

Where censorship is decided upon, Japan offers no exception to the rule that it becomes a dangerous weapon, akin to
a boomerang. Often it has the effect of advertising the hated
ideas. Throughout the 1928 row over university freedom,
the press gave the fullest reports of the situation, spreading
them among millions of citizens. The professors attacked
by the Government gave frank, long statements to the journalists who besieged them to describe "how it feels to be
fired." One prominent scholar boldly told the public that
his students already knew the doctrines he lectured upon.
When, in 1929, a student's debating society was disbanded

at Waseda University, a professor publicly addressed hundreds of students in a protest meeting, the newspapers carrying the picture as well as the incident. The result of all the publicity was delightfully summarized by an editorial in the *Advertiser:* "Japan is probably the only country in the world where students secrete Marx in their dormitories and read him. It may comfort the authorities to know that the effect is soporific." At the height of a Parliamentary debate, the newspaper, *Yomiuri,* called the Diet "a resort of aged foxes."

What the press censors do is not nearly so harsh as one might suppose. I have seen an example of their work translated—a long article by a Japanese, in a native magazine, on freedom of speech, class antagonism and "press muzzling." Here and there nouns or phrases were marked (censored) but the purport was left blunt and plain. Probably none of the magazine readers was so innocent as to be mystified. A better illustration of the "thought control" situation can scarcely be found than a quotation verbatim from a passage in this article: "The traits peculiar to (censored) are absolutism and tyrannical interference. (Censored) are trying to do so, but capitalists energetically strive to keep them down with all their might and main, . . . the action of the Government is founded upon economic reasons, . . . an expectation that a Ministerial change will alter the manner of control is a stupid argument coming from ignorance about its economic basis. (Censored), but the force of control will remain the same as long as the wire-pullers behind them are one and the same." Could anything be much clearer or more forcibly stated?

The fact that the Imperial University of Tokyo published in its *Bulletin* in 1926 a long and impartial account of "thought control" in the academic world seems also highly pertinent. It shows that in the genuine stronghold of officialdom and orthodoxy we may look for plain speaking. The Japanese are indeed not half so "reserved" and "enigmatic" as they are misrepresented to be by people who never take the trouble to read their publications. Thus, in this *Bulletin,* we read how the Government in 1920, learning of T. Morito's essay, "A Study of Kropotkin," in the first number of an economics publication in the Imperial University, jailed him and suspended the publication. Since then, the author continues, "there has never been a lecture on Socialism" in the Tokyo Imperial University, though studies along the lines of the classic economists are permitted. The control of official institutions has been steadily tightened, and more modern economic theories have been relegated to private institutions, such as Senshu University and the Ohara Social Research Institute near Osaka.

Frankly, also, the Osaka *Asahi* portrays in an editorial of May 3, 1927, the long series of stringent measures taken under the Ministry of Mr. Okada (1924-26): "He forbade students to perform theatrical plays . . . set up military training stations in cities, towns, and villages throughout the Empire, prohibited students from organizing associations for research into social science, prevented educators from experimenting with systems of teaching, issued instructions for the control of athletic sports . . . revived the system of education inspectors" and even restricted "art education." Numerous newspaper editorials have openly criticized such actions and have rejoiced when, in a later ministry, a more conciliatory attitude was taken toward the students and reforms were instituted by Dr. Rentaro Mizuno in the examination system.

In spite of the efforts of anxious educators, the fact remains that institutions of learning are more than drilling

grounds for tame minds. The sternest authorities do not
wish to repress all the activity and curiosity of the young;
nor could they succeed if they did. The student mass goes
on growing in *esprit de corps* and interest in the outside
world. Boys—and to some extent girls—are collecting in
debating societies, private study groups, and inter-collegiate
organizations such as the Students' Temperance Society.
They run a large number of newspapers and small local
school journals in which, as a faculty member remarked,
there is an "irritating freshness of criticism" common to all
sophomores. Girls united by several hundreds to petition the
Diet for higher education. And a remarkable degree of student solidarity was demonstrated in 1926, when, following a
governmental measure of control, collegians from several
institutions joined with professors and labor union members
in making public protest.

Just what a lively crowd the students are—and how peril-
fraught they seem to the authorities, who have the task of
keeping them in order—is illustrated by the violent strike,
in 1928, of engineering, medical and agricultural students
in the Hokkaido Imperial University, during which two professors were beaten and the police given a riot call. The
situation was so critical that the Emperor issued a Rescript
reiterating "the high purposes of his forebears in opening
education to his people" and urging "all those connected
with study in the nation to observe diligence."

One understands the magnitude of the problems confronting harassed educators better when one has lived in Tokyo.
For here, in the biggest center of learning in Asia, they are
most concentrated. Here are no less than fifty-five colleges
and one hundred high schools, enrolling 300,000 students.
Under native faculties may be studied subjects as varied as
commerce, medicine, aviation and shipbuilding, engineering,

agricultural technology, forestry, sericulture, Christian and
Buddhist theology, Indian philosophy, Roman or Japanese
law, domestic science, art, music, dentistry, colonial policy,
pharmacy and political theory. Numberless institutions are
specialized: the Butokukai, School of Martial Arts, for instance, inculcates judo, archery, fencing with the two-handed
sword; the Daito Bunka Gakuin instructs exclusively in
Japanese and Chinese classics; one college gives a thorough
grounding in Shinto literature and ritual; several Buddhist
sects have their own theological seminaries; there are military
and normal schools, leading medical institutions such as
Keio's, commercial and technical schools. Senshu University,
founded by a former Mayor of Tokyo, offers a wide range
of courses in economics. Meiji University is distinguished
as the first to open its higher technical education to
women and extend to them courses as diverse as commercial
geography, mathematics, law and sociology, finance and
philosophy.

Within reach of a Tokyo resident, also, are the largest
libraries, priceless collections of documents, museums and
research institutes. In this city the Imperial Education Ministry meets, the Imperial Academy holds sessions, and the
Scientific Research Council apportions prizes. Many of the
institutions publish papers and learned reviews, hold lectures
and give exhibits to scholars and the public. Whatever the
bent of a Japanese mind, Tokyo offers attractions for it.
We may realize this best, by discovering how many organizations have headquarters here: the International Lawyers'
Association, the Japan Sociological Association, the Japan
Chemical Association, the Japan Astronomical Association,
the Philosophic Association, the Sociological Medical Society,
the Japan Geographical Society, the Tokyo Geological Society, the Tokyo Botanical Society, the Statecraft Society, the

Architectural Society, the Electrical Society, the Mechanical Engineering Society, the Great Eastern Cultural Society, the National Physical Culture Institute, and scores more.

Shamefacedly as I admit it, what interested me particularly in all these institutions and societies was their essentially Japanese control and character. Having had originally the vague idea that foreign influence was dominant in education, even imagining that only missionaries ran schools for girls, I was much impressed to discover what a small part that foreign influence—except indirectly—plays in the whole educational system. And it was especially interesting to learn how pioneering natives sought, rather than passively received, knowledge. Accordingly, it meant more to be introduced to such veteran women educators as Miss Atomi, Dr. Yoshioka, Mrs. Shimoda, and Mrs. Hani, who, without traveling abroad, worked indomitably in the education of their own sex, raising funds for the purpose entirely among Japanese, and having no outside connections. The Peeresses' School, the domestic science institute of Mrs. Ōye, and the practical arts academy founded by Baron and Baroness Satano are other striking examples. While Mrs. Ōye is a professed Christian, she is compelled to rely on native sources for the maintenance of her school.

As a symbol of this Oriental atmosphere may be chosen the small chapel to Confucius and Mencius, which existed in Tokyo in 1923, hidden behind the aged trees and guarded by "devil-faced demons." This was a relic of former days when an academy of Chinese classics stood near, to which pre-Restoration statesmen in pursuit of wisdom used to come, bowing at the "Apricot Gate" or the "Entrance to Virtue" and paying homage to the images of the two great teachers of Asia. Although the academy had gone, the shrine was still utilized. Teachers from normal schools in the city were wont to hold an annual service there, expressing an allegiance to classic principles unsurrendered in education.

Peculiarly important is the fact that the leaders of national affairs, brought up through the two chief Universities, receive their training almost exclusively under native guidance. Japan is in a very different situation from other Oriental countries whose prominent men are to such an extent educated by foreigners.

The Imperial University of Tokyo, in appearance, before the recent earthquake, retained little of the purely Oriental, save the mighty span of a red wooden gate, recalling the feudal glory of the ducal family of Maeda. The classrooms were chiefly Western in equipment, and the list of subjects, except for certain courses on Shinto and Indian philosophy, Chinese classics and Oriental law, was genuinely modern in content. The seven Faculties of Law, Medicine, Engineering, Letters, Science, Agriculture and Economics offered students an abundant range of up-to-date fare: the American Constitution, History and Diplomacy; Psychiatry; Surgery; Public Finance; Veterinary Hygiene; and Theoretical Physics—to name but a few, indicating the range. The Imperial University is self-consciously Japanese. It is staffed, with rare exceptions, by natives and its policies are supervised by the National Government. Its scientific men are occupied by many problems peculiar to their people, particularly dietetics and the analysis of tea-vitamins; South Sea dialects; earthquake recording; synthetic rice-wine. The Imperial, moreover, is an outgrowth of two previous schools, in existence before Commodore Perry set eyes on Japan: the "Institute for the Study of Barbarian Books" and the "Institute for Western Medicine." It has taken five decades to create, by amalgamating some other Japanese schools and founding new chairs; at the start, Americans and Germans were invited to organize methods and train disciples to take their places; to-day, they have all been replaced and foreigners are there only as guests, subject to native supervision.

Equally and determinedly Japanese is Waseda University, though in other respects the doughty academic rival of the Imperial. Founded over forty years ago by the liberal statesman, Marquis Okuma, it started off with the defiant motto: "Independence in Learning." Native in origin, it is the same in management. In everything else, the two Universities are bitter antagonists—in sport as in politics, in fund-seeking as in patronage. Neither Harvard and Yale nor Oxford and Cambridge feel such mutual scorn and contempt as this pair. Only two hostile mediæval clans could be so haughtily irreconcilable.

Waseda prides itself on one especial point of interest. While the Imperial has Maeda's beautiful large red entrance gate, Waseda possesses the splendid mansion and orchid-collection of Okuma. When we were entertained by members of the faculty and the honorary President, the present Marquis N. Okuma, adopted son of the famous statesman, the vista from the mansion ended in a garden. Now, across the way is erected a huge Okuma Memorial Hall, containing chimes, and designed for huge pageants. Though this building is foreign-style, it was planned and built by architects and engineers among the faculty; and it possesses, so I have heard, a thoroughly Japanese adjunct: a Shinto Shrine, before which names of honored students are annually read to the "spirits" of departed alumni.

These universities are lively competitors in building. Each has raised large sums among alumni and is "booming" itself into a great new entity. Waseda is erecting spacious homes for its library and laboratories; for its students a swimming pool and clubhouse containing a dining-room, with a view to undergraduate solidarity. The Imperial is just as busy, reconstructing itself from the earthquake disaster, housing the new library with its donations from sympathetic foreign countries, running up an auditorium, engineering museum, and shelters for departments of laryngology and orthopædics, applied chemistry, law and economics.

The two Universities rival each other in the solemnity of their processions of black-capped and black-gowned faculty members, their students chanting to the music of their own orchestras, their field days and lectures. When Imperial secures an Einstein or a Tagore, Waseda retaliates by declaring a five-day lecture-feast open to the public, during which times are discussed such topics as "Electricity and the Universe, A Subjective View of Oriental Culture and Civilization, The General Tendency of Social Education, A Thought on the Labor Problem, The Inevitable Rotation of Business Prosperity and Depression, Liberty and Love, Ancient and Modern Laws, and The Social Foundation for the Development of Art and Literature.

In sports, the pugnacious attitude of the partisans of the two institutions is carried to humorous extremes. So maddened were the spectators at an early baseball game between the two teams that for nineteen years no other match was held; not until very recently did the two Universities meet again around the diamond.

In matters of the mind, this rivalry becomes bitter and intense. Ever since Waseda's foundation, indeed, it has been watched by a hovering Government, anxious lest Okuma succeed in rearing up followers for his own political party. At one time, in a panic, the Government suddenly arrested all the members of the law faculty. But now Waseda has won at least a formal, if not social, equality in position with the Imperial, though jealousy is still active. Today, there is

agitation afoot to abolish the preference given to Imperial
men in Government positions: yet many see in this a trick to
end the "Independence in Learning" of Waseda.

Graduates from either institution carry through after-life
the rivalry inculcated in student years. Imperial men occupy
thousands of posts as administrators, medical and educational officials, judges and lawyers. But Waseda men pour
into journalism, business and opposition politics. The animosity of these "old grads" explains in part the vivacity of
the Japanese press, which detects in every Government move
the hand of some "Imperial man." This, of course, con-
tributes to the already complex "thought-control" situation.
Consequently many of the complications in Japan's mental
and social climate must be traced back to the character of her
student class.

CHAPTER XVI

CAMPUS AND CAFÉ

THE darkly-wrapped, dramatic figure of the student is as striking an apparition on Tokyo streets as the too brightly costumed *moga*. His somber uniform, square cap and winter cape mark him from the multitude as surely as her overbrilliant sash and sandal thongs. He is as conspicuous as she and at the same places, for both are frequenters of newest plays, art shows, dance resorts or sport meets. Both are inseparable ingredients of the modern social complex.

His character fits him to be her companion. About his clothes and manners there is the same touch of bravado; he likes to parade a Russian blouse or French smock and beret just as she exhibits earrings which her people have not been used to wearing for many centuries. With a Byronic gesture, he flings his cape over one shoulder and swaggers on high, screeching clogs along the Ginza. He, too, has an impetuous thirst for novelty, greeting warmly every curiosity from Russian novels to college yelling. He, also, carries his poverty bravely, like a gallant pariah, making a cult of simplicity. He bears himself, as she does, with gay defiance and loves nothing so much as to set gray beards wagging.

The student's rôle in society is indeed the complement of the *moga's*. She introduces Western morals to her countrymen. He acts as filter for Western philosophies. Year after year, waves of "isms" from other lands roll in upon him: realism follows romanticism, liberalism succeeds nationalism,

288

mysticism caps romanticism, communism crowds upon socialism. Through his immature and passionate mind, as through a sieve, all these influences pass to the people. They hear about his "dangerous thoughts" whenever a students' debating society is caught by the police, with resultant storms of press publicity. He teaches sportsmanship by drawing tens of thousands to his stadium for international matches. He supports movements in art or drama by his personal patronage. He brings national questions before the public through his strikes against military training on the one hand and his violence against suspected radicals on the other, especially when a fray reaches the courtroom.

Curious and ill-formed as his personality is, Japanese progress rests on this educated youth. It depends on how much of the ancient culture and of the new can be carried in his overburdened mind. It depends on what his mercurial temperament can make of all the clashing ideas that surround him in these study years. It depends on how well the student, after graduation, can be fitted into society; whether he is to serve usefully as technician or political leader; whether he is to strengthen a great, idle, restless, vainly ambitious, surplus class. He can carry on the work of rebuilding Japanese civilization peacefully—or as in other Asiatic countries he may precipitate a revolution.

A public figure, then, even more than the *moga,* the student is the subject of bitter controversy. He is alternately pitied for the cruel conditions under which he works and reproached for his rebellious nature. He is called "martyr" to the examination system and "peril to the nation" because, when he finishes, he is unfitted for anything but a white-collar job. He is condemned alike for the apathy with which he faces such tasks as combining a knowledge of analytical Sanscrit grammar with astronomical mathematics and for the nervous enthusiasm which, on occasion, he displays for novel theories of State.

It may seem an unpardonable contradiction therefore to insist that the student is withal a truly romantic figure in Japan. Yet around his head circles a halo of almost religious veneration which his nation like all the Oriental world bestows upon the scholar. Similarly in mediæval Europe learning was long a matter of caste and a religious monopoly. Catholics guarded it in the European sector; Buddhists in the Asiatic. Through the dark ages of Japanese civil strife, Buddhist priests were the custodians of libraries and racial records and, in the modern age where thinking has been more secularized, Japan retains more of this remnant of the past than democratic America has kept. The discipline under which a scholar lives, the deep respect he should pay to the "wise man" at whose feet he sits, and the almost monastic type of cell in which he dwells are heritages of the olden days. The student in Japan still feels himself a being set apart. And the nation is inclined to agree.

This "holiness" is however very far from being sanctity. In truth a large measure of rowdy vagrancy belongs with the conception. Many of the Buddhist priests of earlier times had special privileges and the students to-day are sometimes ragged, jovial, hungry Friar Tucks. They surge to cafés and drinking-rooms, flirt with pretty waitresses, engage in boisterous gang combats among themselves and, living as they often do unsupervised and left to their own devices, almost anything has been tolerated except criticism on their part. Many vices produced by liberties have appeared among these young boys turned loose in Tokyo. And descriptions of their lives, especially of a decade or two ago, present pictures of untamed youth reminiscent of England's public schools before Dr. Arnold remade Rugby.

Brawling and hazing and the brutality of older toward younger students led one writer to call his schoolmates "apes in jail." But among the Japanese scholars, by and large, freedom simply tempers learning with a genial, attractive non-conformity. It is this merrier side of student natures which appeals equally with the tragic to the native public. Next to a Hamlet the Japanese dearly love a vagabond.

On the one hand the student is the overworked boy with whom all must sympathize and a person who observes him "on campus" learns what those burdens are and how he assumes them. Amid the "boom" growth of institutions and the massing of youthful students, the spirit of education remains emphatically Japanese. It is unmistakable at the Koto Gakuin, most renowned of the Government Middle Schools and the training ground for leaders of the nation. The stamp there placed on character adheres of course to the university years and indeed is an expression of the scholarly tradition and caste in the Empire.

Accompanied by two students, their mother and their charming fiancées, I had the good fortune to see a dormitory festival as one of the fraternity. This was an annual outburst of student expression by young men from the principal families of the realm, representing nobles, millionaires, artists and scholars, though selected by the route of pitiless examinations and elimination instead of by birth. Here were the types of citizens who, going on through the Imperial University by the same road they had trod to enter the Koto Gakuin, would occupy the best posts in imperial and local government, be sent abroad as diplomats and colonial governors, win coveted positions as bankers, judges, professors, engineers and medical practitioners. And in this key school of the Empire I found a Spartan camp.

A boy's room in a Japanese dormitory is indeed the very

opposite to that of an American "prep" school, both in furniture and use. It lacks pennants, photos, ukeleles; it is devoid of correct lighting fixtures, scientific posture chairs, and soft pillows inscribed "Rah! Rah! '30!" It is a bare and frosty cell; paper windows rattle in winter breezes. It contains little beside a thick kimono for a bed and a foot-high desk where the stoop-shouldered, chilly, undernourished student is expected to huddle over unending tasks, cramming for the gruelling competitive examinations. For ornament and good cheer there may be a scroll with the motto, "Silent Thought," and in symbol a single flower drooping in a gray jar.

Poverty and fortitude, according to student traditions, must be assumed, when they are not real, for the Orient associates these qualities with a gentleman and a scholar just as mediæval Europe did. In part this gallant Bohemianism is necessary because most Japanese students are compelled to live on too little rice and too much learning; a dollar a month spent on cakes is to them wanton gluttony, while books are treasures to be purchased by the pangs of an empty stomach and they are often warned against buying "too luxurious notebooks." Partly, however, this attitude is chivalrously borne. Princes of the Imperial Blood in their student days have ridden third-class on railway trains, so rumors say. Many sons of high family rank deny themselves warm clothing in order to appear "good sports."

Further to demonstrate this tradition, the boys of the Koto Gakuin had made their rooms look worse than ever for the festival by stripping them of movables and littering the floors with paper tatters, peanut shells and rags. The rooms accordingly, each housing five or six fellows, it appeared, looked like bleak and disorderly barns. And there stood the young inmates with aristocratic faces and many-syllabled famous names proudly playing the rôle of "rude fellows." Their lives were stern in discipline; they tried to "eat as little and as fast as possible"; barefoot before winter dawns, they performed martial fencing and wrestling exercises—the so-called "cold practice"—to produce "patience, strength, self-reliance and fortitude." Some came to school with a wardrobe of one kimono, and a much worn garment at that.

For such reasons his countrymen, always responsive to the tragic in life, erect the student into a symbol of mankind's stern search for wisdom. He is romantic to them for the very fact that he is miserable. Genuinely impoverished or subjecting himself to voluntary mortification of the flesh, his force of character is exalted above his necessities by the people at large. Yet he becomes an easy prey to diseases of malnutrition, to colds and consumption, to nervous and digestive complaints. So high indeed is student mortality (a Home Office report estimates it to be 400 per cent above that of non-students) that medical authorities have for some time been agitating for reform in school hours and terms, improved dormitories, food and care. To physical torment is added mental distress born either of the harsh examination system or the perils of free speech. It is no wonder therefore that this "romantic" youth often develops into a melancholy Faustian figure. Sometimes his unhappiness lends only a sensitive wistfulness to his nature; in other cases he is a fanatic, or brutalized, or the victim of despair. So the Koto Gakuin was no American prep-school country club with "prom dances" more imposing than many an ancient regal ball, pageantry around the football arena, parked cars, and rivalry in fur coats and haberdashery. It was a rigorous camp designed for work instead of play.

The very entertainment prepared for visitors on this special occasion reflected the severe economic régime. It was

not a musical comedy that was presented with jazz, glee singing and "he chorus girls" but a dormitory fête. Each room
in the barracks had a window facing the corridor and each
room-group had decorated its corridor window to the utmost of its imaginative powers. Thus the entertainment was
in a true sense a general student exhibition.

Some of these window displays were idealistic, artistic
achievements; others were rough and Rabelaisian in humor.
There were landscapes, jokes about Einstein, then visiting
Japan, and about student behavior. One was a miniature
stage set called "Loneliness," that depicted a winding road
leading up across black, serrated peaks into a ruddy sunset.
Another was a heap of old clothes with the punning title,
"The Student's Lot." A Japanese dressing table, supplied
with eyebrow tweezers and pearl face powder, labeled "To
Make the Ladies Linger," drew attention as a contrast to
another illustrating Dostoyevski's "Crime and Punishment."
There was a charming picture of Maeterlinck's "Blue Bird,"
not far away from a display of humor so Hogarthian as
to defy printed description. There were philosophic windows, illustrative of Buddhist thought, and one, called "Universe," showed a white globe whirling in cloudy space upon
which crawled a solitary ant.

Before two exhibits we halted the longest. The first represented on a tiny stage the famous Western painting, "The
Isle of Death." Blue moonlight streamed on the gloomy
cypresses and precipitous rock. Plainly the designers of this
scene were Christians, for within the room they were chanting, in Japanese, a hymn.

Farther along, lived a different group of boys. Their window was simplicity itself. It contained two images. One was
the figure of Buddha, seated on the fadeless Lotus, with
smooth face and quiet smile reflecting the peace of Nirvana

so that all men might see and seek. Beside him, stretched in agony on an iron Cross, was the body of Christ, His tortured face, bowed on the pierced breast, expressing divine concern —dying for humanity. There was nothing else in the window except a small sign, in English, containing the one word *Which?*

Though much is said about the "Americanization" of Japanese students through baseball and sports and though much capital is made of the fact that an American advised Japan when her educational system was set up, the truth is that the students have more affinity with their brothers in Asia and Europe than with Americans and will certainly retain it for a long time to come. The American of the present day—so complacent, luxuriously housed, supervised, engaged in "activities" rather than intellectual movements, playing with motor cars and week-ends—has no parallel anywhere. There is another significant difference. A Waseda professor has estimated that in the United States there is one college or university graduate to every ninety persons, whereas in Japan there is but one to every three hundred. That of itself makes the path to power through the university more important in the Oriental empire. Furthermore, since the Government through its Imperial Universities molds men to its purposes, forms teachers for its preparatory schools, and exercises enough supervision over private universities so that no degree of doctor, or "Hakashi" as it is called, may be given without consultation with the Minister of Education, both the competition for power and the sense of competence attendant upon achievement are distinctive.

It is rather with the Asiatic and European students that the Japanese may be compared. They resemble them in that they constitute a comparatively small and chiefly masculine scholar caste. The Japanese student is blood brother to the student of the old Latin Quarter, a gallant in a garret. He would be sympathetic with a German of the bygone "Sturm und Drang" period, with its melancholy Werthers and Fausts, its romance about masks and cloaks, moonlight on marble balustrades, and suicide to slow violin music. He would be understood, too, by the students of the 1815 period in Germany, busy with their underground secret *Burschenschaften*, discussing unification of the nation in defiance of the persecuting dukes and kings. He would be understood by the students of Italy, Hungary, Germany and France who supported the cause of popular revolution in 1848. He would be in tune with the pre-World-War German Youth Movement against home and school. And as Dr. Hu Shih shows, he carries on in his restless spirit the most ancient traditions of China whose students were a political menace in the fourth, the tenth and the seventeenth centuries. Unlike his Asiatic brothers, however, the Japanese is trained in technology and practical mastery of affairs instead of being confined to philosophy and theory. He is equipped, no less than eager, to lead in the coming changes in national life and status.

The smoldering fires of youth were encountered in curious ways off as well as on campus. On public highways, distant photographing tours, at exhibitions, the students were wont to gratify their well-known craving for English practice by introducing themselves and offering to be guides. This sometimes paved the way in turn for an intimate foreign acquaintance with Japanese minds, especially when the new friend would be brought home for tea. An incident of the kind may be cited for its flashing self-disclosure. At the Flower Show in Hibiya Park, the most interesting chrysanthemums of the country are annually displayed. I say interesting advisedly, for flowers in Nippon can be individuals,

chosen for personality rather than size. Some chrysanthemums are piquantly irregular, some are ragged pinwheels,
others full mounds of tinted whipped cream, others ladies
wearing fashionable millinery. Our students at this affair
were sufficiently inculcated with the racial love of nature
to explain these personalities enthusiastically but they
soon branched off into general themes and then to their
ambitions, their determination to seek "freedom," to master
science, and what-not. As we filed out of the last tent into
the darkness of night, one of them wheeled abruptly about
and said: "I am very funny fellow. I never marry if I not
find girl with ideas." With bows both students then vanished into the deep shadows. I felt that I knew the great
crowds better when I thought of the innumerable members
who had for an instant or more singled out themselves and
then dissolved into anonymity. If it gave one an eerie feeling, it was also compounded with a warmth of sympathy
and friendship.

The Japanese students are bellicose if not so dangerous as
those of certain other lands. High-school students mobbed
a café whose proprietor had not turned over to them a room
"for literary meetings" and fracases take place on the university campus frequently. They do not always come before the
authorities but recently a fray was brought into the courts
by an injured student, victim of a clash between a reactionary
group and a radical element whose oratorical evening the
former had tried to break up. In more serious affairs, those
who would not resort to violence through rowdy inclination
have the courage of their convictions to a marked degree;
although it is almost suicidal as far as a career goes, numbers
of students have petitioned officials and risked expulsion
from the university to support favorite professors who had
come under the ban. When the well-known sociologist,

Professor Ikuo Oyama of Waseda University, was asked to resign "because of his participation in labor movements," a liberal students' organization passed a protest resolution though wide awake to the fact that the University was planning to "weed out" the dissenting element.

Companions in Spartan endurance to their brothers of the Koto Gakuin and the universities are the girls brave enough to pursue higher learning. Since most of the young women finish their education with the academies of fine arts and domestic science, they are decidedly better off physically than the young men, have made greater gains in height, and possess stronger eyesight. But the increasing numbers who do enter the competition for a career must expect a course even more severe, physically and mentally, than the men. Where no mercy can be shown to male students, owing to economic circumstances, there can be nothing left over for the females.

So Dr. Yoshioka's Medical College for Women was a place which King Lycurgus himself might have designed, so wanting in luxury was it. The operating room was cold and damp without that magnificent array of cutlery and sterilizers, anæsthetic tanks and gleaming white tiles on view in such masculine institutions as the great Keio Hospital which sets the goal for medical men. Dr. Yoshioka founded this school and hospital training for her countrywomen much as Mary Lyon started Mount Holyoke in Massachusetts. She was a pioneer with limited funds and forced down to essentials. Until her journey west in 1929, she had to rely entirely on native conversion to her ideals and native help. In her Japanese-style building before the great earthquake of 1923, the wind whistled down paper-walled corridors into unheated rooms. As I walked along the passage, accompanied by the nurses, I caught glimpses of patients lying on the mattresses resting on frigid matting floors. In the *toko-noma,* or place of honor, instead of the customary scroll or artificial ornament, new-born babies lay, wrapped in brilliant kimono.

Nor are the girl medical students who reside there the type one may see in fine "finishing schools" in Japan—at the annual bazaar, for example, of the Peeresses' School. Those are boisterous, rosy-cheeked girls in fastidiously patterned silks, with sleekest coiffures and radiantly lined sleeves. These are simple young women, pale and strained of countenance, many wearing glasses. They customarily dress in serge, with heavy red sweaters or the plainest of kimono. No pearl powder on their faces; no rhinestone combs in their hastily knotted hair. But their faces are gentle and their smiles, it seemed, still more spontaneous than those of the fashionable misses. In keeping with the stern necessity of their institution, their dormitories are matting-floored cells. At daybreak they roll up their bedding to have the room clear for study after a wash-up in the bathing room which offers only cold water and rows of tin basins—a replica of the Koto Gakuin. These girls have little time for athletics or outside activities; their days are rounds of tasks in German and Japanese medical books, and in attendance at the hospital. Yet, "new women," so intent upon professional positions, were not apparently crushed by the conditions under which they labored. So feminine, moreover, had they remained that the most brilliant scholar in the place, who was assigned as our escort, was too modest to speak a word without blushing. The rest beamed and beamed with affectionate shyness but stood inarticulate, until one of their number suddenly exclaimed: "O, how I want to nurse the miserables!" They have been trained for matters graver than conversation.

There are many other institutions for women in Japan as little known to short-term travelers as this one. Even the Tokyo Women's University is not so commonly described as are some of the mission high schools. This is a great pity because it is thoroughly Japanese in origin and support as well as in the rigor and earnestness of its life. Classes are held in foreign-style rooms to-day with stiff, hard seats; but the dormitories are native in type. The girls do their own washing, cooking and cleaning. In addition they run a co-operative store. Such activities entail a tremendous amount of toil outside the effort to combine Oriental and Western studies and make the girls' schooling more strenuous than that of their brothers in the men's institutions. Women indeed are dogged by domestic duties within the very gates of learning. Once in a while, they told me, they did find an hour or two for genuine recreation. They would then sing. Nevertheless they seemed in fine condition on the whole for they had more athletics than the medical students; in fact some were record-breakers in field sports. They were all a different brand from the anæmic, romantic maidens favored in Victorian England and pre-Meiji Japan and they would look out of place either in furbelows or fastidious kimono. Unlike the boys, they were not bound down to vagabond traditions on the other hand and so scholarly pursuits for them possessed certain advantages.

After much gay practice in the foreign custom of hand-shaking, suddenly at the close of lunch we were informed that the student body had assembled in the auditorium and was awaiting a word from the American guest. What in the world had she to say to her hosts? At least a speaker might for once truthfully allude to the "shining faces before me," for the hall was one mass of sparkling eyes. But gazing down on the expanse of upturned Oriental faces, obviously tense with expectancy, I was only appalled. Though I had learned that everywhere in the Empire—at private parties or picnics no less than at public institutions—every stranger is asked to "address a few words to the assembly," still I caught my breath. What after all, did an American girl have to offer—beyond friendship—in this institution? Could she tell these others confidently that anything American could make them more gently charming or delightful in appearance, than they already were, in spite of their heavy tasks, lightened only by an occasional choral hour or an afternoon of mushroom hunting? That they would do better if, instead of preparing for marriage, they "strove for higher education" in constitutional law or astrophysics, to compete at last in the arena already choked with their struggling fellow-citizens?

Such questions confront the visitor to Japanese colleges of any sort. When the Americans, especially in the South, groan over their taxes for education, how can Japan hope to satisfy the thirst for knowledge of her boys, let alone her girls? And even if heroic efforts enable her to enlarge her schools, what opportunities can she create for the flood of graduates? Already tens of thousands of competent students, successful in passing entrance examinations, clamor in vain for higher education. Already scores of thousands of graduates, having attained that goal, find themselves at a standstill; they can get nothing important to do and must perforce join the multitude of the proletariat.

How awake the educators are to the issue is evident at every great teachers' convention held in Tokyo. At a recent one, in 1929, great debates took place over the question of the girls and what sort of education they needed. Teachers suggested all kinds of things from horticulture and house-cleaning to farming. But when it came to the question of finance, the best they could do in any case was to call upon the government officials for relief. These in their turn urged the high-school administrators to inaugurate reforms. Each interest pushed the issue back upon the other. Finally an instructor in Chinese classics rose and exclaimed: "Without improvement in the political situation no measures for the encouragement of education will attain the desired ends!"

As the President of the Women's University intimated: "We know the problems. We need only funds." Indeed the apparent hopelessness of the situation weighs upon the spirits of educators no whit less heavily than it depresses the students themselves.

Off campus, the student, of the male persuasion at least, merges his educational interest in social affairs of various sorts. Occasionally he becomes something of a *bon vivant*. Cafés are now the same substitute for dormitory lure and week-end engagements in Japan that they have long been in Europe. And no picture of the scholar caste is complete without indications of its social preferences. Thus the streets, the restaurants, the theaters and meeting halls are equally essential approaches to the student mind. They reveal an infinite number of kinds of brains and aspirations within a group supposedly uniform: fastidious æsthetes and royster-ing bullies; baseball coaches and Buddhist theologians; strong athletes whose dream it is to win a prize for their nation at the Olympic Games and coughing, cadaverous scholars who scorn the body and cultivate the mind with meditation on the Sukhavativyuha Sutra; fomenters of for-bidden doctrines; and conservatives ready to help out in emergencies in the suppression of radicals.

Chinese and Korean students, always to be depended on for manifesto-making, add to the color of the Tokyo schol-astic community. The Chinese make demonstrations whenever a stage play or lecture seems to them an invidious attack on their nation. The Koreans battle also among themselves, as when a serious clash took place between Korean laborers and a students' organization; the former, armed with Japanese swords, attempted to punish the latter for deficient social sympathies.

We saw a great deal of the students in their special Bohemian resorts. In a foreign-style place with lace curtains, marble-topped tables, and framed chromos, the air thick with smoke, groups would gather for bowls of spaghetti, cups of lukewarm tea and discussions. Their capes flung back, their thin hands brandishing cigarettes, they would sit far into the night, debating, with all the "high seriousness" of youth, life, marriage, death, art, religion, military service, the slums, ancestors and their own psychologies. Just as European students, having made the cafés their rendezvous, around a glass of wine or cup of coffee spin their philosophies, so the Japanese for a few *sen* acquire study clubs or places in which to map out social campaigns.

Much of the café allure is, however, of a bibulous rather than an intellectual nature. Several times, we came upon academic celebrations of this character. One evening a group of us were dining in a well-known lobster restaurant. At intervals we would enter the small kitchen, kneeling with empty bowls before a low counter behind which a skillful chef would dip fish in batter, fry them deliciously and serve us all we could eat. Then a waitress would glide up with a wooden tub of rice and fill our bowls with this foundation for the fish. Thus we achieved *tempura*—one of the most delicious foods to a foreign taste made in Tokyo. When we had eaten all we could for the time being, we adjourned to our own private room, delicately furnished, where on the floor we could play chess, drink tea in small thin cups, and "converse" until our appetites rose for another bout of fish. This leisurely performance consumed several hours but ours was quite a dignified party indeed. Nearby in an adjoining room, as we very well knew through the paper partition, a group of college boys were celebrating an athletic victory with chorus singing amid the circling wine cups. Shadows of waitresses or swaying celebrants darkened the wall now and then; the chorus swelled and sank; lone voices shouted and were silent. As we left the restaurant, our neighbors pushed open their door and came trooping after us. Enclosing us in a ring, they inquired the names of our respective alma maters and saluted each with a cheer that shook the rafters. "Banzai, Colombia! Banzai, Vassaru!" Not to be outdone in chivalry we stood up in the doorway, one shoe on and one shoe off in the hand, replying with the forceful "Banzai, Waseda, Banzai!" Then as we picked our way through the dark lane, we could hear fainter and fainter in the distance, the slightly maudlin but joyous cry: "Banzai, Colombia!" "Banzai, Vassaru, Banzai!"

Drunkenness has become of late so widespread that students have assumed a leadership which German boys of the Youth Movement took in tackling the question with a vim. Not under missionary urging but of their own volition in 1927 a "Student Federation for Prohibition," composed of representatives from 29 universities and colleges and supported by college presidents and scholars, launched a campaign in favor of a bill to extend the "age limit of the Juvenile Prohibition Law from 20 to 35 years." They made house to house canvasses, called on members of the Diet, and issued a declaration which read in part: "The neighborhoods of universities and colleges are infested with countless bars and cafés. The districts, in which these educational institutions are situated, are veritable drinking zones. There are 1,200 bars operated in connection with cafés in Kanda where there are four universities. . . . We cannot ask the bars to leave the districts for us. Nor have we the liberty of obtaining better sites free from liquor in our school districts. Often it is the case that we cannot take three meals without associating with liquor. . . . The general awakening on the part of the students to the danger of liquor is important but it is still more important for the community to help them by the adoption of law."

As a substitute for café idling, dramatics is so actively fostered by students that the Education Minister even had to limit that. They have formed many societies; written and presented their own plays. Among the girls, Western plays have been very popular for the release they afford. No Japanese girl, they themselves told me, who has once essayed a Shakespearean rôle, swaggered and mouthed grandiloquent passages as a hero or uttered defiance like Katherine the Shrew, is ever the same again. Neither is her audience. At one such production of "Midsummer Night's Dream," excellently given by Mrs. Hani's school, the theater was filled with boys in student uniforms, relatives and others who came for the English. They fairly rocked with merriment at every touch of feminine bravado, every brandishing of a wooden sword, every shriek of girlish rebellion.

Sports form, of course, still another natural outlet for energy. By the thousands, students flock to the baseball games between universities; here you may hear vociferous cheering, and see innumerable pairs of shining eyes in the faces of "impassive Orientals" massed around the grandstands. Little boys, in the approved fashion, climb tall trees and so obtain a free view. I saw one of the first big games ever played in Japan—between a visiting American team and Keio University. The Japanese lost the series; but then they started in to work and soon afterward vanquished American teams with tremendous éclat. It did not take them long to develop enthusiasm, fans, methods, cheering, skill and an organization which pays enormous sums to combatants. Some baseball games have netted 25,000 yen—in Japan a huge sum. A few weeks ago the Emperor graced a game by his presence, setting a sensational precedent.

Nevertheless it would never do to suppose, as so many foreigners do who witness such mass spectacles, that Japanese students are plunging in wholesale for athletics. That is beyond their means; equipment is insufficient. Only the teams of skilled players really study games. The mass of students in the universities are left stranded and much of the evil of the American system is thus carried over the seas —specialized actors in arenas and no physical development for the spectators.

CHAPTER XVI

BUDDHIST MODERNISM

THE Westerner who alarms himself with the bogey of an "Asiatic Peril" usually foresees physical dangers: a struggle for power along the Russian border or an armed clash in the Pacific. Not so Easterners. Quite as often to them the more immediate menace of the "Pale Peril" is purely mental—a threat to their civilization rather than to the possession of their soil. It is not armies they now dread so much as the less tangible invasion of ideas; they shrink less from conquests than from the consequences of an inferiority-complex. They watch the intolerably haughty West, puffed with pride in its riches, knowledge, and technique, vociferously engaged in propaganda to batter down, not their government, but their self-respect, their faith in themselves and in Asia. If they would resist this mental encroachment, they must join a combat in which the weapons are lectures and books loaded with theories about "racial characteristics," "cultural missions," "innate superiorities," "spiritual versus material outlook"—a modern warfare of words that knows no armistice.

Driven to shield his brain as well as his bodily existence from attack, the Asian seeks new ways of justifying himself to the world. He has had practice inferior to that of the West in the arts of verbal defense. His forebears did not develop the oration to a high point, lacking the necessity to sway mobs, which the Greeks experienced, or incite hordes to a crusade in the manner of Europeans of the middle ages.

307

Nor were his thinkers stirred by the close pressing of one great nation upon another as in the European continent; for on the immense reaches of Asia civilized groups were separated through the centuries by natural barriers or wildernesses inhabited by rude tribes. India and China were too far apart to fight. Political philosophers of Asia, unhampered by travel abroad, could in general spin theories about ethics, the State and even world peace of the vaguest application. A supporter of the reigning dynasty, yet Confucius did not glorify the Chinese as such; he seems indeed to have looked forward to a "Great Fellowship" of human society.

Only the Japanese appear to have had a training adapted to recent needs. The most elaborate, consciously nationalistic system of religious philosophy in the old East was apparently that erected by the vehement saint, Nichiren, just before the Armada of the Mongols thundered against the coasts of Japan. And that philosophy, Nichirenism, had a clear basis in the necessity for national defense. All Asia had begun to tremble before the Mongols and refugees from China had told the Japanese what horrors they in turn might expect. Then Nichiren rose to shout his prophecies of doom unless his people reformed their Church and State in time. He envisaged an enormous system of universal salvation in which a remodeled Japan was to be the center of a new world with Fujiyama as its heart. He climbed to the peak of this holy mountain, buried his written prayers at its summit, and so, certain Japanese maintain, made it the national symbol it remains in the present age.

That Japan still, as in the thirteenth century, should be conspicuous in "mental defense" need occasion no surprise. She was the first among the Asiatics to set up a formidable modern army and navy against foreign physical might. What more natural than that she should also lead in the search for a Great Answer to the challenge of the Western mind? That search carries the Japanese along at least three distinct trails.

The first is the glorification of racial or national traits. All Asian countries have vaunters of the racial soul, crying "mystic India" or "China always absorbs her conquerors." But as I try to indicate in a later chapter, the Japanese have gone farthest toward creating a national synthesis, on a concrete basis of Shinto religion and emperor-veneration. This is partly because neither India nor China finds it quite so easy to simplify its ancient heritage and adapt it to the modern life. Chinese revolutionaries, in fact, repudiate Confucianism and its family connotations. Hindus find an excessive number of customs sanctioned by religion that must be abolished, such as child marriage and harsh treatment of widows. Shintoism, however, requires but little modification for the hour. It was even possible for Japan to revive Nichirenism, in the last century, and establish a "joint stock company for the spiritualization of industry according to Nichiren's idea of the synthetic creation."

A second trend in Oriental thought is toward compromise. Many thinkers wish to blend "Western science and humanism with Eastern art and insight," or the teachings of Gautama with those of Jesus. Here also the Japanese are fitted to lead, since they possess both ideologies in greater degree than their neighbors, being at once more Buddhistic and more industrialized.

And there is a third path open to the Asian mind. It may disdain compromise with the West and yet shun nationalism, by exalting Asia as an entity, with Buddhism as the highest expression of Asianism. In this movement again the Japanese are competent leaders. Buddhism is a living force in the Japanese nation and capable possibly of reviving a pan-

Asian enthusiasm for a religion once common to the great cultures of India and China. Buddhism, it is true, is actually extinguished in its pure form in the Indian peninsula, supplanted by the native Hinduism; while in China it has sunk to a very low ebb and status. There are two existing Buddha sects in China whereas about a dozen distinct and flourishing ones exist in Japan. In China a strong reaction against the temples has resulted in revolutionary outbreaks during which images have been lassoed with ropes and then sawed asunder. But, in Japan, popular violence against the church spent itself two generations ago. Furthermore, Buddhism in Japan, according to both native and foreign writers, is expressed in forms older than those which prevail in China, harking back to original Indian tradition on the whole. Consequently Japanese leadership in a pan-Asian Buddhist movement is logical. There is no question of a mere survival of the faith within the nation; it has sunk more deeply into the life of the people than elsewhere. Possibly by reason of the Japanese veneration for the Sun Goddess, such monks as Shinran made a better place for women in the system than the Indian doctrine had allowed. Beside, Buddhism has been more of a political factor in Japan than in China and, while it is not a State religion there any more than in other Asiatic countries, it has been subject to external direction in a marked degree. Now its priests are working hard at executive reforms within the hierarchy and its scholars are making profound researches into its ecclesiastical history.

Those Japanese who aim to effect a compromise between the warring creeds of the hemispheres are, let us note, met with a really remarkable tolerance on the part of Christian missionary leaders. That is, in fact, one of the most interesting features of the whole situation in Japan—that it is

not natives alone who feel the need for more tolerance
and mutual concession. The resistant and yet calm attitude
of the "paynim" toward conversion has had far-reaching
effects upon the Westerner's own mind. Western evangeliz-
ers are rapidly abandoning their blind scorn toward the
"paynim" and publicly stating their new interest and sympathy. Thus the reaching of the Japanese toward compromise is of more than local importance—it sends echoes far
and wide.

As Christianized Indians are demanding a "Church of
India" and the Chinese a "Church of Christ in China," so
the Japanese are growing more insistent upon taking Christianity upon their own terms. They have already won self-
government; three of the four largest Japanese Christian
churches are absolutely independent of foreign control and
are seeking adult status in money matters as well. At a National Convention of Christian Workers, Dr. Ibuka declared:
"The tendency at present is for the local church to assume
the leadership with foreign missionaries under it." They not
only want to lead and if possible own their churches but to
direct their work and shape their own creed. Japanese head
their own national branches of the Y. M. C. A., the W. C.
T. U., the National Temperance League, and the Salvation
Army. A Japanese professor framed a program of social
welfare with humanitarian legislation, abstinence and other
planks and had it adopted by the Methodists in 1928. And
at another convention the same year, Japanese delegates
criticized mission workers for trying to evangelize only in
cities (where life is comfortable) and leaving "the vast agricultural area occupied by more than 30,000,000 persons . . .
practically untouched by missionary activity." The Rev.
Sugiyama declared, further, that "such terms as God, sin
and Jesus are not attractive to farmers, and Christian work-

ers must learn to approach them through instructive talk on the care of plants, chickens . . ." Will Christianity, under native supervision, make greater progress than hitherto? It is at least an experiment that will be tried.

Other Japanese, attracted to the study of comparative religions, are eagerly blending doctrines. They called a Three Religions Conference in 1928, at which Buddhist, Shinto and Christian delegates spoke on possible bases of unity; since then a threefold association, the Shukyo Konwakai, has held regular discussion meetings. But the Japanese are not peculiar in their intense interest in comparative faiths, for the Chinese have also concocted many combinations of Christianity, with Taoism, Confucianism, Buddhism and Mohammedanism. They have simply advanced farthest from theory to practice. At least one little church in Tokyo has made compromise workable. Kaiseki Matsumura, creator of a "synthetic religious service," holds Sunday meetings for an audience of a few thousands, mostly students, in a chapel decorated with the Shinto mirror, Buddhist incense burners and a Christian altar. He discourses on texts taken from the scriptures of all three faiths, assuming the liberty of eschewing any doctrines he cannot accept, such as the virgin birth of Christ and, presumably, the miraculous conception of Buddha. But instead of exciting horrified opposition among Christian missionaries, in fact he has a colleague in the person of a German missionary at Nanking, who, though remaining a devout Christian, yet believes he cannot lure Buddhists unless he gives "full credit for the real values which they possess." The Rev. Karl Reichelt has a baptismal font in the shape of a lotus flower, a representation of the Cross standing on the lotus, and chapel murals combining Christian texts with Buddhist sutras.

It is doubtful whether Buddhism can again fully be separated from the strong influence of Christianity. It has always received tints from the beliefs of each country through which it has passed; and it seems that the active, humanitarian character of missionary movements in Japan has once more altered it. But, on the other hand, apparently Christianity will not be what it was before it was taken to Asia either. The blind fervor of the evangelist, a generation or two ago, who meant not merely to baptize the millions of heathen but entirely to refurbish all Asia, reclothing its people in calico suits and wrappers, burning their idols and libraries, rebuilding their homes in Victorian styles, and substituting the organ for the lute—these types are not replaced, as they perish, by the younger emissaries. On the contrary, striking modifications have came in the missionary movement itself.

Perhaps one of the most clear-cut symptoms of change was the census of opinion taken in 1928 by the *Japan Christian Quarterly* among some 400 missionaries. By 322 to 34, they agreed "that in all important respects the cultured people of Japan are the equals of corresponding groups of Europe and America." By 339 to 28 they voted that they would not object to Orientals sending, in return, missionaries to teach the West. If they felt that much remained to be condemned in Oriental life, they at least voted, by 229 to 119, to deny that "all progress in the Far East in the past 100 years is due to Christianity."

Whoever follows the various international religious conferences will be impressed by the remarkable alteration in tone. More and more, Christian mission leaders confess their sympathy with and respect for the "heathens'" personalities. And they know, now, that they will never succeed in their appointed task unless they develop fresh methods and attitudes. Thus the assembled representatives of fourscore sects of Christianity, at the world religious unity conference at Lausanne, in 1927, met to discuss a common basis of faith, were told by a Bishop of India that "unity may be forced from abroad" on Christian churches, as Orientals have grown weary of the bickering of sects. At another world conference, in Jerusalem, it was openly and frankly declared that future missionaries to the East must be aware of Eastern culture and be prepared to learn as well as teach. And at a Pan-Pacific Conference, a long-experienced missionary of high standing, Dr. Edward Hume, is quoted as saying: "We must secure, as representatives of Christianity in the Orient, men who are willing to seek a new understanding of the Oriental religions and who seek to bring these two into harmony. They must approach the Orient as humble students of religion and must remain students all their lives."

But what of those who find in the concepts of Asia, and in the figure of Buddha especially, their answer to the West? It is apparent to many Japanese that their best armory stands here. For every purpose there is some weapon in the treasure house of Buddhist aphorism, precept, metaphysics, and incantation compiled during the ages—a treasury so vast that the scriptures fill from five to seven thousand volumes while the death-bed sayings alone of Buddha, so a Japanese states, amount to ten times the bulk of the Bible, Old and New Testaments together.

Asia, to her glorifiers, is the mother of religion, the nurse of civilization. She is spiritual, profound, intuitive. She is eternal; forever mysterious yet forever comforting. Compared with her, the shallow, practical West is but a chattering child. Western civilization, insist the Pan-Asians, is skin-deep only; it consists simply of conscious knowledge or of logical philosophy. All its efforts lead nowhere; its technique solves no problem of the weary soul; its democracy is a jest; its religion is effete. But the East's culture is rooted in the darkest, deepest instincts and so is immortal. Take-nobu Murobose in an article in the *Kaizo,* called "Asia the Victor of the World," maintains that "the mystery of life can be understood only by deep instinct" and thus it must be to Asia eventually that the world will look for liberation.

Rabindranath Tagore, though a Hindu rather than a Buddhist, has flung the Asian challenge to the world through the medium of lectures and the written page. When he addresses the Indo-Japanese Society, he argues for the formation of an Asiatic consciousness of kind; for a new spiritual international force, Asiatic inspired, to salvage the soul of mankind. And the Japanese Buddhists in their practical temper called a conference on the subject to see what more could be done. Abbots were invited to attend from China, Korea and Formosa, though Southern Asia was not expected to participate owing to the great divergence in religious opinions and creeds between the two sections of Asia, corresponding somewhat faithfully to the sectional divisions in Europe. When the congress assembled, the abbots discussed the possibility of spreading books and pamphlets "so that mankind may be benefited by the grace of Buddha." They urged missionaries to go West, fearless of persecution, and yet warned them how to act: "The conservative class of Christians will be rather difficult to deal with because they are bigoted. In such cases it is essential that we be broad-minded in our treatment." They wished to repudiate the efforts of Christians to make Buddha a kind of forerunner, a "tutor leading up to Christ." Very gravely an abbot explained that, in fact, Christianity is included in Buddhism and is a mere branch of that faith—about "the middle section," he had determined.

This hope of sending evangelists to Christendom naturally lays strong hold on the imagination of Buddhist priests. Nor can one blame them for thinking it would be high adventure. Count Otani, head of the most powerful sect in Japan, the Nishi Hongwanji, expressed his ardent wish to extend toward Americans "rest, peace, repose . . . in the midst of their busy lives." But the West also colors local developments: Tokyo held a song contest with the object of creating a new Buddhist hymnal, because the method of chanting the inherited music, the Sambutsuka and Goeika, seemed "out of keeping with the times." New music was required, and especially to be played on Western instruments, as the leader said, "because Buddhism is to be propagated throughout the world and I am of opinion that the music which is bound to play an important part in this missionary effort must have an international value."

The Pan-Asian doctrine, in one form or another, finds emotional response among many Westerners, previously prepared for it by the widespread glorification of Eastern virtues which has been prevalent in Europe ever since the invasion of Chinese influences in the eighteenth century. To-day there are Buddhist temples in the United States, as well as in Paris, Berlin and London. Ardent converts have been made among foreigners. At least one Englishman became an Archbishop in Japan, entitled to the "purple robe of the second class" with Imperial chrysanthemums. He believes Buddhism "correlates perfectly with chemistry, physics and astronomy" and hence is especially agreeable to that "scientific people," the Germans. The Japanese-German Cultural Institute's director praises the Buddhist method of salvation by "analytical dissolution of all concepts which to ordinary men constitute the universe." Western women have become nuns in Japan; one Englishwoman is buried on the holy Koya Mountain, and her name tablet stands among those of the proudest native abbots.

Certainly, too, the Buddhists of other countries than Japan are making efforts to appear vigorous. The King of Siam solemnly exchanges statues with the Japanese. The Buddhists held in 1927 conclaves of the brethren in the Buriat-Mongol Autonomous Republic and the Kalmuck Autonomous Area. The Pan-Asia Congress in Tokyo was attended by fiery speakers from remote corners of the East. It all sounds very impressive—far away. But how much is behind the organizations, sonorous phrases, and splendid gesticulations is a question.

Several steep hills seem to rise in the way of any general Buddhist revival in Asia. In the first place, Asia is no longer Buddhist; one would have to re-convert all India and re-vitalize all China. Where Buddhism survives, the church has degenerated and needs thorough reorganization and revision for modern needs. But if Asia could be evangelized and her churches regenerated, what about Buddhist doctrines? At present they are in a confused, antagonistic condition. A vast amount of research must be carried through by a generation of scholars in order to clarify creeds, after which, if some common basis should be agreed upon, the ancient antipathies of quarreling sects, transmitted through priestly families, must surely be reconciled. It is a monstrous task that the Japanese Buddhists are setting their minds to perform.

The Japanese priesthood has started its work by cleaning house. To compete with Christianity, Buddhism must be given a popular appeal and modern flavor. It must be made a social agent. Though its tone has always been gentle and humanitarian and though many charitable works may be credited to the mediæval church, it has not been an aggressive, creative force among the downtrodden. Its emphasis has been placed on escape rather than reform.

So we now find "modernist" abbots in Tokyo reading papers at meetings on the "Relation of Buddhism to the Community" or "Problems of Women and Children." They run kindergartens; they give lectures to "improve the cultural appreciation and religious life of factory workers" and benefit concerts of Noh and Nagauta to buy New Year rice for the poor. The venerable, though progressive, Lord Abbot of Zojo Temple was inspired to send aloft an aeroplane, scattering religious handbills over the city.

Finding out by questionnaires that women are more religious than men—a trait in which Japan betrays similarity with the West—they strive to intensify feminine support. Consequently nuns of the ancient orders come forth as leaders of discussion groups. More schools have been founded, and the Y. W. B. A. is as active as the Y. M. B. A. In the "Sympathy Week," sponsored by the Buddhists in 1920, a score of women's religious organizations took part, helping to sell "Sympathy Stamps" on the streets.

They have endeavored to bring the dramatic element into Buddhism by great public masses and services. An immensely impressive memorial service for the earthquake dead may be taken as an example; 400 Buddhists and 90 Shinto priests intoned the liturgies, while thousands of lanterns in the shape of sea-gulls or red and white lotus blooms were sent floating down the Sumida River after the departed spirits. Of course, the revival of celebrations of Buddha's Birthday is a direct answer to the popular appeal of Christmas. It is now celebrated in Paris, Berlin, China, and India, as well as Japan. But, according to one of the highest Buddhist authorities, they have so far failed to excite the youth of the nation by their ancient rites, such as pouring licorice tea over the head of the infant Buddha.

Buddhism wants to hold the children no less than their mothers. One very typical attempt to do so was the Buddhist mass held before hundreds of primary school children for the spirits of their broken dolls. A Dolls' Tomb was erected in a courtyard; incense and flowers were offered; and then "the chief priest of the Sofuku Temple and his assistant read a sutra to comfort the spirits of the forty-five broken dolls." He said: "This is a spiritual movement encouraging the children to love and think tenderly of all things that have been the source of their joy."

But all these activities cost money. They mean heavier outlays. At present the majority of Shinto and Buddhist edifices are maintained by land-holdings or local communities; the Government supports only the chief shrines of the Imperial Family. Each sect is thus a self-governing body, and, though there is a Federation of Buddhist Temples, there is, so I understand, no national system of finance in either religion. Some city temples are very prosperous and the office of head priest, it is said, may be "sold at a price as high as ¥50,000"; such temples try to raise funds in a very modern way—"sell the temple lots in cities at a high price and move the temple to suburbs where the price of land is very cheap." However, the vast majority of Buddhist temples are poor, especially in rural regions from which so many families have moved away to town. There is no immediate agency for helping them, and the movement to recover confiscated lands of the church, led in 1928 by the National Council of Temples, met no success.

Poverty is common to the Shinto and Buddhist churches. Pitiful stories are told of old priests who once could enjoy four eggs a day, but now have a single one; counting families and dependents, there are close to a quarter of a million Buddhist clergy—far too many. They are poor; they are also often ignorant. The churches have had to take what leaders they could get; in cities they find well-to-do *bonzes* inclined to riotous living, eating flesh, drinking, leading fast lives; while in the villages ignorance is a greater foe than dissipation. S. Venoda says: "There are thousands of institutions which are operated by priests and priestesses who have no more than primary school education . . . certain sects of Shintoism are well known to have been making priests and priestesses in a wholesale fashion by selling certificates."

All sorts of difficulties exist. The question of including the "outcasts" is a serious one; in 1925, about 10,000 left the Hongan sect because of alleged discrimination. The sects at once drew up a "social program." In rural districts, the quarrels of tenants and landlords are now so bitter that the stand of the Church angers both sides. There is the question of "superstitious practices" which bring in large revenues to many temples; intelligent priests would like to give them up, but must they face starvation by failing to provide the multitude with its anti-thunderbolt talismans and similar tabus? There is also a vast amount of personal antagonism and rivalry within all the sects. As the Secretary of the General Federation of Temples said: "The bone of contention (between two sects of Hongan) is not doctrine but personal animosity of the leading priests of the temples." A very curious illustration of these family quarrels was the rift in the Hongwanji sect. Its head, the very Count Otani who wishes to convert the West, is the lineal descendant of that Saint Shinran who, like Luther in Europe, advocated marriage for the clergy. Greatly disturbed by the denial of salvation to women, he founded a sect of his own in which family life was obligatory; his descendants intermarried with members of the royal family in Japan; the present Count's wife is a sister of the present Empress of Japan. Yet this royal-saintly family has had great trials over the headship of the sect; the same Abbot was excommunicated on account of financial irregularities in the temples and his son, elected in his place, finds a divided allegiance awaits him. Indeed, feeling has run so high that two aged priests recently indulged in a dagger fight.

Faced with such problems of internal development, Buddhism has made a swing toward political affiliations. Its directors wish to regain some of the influence over State affairs which was taken away during the Restoration when the Church was disestablished and much of its wealth confiscated. The various sects have united to push through a bill requiring more supervision of religion and higher educational qualifications for the priesthood. During the first election under nation-wide suffrage, the Church tried to create a definite Buddhist party and two score high priests of Kyoto, Osaka and Tokyo took a survey of political interests among their reverend brethren with that end in view. The big Hongwanji Temple launched a campaign to teach priests how to vote; lectures were given on the "Operation of the Manhood Suffrage Law and the Destiny of the Nation," to which all the priesthood and eight million devotees were invited to listen. This was the first time a religious body in Japan had made a move toward political education. But a Church which is not automatically represented in the House of Peers as in England or granted the place it holds in European affairs has far to go to overcome a formidable opposition in the nation to its political assumptions. It has been shaped by politics more than it has itself affected the course of politics and whether it can again count in that field is a matter of pure speculation.

Buddhism presents spiritual as well as practical issues to its believers. Scholars must toil beside organizers if a powerful Church is to arise. In the realms of study and discussion, the pioneering work which the scholars have done is therefore of the utmost importance. Dr. Kimura wrote in the University *Bulletin* of 1926: "The study of Buddhism in present-day Japan is epoch-making in the history of Buddhism." It is also attracting the attention of Western students of comparative religions, who have hitherto studied Buddhism chiefly through its Indian scriptures, which are easier for them to read, and have not paid enough attention to the equally important northern branch of the faith.

This work is carried on by many agencies. Sundry sects have founded ten colleges and four institutes of university grade, in which the modern technique of scriptural analysis is taught, together with the history of Buddhist culture; some of these teachers have studied comparative religions abroad. All the Japanese universities, including that for women, maintain non-sectarian chairs of Indology, and the Tokyo Imperial has an especially active group of scholars in this field. Beside these the Toyo Daigaku, the only institute of its sort wholly independent of any religious sect whatsoever, conducts impartial research into religion. Such efforts to break away from age-old sectarianism mark, of course, a great rift with the past. But the public heartily supports the movement for a modern appraisal of Buddhism; it attends summer schools and maintains more than thirty magazines devoted to that subject alone. The scholars, according to Dr. Kimura, are doing three things. First, of course, they are analyzing the wealth of Eastern religious literature, issuing new editions, comparing texts, disputing age and authorship, examining the evolution of doctrines and the history of the manifold sects. A tremendous task lies ahead, because all religious thought was heretofore sectarian; "as for studying the general spirit and creed of Buddhism with the eye of a critic, it was never thought of by any of the Buddhist students of ancient days." So they are making, in this way, contributions to the history of world thought.

While such purely critical studies of the faith itself go on, other scholars are taking a little wider view. They have become interested in the influence of that faith upon the life of all the peoples of Asia who fell under its sway. For example, they are seeking to know "how Chinese thought assimilated itself with Buddhist thought, how the Chinese people established a Buddhist creed peculiar to them, and what effects Buddhism had on the then new philosophical ideas of the Sung and Ming dynasties." In other words, they are investigating the social, cultural and political background of this religion.

A third and greater task also invites the Japanese. And that is the evaluation of Buddhism for modern needs. "What thought and what science does Buddhism contain? . . . What is the attitude of Buddhism toward life, toward the theory of cognition, toward psychology, toward morality?" In other circles, according to Dr. Kimura, "the relation between the Buddhist spirit and social affairs, what measures Buddhists should take to promote the social welfare, and other problems of a practical nature are being discussed with zeal."

Is the East in truth more spiritual than the West? Innocently before I sojourned in Japan, I imagined one might discuss such a question, provided one were "acquainted with Buddhist scriptures" or had "delved into Eastern lore." While I knew the highest esoteric thought would be beyond me, I at least planned to read such books as formed the basis of Buddhist faith, supposing them condensed into some such size as the New Testament. To my consternation, I found that some Buddhist sects accept most of the gigantic bulk of sacred scripture, while others select a few doctrines and a handful of writings, and the Zen sect, adapted to the abrupt minds of warriors, rejects all literature and all dogma as unnecessary! I had supposed that, to approach Buddhism, I must study its metaphysical speculations and ponder on the "Twofold Suchness of Reality," but I soon learned that, in the views of many Buddhists, Buddha himself disapproved of all metaphysics and wished by simplicity to reach the masses.

The average Chinese Buddhist priest cannot understand the very liturgy he intones, for it is in Sanscrit, with Chinese pronunciation. Naturally, therefore, ordinary laymen are helpless before their scriptures written in a calligraphy so ancient. The Japanese have not yet translated more than a fraction of this literature into their own tongue; and only by arduous industry did they issue an edited version of the Chinese Canon even in the original in 1928. Moreover, if all this material were accessible, it would not aid us in knowing just what Buddha taught, since he wrote nothing himself. His sayings were written down about a hundred years after he died, and in a language he did not speak. The most various interpretations can be and are made of his philosophy.

What difficulties block the way of a layman trying to understand the religious background of Chinese or Japanese minds are excellently summarized by Dr. Bruno Petzold, in a review of the new Japanese edition of the *Tripitaka*: "Chinese Buddhism . . . like its offshoot, Japanese Buddhism, has only accidentally been considered by European and American scholars," and those able to read the literature of this northern branch, written in archaic Chinese, "are and will also in future be a mere handful . . . it will require several generations and a phalanx of scholars to make noteworthy progress in translating the Chinese Canon." In brief, Occidentals who can read both northern and southern Buddhist literature are about as rare as mortals who understand Einstein; moreover, those very Orientals learned enough to know its contents, disagree on the truths preached therein.

But worthwhile general impressions may be caught even by hasty and bewildered aliens. Quite vivid and understandable is the story told by Dr. Masaharu Anesaki, of Tokyo Imperial University, in his small book called *Quelques Pages de l'Histoire religieuse du Japon.* And for the general reader of German, a picture is given of the Asiatic world as a whole by Dr. F. E. A. Krause, in *Ju-Tao-Fo: die religioesen und philosophischen Systems Ostasiens.* Whoever reads these alone may not "understand Buddhism" or trace every doctrine to its source, but at least he can watch it fashioned by the zealous and intelligent or manipulated by the shrewdly unscrupulous. It will seem to him not a strange doctrine only, tamely accepted by vast multitudes of Easterners, but a name covering the most divergent and antagonistic views of the universe, attained by a variety of nations, in widely different epochs and economic circumstances and characterized by centuries of spiritual longing and mental struggle. It will seem to him more than an Oriental phenomenon—a vivid human story.

One of the conclusions we are led to draw from these writings is that religion united the East no more firmly than the West. Racial or national traits strikingly persist, despite international ideals. Japan is no more likely to unite with Ceylon on a mere basis of their common Buddhism than the

Scotch and Sicilians on a basis of Christianity. The Koreans, who have their own sectarian views, are linked in no bonds of Buddhist amity with the Japanese rulers. The Tibetans are isolated not only by deserts but also by their weird, magic-ridden schools of Buddhist faith. In the three greatest Buddhist countries, Buddhism never completely supplanted the older, native beliefs. There never was a time, according to Krause, when Buddhism "wholly and exclusively ruled India," and to-day, of course, it has about yielded the last trench to its ancient foe, Hinduism. In China, it failed to supersede Confucianism; in Japan, to eradicate Shintoism. Impassable gulfs separate North from South; Mahayana from Hinayana schools of the faith. Northerners have evolved more practical, social-minded, life-affirming creeds than the mystic, despairing South. Great multitudes of Northerners believe in a real paradise, rather than a Nirvana; in a ship of salvation; a compassionate Buddha to be approached by prayer; and, especially in Japan, a haloed feminine Kwannon, the incarnation of mercy. It is with this Northern teaching that an eminent German Buddhist authority has noted "wonderful and delicate and striking similarities and parallelisms between Buddhist doctrine and European philosophy and Christian theology."

Buddhism differed from country to country. It also changed from age to age. Even Tibet has been torn by inner strife, a Yellow Church, favoring marriage for the clergy, disputing with a "reformed," celibate Red Church. In Japan it has undergone ceaseless transformation. Up to 1000 A.D., aristocratic devotees were happy in the sheer beauty of the ritual, hymns, dances, phœnix halls and gold-sheeted statues; it took a civil war to shock them out of their æsthetic trance and send them flocking to the forest hermitage of Saint Honen, seeking salvation. When, later, a strong military government arose again, Buddhism took on a political tone in the preachings of Saint Nichiren and also lent itself to the needs of warriors. These wanted "instantaneous enlightment" and a kind of meditation they could practice in camp or before battle; such they found, strangely enough, in the faith of the merciful Buddha. Zennism began to teach them what I should imagine to be the perfect creed for a fighting man—"Silence, over the Incommunicable."

Clearly, in Japan, religion has been molded by men, as well as quiescently accepted. We see how aristocrats chose the artistic sect of Shingon, which delighted in ritual; and how the humble folk in the twelfth century, after the civil war, joined the Jodo sect, which promised help to all who simply called upon the Buddha's name. We discover why Japanese monarchs in the early days took the faith from China; because they insisted "the unity of the nation was but an application of the Buddhist conception of the unity of all existences"; it offered them an excellent excuse for ending the power of clans, each of which had a different divine ancestor. Especially is man-made religion evident in Japan, where Buddhism up to modern times was more of a political factor than in either India or China. Very early, by the end of the eighth century A.D., Japanese monks and the monarch were coöperating in organizing a hierarchy of clergy, closely bound up with the State. As Dr. Anesaki points out, they were called to the same task as their European contemporaries in the age of Charlemagne.

And yet another realization comes to one, a sad kind of knowledge. There was never a prolonged "golden age." Always, in the Buddhist world as in Christendom, prelates were disputing theological points, leaders were trying to shape doctrines to the ends of statecraft, hermit thinkers were wrestling with temptation in dark forests, literal folk were insisting upon good works being as essential as faith. Worldly affairs were all too soon mingled with spiritual, and proud bishops of Japan, resolutely as Europe's militant monks, meddled in the quarrels of clansmen and led their cloisters to war, armor under their monastic robes and cowl-like scarves bound over their helmets. Early as the eighth century A.D., corruption had gone so far in the hierarchy that the Imperial Court moved away from Nara to escape clerical machinations and build a reformed church. In the twelfth century, the gentle Honen wrote this melancholy reflection: "Think, you live in a century full of deprivation; the only door open to all, . . . is the door to the country of Beatitude." Warriors weary of bloodshed, court ladies sick of vanity, and poor folk impatient both of warriors and court ladies, all trudged to hear him gladly.

In both hemispheres, religion was a light amid darkness. Learning and charity were kept alive through dark ages of conflict by the Japanese as well as European monasteries, and we owe to them the preservation of remarkable documents and literature. In both hemispheres, on their common basis of Greek inspiration, arose a glorious art, fostered by religious edifices. In both, scholars obscured with abstract speculation the simpler words of earlier scriptures; and in both, the common folk cared little for what scholars said, as they knelt at the ivory feet of their Christs or the bronze feet of their Buddhas. To be sure, there was a world of emotional difference between the peace of Buddha who, seeking the "way out" for humanity, sat under the Bo Tree and smiled, and the agony of Christ preparing in the Garden of Gethsemane for ultimate self-sacrifice. But the populace, hungering for divine sympathy rather than metaphysics, found consolation alike in that smile and in that agony.

Whoever would compare the two "souls" of East and

West must bear in mind a mass of pertinent reflections. He must be ready to answer this question at any rate: In what country, at what time, among what class exists the "soul" under consideration? Otherwise, if he draws a line dividing those millions of worshiping hearts into a "spiritual" and a "non-spiritual" hemisphere, he may be accused of "gerrymandering" in the non-political realm. And, of course, how much rasher must he be who tries to estimate fairly that Oriental culture of which religion is but a phase!

CHAPTER XVII

THE PROUD PEASANTS

THE pride of the peasant surpasses the much-discussed "honor of the samurai" in holding the Japanese nation together. Indeed, Japan manages well enough notwithstanding the fact that her knighthood with its chivalric code of "bushido" has diminished. But she would find it a true calamity if the peasant were to lose the complex loyalty, woven of village and family patriotism and religious devotion, which keeps him willingly busy terracing and sluicing the mountain sides for rice, until they seem to lift thousands of gleaming and brimming cups to the very sky; while his wife as patiently rears those blind, voracious worms which yield the single thread, slender and silken, that is strong enough withal to support the flourishing cities, the developing culture, the army and navy and ambitions of a mighty Empire.

It is code and sentiment that still bind the peasants of Japan to their rice paddies, tea hedges and mulberry patches. They are real characters, the peasants, comparable in individuality to samurai or Shinto priest. They are shrewd, nimble, literate, possessed of dignity and a certain dry humor, as well as ability to organize and conduct their own community affairs. Above all, they have a spirit that generations of oppression have been unable to quell; for centuries, as modern historians disclose, they have shown themselves astonishingly stubborn in defense of legal rights, rallying time and again about their "straw flags" and rising desperately, with sharpened staves of bamboo for weapons, against feudal overlords. To-day they are quick to organize or dispute and actually have appeared much keener than city men to exercise the new power of the ballot. The women are equally individual; they have long been freer than the conventional "ladies" of upper-class Japan; for generations they have been inheriting property and, at times, raising voices in village councils and joining in the election of local officials. Now they actually lead their men in violence. Women started the famous "rice riots" in 1918. Women, a hundred and fifty strong, leaving sons and husbands in the fields, journeyed alone to Tokyo to besiege the prefectural governor for three solid hours with shrill demands.

If we need concrete proof of the quality of Japan's peasants, we have but to recall that Hideyoshi, the great unifier by force of the nation, was the son of a poor farmer in Yasu-suke, and one of the famous incidents of his life was his clapping on the shoulder the statue of proud Yoritomo, crying: "You and I alone have held all the power of Japan in our fists! Yet you were born in a palace—I in a wretched hut!" The other great military leader of Japan, Ieyasu, buried among the magnificent temples at Nikko, was the son of a village headman in Mikawa province. The founder of Japan's greatest religious sect, Nichiren, was the son of a poor fisherman, who denounced the sect of the knights, Zennism, as "the Devil's own." In modern times, a peasant woman founds a new popular sect, the Church of the Heavenly Reason. Viscount Shibusawa, "father of banks," was a farmer's boy. And there has been at least one poet in Japan, Issa (about 1750), bold enough to sing: "The most finely ornamented sword can hardly bear comparison with the homely spade." "Let us prefer the yellow ears of barley or wheat to peonies or roses or morning-glories."

Obviously, forty or fifty millions of such folk cannot be kept content with their miserable life of drudgery by force alone. Creed and code must fasten them like velvet-riveted handcuffs, for their misfortunes are appalling. Toiling on farms so small that three acres make a man "middle class," a family is lucky if it clears $50 for living expenses in a year. Dwelling in villages devoid of sanitation and generally of medical service, often physically undermined by intermarriage—especially in hundreds of "outcast" communities—the peasants must keep anxious watch on shifting rice and silk markets, must sell their rice to city folks while buying cheap barley for themselves, and must see their children in huge numbers die of intestinal troubles for lack of milk, eggs, or other foods. Every year they must strive harder to feed increasing millions of mouths by winning a few more irrigable inches from volcanic hills, bettering silkworm care, or improving rice growing—already said to be in their hands the most intensive form of agriculture in the world.

And all their efforts benefit the cities. They defray the costs of a progress that others enjoy. According to a Japanese estimate, they pay taxes "proportionately double" those of the merchant and triple those of the manufacturer. Yet this wealth remains in the cities; instead of returning to them in good roads and farm loans, it goes to subsidize shipping, banking, armaments, and industry—an industry so slight that an observer states: "If all our big factories that employ more than one hundred workers go to ruin to-morrow, scarcely five per cent of the population will lose their means of living." Peasants must scratch soil frequently inflated in value by city speculators and at the same time give direct aid and consolation to urban dwellers—their relatives—for discharged dockyard laborers and tuberculosis-infected mill girls are sure to travel back to the old country homestead in time of need. There is nothing more striking than the way the country people reëquip the city relatives after a fire or an earthquake. Processions of homeless folk stream out to the hills and straggle back again, bearing on their shoulders wood and new garments and utensils with which to reëstablish their homes; unless they push into the rural dwellings to abide as non-paying guests.

How long it will be before the changes now sweeping over urban Japan spread into the country and demoralize these patiently suffering, touchingly loyal burden-bearers, is the wonder. With characteristic means and determination, Japan would prevent such a catastrophe. Her Government, by organizing the Seinenkai, or Young Men's Society, with a representative in nearly every village of the Empire, directed by ex-army officers and pensioned teachers, is trying to keep alive by persuasion—with the fervor of a Henry Ford—old-time dances and ballads and to preserve the socially useful sentiments of the "good old days." But will this attempt be successful against the lure of city lights? Against factory recruiters, rural labor propagandists, the radio voices, the furious discussions of campaigning politicians? Can any number, however determined, of kimonoed Canutes stay the rising and whispering tides of change?

In any case the conservative power of the peasant is still very great. Something substantial, strong and wholesome still lives in the bamboo forests. All the landlords are not busy summoning Korean strikebreakers and evicting tenants, nor are all farmers engaged in combats or being dispersed by police. Without overemphasizing the happiness of Japanese peasants or attributing any false "arty-ness" to their life, I would insist that, however poor by our sociologists' minimum wage standards they are, qualities seem to persist among them that the West has either lost or never possessed.

How could one by tables and percentages, for instance, estimate the smiles of those weazened old fellows who would lay down their bundles and lead us up a path to point out the pure shape of the sacred mountain with a sweep of the arm as proudly expansive as that of an Iowa farmer displaying his broad acreage and crops? Did not Fujiyama, from purple foot to silver summit, indeed belong to them? Is the mental ownership of a holy peak nothing compared to the physical possession of a motor car?

One picture of rural peace can never leave me. In a far fold of the blue hills to the east of Kyoto, on a small clearing won from the forest, lives the owner of a tiny bit of land who specializes in grapes, melons and chrysanthemums. Even by the standards of Europe his estate would be considered cramped, and by California fruit-growing standards the owner would seem almost destitute. But he was a poet-farmer. Such grapes! Such melons! Such flowers! Every bunch of purple splendor, every superb melon, every individually named chrysanthemum was a personal joy, and those which we were given on our departure were offered almost as beloved children from whom one separates only with tenderest affection.

A Japanese peasant who saw Millet's "Gleaners" as an illustration of agricultural life beyond the seas would probably observe that the women seem remarkably fat and overfed; that they wear warm garments and that their petticoats would suffice in cloth for a whole family's wardrobe on the island; that the harvested field is many times the size of his own holding. But he would also notice that there is no single, beautiful object in the picture—no headkerchief patterned with bamboo leaves, no flowing sleeves looped up with cords, no white heron standing on the rim of the paddy, no fox-shrine nestling among the roots of a nearby tree.

In that still more famous picture of Millet's, "The Sower," beauty lies in the large, free gesture of the grain-scattering hand. The clothes the man wears are coarse and bare of design—since European peasants toiled in the roughest garb and reserved embroideries for Sunday and fêtes. Japanese laborers, on the contrary, have even in the fields some touch of symbolism. How they kneel and wade in the thick muddy ooze of the rice paddies, getting chilled and cramped, as they tend each separate sprout by hand, possessing few tools! At the same time there are fine patterns on the tucked-up garments; the peaked sedge hats reflect the curves of the nearby roofs; and young girls at their planting sing ceremonial chanties. Perhaps in lieu of the large free gesture the spirit achieves what it can.

Another contrast is afforded by Gainsborough's "Harvest Wagon," carrying home a fat family behind a burly-flanked horse at dusk. Scarcely does it seem to belong in the same category as those thousands of peasant carts that fill the streets of Tokyo every day, bringing in vegetables in small parcels instead of by trainloads and moving out, carrying the human night soil in wooden tubs miles away to the fields for fertilizer—a custom befitting a land with so little animal-husbandry as Japan. Here nobody rides the little carts drawn by slender bullocks; the peasant stalks even ahead of his horse, arms folded on his chest, head high, treading with the soft step of one who has never worn heavy shoes. On rainy days he looks like an animated haystack, in his straw sandals and bushy straw raincoat topped by a straw parasol-hat. Hundreds of carts have no animal attachments; they are pulled and pushed for miles by men and women, their kimono tucked in their girdles, heaving and straining to get the clumsy wooden-wheeled affairs over mudholes and moon-shaped bridges and through long lanes into the country. A painful sight, the strain and tug of these tired folk, hauling the loads of none too æsthetically odoriferous tubs miles and miles away. But the towels knotted about their swarthy sunburned faces have "tie-and-dye" patterns so charming that Americans use them for luncheon scarves and curtains—patterns more subtle and fine than anything possessed by an English peasant of Gainsborough's time. In the midst of their severe toil, the Japanese peasants exemplify the fact that poverty and drudgery alone do not make a cringing human being—not so long as some discipline and creed still give life a meaning for him. Undoubtedly much remains to furnish comfort in Japan.

Local patriotism for one thing still enriches the sentiments of the provincial folk over the whole nation. Each region retains some legend, perhaps about a giant woodman so thirsty that he turned into a dragon and drank up a lake; possibly a shrine, known if seldom visited, hidden in a wild desolation of lava rock or within an aged forest, but handsome with rarely carved porticoes and containing an important family portrait, some famous "vendetta sword," or a lacquer bowl brushed by a master hand with a painting of parsley. Each region rejoices in a local nature wonder—for they are plentiful in Japan—curiously shaped and devoutly worshiped rocks, a valley like the "Giant Hell" near Hakone where weirdly molten forms and steaming sulphur fumes make a mad foreground for Fuji, or some cascade such as the "Thousand Thread Waterfall." Each region has a specialty of manufacture: an oddly cut sleeping robe, unusual towel, bean candy, or peculiar dish, as, for instance, the buckwheat rolls and soy sauce eaten in the volcanic plain of Miyagino. Or it has a town famous for a special craft, say

Shinjo's remarkable tortoise-shell-patterned silks, Noshiro's light orange lacquerware, made by a secret process owned by two master artisan families who go "far out to sea to ensure absolute absence of dust from the air," or Hirosaki's cloudy lacquer made in layers of different colored juices. Each region has its special harvest dances, its songs of cattle drivers and rice planters, its ballads of dimly recollected wars, two hundred of which the Seinenkai brought to Tokyo at one time. Thus the peasant feels that he has a history of his own and a development behind him, whether it is inscribed in books beside the history of the knight or transmitted directly from generation to generation.

The fact that his labor is essentially handicraft in character explains some of the peasant's peculiarity. He is no heavy-handed ploughboy, plodding through furrows with ox or horse, or pitching tons of hay. He is a craftsman, tending each rice stalk by hand, picking tea leaves tenderly, so that Tokyo connoisseurs may have unbruised fresh spring brew. The women must mate moths and feed silkworms so delicate that the Chinese say they are afraid of strangers in the home. Moreover, until very recent times, families used to make their own simple furniture, dye and weave clothes, and shape earthenware cooking bowls. In connection with all this craftsmanship go legends and observances to make life a ritual-accompanied toil. The peasants sing a certain "bushi" to drive away insects; they offer libations to the gods; they remember the dead on All Souls' Day with candle-lighted ships set floating; they make pilgrimages, five hours long, up the summit of Oyama to pray for rain.

Part of his dignity is also due to the fact that the Japanese peasant has an unusually honored place in the national social scheme—lowly, but assured. In the feudal past, though bound to the soil, he owned his narrow field, and his rights in community water and forest were conserved; often his property had been registered for generations at the local temple. In Imperial files are preserved maps of farms and village census figures of the eighth century A.D. A long training in self-government under the Tokugawas, combined with a settled life, has bred in him a sense of responsibility. Law codes and story books give the records of independent folk, enjoying considerable democratic freedom, electing their own headman to coöperate with the Government in the assessment and collection of taxes, judging local disputes, registering wills at the temples, caring for bankrupt brethren, and presenting claims for relief to feudal lords in time of famine or flood. In many parts of old Japan life had its attractive aspects; there are communities like Kamashima-shinden where the relation between the lord and the villagers has been "peaceful and harmonious for the past 270 years." Many headmen have risen to fame: Sugihira, one of the celebrated, was elevated to the rank of a samurai for serving his village during forty years of devotion; another, the blind man of Toyooka, inspired his neighbors to temperance, thrift and coöperation through his "Moral Bank"; while others have raised the skill of their respective communities.

Taxation unfortunately took from fifty to eighty per cent of peasant earnings, but at least the assessed were responsible for gathering the crop, labeling and packing it, and delivering it to the Government. Under the Tokugawas, Japan was seldom looted by brigands or laid waste by tribal warfare, as in luckless China to-day. However hard life might be, it was at least organized. In the old records of Yedo, farmers are shown complaining of persecution to the Shogun's officials and obtaining redress. Recently the force of this tradition was exhibited when the Governor of Gifu Prefecture and all his officials, believing that the people were defrauded of land by a Government irrigation plan, resigned in a body as a protest, leaving the district unpoliced for a time.

Honored by Church as well as State is the peasant. His crops are blessed both by Shinto and Buddhist rites. His first harvest fruits are laid at the door of the Sun Goddess and of Buddha. There is said to be a remarkable dearth of city gods or saints in Japan, such as watch over urban destinies in Europe. The whole civilization retains a rural cast and its best art is yet based on profound nature-appreciation. In ancient times even warriors, on certain days, dressed as peasants and danced in praise of agricultural deities; one great feudal duke, Rekko, offered a part of every meal before a copper doll he called "Uncle Farmer."

Shinto plays a great part in holding the peasantry together. This is sometimes called "ancestor worship," very superficially, for such a label does scant justice to its agricultural symbolism, and gives too static an impression. Shinto is not the worship of the past only, but of the future, too; it expresses a feeling of the divine continuity of all life, human or inanimate. An ancient cult of fertility is embraced within it and appropriate rites survive in many rural places in unabashed archaic simplicity. The West merely throws rice after the bride in these times, but in Japan Inari, the Rice God, guarded by his all-too-symbolically-tailed foxes, keeps the original meaning clear.

Devotion to the Emperor, which is the high peak of Shinto, is also agricultural in foundation. And the peasant continues to see in the Emperor both the temporal ruler—economic monarch and head of the national family—and high priest representative of divinity. Statesmen and warriors, having no such need of his economic blessing, lost the awe connected with the notion of temporal power and retained but the spiritual worship. The force of the more complex peasant worship is impressed upon one in the Imperial storehouse at Nara where, among ivory scepters and spotted sapphires, rests a royal hand-plough of the eighth century, ornamented with crimson and gold, and thought to have been used by the Empress Koken in field rituals.

The recent coronation of H. I. M. Hirohito was almost purely agricultural, a genuine rustic idyll. To be sure it is so encrusted with poetry and legend that many people ignore its profounder meaning. But it is more than pageantry when in solemn procession, to the scream of flutes and the thud of muffled drums, are carried the Emperor's three sacred insignia, or "treasures": the sword, the mirror, and that long gem commonly called—euphemistically, some German scholars consider—the "jewel."

The climax of the coronation takes place in two huts, called Suki and Yuki, from the two divisions of the Empire. They are peasant huts, built of rough bark-covered logs bound with tough vines and hung with plain, clean, white cloth. In each hut is offered rice from chosen fields in the Suki and Yuki regions, respectively—fields, belonging to peasants noted for "moral integrity," chosen by diviners from the marks on burned tortoise shell, consecrated by flower-crowned shrine virgins and chanting priests and then planted by singing girls robed in holy green. In the second of these huts, to which the Emperor goes late in the afternoon, feminine toilet articles and a couch spread with silken coverlets are prepared for the divine invisible guest, the Sun Goddess ancestor of the Imperial Family. Here the Emperor performs alone and in secret the mysterious rites of homage, including a libation of rice wine. It is a ceremony known to all ancient religions; it goes back to the very dawn-age of society.

SHINTO PRIESTS WITH ANCIENT IMPLEMENTS PERFORMING RITES AT THE SACRED RICE FIELDS

No wonder that the distinct essence of Japan is in the safekeeping of her peasants. Industrialization and urbanization would spell disaster for the imagery, the intent, of her racial culture. No wonder, either, that the stanchest loyalty to-day is found among the peasants. Their deep sentiment finds expression in pilgrimages to Imperial shrines and in the festivals of the Seinenkai. And it is systematically cultivated by the instruction the peasant boys receive at barracks during their compulsory military training period—a device for maintaining conservative concepts Europe has also been adept in utilizing. How profound their reverence is, I first realized when I talked with some country soldier boys who guided us through the dismantled fortress of Hideyoshi at Osaka.

With an emotional, non-rationalized attachment, the peasants cling to their locality, its landscape and its climate. So fond are they of established habits, accustomed sights and the clan spirit—all that goes to make a strong home complex—that the Government has been balked in its dream of colonizing Manchuria, Formosa or indeed the more northerly island of the small Japanese group. But, of course, Japan values this sentiment as a precious part of its national stability and would be loath to see it dissipated.

It is indeed a singular countryside to which the Japanese are attached, a land whose very infertility endows it, by way of compensation, with a wild and often lofty beauty. Each locality, as the peasants proudly recognize, is quite different from its neighbors, largely on account of volcanic action. The country as a whole is unique, too, in its combination of cold northern austerity and southern luxuriance.

But its jungle richness is illusory. The truth is it covers a volcanic soil. Some eighty-five per cent of Japan is non-arable and the sharply outlined hills produce only trees or a sword-like grass that kills sheep. And thus, while about fifteen per cent is tended like a tidy garden, the great mass of the country is left in forest wildness, undisturbed even by grazing animals. The fact, moreover, that much more than half of Japan-proper's sixty million acres of forests is owned, not privately, but by Crown, state, church, and communities, gives it a still more spacious and unparceled appearance. To know Japan, therefore, one must have rambled in her deep forest preserves!

Countless legends circle about the forests. "Freedom," they say, came from the groves of Tosa where, in the last century, the Restoration movement started. They describe the days when towns were mere camps set in primeval woods. How huge these early forests were may be somewhat judged from the giant cryptomeria trees forming the Shoso-in, the world's oldest wooden building, a stupendous "log cabin" that stands at Nara. And Japanese houses retain the light, camp-like, out-of-doors character typical also of China, when China herself was forested. Animals dear to native fancy—the badger and the fox—dwell in the cool, mysterious depths of the woods and make prank-playing their avocation. There, too, lives the alluring, dangerous "fox-woman," whose love is death to a mortal man, amid the elder gods, deities of stream, rock, tree, and hill, who had their sway long before an alien Buddha came to Japan. Not with stone but with wooden and thatched structures is the Shinto faith identified, employing in its rituals fir, bamboo, vines, water, straw, and paper. Of course, city dwellers remember the forests. And at certain seasons, such as Star Day, when bamboo stalks hung with paper prayers are planted by children at doorways, or at the New Year, when pine trees, pagan survivals in Western Christmas ceremonies, are tied to gateposts—at such times, it seems, the forest has moved straight into the city.

The character for tree seemed to me in my hasty and superficial surveys to form the root of many words in Chinese-Japanese writing. Certainly in Japanese painting, inherited from the forest-loving, southern Chinese traditions, a favorite theme is the picturing of mist and rain on hills, of lonely hermitages on crags; while literature recounts the wood wanderings of outlaws, runaway geisha, or sportive feudal parties. To-day, stress is laid on the economic value of these remarkably varied forests, combining northern pine, beech, chestnut, and cherry with southern fig, magnolia, mulberry and camphor. Within the past thirty years the Japanese have acquired great skill in modern practical forestry, and now the State alone draws tens of millions of dollars annually from well-administered property. One of the indisputable benefits of Japanese colonial administration in Korea, Manchuria, and Shantung has been the wholesale re-forestation of long-denuded areas or careful tending of timber planted by the Germans. These woods have already, it is said, aided the rainfall in Korea; whereas in Shantung, Chinese statesmen are trying to save them from the ravages of peasants, who dig up the very roots for precious fuel and would leave not a splinter behind, if they had their way.

Dashing through the forests are streams too rapid and tumbling for navigation, but now, like their protecting trees, turned by science into wealth. In "white coal" production more capital is invested than in any other Japanese industry. The Fuji River at the base of the holy mountain and other sacred waters where once, legend relates, goddesses delighted to bathe, now serve to make Japan one of the most highly electrified countries of the world. She exports yearly hundreds of thousands of dollars worth of electric lamps to

America—"typically," one exclaims, "miniature lamps," such as are used on Christmas trees and dashboards of automobiles.

"Two voices there are; and one is of the mountains and one is of the sea; both are mighty voices," wrote an ancient Greek. His words apply beautifully to Japan, deeply indented with bays in the manner of Greece itself, so that one never gets far away from the murmur of those waters across which the ancestors of the Japanese sailed in tiny skiffs from a former home, as much disputed as that of the early Grecian tribes.

Throughout Japanese conventions, symbols of the sea are encountered. Crab, long-life tortoise, heron and waterfowl, lobster and *tai* (fish) remain intimate signs of human affinity, both in town and country. The white triangle of a sail on the horizon and the crisp curl of waves are deeply realized facts to a Japanese mind, and not mere strokes on bowl or skirt. The people know that their sea is magnificent—the Inland Sea vies with the northern Mediterranean in the splendor of blazing water and the keen profiles of volcanic cones and pine-set lava rocks along its shores. They also venerate it for protecting them, as it has for centuries, from invasion; moreover, it has furnished them with the fish so extremely necessary to the vegetarian and vitamin-poor national diet. The land alone, in spite of the toil of the farmers, does not produce a satisfactory nourishment for the nation; its people are compelled to search the seas.

Sea and pine forest, waterfalls and fog-wrapped hills, cool and austere in effect, make the islands of Japan predominantly northern in aspect. Different in composition from the steaming jungle of southern India or the vast yellow plains and eroded, bare-sloped hills of northern China, Japan cannot be represented by the Oriental palm tree and gold-roofed temple. For her the pine tree and thatched shrine must stand as the embodiment of beauty. Such are the Arcadian—or Spartan, if you prefer—surroundings with which the peasant must cope for a living. And he has wrested from them more than a living—verily, a civilization.

With heroic toil the peasant has made out of Japan's countryside one vast garden for himself and his gods. If the rural scenery of the island of England impresses Americans as an incredibly tidy patchwork of lawns, hedges, copses, dingles and hamlets, yet England is no longer a great agricultural country and most of her tillable land lies idle in hunting preserves or decorated estates. Except in the frigid north, Japanese cultivable land, however, has been worked with amazing intensity, such as we hardly see in the famous vineyard regions of southern Europe. Its wildernesses are trimmed and the deep forests combed of every twig or cone. High volcanic hills are ingeniously hollowed and mounded for water-paddies until they flash light as from a thousand facets; and in autumn they are studded with drying racks, on which the rice straw hangs in bundles, each tied as neatly as a Christmas present. Over the rushing streams are flung humpbacked bridges and beside them kneel women washing the long white radishes, or *daikon,* that look like piles of baby elephant tusks. Miniature shrines nestle by every curious rock or venerable tree until it seems that there is no longer an inch left unclaimed by man or god.

Everywhere the skyline, as in all ancient countries, is italicized by temples. The rise of a hill is matched by the jut of a peaked roof. Everything seems emphasized and intentional, so that the very shadows in the hollows appear planned to mantle some low statue. And, also according to the rule in long-inhabited lands, every path seems to lead somewhere.

The brown ladders worn by barefoot generations up the steep mountains will not merely take you to the top, but usher you into the presence of some "elder god," who sits meditating among the gnarled roots of a sacred tree, apparently oblivious to the garment of moss-flaps growing on his shoulders or the moldered coins cast at his crumbling knees; so patiently he awaits the *Götterdämmerung*.

Every mile of Japanese territory has been worked over—and dreamed over. Generations of wandering *bonzes* and knights errant, poets and hermits, together with the pilgrimage-loving peasants themselves, have studied the countryside, learning every profile of its face. If patient hands have turned the soil and diked the streams, sensitive hands have recorded, on spreads of pineapple silk, or porcelain, bronze or gold leaf, their love of land and water. If the earth looks like a garden, it is loved like a garden by men and women who know with astounding intimacy its component parts: the rough, protective gesture of a pine branch over a pond; the curl of ripples and foam-topped waves; the somber richness of the wings of marsh fowl; the steep hats and bowed backs of peasants in the rain; the various soft ways that snow takes with temple ruins; the humorous melancholy of waiting toads in dew-globed grass. Thus the visitor experiences in Japan what he also feels in Italy—the perpetual joy of recognizing a peculiarly national quality in every spot and object.

Farmhouses blend into the trees and hedges, for they are built of unstained timber and thatch in sloping curves. Small, spare and cold, they have the faults of all pre-modern homes, but they have also the virtues of simplicity, cleanliness and order that save the meanest from being uncivilized hovels. Approaching an old house, one notices how thick the thatched roof is, peaked like a gnome's cap and weathered

THE MINISTER OF AGRICULTURE AND FORESTRY VISITING THE
SACRED RICE FIELDS

PRIESTS OF MEIJI SHRINE DEDICATING POEMS WRITTEN IN
MEMORY OF THE LATE EMPEROR

to mahogany brown, on which golden melons clamber—for even the roof is sometimes gardened here. A hedge of tea bushes defines the courtyard, containing color enough in the bright blue kimono of children and the red comb of the solitary rooster. Out from the verandah totters an aged woman with kerchiefed head, who surveys the funny foreigners with a twinkle, and then, with the poise of a lady making a present of a silk fan, solemnly picks and offers a flower from the hedge. How many American farmers, seeing a Japanese walking by, would show so quick and instinctive a courtesy?

Isolated farms are to be met with in valleys and uplands, while occasionally at a "crossroads" stands a lonely "emporium" crammed with varied goods. Villages are usually built in the American style, not around the plaza of a house of worship as is often the case in Europe, but along a crooked trading lane. These Japanese Main Streets are lined with shops not very different from those in cities, offering clogs, pottery, tubs, baskets and unpainted, diminutive coffins. Homes, broad-eaved and paper-walled, open to the lane verandahs crowded with babies and grandparents. Oxcarts come and go, guided by farmers who, in blue tights and jerkins, might have stepped from fourteenth century Europe. Their children, with hieroglyphic textbooks under their arms, cry in kindergarten English a gay greeting: "Goodaday!" In the New Year season, all the inhabitants will be lined up along the road, men on one side and women on the other, playing battledore and shuttlecock with much laughter. They will admit a genial foreigner to the game and streak his cheek, too, if he loses, with their inky brushes.

In such secluded places, approached by rutted trails, one may easily fancy the centuries rolled back. On Boys' Festival Day, in March, I have seen flying above the low roofs of sea-coast villages swarms of giant, gaping-mouthed, gray-scaled cloth fish—ceremonial carp that nowadays city folk declare interfere with their radio ground wires. And in some islands, especially off the coast, ancient revelry still goes on. Villagers in festive robes carry sixteen pairs of gilded lions through their streets, and rows of chanting young men bear on their shoulders the shrine of the elder brothers of the Sun Goddess down to the shore and into the waves for a symbolic bath in the sea.

In the *Bon Odori* season, particularly, a kind of harvest madness continues to descend upon many isolated villages— just as in southern England, in Thomas Hardy's youth, rustics were yet celebrating the maypole dance with a lingering pagan impropriety. As the harvest moon brightens, the throb of drums in hills grows more insistent, until a night comes when the half-forgotten gods in forests—the pre-Buddhistic gods—steal out to play among mortals. Then men in pumpkin masks (like our jack-o'-lanterns), in flower garlands, in women's clothes, or sometimes simply in soot, assemble in forbidden circles in the hills, blue-lighted by the moon. And there the wild scream of flutes and flare of bonfires repeat the revels of archaic Greeks. The deep chorus of the men is answered by the soft voices of maidens singing: "Though the moon shines, come visit me. It is always inky dark beneath my roof. . . ."

The forest-dwelling gods of Japan are remote from the proud, discreet, modern divinities. Closely they resemble those of Arcadian Greece, whom mænads worshiped in sacred groves. But up-to-date nations, such as Japan and Greece have both become to-day, have less time and temperament for such archaic ecstasies. Wine and cymbals no longer allay agrarian unrest; landlords no longer listen to the pipes of Pan or the eerie laughter of the fox-woman. And thus in spirit, if not in architecture or costume, the countryside of Japan is rapidly and permanently altering.

Bon Odori are disappearing just as Passion Plays and other festivals are vanishing from western Europe. People cease to be so careful in Japan to give the precise kind of lacquer boxes filled with tinted candy on the birth of a peasant proprietor's grandchild. In Europe, swains lose much of their ardor for planting birch trees in front of their sweethearts' homes. Women's pride in making fine festival robes wanes in the "flowery kingdom" just as the silver ornaments and local caps grow less common among Brittany or Frisian village belles. Much that went to make up the "pride of the peasant"—the loyalty to landlord and gods, the feeling of oneness with nature, community and empire—is surely doomed in two continents, while Americans have had much less of it at any time.

Bon Odori, for instance, are now regulated by edicts from Tokyo, center of changing religion. Local municipal officials supervise the dances, presented on formal platforms, before people politely looking on the way moderns would, without betraying primal animation. Villagers must not "sing their wild songs nor wear fancy costumes after midnight." If everybody behaves, there may be municipal fireworks. And the people are more inclined to meet the Government's wishes every year; they are not wholly suppressed by Tokyo; they are altered from within. Yau Yokose in the *Bunsho Orai* (Literary Intercourse) says: "Now there are no more village feuds or happenings such as a whole village raiding another for their women. The people are more far-sighted and deem it more fun to go to some popular place four or five miles away on new bicycles and in their best rig . . . than do such mad things as they did twenty years ago."

Religious exaltation, moreover, melts away among the

Japanese peasantry in proportion to the energy of the Buddhist Church, drawn into their legal squabbles, in assuming secular control. Being a landowner itself, the Church has trouble with the rural folk. They want to use temples for meeting places—the only big rooms, often, in a village. So the temples have become centers of conflict, the peasants claiming the right to them for their union meetings directed toward redress of grievances as a "party of the first part," and as the second party the clerical landlords trying to hold the village priests in line with their superiors. One Japanese writer claims that although social workers were formerly largely Christian in the villages, "at present they are more Marxian in theory," and thus the trend among the Japanese peasants is probably further away from orthodox religion than contemporary agrarian movements in the West.

Inevitably the peasant in all countries begins to feel attached by more important ties to the city than to Nature, so long his sovereign. We know that Tokyo censors his gods and watches over his morals, compels his children to enter schools and dictates what they study, fixes his taxes, booms the price of his land and regulates the prices of his products. If he has a grievance, he inclines to believe that it is not to some local god or ducal castle on a nearby hill that he must go for help, but to the capital, where city politicians will trade for his vote at least an "inquiry into the rural situation." He becomes acquainted with urban laboring men, less numerous than the peasants but more aggressive, who urge him to make common cause in a class strife. He realizes that the city is his ruler and antagonist; that captains of industry and political leaders in Tokyo parade plans to industrialize the country and would, if they could, blacken with factory smoke or line with electric wire his landscape and make a clean sweep of his occupation and home. Through

Tokyo, finally, the peasant feels intimately connected with the world at large; perhaps more than other peasants, he actually depends on the outside world. His indigo plants must wither when "foreign devils" invent synthetic dyes; his family must suffer when silk goes down in price in America or when Javanese tea leaves instead of his own are steeped in foreign bowls. It is no longer enough to watch the weather—he must watch the latest quotation on the rice and fertilizer markets. It is no longer enough to pray for success before an Inari shrine; he must study Tokyo's newest method of standardizing silkworm egg cards.

Contact with the city increases with every year. Roads now bring pleasure seekers on motorcycles through the former dense forests to the foot of Fuji, where once Nichiren and other anchorites communed in silence; they spread their dust and noise along the quiet sea-coast villages as tourists ride to temple groves. The nation-wide road-building program, though slowly, yet steadily is pushed ahead. And the well-off farmer has a bicycle himself, on which he may ride to a meeting of the Japan Peasant Union. Periodicals bring his daughters fashion knowledge from the metropolis and make them long to exchange their blue scarf headgear for "modan" hats and accessories.

Developing urban suburbs threaten to devour the countryside, boosting land values so high that it no longer pays as well to till the soil in the environs of a city as to rent the farmhouse for a summer villa. Tourists from Tokyo and "summer people," the Japanese having recently acquired that classification, diffuse in the villages luxurious ideas and desecrate the shrines with postcard booths, in the manner of New England resorts. Country folk go to the city just as the city comes to them, permanently or for seasons.

In the beginning the girls seem to have regarded the shift

to town as a temporary exigency—to meet a dowry need or to tide the family over a crisis. Indeed, so prone were they to forsake the textile mills, greedy for cheap operatives, that the plants generally installed dormitories surrounded by high walls, in order to hold them, at least until their contracts had expired. Waitresses and servants in like manner often expect to return to the villages with their savings, whether they actually do so or not. Successfully, or unsuccessfully, hundreds of thousands of country girls thus establish town contacts which leave imprints on their spirit. The females outnumber the males in Japanese factories, and office and restaurant workers are conspicuously feminine these days. Several thousand boys go annually to municipal or private or Imperial schools to study agriculture, sericulture or forestry. So that every year more young people catch a glimpse of lives softer than those lived on the soil and, if they return to the land, they infect it with ambition for higher standards of living. By no means do all the fugitives return. In Japan, as with us, a boy who studies agriculture at a university is apt to teach in the city, rather than go back home to practice. What a demoralizing effect this trend toward the cities is having may be realized from the fact that in the past two generations the proportion of the Japanese population on the farms has dropped from eighty to forty-eight per cent of the total, and is rapidly sinking further. Much land is suffered to lie idle; crops other than rice are declining; peasant proprietors decrease at the rate of 10,000 a year; both the landlords' and the tenants' offspring seek the cities, and now it can be said that "Today for the first time in Japan's history, the population of the cities and towns above 5,000 people is greater than that of the country." The census of 1925 shows only forty-four per cent of the nation is living in places of less than 5,000 people.

Great cities, if few in number, throw their shadows far across the landscape. They control the habits and fortunes of country people more and more tightly; they inspire them with new desires and restless quests; they lure them to paved streets and there stamp them indelibly with an urban brand, The Japanese resemble the Europeans and Americans in never regaining, once lost, the peasant heart and mind and body. The long-enduring strength passes out of their systems. Nor is this urbanization all that happens to a peasant class. The modern age creates a tendency toward consolidation and more efficient management of the land in two hemispheres. Thus Japanese landlords are trying to standarize fruit, grain and cocoons instead of perpetuating the careless handling of strains, varying from town to town, even from farm to farm. They are also trying to merge small holdings, save the wasted boundary space and cultivate such enlarged areas by hydro-electric power or, failing in this expensive operation, by more efficient man-power. In one experiment it was found that a simple farmer could cultivate alone an area formerly employing six men. In the country as well as in factories there is less and less room, it is claimed, for inefficient labor—notwithstanding the fact that overcrowding and oversupply increase alarmingly. The more mouths there are to feed, the fewer hands need be employed. The result of this process is already visible: two extreme types of landowners multiplying—those holding more than one thousand acres and those tilling less than one and one-quarter acres. The former middle-class peasant proprietor who used to own and manage from seven to twenty-five acres is being squeezed out, partly, some say, because he is losing his taste for the double responsibility of rice and silk production, which a rich man can assume through his command of extra labor and which a very poor family is wont to take upon itself. Consequently, in the country and in cities, the class rifts broaden, upper and lower, employer and proletariat, landlord and tenant grow in number, while the former self-sufficient yeoman with the petty tradesman and artisan is dwindling. In the midst of intensifying poverty, congestion of population and weakening of familiar standards comes an ever-sharpening consciousness of class to prepare the way for conflict.

For conflicts, however, such as fill the years with ever-swelling din, the upper classes in Japan have apparently their own provocation to blame. Landlords, by exercising during the Great War the right given to them by laws, copied from Western codes, to evict tenants from lands that had been tilled by their ancestors since almost immemorial times, taught peasants to organize their animosities as a means of survival. Courts, by upholding this break in mediæval custom, made clear to many a slow-moving rural mind for whose benefit his country was being ruled. And thus the city became responsible for the cry of the country, voiced in the platform of the All-Japan Farmers' Federation in 1926: "We deny the unhealthy culture and civilization of the cities, but we are determined to realize a new culture and civilization in the rural districts."

With startling rapidity the antagonism of the peasantry has taken shape. The Radical Japan Peasant Union in 1922 had less than 300 members, but five years later had enrolled nearly 60,000. The number of tenants' unions increased from 376 to 3,926 in 1926. Meanwhile, during those years, unions of landlords tripled in number. The annual crop of disputes augmented in size and in bitterness. In 1918 there had been eighty-five disputes brought to court, but a decade later there were more than two thousand.

Up to 1922, in the worst of times, only two or three hun-

dred disputes a year over rents or other matters had been
carried into court. There was still much confusion as to the
exact rights of landlords. Title deeds were often non-exist-
ant, the peasants holding fields by immemorial custom rather
than by legal warrant; it has been a tradition that no one
might thrust them from the land and let them starve, even if
they failed to pay rent, for the Tokugawas shrewdly reasoned
that it was better to support peasants than build up the power
of landlords. Not until scores of legal fights in the courts resulted in a series of victories for the landlords did the sudden
rise in the quantity of disputes begin, spreading from prefecture to prefecture. Month by month, in that year, tension
increased. Mobs of angry villagers were collecting here and
there, planning retaliation in secret or openly menacing the
local landholders. In vain the village merchants attempted
to act as mediators. Sabotage and strong-arm methods were
more frequently employed. Believing the landlords would
not evict them from fields where rice had been planted, peasants banded together to rush through the planting work. To
prevent them, landlords forcibly occupied the fields, imported Korean peasants as strike breakers, and, finally, went
to the length of seizing the already planted rice and auction-
ing it in the fields. Faced with starvation by such extreme
measures, thousands of villagers in one prefecture, that of
Gifu, attacked landlords' homes, burning one, and mobbing
the police station when they heard that the frightened landlords had called for soldiers to protect them. Children dramatically joined another strike at Kizaki Village, refusing to
study beside the landlords' children; the Farmers' Association built a special school for them, Toyohiko Kagawa,
the noted Christian reformer, acting as principal, aided by
three Waseda University graduates and a woman social
worker. Other villages took up the idea. In some places

warehouses were erected to store grain with which to support the dissidents in time of strife. The new independent spirit is shown by the several "bone-dry" villages, such as Kawai-tami in Ishikawa prefecture, where all the households agreed to go without liquor, fastening scarlet "Prohibition Here" signs on the doorposts, while the liquor dealers voluntarily withdrew from the business, enabling the village to collect eight thousand yen ($4,000) in a few years for a new school-house out of the savings on saké. When steadily growing unions of peasants were answered by hastily formed land-lord associations, the small peasant proprietors, who had a plot or two to rent, faced the question whether they would join the big fellows or the tenant dissenters.

A sudden turn toward political action checked the trend toward physical violence. The Manhood Suffrage Bill passed in 1924 was a safety valve for popular excitement. Peasants now directed their energies toward campaigning for local elections and secured increasing percentages of proletarian members in country and town assemblies. In some com-munities they secured a majority and at once lowered the rents so drastically as to ruin and exile their enemy land-lords, taking revenge with perfect legality. In 1927, aiming higher, they helped elect a score of proletarians to prefec-tural assemblies.

Popular leaders began to appear, men fresh from fields and seldom with more than the primary education of their neighbors; such is the politician, nicknamed "Matsu the Moustache," who finds "making speeches the best medicine for his illnesses," and the equally popular Ichitaro Hirano, whose children cry: "Father loves disputes better than mother and us." As the unions grew stronger and the leaders bolder, they started to invade the cities, summoning urban labor to their aid and trying to mix in national politics and even international affairs. They brought pressure to bear on Diet members, asking them to meetings and sending delegates to theirs. Exciting physical brushes occurred; for example, when a Minseito party man, a former Minister of Agriculture and Forestry, publicly attacked the Government policy before an audience of farmers, men representing the criticized party rushed the platform, only to be "gathered in" by watchful guardians of the peace. Demonstrations grow more frequent in the capital and farmers' wives come in to parade, met at the station by urban men with banners.

No united front, however, have they learned to present. And so the landlords and capitalists enjoy the advantages of their disunion. In a bewildering succession they form, reform, and dissolve political parties and unions. They can neither agree on what they want for themselves nor on a joint program with urban labor. One of the four leading farmer unions supports the Labor Federation, whereas the All Japan Farmers' Federation refuses to coöperate with city labor, while another denounced indeed "any form of centralization on cities" demanding the "founding of rural community centers" and the development of a rural "culture." Only one real national union has been formed, the Japan Agricultural Union—a merger in 1926 of the Tokyo and Osaka labor-farmer groups led by Suzuki and Kagawa. Its appearance was significant though its membership is still small.

Great diversity reigns also among party platforms. They do not agree on any set of solutions for their problems; but they all make clear that dozens of reforms are called for. Thus the moderate Farmer-Labor Party wants woman suffrage, freedom of speech, military retrenchment, abolition of secret diplomacy, revision of factory and tenancy laws, the right to strike, fixing of the price of staples, abolition of

licensed prostitution, old-age insurance, and many other
things. One politically active, radical Union voiced opposition to Japan's interference in China. Another Proletarian
Party of peasants and workers, which was dissolved in 1925
by the Tokyo police, demanded a thoroughgoing change of
the Japanese government—no less in fact than the sweeping
away of the General Staff, Office of Admiralty and Privy
Council, House of Peers and Genro, as well as disarmament
and colonial autonomy. But such proposals failed to secure
unanimous consent within its own ranks. They evoked a
storm of stone-throwing, hissing, and protest when they were
presented; the tramcar workers left the meeting in disgust;
and the police "quietly but firmly" proceeded with the work
of "gathering in" the leaders. Racked by dissensions between
communist and moderate, peasant and worker, and torn by
vague, visionary longings for a better world order, coupled
with demands for immediate satisfaction, it is plain that the
peasants do not yet count big in Japanese politics.

Nevertheless, they have struck alarm in high places. In
1926 there were thought to be nearly 350,000 members enrolled in tenant unions, whereas labor unions totalled a
membership of only 260,000. Shocked at this portent, when
a "communist plot" was unearthed in 1928, Premier Tanaka
issued a solemn warning to the whole nation that it was
"designed to replace our glorious national policy with an
autocracy of laborers and farmers." Whatever the peasants
have failed to gain, they have at least drawn attention to
their potentialities.

Unable, in the style of a Mussolini, to order the young
men of the nation to stay contentedly on the farm—for
Japanese autocracy, despite its bravado, hesitates to exercise
such far-reaching power over the multitude—the political
leaders rush to and fro with assorted schemes for control.

Some wish to solve the problem by developing finer agricultural economy; others would simply suppress, by the sword if need be, every uprising; yet others would like to industrialize the nation and thus abolish all annoying agriculture. There are propagandists who advocate prohibition as an aid to prosperity; some point out the savings that army and navy reduction would bring; the Kenseikai party advocates a wholesale government monopoly of land; and again and again, a small minority proclaims the inevitability of birth control as the great solution.

The Government itself has done little in return for rural votes. At first it attempted to form arbitration boards in the country for the settlement of disputes. Then it planned special school readers to encourage youth to stay in the fields, selecting such topics as "Honor in the Agricultural Industry," "Roots of Pine Trees," "Love Living Creatures," and "Harmful Insects on the Farm." It voted various subsidies to aid agriculture, encourage farmers to produce more eggs in order to compete with Chinese imports and rear cattle, carp, and frogs for food, and help silk growers by teaching them to breed better winter worms. It adopted a "health program," if pitifully meager compared with the billions of yen disbursed on reconstructing Tokyo and Yokohama, when it proposed to build only a few maternity hospitals, study some rural diseases, erect a single "model village" and equip three other villages with "model plumbing." The proposals failed to appease the Peasants' Union. Another scheme, more grandly sounding, offered aid to peasants seeking to reclaim by irrigation and own land, but this proved both an expensive burden to taxpayers and a help to landlords in disguise. Ironically enough, the Seiyukai, or Government party, supported by the mass of unorganized farmers, has had as its chairman Premier Tanaka, who advocates wholesale industrialization. He would turn the country over to the business man.

Whether any compromise is possible, no one seems to know. Neither landlords nor peasants are well off with land at its present high prices; even though they may exact sixty per cent of their tenants' crops every year, the landlords can scarcely pay their taxes and daughters' dowries. There is no room for all the peasants, let alone for idle landlords, on the intensively worked Japanese islands. Nor is it possible to increase rice production so very much; the limit has almost been reached both in Japan and throughout the warm, wet regions of south Asia generally. Korean farmers begin to want rice instead of cheap barley to eat at their own tables, and that fact complicates production and exchange. Mere tenancy laws or arbitration boards are but trifles in the face of the desperate realities. Japan will not support both peasants and subsidized industry. She must choose between them to some extent at least.

The line-up in the contest between city and country, business and agriculture grows every day more distinct. They are irreconcilable foes. *Bushido,* the chivalric code of the knight, was not incompatible in mediæval times with the pride of the peasant, but to-day the demands of the industrialists and merchants are crushing all that once made life tolerable for the toiler in the paddy-fields and for his helpmate coddling the silkworms.

CHAPTER XVIII

THE UPTHRUST OF MASSES

At almost any hour of the day or evening, a familiar tap might sound on the door of our living room in Tokyo and presently there would stride into our midst a stalwart man, unwinding a bright muffler from his neck and swinging a long cape back from his heavy shoulders as he roared the greeting: "Here am I, just Honda! No bother!"

Unlike the cautious aristocrats, Honda, a hearty plebeian, was wont to shrink neither from laughter nor from self-disclosure. He would settle upon a chair and for hours, perhaps half a day, pour forth a steady stream of speech in his vivid English, which consisted partly of the classical forms learned at college and partly of queer, rummy oaths which he had picked up in his youth as a rickshaw boy, hauling Englishmen, it would appear, from one taproom to another. At times he would apologize for some unusually pungent bit with the booming: "No bother! Just Honda!" Often he asked about incredible America, where women, he heard, might actually be judges. I don't think he believed our tales, but he welcomed them with good-humored laughter, so loud and infectious we usually joined in. He recounted stories in return. He heard a lecturer tell a group of Buddhist priests that an American President once chopped down a cherry tree—yes, a cherry tree! Probably in blossom, at that! And then the prospective President said, as he put his sword back through his *hakama:* "Father, I cannot tell a lie!" The priests had thought this a curious anecdote but Honda jovially roared: "It won't hurt them!"

He brought his daughter one morning, a shy mite of a baby with a fresh pinafore over her bright kimono. He was exceedingly proud of her and across her head, glossy as a doll's, he shouted: "Yes, she may be a judge some day! But never a geisha; not if Honda lives!" Often he arranged parties for us, carrying us off to visit schools and be introduced to sundry illustrious persons for whom he acted as interpreter. On returning by motor from such events, which he hugely enjoyed, he used to rock with laughter, crying: "Did you see the Countess? Did you see the Dean? They were there, weren't they? And you were there, weren't you?" He would fairly double up with happiness. "And there was I—just Honda!"

Our acquaintance with this merry personage began in the best romantic tradition. We were strolling, after the fashion of Haroun-al-Raschid, in search of adventure through the city at night. By a bookstall where we had halted and, just as the lanternlight revealed our faces, a tall stranger, recognizing us from snapshots in newspapers, addressed us, begging to be excused for his boldness as an interested teacher of English in a Tokyo High School, and forthwith invited us to his home. Along many a lane we followed his flapping cape, down the dark and narrow alleys that lead to the homes of the people, and finally through a low doorway into his "foreign-style" parlor. Here, while hours fled by, we listened to the story of our friendly host's life, learning how he rose from rickshaw-boy, through study at college and, owing to an unquestionable aptitude for languages, to a post as teacher and interpreter. Now, in this capacity, he could mingle with the rich and great and had moved in the company of lords and ladies so splendid that, every time he breathed their names, he must perforce raise his hand to his mouth in humility. The story of this rise in life was of the freshest wonder to him. The genial giant never wearied of relating its incidents and his climax was always the same jubilant outburst, a veritable explosion of delight: "And there was I . . . just Honda!"

The career of Honda-*san* may seem exceptional to one who imagines Japanese society to be rigidly stratified. Nevertheless, under proud titles and in high offices, are numerous men of humblest origins. The crested coat of a prince and the epaulettes of a general may grace non-aristocratic shoulders, even in the proud island monarchy. Titles are very misleading in fact; so famous a man as Viscount Shibusawa, one of the "grand old founders" of the modern nation, is said to have begun life as a farmer boy; in time he was received into the ranks of the samurai and thence promoted. A number of rich merchants have been given "court rank," which, though not strictly a title, is a claim to social precedence peculiar to Japan and much coveted. Wealth is not inevitably the possession of the noble for, out of fifteen highest taxpayers of Tokyo recently listed, only two were titled. Counts, millionaire magnates, political leaders and many others may be whispering beneath their breath, while they enjoy the favors of fortune: "Here am I—just Honda!"

A glance about the political field is illuminating. One learns how eight Proletarian members of the Diet were compelled to refuse an invitation to the Imperial Cherry Blossom Party because they had no silk hats. Startling is such information as Santaro's: "Almost every one of the fifteen Premiers Japan has produced in the past half-century was the child of poverty, if not indigence." Elsewhere we find that ex-Premier Wakatsuki, for instance, began his career as the poor teacher of a primary school; that ex-Premier Takahashi

toiled in America as "farm worker and domestic servant";
how the late General Tanaka's father was the humble porter
of a palanquin, a trade closely resembling that of Honda-
san's youth.

If we look at the 1929 Cabinet, we may discover a most
dramatic character, "Wild Man" Koizumi. He started public
life as a small-town fireman, married to a beautiful geisha.
Gradually he worked up as janitor of a politician's home, as
teacher in a lowly post, as town councillor, and finally, as
leader of mass meetings, to political influence. With none
but the most elementary education, without important official
status, and moreover so poor that he was long in arrears with
his rent for a forty-yen-a-month home, he seems to have
proved himself indispensable to politics by his gift for inspir-
ing crowds. Probably, like Honda-*san,* he had the plebeian
force and volubility that equipped him for political management. For twenty years, it is said, without pay, he fought for
the cause of manhood suffrage. He was appointed Minister
by Premier Hamaguchi. The newspapers played him up then,
telling the Japanese world how, when summoned to the Premier's villa, his wife helped him into a worn frock coat but
didn't know how to arrange his necktie; how abashed he
looked at the title of "Excellency"; but how relieved he felt
at being safe from his landlord. He was pictured in the ceremonial group of the Cabinet, wearing a pleased, puzzled look
on his face which might very well have meant: "Here am I,
just Wild Man Koizumi!"

The Premier who chose this man of the people had himself been a boy as poor and plain as Calvin Coolidge. "Lion"
Hamaguchi, as he is called, was born in a remote fishing village and his youth was as thrifty and industrious as any in a
storybook. He was adopted into a good family—a common
occurrence in Japan—and when he rose, through the Finance

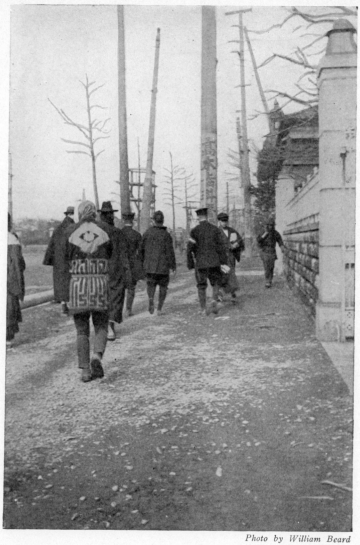

AN ARREST DURING THE VOTES FOR MEN CAMPAIGN

Ministry to power, the villagers had to raise a fund for his seventy-five-year-old brother to go to Tokyo and visit him. "Lion" Hamaguchi has another resemblance to Calvin Coolidge; he is renowned for his ingenuous silences and his dislike of society. They say he never spoke to a geisha but once in his life and that was to enquire in his abrupt way: "In what fiscal year of Meiji were you born?"

The Lion and the Wild Man came into office in 1929, taking positions just vacated by high officials with titles and wealth much more imposing but of origins similarly obscure. General Baron Tanaka, the retiring Premier, for all his military pomp, had come up from the lower ranks, acting at one time as "student-servant." In his upward climb, he was aided by a friend, Kuhara, who, originally a warehouse keeper, finally made millions in copper mining, real estate and fertilizer. From gratitude, Tanaka made Kuhara his Minister of Communications, and it was this millionaire ex-warehouse-keeper whom the Wild Man replaced.

Colorful as are the stories of individuals who have risen from the mass, there is another and more significant tale to be recounted: the slow but general emergence of the mass itself. Famines, plagues, the tyranny of lords and the terror of local wars have become historic memories. Consequently life in general is safer, healthier, and more hopeful than it was in the "good old days." For great numbers there is yet more to be reckoned as gain: a higher material standard of living and a constant growth of self-respect.

Perhaps one cannot do better than to quote, in illustration, the remark of a guardian of clogs in a Tokyo theater, who was interviewed, among many other greater and lesser citizens, on the occasion of his first balloting in the year 1928. What Sadanji Mori, humble watchman, said was this: "I was free to vote. I wouldn't listen to anybody whatever he said. I voted for the man I liked best. Judging from the way the new election law was adopted, I think the time we laborers dominate will come earlier than first thought. I tell you we laborers don't lie. The world is becoming interesting." And that last sentence is indeed the point; for millions of Japanese people life is now not merely safe—it is even interesting.

Materially, Japan is so much better off than her Oriental neighbors that Japanese capitalists, looking abroad for cheaper labor, consider moving to Korea, where wages are almost half those of Japan, or to China, where men work longer on less food. While the curve of industrial production has for half a century risen faster than the population, the per capita consumption of rice, grain, and fish has mounted in the past generation. According to the Bureau of Fisheries, "fish consumption has doubled every ten years for several decades" and the increased stature of boys and girls of school age bears testimony to improved nutrition. People who once were forbidden by sumptuary laws to wear socks in winter, now wear *tabi;* they buy charcoal and school textbooks; they read by electric light at night; they use water from public works. Conditions in several large factories already show a considerable improvement on the handicraft system where no supervision could successfully be carried out; if Japan's factories leave much to be desired, so do the little, old-fashioned sweatshops which are mostly dark, damp firetraps, in which children may be mercilessly overworked. Several labor leaders, I found, are inclined to regard the factory system favorably, for at least legislation may improve factories, but what can anyone do with homes? Moreover, common people, whose surplus earnings were rigorously taxed away by the feudal shoguns, now make up a list of thirty-one million depositors in savings banks, divided into

classes, as agriculturists, laborers and school children, with
a billion and more yen to their credit. Labor has scratched
together coins for coöperative associations and election campaigns; mutual aid has kept up several long, hard strikes,
such as a seven-month Noda battle; a laborers' association
now has a small bank of its own.

The people's mental status shows equally definite gains.
Where formerly not one in a hundred, it has been estimated,
could read, to-day hodcarriers may peruse election pamphlets
and write their names on voting lists. In the new jury system, humble men sit in judgment, bewildered but proud.
Remarkable advances have been made all along the line in
the past dozen years; in labor organization and legislation,
and in public care and consideration. Even the despised *Eta,*
or "Defiled," feel the stirring, for some of them now teach
in universities; peers aid their "Water-Level Society" which
denounces social—there are no legal—discriminations against
them. They scrutinize textbooks for objectionable references
and in fact they confiscated gramophone records of a certain
melodrama I had seen at the Imperial Theater, showing an
outcast in none too pleasant a light. With a pride, indicative
of their self-respect, they cried out in their manifesto of 1927,
that their ancestors "were laughed at, cursed and spat on, but
bore their lot with unbending souls. Their blood runs in our
veins, and now is the time for us to arise, and cleanse the
brand of martyrdom from our brows. . . . We should be
proud of the name of 'Defiled Ones.' " In this declaration is
compressed the folk-history of Japan: the people have long
been stubborn, and at last they are defiant.

Steadily these masses have been taught coherence and
expression. A national system of education has forced a
common speech, wiping away many dialects; it has impressed
upon them also the national ethics of Shinto and has taught

them, under the guise of history, the consciousness of a uniform heritage. Military training has increased the pride of the plebeian who now bears weapons, once the privilege of the knight, and feels himself responsible for the defense of the Empire. Industrialism, herding country people into the smoky area of the Southern cities, has made homeless and restless groups of proletariat; within a generation, labor has stretched its ranks from a few hundred thousand members to over four million. Foreign wars with their booms and crashes and the incoming tides of "dangerous ideas" from abroad have done the rest. And finally, so advanced has this consciousness become that the Government with serene determination gave nine millions the vote, and thus took them into partnership. Out of the masses has been thrust a group unique in the Oriental world—a public!

A public! A great body of men and women able to read and able also to buy considerable quantities of printed matter; having strong and definite interests in place of resigned philosophy or apathy; having, too, a sense of cohesion drawn from the possession of common symbols, a common language and background, and at least a tolerance in matters of religion. It is not a mass of indifferent fatalists, nor yet of rabid revolutionaries; in the truest sense of the word it is a public —a great society, not on the march but on the watch.

Above all, it is held together by hope. In neighboring China, there has been insufficient stability for public enterprise. What use to improve a civic water-supply plant if to-morrow the bandits will occupy the city? What use to be an honest government official if one's predecessor has already collected the taxes for seven years to come? But in Japan, gloomy as the horizon may often appear, there is room and security for movement ahead. Men continue to rise in office; merchants develop trade; workers win strikes; ships sail on appointed days; trains run on schedule; interest is paid on loans; schools open on the hour. To employ an abused phrase, the Japanese public is "forward looking." The undertones one detects in newspaper editorials, it is true, are very often skeptical and embittered; nevertheless there is a general feeling that improvement is possible, that things must continue to get better—that surely the rise of the masses is not in vain—surely there will be no descent.

"How large is this public?" one may ask. It is capable of absorbing five million copies a day of newspapers—and each paper is read by frugal neighbors. A single paper I have seen suffice for a score of rickshawmen. Of magazines, astounding numbers of copies a day are sent through the mails alone, not counting the sales from the stands.

The public purchases the copies of 20,000 new books each year, and the output of more than 5,000 periodicals of widely varied kinds. Some other figures may be given to indicate the size of this audience: three cities in 1928 estimated that they had 370,000 listeners for their radio stations. Equally impressive have been the successes of several series of popular literature reprints, a single selection of modern plays securing 400,000 subscribers.

The enchantment of the past had been successfully preached to me and only gradually, as I listened to the old people, who had lived in the early Meiji days, did developments acquire any meaning. I heard a grandmother describe the Meiji theater, when crucifixions were presented in a manner so lurid that modern citizens would certainly not endure it, and grandfathers rehearse the bitter hardships which were commonplaces of their youth. Reading helped to render graphic the rougher period when beggars fawned by the wayside, when corpses were flung into the Sumida, when executions were as much a public show as in the London of Samuel Pepys. Furthermore, on the stage, in classical plays, I saw represented the "toughs" and bullies of Yedo, swaggering buccaneers, flaunting gorgeous kimono, drinking, roaring, insulting the meek citizenry, and trying their blades on criminals. A samurai might test the edge of a new sword on a beggar or a dog—but he preferred a beggar, for the hair of a dog was apt to turn a fine edge.

Plenty of unimpeachable witnesses arise in the press from time to time to testify to progress. For instance, Professor Namae contrasted the period when a family was delighted just to have food—a little rice and a bit of fish—with to-day, when humble folk feel amusement and recreation to be their natural right. Viscount Shibusawa, after a careful weighing of losses and gains in his "Hundred Days," concludes that, on the whole, the level of wealth and general well-being have both been lifted. So authoritative a person as Dr. Washio makes the striking statement: "There is not much of that sneaking, lean and hungry, haunted sort of air which we used to see on the face of every plebeian of middle Meiji. What big heroes men like Admiral Kabayama and General Oyama looked among the small ill-fed commoners of the time!" It is his opinion that, if the standard of men at the helm of state has gone down, that of plebeians has "come up marvelously." The late Count Oki, an early governor of Tokyo, is quoted as saying: "You speak of the people of the slum quarters being hard up in these days, but the poor in the first two years of Meiji (1868-9) were in a condition which almost passes your imagination."

Bunji Suzuki, the famous labor leader, referred in a speech to the years when his followers shrank in the presence of a visitor in splendid uniform if such happened to attend their meetings. Now, he said, they would "make fun" of a pompous dignitary and he concluded: "In those days laborers were conscious of their position. To-day they are morally and intellectually elevated much higher and their efficiency has also been raised accordingly."

Their advances, to be sure, have largely been a case of luck. The "founders" of modern Japan were probably as sublimely unconscious of the long future as our own "founding Fathers." Historians generally presume that those who wrote the famous oath of Emperor Meiji, which corresponds in importance with the American Declaration of Independence, were unaware of the full import of their words when they said: "All measures shall be decided by public opinion." They were so aristocratic that it doubtless never occurred to them that the "public" might some day mean, not a feudal aristocracy, but clog-keepers and carpenters. If the clause was stretched, later, to take in millions of plain folk, it was because a disgruntled knighthood, excluded from the Government and left without arms or estates in a world of money-grabbing, formed the first "Liberal Party" and raised the dangerous cry of "the people." They meant themselves, but friends of laborers, merchants and commoners joined them until no line could be drawn any more. In Japan, as throughout the nations, slogans tend like water to run downhill.

Unintentional on the part of labor too has been the rise, for the most part. Helping hands have been extended from above. Kagawa, missionary to the poor and organizer of farmers, was no worker to start with; neither was the industrial workers' organizer, Suzuki, the "Samuel Gompers" of the East, who came through the Imperial University and newspaper reporting to his social enterprise. The first labor unions were inspired by a benevolent capitalist, Teiichi Sakumu, in 1884. Middle-class women have been the investigators of the conditions of their sisters in mines, factories and domestic service. Waseda University professors formed a Fabian Society and Association for Political Studies—nuclei for socially-minded intellectuals. Professors from various seats of learning, joined by lawyers and officials and frequently aided by students, worked hard for humanitarian legislation. A Waseda professor organized the Farmers' Union; three professors, Abe, Horiye and Yoshino, in 1926 formed a party advocating "the establishment of political and economic institutions for the intellectual and physical laboring classes."

Religion played the same forceful part in the early labor movement in Japan that it did in England. The first Labor Federation started in a Unitarian Church and in fact the police of Tokyo thought it must be a species of religious sect. This religious zeal still inspires Kagawa—an evangelizing influence such as the West hardly knows any more though it was a decided factor in English labor history.

Horror at the effects of the industrial revolution—a horror part æsthetic and part moral indignation—turned the sympathies of comfortable bourgeois toward the sufferings of other persons, suggesting another analogy, that of Ruskin and Matthew Arnold. Middle class were the novelists and essayists who "exposed" the "underworld." The first investigators who went "slumming" were as fearful as New York society beaux when they ventured to Hell's Kitchen among the "Plug-ugly Gang." Yet year by year the exploration went on until of late an Imperial Prince and a mayor paid visits formally to the people in municipal lodging houses. What began as a kind of curiosity has become a gesture of deference exacted of the great.

All this, it seems to me, shows a remarkable kinship between the Japanese and the Western development. But despite these similarities the background of the Japanese story has its local color.

Chanty-singing, for instance, still echoes along the lanes wherever builders are at work on superstructures or piles are driven into the ground. And one still sees singing workmen clambering up the bamboo scaffolds, like copper statues against the sky. Delivery boys continue to wear the blue cotton jackets elaborately inscribed with the insignia of their masters' houses. Little maidservants, flopping out of houses in every alley, wearing nondescript brown kimono and carrying kimono lengths stretched on wooden boards in lieu of ironing, appear to pursue customs as non-modish as their looks; most of them have but two holidays in a year when, as in days of yore, they visit the temple of Emma, Judge of Hades.

Especially Eastern seem the handicraft shops where the larger part of Japanese manufacturing still is carried on. Deep in the caverns of buildings where the casual sightseer would never spy, working in damp and dark wooden cells in cramped position and half blinded by close application in the bad light, children were shown us who dared not take time to look up as we slipped in, so pressed were they with their weaving, embroidering and inlaying. Without, in the shop part, the silk-robed master, bowing, displayed the heaps of finished silks with their golden dragons and other hand-made goods. Like the maidservants, these apprentices get two holidays a year. One in January they spend in search of more skill and to obtain it they run through the streets in the cold night to a Fudo Temple where they pour icy water over themselves and then run, run, home. The only sign of the break with ancient habits is the fact that now they wear thin white kimono as they run whereas, formerly, a birthday suit was deemed sufficient for the ceremony. Blessed handicrafts!

Shelter is sometimes but nominal. The 350,000 persons officially listed in Tokyo as "poor" are packed into slum districts of which more than a dozen are scattered about the city. Some 40,000 are said to lack family care and self-support; thousands depend on charity; droves of unemployed besiege the municipal lodging houses in winter and in summer try to sleep in the parks. Great numbers are glad enough to give the name of home to any square box in which certain members of the family may lie down while the rest curl up as best they can in the absence of full-length space; they are grateful for the money merely to rent a quilt for a cold season, from usurious brokers.

In quarters where the average daily expenditure is fifteen cents, live many of the "characters" whose personalities enliven the congested lanes: such as the vagrant son of a samurai who knew too little of arithmetic to become a great trader and bureaucrats cast out of office in middle age and compelled to give up the white collar for the coolie coat. Hedge-priests ramble to and fro with perhaps a mumbling sorcerer at their heels, presenting that other side to Eastern mysticism—the saintly beggars who live on coins lured from hungry women. Here are the story tellers who entertain the poor with anecdote and ballad; the little girls sold as apprentices to tight-rope walkers and geisha; ragpickers; the hairdresser out of work because of the craze for bobbed locks; the sedan carrier displaced by the taxi service. Bold robbers lurk about in the daytime and at night pry open the wooden shutters of the plump burghers; while the Preaching Burglar, or the evil impostor who steals from the blind, may operate day or night. Gangsters and gamblers are the activists; the everlasting blind of the East are the passivists who wait in these tiny cells for the end, supported meanwhile by the labor of child drudges or aged crones. Thousands of these

WATER GYPSIES

brave, simple folk work as hard as they can. Others, on the brink of failure, clothe their children in their best kimono, buy them toys and take them to the movies, before they put a ceremonial finish to their tragic lives.

Moreover the boat people, "water gypsies" as someone has named them, are part of the abounding poor. These river folk, whose only connection with land is by a narrow swaying plank, live out their days on the water in barges, buy incense and worship in boats, and keep their children safe from truant officers of the schools. A friendly folk they are, glad to welcome a foreign guest down the slippery runway and pass him from vessel to vessel with jests, or pose for snap-shots—less afraid of the evil eye than the boat people of Canton in China.

Great, flat-bottomed barges are theirs, splashed with de-signs in black or red, cumbered with cargo, sails, poles, and straw bags. The entire wealth of the family is compressed into one small hole in the stern deck—a diminutive cabin containing a pot with a bit of charcoal for cooking, a few yards of cloth, a brush or a knife, nothing more. From the corner ooze babies; a mother squats in it cooking; wrinkled granddad and grandmother watch the little boys who wriggle on deck or fish in the gray-green waters of the Sumida. On New Year's Day, even these boats become festive. A barge would be destitute indeed that could not afford a tiny sprig of pine or a straw rope with a paper zigzag prayer tied upon it.

Many an afternoon I have watched the river people in the canal region near old Tsukiji, which used to be the foreign settlement, full of little brick houses, its sky fretted with masts. Ruined balconies with shuttered windows or bits of gay clothing hung to air loomed over the water—Venetian regions of boats and pageantry. By the Naval Arsenal

garden the barge groups can be quietly observed, sitting on
the simmering hot decks, smoking tiny pipes, chattering a
lot. Toward evening, they light the red lanterns and pole
away with a swish of dark water, singing ballads, mostly, I
suppose, about homesickness, for to Tokyo come drifting in
from all corners of the Empire the folksongs of Korea or
Formosa, ballads about teacher Ono who died saving her
pupils, of imprisoned geisha, of tea pickers toiling in the
fields, of fishermen in northern seas. One hears the song the
boatmen sing on the Yalu River:

High-swinging is the iron bridge over the river—
　The pale, great river dividing Chosen from China;
Through its dark framework see a thousand junks gliding,
　Far below, with swelling sails, down the river-way of prosperity!

For all the revolutions that have broken over them, the
Japanese masses have retained, to a degree that is amazing,
their heritage of simplicity, sentiment, and song. Where else,
for instance, are strikers' wives accustomed to make barefoot
pilgrimages to shrines to pray for victory? Where else would
electric workers, struggling for higher pay, rent three temples on the summit of most holy Koya Mountain, move in by
the hundreds, and refuse to leave until their demands were
granted, thus enlisting the aid of priests as mediators?
Where would one find despised folk, such as the outcast *Eta,*
banding together to avenge an insult to one of their number
and, before the attempt, pledging one another in cups of cold
water—the stern old Japanese way of saying *morituri salu-
tamus?*

Types, traditions, and incidents of mass life are distinctive
in countless ways. Striking delivery boys stand before a big
department store crying: "Ladies, beware of the Palace of
Vanity!" while their confrères slip inside and set snakes loose
among the shoppers who refuse to heed their warning. Some-

times strike sympathizers fill the shop in such throngs that no one else can pass through the door. Or "pestering" tactics are employed whereby tramcar conductors arrange for such a slow movement that the cars pile up all along the line. Kimonoed boy apprentices at the Labor School in Tokyo not only listen to lectures, study and discuss but play folk ballads on the *biwa*—a melancholy, moon-shaped guitar—and present with vivacious dramatic skill the plays of their own construction based on the life of the people. To these incidents are added the episodes which indicate the ramifications of the upthrust of masses, such as a landlord's daughter opposing her father's candidacy on account of his hostility to the demands of his tenants and committing protest-suicide when persuasion was of no avail. A high-school boy, fully aware that criticism might mean the wreck of his life career, turns his commencement address into a stirring denunciation of his school authorities' prejudices. An old rickshawman, who has spent years collecting case-histories of unfortunate people, stands up in a meeting, after various officials have finished congratulating one another on their excellent rule, to brandish his bundle of facts in their faces. An *Eta* soldier, in 1927, tied to his bayonet a petition, written on ceremonial rice paper, and kneeling held it out to the Emperor who rode by in review; to the credit of the Army, the soldier was dealt with lightly and the Minister of War issued orders that *Eta* should not be discriminated against. But how Japanese was the whole procedure: the hero, bent in his cell for many days in meditation; the company commander, overwhelmed at the incident, locking his front door and remaining inside for an equally long period!

In an Eastern milieu and in a peculiar manner, the work of helping the people up is carried on. Usually the atmosphere of social conferences was at first very solemn and it lightened only by degrees. This was largely due to the terrible cold of the Tokyo winter, unmitigated by heating arrangements, which made half the group sick. The participants—mostly men, with a sprinkling of women in somber garments—would sit for a time in melancholy groups, eyes downcast, like patients in a doctor's office. Occasionally a noted poetess would be present; ill with cold, she would shiver and wrap her thin hands in her sleeves. Another would be rubbing wrists swollen with chilblains, or rocking to and fro with coughing, wiping the eyes continuously. The types were always varied: tall, dark, morose persons; short, brisk individuals with white, stiff hair and twinkling eyes, bundled plumply in many layers of winter kimono; anæmic, thin idealists; the handsome, quizzical-looking elderly people, filled with an extraordinary zest for living, who would look around at the illnesses of the younger folk, as much as to say: "Well, well, dear friends, you should have had *my* Spartan discipline in youth! You should have seen the cold in early Meiji!"

Gradually, under the influence of conviction and companionship in effort, in spite of personal discomfort, the little party would begin to unfold. Eyes would brighten, arguments would commence, hands creep out of sleeves to emphasize a point. I heard one lively dialogue between a man who insisted it did not hurt women to drive piles, when they had babies strapped on their backs, and a fiery little woman who inquired how men would like to try that experiment. A quiet man in a corner would ask me some strange question, about feminine I. W. W.s in America it might be. And sometimes the most precise of the persons in the conference would rise, cough, and make a long speech on birth control or some such debate-fraught topic.

A DAY NURSERY IN TOKYO

Frequently I learned in these meetings the background of
the workers in social causes. For example, the Editor of the
Woman's Journal was inspired to his work of emancipation
by the woes of an elder sister, an abused slavey, who died of
grief. Some had come to social work through personal tragedies; others through theory alone. And there was usually
a rich person in the group—a vagabond-rich type so especially a Japanese product—who was lending a helping hand
and a ready fund of anecdote. Such was the merchant prince,
a benefactor of several societies and publications, who met
us with so hearty a handshake that it made one feel exactly
like a pump handle. He was the jovial, quizzical species of
Japanese, in whose presence one never is sure whether jest or
earnest is spoken, fond of sallies, telling about the home he
makes in one of Tokyo's worst slum quarters where no one
ever molests him. "I am very radical. I am more so than
Lenin or Trotsky. But I am, oh, so conservative in practice!"
He would chuckle, and then, quite suddenly declare: "I am a
pioneer of women's movement. I have read Olive Schreiner's
Woman and Labor fourteen times. I am probably the only
man in Japan, if not in the entire world, who has read Olive
Schreiner fourteen times." I found just such individual
stories and points of view among all these groups—no two
persons had had an identical approach to the social movement.

Though he was not a personal acquaintance, Mr. Zenze-
mon Iwasaki may be taken as a good illustration of Japanese
genial eccentricity, which is so general and so striking to an
outsider. Iwasaki is a poet and has had all sorts of adventures from jail to rickshaw pulling; he and his wife, a former
waitress, run a little restaurant to make the money they devote to a small, private home for the aged poor. And how

typical is his way of expressing defiance for bourgeois society! He dresses in the costume of a fishmonger, but on his shirt front, with the decorative Japanese handwriting, he has splashed two slogans, which all who meet him in the street or his home must read—"Those who do not work have no right to eat" and "Those who cannot work must be helped."

CHAPTER XIX

COMPETITION FOR POWER

VERY small, in comparison with the close-packed millions of the peasantry, is the group of men who actually rule Japan. But though few they have been extremely competent. They have guided a huge, complex, modern, governmental machine, which is rather insufficiently lubricated with money and somewhat overloaded with citizen passengers, for half a century, steering skillfully past the brinks of bankruptcy and across a terrain seamed with diplomatic pitfalls. The will and ability of Japanese political engineers have been the inspiration and envy of the whole Orient; many a Chinese statesman, such as Chiang Kai-shek, has come to study their secret at firsthand in Tokyo; in India the revolutionists have pointed to their work as the shining exhibit of Oriental independence; as far away as Turkey, Kemal Pasha has avowedly been strengthened in his war on ancient customs by their example. And numerous Westerners have been thrown into a panic by what they thought was an unnatural and portentous sight—an Eastern governmental machine that grinds steadily ahead, under its own steam.

Because this ruling body of men in Japan is so select, a great many outsiders have the idea that their government is a harsh, formal, military autocracy and nothing else. They imagine ruthless commanders issuing orders while, below, the masses obey with blind subservience. Because the Emperor is still a high priest, interceding with deity for his folk and their crops, they suppose the whole atmosphere of poli-

tics in Japan is charged with religious awe and befogged
with magic. Because the Japanese are famous for their courtesy, they presume all procedure must be coldly ceremonial.
Lest such remain in error, it would be well to quote from a
report of the proceedings of the Diet for January 4th, 1929:

The Minseito members' response added to the disturbance of the
floor and so seriously that one stout man in the public gallery suddenly exclaimed: "What can all this mean, gentlemen! We people
do not remember that we returned Beasts in the Menagerie to the
Diet!" No sooner had he finished than he was arrested by the Parliament guards. The Minseito group shouted for the Speaker of the
House to act, but in vain, until the guards interfered and order was
barely restored.

All the cheery, rowdy side of the Japanese nature, which
is suppressed during Noh dances or tea ceremonies, seems
to come out in the House of Representatives. The man who
acts like a graven image of sobriety at a reception can throw
inkwells with the best of them in the Diet. In their talent
for epithets, the Japanese politicians compare very favorably
with Washington Senators. And if Tammany Hall methods
did not prosper in Tokyo when a bold American-trained
Japanese sought to introduce them, a little while ago, it was
not because Japanese politicians are so holy or so religious,
but because they need no instruction in bossism or the
"ropes" of contract letting. Indeed I would say encourag-
ingly to all who fear the ominous might of Nippon that the
course of her political life is refreshingly human in fact.

The more one associates with the men in power and the
more visits one pays to Parliament, the quicker bookish concepts fade away. The notion, for example, that "mikado
worship" is the mainspring of government becomes positively
ridiculous. A reader of solemn dissertations on the "Theory
of the Japanese State" may assume that the nation is kept
together solely by devotion to His Imperial Majesty. Unques-

PREPARING A POSTER FOR A POLITICAL RALLY

tionably this sincere piety exists and indisputably the multitudes continue to kneel at his passing and to mention his title with their hands to their lips. But this veneration does not now, nor has it in the past, made of Japan a going concern. Warriors and statesmen have steadily diminished the monarch's temporal power. The most holy awe failed to prevent a strong-handed peasant, Hideyoshi, or a village headman, Ieyasu, from grasping all power in their own fists and confining the priest-king to compulsory exile. Princes and shoguns quarreled for generations over fiefs and revenues without so much as a transient reference to the sacred Emperor; strong men married their sisters and daughters to the rulers, or, like the last shogun, demanded the daughter of an Emperor as bride. And at the moment, the "sacredness of the throne" serves political parties either as a convenient pretext for upsetting a Cabinet or campaigning for offices. The slogan, "disloyalty to the throne," operates as an excuse for jailing a political opponent or for terrorizing a rival. To-day, as yesterday, despite sentiments and beliefs, the ruling class of Japan, behaving according to the code of its kind, has fixed its firm and keen gaze upon the division of national spoils. Its members still rally around the sources of power, seeking for contracts or subsidies, tariffs, places for sons and nephews, as heartily as their noble mediæval forebears sought Government aid against usurious merchants or rebellious guilds. And if at this hour military men, landed gentry, bankers and politicians, nobles and plebeian merchants work together so remarkably well, it is not merely because they are consumed with pious fervor, but because no one group among them is strong enough to rule alone. They must "hang together or separately."

Another favorite concept that is shattered on closer acquaintance is the rigid nature of the Japanese system. The idea arose from the fact that the military men have so much to say in affairs and the habit of drilling and marching is so much in evidence—thousands of school children are even brought out to tramp and salute on important occasions. It cannot be denied that the bristling, martinet type of official and his underling is a very real phenomenon. Like many travelers, I have met the sword-rattling, mustachio-twisting "inspector" who brusquely endeavors to discover "dangerous thoughts" and menacing personalities. But one need not be too hasty in calling the Japanese a "peril" to the West for such a reason; often an irresolute and inefficient man holds a gun and salutes; arrogant officials and underlings are usually just retainers of those who hold the reins of power.

The men at the helm are generally quite the reverse of these tourist inspectors or guardians of the public morale. One may be a jolly, luxury-loving bacchanalian, a sort of Tammany politician tinged with æstheticism, who, kneeling in his beautifully decorated palace, clad in flowing, easy robes, supporting himself by one plump elbow on a porcelain brazier, puffs at a big black cigar. Others belong to a more mellow and aristocratic lineage; they are exquisites, fond of collecting peculiar stones for a favorite garden path or practicing the subtle art of incense burning. And as in every government, there is a certain percentage of figureheads whose office is obtained through a "pull" and whose work is done for them by conscientious, hard-working civil servants alive to the public weal.

In illustration of this latter type, a true story was told me by an American who tried to get information concerning, let us say, the tramcar system in a small town in Japan. The official in charge sat silent, fixing him with a glassy stare, but at intervals replying, "Ah-h-h, so!" Every question received the same ambiguous reply. After a vain hour of inquiry, the

American arose, much annoyed, remarking: "Well, that was interesting. Old fellow wouldn't say a word! That's the silent, cautious samurai for you—knows a pile but keeps it to himself." But the subordinate in the office only smiled, knowing the official to be of plebeian origin and that he was silent out of perplexity—for how could he admit that he knew nothing whatever of the subject, that he had been placed there by politics and relied entirely upon his faithful secretary?

The bogey of the irresistible, deadly juggernaut raised by Western sensationalists is laid when one sees at closer range the scandals, corruption, inefficiency, inexperience and lack of foresight of everyday Japanese business and politics. It reminds us too much, in fact, of familiar Western politics when we get the news of decorations sold, titles bought by a wealthy brewer, city councillors languishing in jail, venal M. P.s pilloried in the cartoons, elections contracted for by "brokers" of votes. All sorts of scandal fill the air—about a certain railway that paid election expenses in return for favors; about M. P.s involved in forestry steals; about corrupt practices that have overthrown Cabinets and shocked the voting populace; about the prices paid for peerage by wealthy parvenus. Their Government often seems to the Japanese themselves discouragingly human indeed.

Then how does it manage, so corrupt, to be so stable? It survives instead of sinking like that of Oriental China or of Korea which it supplanted—because it is never *too* corrupt, never *too* inefficient. Because there are always in Japan enough loyalty and common sense among the ranks of bureaucrats, petty officials who administer laws, judges, the police, and technicians who oversee waterworks and transportation, fire-fighting machines, and hospital edifices. There were doughty men of honor in the wildest turmoil of Restoration times when grafters sought to take advantage of the Government confusion, going to the length of sending an assassin in pursuit of a certain over-ardent reformer. Brave men like Viscounts Inouye and Shibusawa are said to have risen in public defiance of the reckless management and spoils system of the Government, resigning from the Finance Department, publishing in a newspaper a full account of what they had experienced, and demanding the introduction of a budgetary and accounting system. This was so shocking an act of disloyalty, it then seemed, that the two were arrested and heavily fined; but none the less, they had the satisfaction of seeing their budget scheme ultimately installed. Such men and such deeds have saved Japan. And there have always been, in political life, sufficient hope and initiative among a nobler element to keep things moving forward; there have been social workers willing to campaign for a generation to carry a bill through the Diet, citizens uniting to force a "purified politics" election; liberals in the Parliament bluntly and persistently interrogating the ministers and premier—in short, there is enough criticism alive in Japan and enough integrity of character to make the reigning party forever uneasy in its seat. Politicians can "get away" with considerable amounts of loot in Japan, as in other countries, but they cannot take it all.

Thus the political picture that Japan exhibits is in reality far from the simple one commonly drawn. We are usually shown an iron rule, superhuman and relentless. We are asked to behold the contrasting humble piety of the folk and the aloof disdain of the aristocracy; awe and majesty; groveling obedience and superb command. Instead, what a picture business and politics actually present of intrigue, chicanery, log-rolling, wheedling at dinner parties, buying off behind scenes, even hand-to-hand conflict as in the memorable fist fight in the Diet in 1927, when sixteen members of the Government party were charged in court with man-handling opponents who attacked an alleged misuse of military funds in Siberia! In truth uproar often occurs in the Diet and sharp sallies in the never successfully muzzled press. Sweeping assaults are made on the Government. Visionary schemes, meaningless slogans, extravagant campaigns are mixed inextricably with practical programs, hard work, generous intention and devotion to public interests. As a matter of fact the Japanese Government is a chip off the same block as other governments. It is, after all, not really a machine. It is a contraption.

What manner of men have in their keeping this "contraption"? I became acquainted with a remarkable variety of them: colonial administrators at their posts in Formosa, Manchuria, and Korea; parliamentarians shouting in stormy debates or sitting immobile amid the din; city and imperial bureaucrats, gathered in solemn State banquets, busy in office or institution, or relaxed in the jovial informality of a geisha dinner; military men displaying their medaled chests at an Imperial Garden Party or, sword by their side, teaching savage aboriginal youth in the mountain fastnesses of Taiwan; business men of renowned aristocratic or commoner merchant families at home and in mammoth meetings of bankers, boosters, or manufacturers of celluloid dolls and dynamos. And as, in memory, those hundreds of faces float, cloud-like, before my eyes, I wonder what composite portrait may be painted of this extraordinary Oriental ruling class— of these "men behind the miracle."

As a whole their cultural background at once differentiates them from other ruling classes round the world. They still possess the tastes and practice the arts of their feudal forebears. Even the Japanese who have risen from plebeian ranks to wealth—at least, the older crop, if not the younger, of new-rich—have been assimilated into this cultural atmosphere, and have begun to build tea pavilions, while their wives take lessons on the harp and their daughters, at the most elegant finishing schools, learn etiquette and how to write poems of the dawn on gilt-spotted cards in the most elegant, spidery-thin, ladylike brush writing.

In other countries the ruling class makes itself socially agreeable and tempers its rule by other means: in England by sports, bird lore, hobbies and "tea fights"; in America by public benefactions; in pre-Republican Germany, by the splendid pomp of military display. But the Japanese do not have a "society" in the French sense; the Imperial Court makes extraordinarily little parade of itself; and the rich people as a class are rather inconspicuous in public.

This may be illustrated in the personality of a manufacturer living in the hills near ancient Kyoto. We had walked up his huge garden, beside the ladies of his family—the types of patrician Southern beauty, with the extremely long, pale face, small mouth, slender nose, and high, thin eyebrows—the prints incarnate. On the gardened hill, we had quaffed foaming green tea from rare bowls and eaten thick white sugar-paste in the tea pavilion, a charming cottage nestling at the foot of a pine tree. Then we had dinner under an awning, *al fresco,* in splendid style, on the very brow of the hill. Here our host, elderly, with the twinkling eyes of alert maturity in Japan, sat clad in a kimono with his small neat fan in his hand at the head of the table. From the viands we could look far away across the valley in which Kyoto lies, with its crystal river spanned by many arched bridges, with its dark roofs of palaces and temples, and with the chimney stacks of our host's factory rising incongruously in the panorama. Indeed the whole scene was characteristic

A GLIMPSE INTO MARQUIS OKUMA'S HOME

—factory whistles blowing over temple bells. But—instead
of a bourgeois Babbitt as owner, the factory possessed an
æsthetic patriarch!

Many another time I recognized this continued sway of
the antique. The late Baron Okura for instance was a thoroughly Japanese model of wealthy man. He had risen from
poverty to fortune and title; he had come to the big city with
a few yen in his kimono sleeve, had worked as apprentice,
and soon found himself selling supplies to the Government
during the Russo-Japanese War, making a huge income and
spending it regally. His collection of mediæval angel statues
was superb. But he practiced some of the arts, as well as
patronized them, especially the writing of humorous poetry.
On the occasion of his eightieth birthday he spent a million
yen in entertainment of the public, one of the chief attractions being the Chinese actor, Mei Lan-fang, imported for
the festivities. Younger members of his family were thus
bred in a new-old tradition. We sat with some of them at an
elaborate tea-banquet which should precede the tea ceremony
according to antique formality, but is very rarely tasted in
these days because few cooks can master the secrets of its
cuisine. Baron Okura's cook was such an artist. Countless
lacquer trays were slipped beside each of us, bearing arrangements of bowls, with odd foods beyond identification covered with sauces that struck as strangely on our palates as
Oriental music first strikes the ear.

Through the friends of Count Goto, we saw several show
places. The Yamamoto's, supported by trade and copper,
was a lovely native-style mansion surrounded by an enormous garden, in which the twilight tea ceremony was performed by the crimson-robed young daughter of the house.
This was followed by a banquet, again spread under an
awning in the open, with fish brought especially from Lake

Chuzenji to grace the feast. On this occasion, however, tiger hunting in Korea was the chief theme, for the mine owner was devoted to the sport. Another great establishment, English in type, belonged to the coal mining magnate, Baron Furukawa; for the entertainment of his guests, jugglers arrayed in wide, flowered brocade pantaloons, such as servants and attendants in classic comedy wear, balanced teapots on the ends of parasols. At the home of an electric magnate, Mr. Sasaki, who recently stood for Parliament, the wife performed on the lute, demonstrated flower arrangement and sand painting and beat us in a game of ping-pong, while her husband defeated us at tennis and took moving pictures of the events of the visit. In such wise, the industrialists of Japan indicate the social ends of their business strife.

Gradually, of course, the traditional background is receding. The arts are left to the women in an increasing degree; the men give more time to stocks and elections, to foreign politics and economic expansion.

One of the things I first wished to know about these circles was their aristocratic sincerity. Were they all of samurai origin? For I was American enough to be deeply impressed by the talk of samurai and cherry blossoms rather than of pioneering and plunder. Having heard that the "samurai spirit" was Japan's most precious heritage, it was logical to imagine the samurai as the embodiment of *noblesse oblige*. What was my dismay then to meet the daughters of feudal dukes who spoke of mere samurai with contempt, as a feudal duke might speak of a lackey! Confusion was only confounded at the discovery of how many commoners bore noble names, which they had acquired by Government favor; also how impossible it was to know whether a plain *"san"* (Mr.) was of samurai blood or not, since the Japanese give it no distinguishing prefix.

Before attending business men's gatherings and visiting in homes of merchant princes, I had also labored under the delusion that only plebeians in Japan were engaged in manufacturing. All I had heard concerning the samurai tended to emphasize the disdain of the knight for the pursuit of gain. Books had related how Mitsukuni, great feudal lord of Mito, in his "Instructions to Retainers," explained the position of the samurai class: "The people of the other classes deal with visible things, while the samurai deal with invisible, colorless and unsubstantial things, such as honor, justice and ceremony." Stories had told of samurai who discharged tutors discovered to have taught their sons elementary arithmetic and of others who left all pecuniary matters in the hands of their womenfolk, transmitting the famous remark of a samurai to the rising generation: "There is one game, my son, in which it is a disgrace to be winner. That game is called trade. See that you know nothing of it." So I had arrived at the belief that whatever the plebeians were doing in the East, it must be reprehensible.

However the lesson was to be learned that Japan is a sea of social and "spiritual" contradictions. What actually occurs is a large interplay of plebeian, samurai and aristocrat. A Peer is ready to act as dummy president and lend the prestige of his family name to a commoner's corporation. Again, behind some noble title in politics may lurk the powerful support of a plebeian business man. Nobles with their wide clan and family ties shape Japanese trade and politics, while "vulgarians" alter the very complexion of the nobility with titles and decorations, their marriages into old families, their radical legislation. On one side, grows the strength of commoners in the Government, plebeian business men obtaining Cabinet appointments and being named as premier; on the other, the inclination of noble families toward a business, rather than a bureaucratic, career increases. Thus a poor farmer boy has become samurai and then risen to world-wide recognition as Viscount Shibusawa, one of Japan's first bankers. So sons of a general, an admiral, a baron, and a supreme court judge went as a quartet to work "from the bottom up" in a shipping concern.

In short, there is no longer any real dividing social line of power in Japan. Classes have astonishingly amalgamated. Among the lists, for example, of the fifty wealthiest men, one reads not only names of old ducal families, Maeda, Matsudaira, Tokugawa, representatives of clans of Satsuma and Sendai, and scions of the ancient Kyoto court nobility; one discovers also that the immensely rich and dominant Mitsuis are of merchant, rather than knightly, origin. Baron H. Mitsui, though now a noble and one of the score of wealthiest men alive, classed with Rockefeller and the Gaikwar of Baroda, is of plebeian ancestry. Everywhere appear titles in public life that may or may not indicate ripened aristocracy— Baron Koi presiding at a World Engineering Congress; a Prince addressing the Rotarians and some of the brethren doing a samurai sword dance at their festival; Baron Goh representing electricity on an Economic Council. Sons of warriors, who would normally have been arrayed in rival camps, are now forced to coöperate in marketing crabmeat, tusks, twine, or tangerines.

Among the groups gathered around the golden oak tables in Kobe's modern Chamber of Commerce, conversing on the outlook for exporting potatoes and onions to the Philippines, clad in variegated costume, dark kimono or well-worn cutaway, plebeian and aristocrat sit elbow to elbow. Here are men whose grandfathers were forced to store away their whiskered, wooden, fighting masks and winged helmets and apply themselves to the production of soap and harmonicas.

Here are men who by right of birth should be manipulating tasseled spears instead of stocks and bonds, and, of course, they have not wholly forgotten the fact.

The differences among samurai themselves can in time be traced. There are knights of the true storybook pattern, living impoverished, disdainful, in retirement behind the thick doors of their dwellings, surrounded with heirlooms of a "golden age." There are samurai children who play golf and jazz at country clubs, whose fathers ride down, resplendent in high hat, pearl-gray gloves and spats, to the Tokyo Exchange, in limousines.

How diversely the samurai reacted at the overthrow of the Shogunate! Some had foreseen the coming of machine industry and had rushed more keenly than any of the existing business men to welcome it. Ex-feudal lords built and owned ships; a samurai sailed the first Japanese vessel across the Atlantic; samurai conducted banks, railways, cement plants, telephones. It was they who, finding themselves penniless, were quicker than comfortable plebeian business men to experiment with the new modes of winning a livelihood. So the plebeians are not responsible for every change. Even in the earlier days, there were two kinds of samurai—conservative and adventurous. The former, it seems, detested all the works of the foreign devils and especially electricity; when they were forced to cross a street and go under the overhead electric wires, to ward off the evil influence they would open their fans with a smart rap and hold them over their topknots. But it would be false to use such an anecdote as conclusive of the "samurai spirit"—for two knights were the first to bring electric bulbs into Japan and to exhibit them on the Ginza in 1886!

One quality in common the Japanese have—prince or plebeian—a certain stoicism. In the softest, most poetic, there is a hint of steel. This is what antagonizes many foreigners who feel the innate power and do not know what to do about it. Yet as among all mediæval peoples, it has been quite direct and unabashed in expression. In early diplomatic exchanges, the Japanese were often amazingly blunt— quite the opposite to the sly, secretive Oriental of fiction— and they never did quite learn the art of palaver. When they do not wish to reveal their real purposes, they avoid the Anglo-Saxon habit of making an oration on home and fatherland; they remain silent. How silent a Cabinet minister can be, when a parliamentarian interrogates him! And nothing is more characteristic than the silences of Prince Saionji, aged adviser to the politicians; when he has no order to give, he is speechless and the countrymen who visit him are as baffled as any foreigner might be. The Japanese have practiced arts and etiquette enough to make them refined and polished; but they have missed the *bonhomie,* the often critical persiflage of the Anglo-Saxons. They are statuesque, simple and unaffected.

Occasionally this stoicism becomes arrogant ramrodism; it is a "stiff-necked generation"; and some men, once they get set in their ways, cannot be blasted out by all the logic or dynamite in the Empire. Severe, even brusque and offensive, a Japanese may be in his bearing. But the quality of steel can also be superb—a sheer moral force that puts the impossible through to practice. Frequently an awful pride is covered up under this desperate quietness of theirs; this glinting metallic personality

Is it leaving the rulers? Many Japanese think it is; that the feudal quality is softening rapidly. They blame the plebeian alloy, or the times that are excessively enervating. They declare the habit of *hara-kiri* is losing its hold. But others say that *hara-kiri* was never general and that in truth it was sometimes a mere "face saving." A knight condemned to death would just make a motion of his own, before the executioner cut off his head—a motion denoting suicide, while establishing an "honorable" death.

There are critics who state that Japan has no more the terrible spirit of the early heroes who all faced death. Santaro writes: "It is hardly an exaggeration to say that nearly all the men who had labored on the Imperial cause either committed suicide or were assassinated by political adversaries or made narrow escapes from death," instancing the violent end of Saigo, the assassinations of Ito and Okubo, the attempt on the life of Okuma, Inouye scarred for life by ruffians, Itagaki wounded. Uncounted are the men who died for the Restoration, who pursued forbidden knowledge and accepted the death penalty; who voyaged abroad and returned to confront the Shogun's vengeance; who led forlorn causes; who championed dangerous theories. Is this steely quality, that has again and again saved Japan, passing away under plebeian alloy? Or is it itself a cultural tradition capable of wider diffusion? These are moot questions in Japan.

Force alone and unadorned gets nowhere and in studying the strength of Japan's rulers, one finds amalgamated with their steely fortitude another potent quality: ability to compromise. They are first-rate combiners, discussers, go-betweens and middlemen. They know how to pull together and hold together. And this, as well as their samurai grit, has been responsible for their success.

They are accustomed to working in companies, societies, guilds, associations. Partly because so few individuals in former times had enough wealth to operate alone, the Japanese started their first businesses as companies. Moreover, the inherited feudal sentiment of allegiance compels those who might stand by themselves to work in combination; a *ronin,* or masterless man, is an idea repellent to them even to-day. Gradually men like Kikuchi or Tsurumi are earning democratic money by their pens, but this is a veritable anomaly. Most *ronin* are considered bad fellows by reason of their very independence—living by blackmailing or other underhand methods. So strong is this notion that, until recently, the more sensitive Japanese felt happier in a poorly paid Government post than in business; they wanted to stand close to the central power, to have no master but the highest. Yet this very willingness of rich as well as poor to do some kind of work, and to pull in team is what preserved Japan.

Not only are individuals forced to labor together on very close terms; groups must also combine. The caste of aristocrats, for example, though they would like to stand alone, find it very difficult to do so. They are held fast to the Government by monetary ties; they dare not be too anti-democratic and obstruct too much legislation in the House of Peers, because they can so easily be attacked through that peculiar institution, the Peers' Bank. This very exclusive affair in which, at least at first, no plebeian was permitted to own a share, has held the worldly wealth of many an ancient family: of the *daimyo* whose feudal revenues were converted into bonds; of old court dames whose hoardings were invested there. When it crashed in 1927, the Peers, through activity in their political party, forced the Government to salvage their fortunes by taking over the bank's debts though other victims in plebeian banks were left to suffer without relief. Had not the Government stepped in, disaster would have spread havoc throughout the ranks of the nobility. In this way, and through the fact that its bank funds have been used to finance many undertakings, such as shipping and dockyards, the peerage is closely allied to business no less than the Government. And so nowadays the dreamiest Peer must pay some attention to the ticker tape as well as the tea ceremony.

The Imperial Family is also heavily interested in business ventures. It has millions of yen invested in the stocks of steamships, gas companies, electric plants, and Formosan sugar concerns. In the Imperial Hotel the Imperial Family and the Okuras are the largest stockholders.

Japanese business is perhaps more closely allied to Government than in Western countries, because most basic industries are carefully subsidized or protected by the Government paternally. Banks are rescued from crashes through timely aid; shipping lines are extended a fatherly hand; whenever a prominent adventurer is in trouble, he involuntarily looks to official aid and comfort. Rich people in general have achieved wealth through just this close connection with the Government, rather than by individual effort. Most of the richest men are bankers, and banking is a "pet" of the Government. Often a family has money because it holds land in the heart of some big city, which the Government tactfully classifies as "bamboo grove" or "rice paddy." The Mitsubishi family is affluent by reason of the fact that an ancestor, as soon as he saw a chance in Restoration days, managed to get close to power and monopolize shipping. The Okura fortune came in the beginning from military supplies. Indeed, Yukio Ozaki publicly declared that most of the wealthy families of Japan had amassed their gains during some war or other. Business has a large stake in politics, and helps to defray expenses of political parties. It has happened that one Cabinet fell because its Finance Minister was not "in close touch" with business, sufficiently to float bonds after the Chinese war.

The usual connection of industry with Government, such

as contracts, low taxation and high tariff, or the aid of diplomats in furthering trade abroad, Japanese men of business enjoy. But they have other ties, curious and peculiar to themselves. For instance, there is the case of the dissolution, not long ago, of a political party because its president, involved in a big business concern subsidized by the Government, was told by the Government party to turn over his followers or lose his property. He was compelled by this manœuvre to retire from political life after wrecking his party.

Thus by strong economic ties is the ruling class of Japan made compact and united. Its leading men are ranged together by complicated sets of influences. A man's party may occasionally conflict with his business interests, or his clan and rank may antagonize his party followers. Adjustments must be made. The whole course of affairs is determined by just such subterranean and complex bonds, that vary from year to year and even month to month. Parties dissolve and re-form with bewildering rapidity; businesses go into bankruptcy and are salvaged with astonishing celerity; and a spectator often fails to discover from the sidelines who is responsible.

To such conditions, methods must conform. We should expect Japanese business and political processes to be distinctive, and they are. For one thing there is a tremendous amount of "dinner dalliance," if one may call it so. Elaborate and expensive "treats," geisha banquets, serve as opportunity for *rapprochements* and new alignments. Frequently a man owes his position to his genius in giving feasts, to his charm of conversation, or his skill in singing. One politician, it is well known, on principle refused to offer anything but rice and beans at his dinners; he soon found himself out of the office. Perhaps a story, if oft repeated, is not amiss.

General Tanaka, it seems, made a life friend of the late Marquis Okuma, by inviting him to lecture to his soldiers and by greeting him on his appearance with a fanfare of trumpets; this little attention so surprised and delighted the Marquis that the political career of Tanaka was at once assured. Gossip distributes numerous tales of beans and banquets, lutes and trumpets, or the dazzling smile of a geisha that aided at a crucial moment.

What might be called "go-betweenism" is as characteristic as dinner dalliance. Japanese great men, in nearly every case, have the feeling inherited from a feudal past that one is superior if one may delegate one's affairs to a *major domo,* and when they travel it is with a retinue resembling that of a prince. The go-between is therefore a very important character in the situation. To rival clans, factions or parties must endlessly run various little-known but necessary "bosses," or professional "fixers," who arrange line-ups, bring enemies together, achieve sudden *coups d'état.* The "brokers" who deliver guaranteed quantities of votes are the mainstay of political candidates.

Inevitably, with such methods, should occur all those apparently irrational delays so painful to the hustling American "go-getters." These are not due to racial character merely—for I think the Japanese would like to be swift of decision and rapid in action if they could. Some admit it indeed. Delays are due rather to the complexity of their situation. A Japanese really must consult many people before he makes any important move. He must advance warily, lest he hurt someone's feelings or ignore a vital contact. To certain persons he may telephone; to others he must go in person, which means long and difficult trips and interminable calling; to a few, for sign of respect, he must give expensive dinners before asking advice. He must see his political "little father," his clan or family head, and summon all his friends in politics, business or journalism. Little can be done directly; almost anything may be "arranged."

In many ways, this has been a good thing. It has hampered enterprise, but it has kept the country consolidated and has made for reasonable consideration. Everybody—within this small ruling class—feels responsible for everything and works hand-in-glove with everybody else when a crisis arises. It is just this very lack of coöperation that makes China a war lords' prey.

From the ruling group emanate all sorts of ties to the white-collar underling groups. Both in business houses and in government offices, the veriest clerk is as closely bound to the "system" as the highest official. This is partly a result of the feudal custom of rallying around an over-lord; so a manufacturer, like a party leader, collects unto himself devoted bands of "spearsmen" whom he may direct in public life. Another bond is the pension and bonus system. Once a man enters an office or concern he must remain faithful and loyal to a romantic degree or lose not merely his job, but forfeit his bonus and pension beside. No wonder that men are obsessed by this factional loyalty; that students of the Imperial University are arrayed against Waseda University; that rivals of two business colleges carry their animosities into practical life; that there is such combat in party groups. It is excellent in a way, for its patronage system has so far spared Japan from serious unemployment; everybody is dependent on somebody. But it is responsible also for about as much factional strife as for national loyalty.

It is obvious therefore that in Japan we do not actually have a helpless, undistinguishable mass of humble folk bowing before an absolute monarch. We have rather a folk intimately divided within itself into tiny groups, and these in turn gathered into curious larger entities pulling apart and together. All in all, a stupendous engine is in operation. In spite of the furious animosities among business, political, military and noble groups, what a united front they present to the people! They squabble among themselves, but remain consolidated. Below this organization, factions of labor, Right and Left, and peasant and industrial workers strive to maintain the same united front against the ruling organizations.

How long can these small groups at the top continue to divide among themselves the privileges and prerogatives of office? How long can they confine the scramble for power to their own ranks? That is the main question. Already the rule of so small and exclusive a group is challenged by groups below, seeking to capture power.

Opposition to the governing class, in truth, steadily and strikingly intensifies. Animosity toward the favoritism of the Government enlarges: the middle class who were so hard hit by bankruptcy—a series of crashes in 1927—felt a lasting bitterness toward the plutocrats; they realized that "big" men "saw what was coming and withdrew," leaving the little ones to bear the brunt of disaster; that the Peers and Dames at court were saved at their expense. It was only after an exceedingly desperate fight that the Peers succeeded in securing relief for their Bank; the public opinion against them was so strong that the Government hesitated. Moreover, successions of scandals, thoroughly aired in public by a delighted press, have done much to diminish the awe of the people. They are still devoted subjects of their Emperor who holds himself aloof from politics and remains on a dignified height; but they are not duped by the politician. An atmosphere of political skepticism is very general in Japan.

One important sign of the times is the growing appeal of

business over political careers. More and more a commercial spirit is surging up. Rich men begin to flaunt their wealth, instead of hiding it in a warehouse behind a high wall; they now build enormous banks with bronze doors and marble pillars, that stand out in vivid contrast with the humble people's homes; they engage in public festivals of Rotary; they ride in limousines. And correspondingly, the people begin to feel arrayed against wealth, rather than against the Government as such.

The change is gradual. It was foreigners who started much of the prejudice against business for, when firms were first opened in Yokohoma and Kobe, they allowed Japanese to enter to transact business only through a side entrance, never the main. Once speculation in stocks was disgraceful; "brokers were stealthily visiting their clients' houses by the rear entrances to inform them of the market tendency." Now it is something to boast of. If nobles are going into business, so are plebeians rising to power. The disappearance of Japan's upper crust is certainly conceivable. It may happen. It has happened before—in early Tokugawa times, after the civil wars, frequently a knight was thrust down to live among the beggars on the river-bank, while now and then a common soldier was elevated to the command of castles and mustered spearsmen.

Opposition certainly takes dramatic forms. In January, 1929, for example, in the House of Peers, a member openly demanded the creation of a labor ministry. In the Lower House, an opposition member sharply interrogated the Government, pushing questions as to its foreign policy, and when the Premier gave evasive answers, Bunji Suzuki, the zealous labor leader who also sat in the House, rose to declare: "If you cannot answer his questions you had better resign as State Ministers." Then Suzuki went on to demand why the

Government delayed the Trade Union Bill, to criticize police authorities and foreign relations, and to keep three ministers busy answering him. Numbers of ringing attacks on the Government have been heard in that public forum of the Lower House. And they have all been broadcast through the press.

What answer does the governing class make to its challenges? Three sorts; force, economics, and politics.

As to the forceful or strong-arm methods already used, all sorts of stories are current. Dr. Washio reports how conservatives conduct such campaigns in rural communities, though they may not dare to in big cities. Rivaling former American election methods, bullies and gunmen are sometimes brought into play. There have been murders in election rows. Miners' wives have been jailed for pamphlet distributing. In a village whose life is dependent on a big manufacturing company, the whole place was made to suffer for its political wrong-headedness. Trade was cut off from retailers, and employees were threatened with discharge if they voted for proletarians. The whole town was frightened, and one person would say to another: "Have you washed your neck clean?" meaning, "Are you ready to receive the discharge notice?" And the other would reply: "Yes, mine is washed every day to receive the company's sword." A candidate declared: "The shadow of death hangs over this mountain community and the people are afraid of universal suffrage." He wound up with the cry: "What terror have you given us in the name of universal suffrage!"

But force is not the only weapon of the ruling group. They have sought subtler policies. They have hoped to solve the situation by economic improvement. They have tried to increase prosperity and allay the discontent. The Seiyukai Party, with its motto of "Go-and-get-it" and "Deeds, not

Orations," has drawn up grand programs for industrialization. They have planned immense subsidies for industries,
attempted to conserve the nation's iron and coal, store oil
reserves, or utilize water-power—the latter scheme failing,
it is said, because the water-power is too scattered for enormous plants. They have looked abroad for markets, trying
to establish trade connections with the whole Far East; to
compete in cement with the Dutch and British in Java; sell
patent medicines in Russia; ship rickshaws to Africa; rival
the British Lancashire in the Orient and expand cotton and
woolen production to formidable proportions. Combines
grow; centralization and politicalization sweep forward.
The age of trusts and corporations and mergers has arrived
—bigger business growing greater and smaller sinking down
to diminutive size or passing out of existence.

So far the Japanese governing classes have had astonishing economic success. They have brought a nation of warriors and peasants, without much money and only rice and
silk for exchange, unused to machines and cities, to dizzy
heights. This has entailed enormous burdens, forty-five per
cent of the national budget being spent on armaments alone.
And there are questions as to how much further the expansion can go. But the apparent necessity for expansion has
brought a radical shift in policy: from antagonistic to peaceful trade penetration, to conciliatory methods, to an enlarged
participation of business in the Government.

Conscious that the public may be offended at the irresponsible flaunting of wealth, which tends to increase, the rich
men of Japan now make attempts to placate public opinion.
Z. Yasuda, a plebeian millionaire, was shot by an assassin
who on principle hated rich men; ironically, his will disclosed
the fact that he had left a fortune to found the Institute for
Municipal Research in Tokyo. Others entertain the people

with exhibits; such was one we saw in Osaka of rare old prints which a merchant had brought back from European countries. Some endow and patronize colleges for peasant girls, or business boys; their foundations include a fine art school for women in Tokyo. Prince Konoye directs a Symphony Orchestra and helps finance it. The upper class used to be known as art amateurs; now they aspire to be praised as public benefactors.

Since the last war, with its attendant strikes, riots and unrest, the increase in humanitarian legislation—the third or political reply to challenge—has been notable. Osaka and Tokyo established bureaus for social work. The Imperial Government, as well as the municipal, founded a Social Affairs Department. Expenditures on all forms of welfare work enlarged from one to fifteen million yen a year between 1912 and 1920. How striking the new activities are may be judged from the fact, pointed out by a social worker, that in Tokyo in 1919 there were but one almshouse, a reformatory, a hospital and some employment exchanges, whereas now, there and in other cities, help is rendered in varied and elaborate forms—maternity hospitals, lodging houses, markets, baths, day nurseries, dispensaries and employment bureaus of broad scope.

The piling up of labor legislation during about the same period has been equally rapid. The "labor exchange law, the age limitation on juvenile workers, the renewed factory act, the prohibition of women and children from night work, protection of mothers," health insurance, and other measures have followed in succession. In 1923 the juvenile law established separate courts and houses of correction for young offenders. In 1929 the law, called "Save the Poor," appropriated several million yen for the needy, young and invalid in towns and rural communities; it occasioned rejoicing among social workers, who had been campaigning since 1889 for such a law, but had met the continual objection: "It will make workers 'lazy.'" In the same year the Commission for Social Politics was set to investigating the unemployment problem, undertaking public works for relief and aiding village local relief enterprises. More and more, too, Japan is aligning itself with a large part of the world in ratifying labor conventions and improving safety devices.

The governing class made one drastic experiment—a magnificent act of abdication—enlarging the electorate to include all able-bodied men over twenty-five, thereby creating a new voting population of nine millions at a stroke. They determined that the menacing unrest should take the channel of politics instead of revolution. They thus gave evidence of being a far-sighted body of men, by no means so stubborn as the Russians of the old régime; but rather prepared to face realities in plenty of time and with good grace. The people had not demanded the ballot *en masse;* they received it as a present and were gratefully surprised at the gift. It appears that the governors, for all their dillying and dallying, have a common mind, are capable of evolution, can compromise and execute with quiet determination. And now they face the result of their experiment—an ever-widening circle of power.

CHAPTER XX

CRIMSON CANOPY AND PAPER BANNERS

WHILE the ruling class alters in type and method and the restless urban and rural masses reach out for power, politics engrosses a larger share of Japanese thought and effort. Such interest as people have so long diffused over moral, cultural or social conflicts has now begun to collect and concentrate on the transcendent strife of lawmakers. This new era may be said to commence on February 2, 1928, for on that day nine million recently enfranchised voters were invited by the vibration of temple bells and the shriek of factory whistles to the polling booths. Workmen in cotton blouses came bowing low and timidly, followed by silk-hatted magnates; chauffeurs cast votes with their employers, and messengers with teachers and matinée idols. No disorder marred the occasion which passed in typically Japanese solemnity. The ruling group had granted the ballot to all men and a dazed, overawed multitude had accepted its privilege of sovereignty.

For weeks, Tokyo agitators had looked forward to the momentous contest in Parliament which inaugurated manhood suffrage. Mass meetings had been sponsored by newspaper men whose liberal convictions were doubtless intensified by the knowledge that more voters would make additional readers. A monster parade had wound through the city, along the old moat and under the fortress walls of the Palace; curious onlookers had crowded the roof ledges or filled the streets with billowing sleeves as they marched be-

407

authority of his family head who might be his grandfather or, indeed, his great-aunt. So much feeling was aroused by this argument that telegrams and letters had deluged the representatives, urging that the ballot be granted only to family heads. Before the second debate on the Bill, a fanatic was seized for an alleged plot to blow up the Diet building and assassinate the Premier, so strongly did he resent the threat of suffrage to the nation's family life.

The men who, in this Oriental forum, ultimately decided for democracy, belong to a sphere of life quite distinct from officialdom. Very few of its members, less than seven per cent, have been employed at any time in the civil or military branches of the Government; years in passing civil service examinations leave little time for a political career. Hence these are not bureaucrats; on the contrary, they are often hostile toward the occupants of comfortable, pension-paying posts, and tense opposition sometimes develops between Japan's lawmakers and her administrators. Business men make up the largest group in the House of Representatives; farmers the next; then lawyers, with journalists a steadily augmenting group. The members are an educated body, as a whole, the majority holding college or university degrees; consequently Western theories of State and society have played a part in the formation of their minds. Such considerations may have influenced the coming of suffrage, though only an expert could say to what extent.

But that does not mean they are students hot with the fires of youth. In fact, their average age tends to mount. By far the majority are much older than the Parliament in which they sit. Some of them can remember the days of Old Yedo, when speech-making in the Western style was a brash adventure and championship of a national assembly called for high courage. Ozaki took a seat in the first session, in 1890, and has been sitting there ever since, watching the working out of his favorite experiment. He has seen the Parliament, composed originally of men from the heart of a feudal age, successfully meet three wars and a devastating earthquake with their attendant troubles of conscription, reconstruction, and finance. Now he stands watching it face the great problems of democracy: freedom of political association, liberty of the press, expansion of public-school education, extension of the suffrage, and reform of the House of Peers on which the grip of titled members has been somewhat relaxed.

The House of Peers is usually a much more solemn affair than the Lower House, although when Prime Ministers are challenged by its members it can also enact stormy scenes. The hall is smaller for, while there are theoretically four hundred-odd members, in practice the Princes of the Blood wisely abstain from politics. A division into antagonistic camps is absent in the Peers, which has no clashing political parties if some members have grouped themselves into cliques.

While the Upper Chamber is generally in opposition to the more democratic House of Representatives, the cause is not aristocracy. A good half of the men in the Peers are commoners by birth. Some represent the highest taxpayers of the nation. Others are officials retired to a life-long berth. Of late has been added a group of scholars chosen from the Imperial universities. If there is community of purpose among them all, it comes less from noble blood than from economic station; more professional than inherited is their common attitude of support for the Government and the bureaucrats. No strict political dividing line can be drawn between the titled and the untitled, for those who descend from the highest courtier families are sometimes more liberal in their views than the scions of richer but less esteemed families.

The striking feature of the House of Peers was a crimson velvet canopy spread above a kind of opera box, in which sat members of the Cabinet, representing the program of the Japanese Government, ready to undergo interrogation from members. Bolt upright sat the ministers, beneath their canopy, prepared with unflinching gaze to meet all criticism. Wondering why they looked strange, I sought to remember group photographs of men assembled at congresses or conventions in Washington, London, or Geneva—faces of mortals deputed to make and remake worlds. Why did these seem different? Perhaps because one missed the familiar heavy or irregular types: Lloyd George with his bushy hair, the cherubic Churchill, or Borah from the "Wild West." These were thin, neat, nervously constituted citizens. Arrayed in dead-black silk robes with white tassels, fans in hands, their type is the very essence of ancestral formality. Even the more generally worn frock coat fails to alter that impression of tidy austerity.

The President of the Peers is no less a personage than Prince I. Tokugawa. If not such a parliamentary fixture as Ozaki, he at least has held his post for a quarter of a century. Placidly as a Chinese god he presides, plumper and cheerier in appearance than the row of Government officials. Of course! They had relieved him of the cares of State. Had not the Restoration come, this genial man would have inherited the despotic power of his ancestors, the Shoguns. He would have wielded authority, strong as a mediæval king's, over all the Japanese; and he would have been sitting, crowned with black gauze, in some gold-screen hall filled with kneeling knights ready to knock their foreheads on the floor at his slightest beck. With a good grace, however, this descendant of feudal potentates has accepted the new order; clad in a machine-age suit, he has long presided over a con-

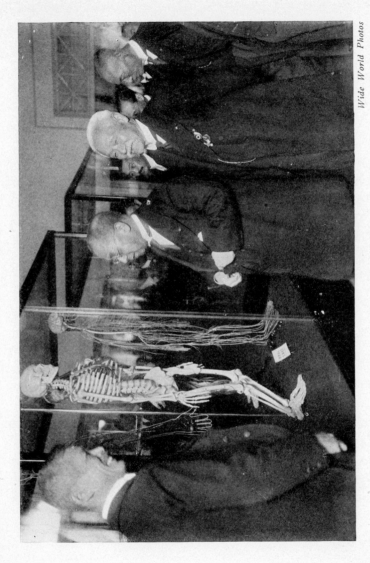

Wide World Photos

PRINCE I. TOKUGAWA AT THE OPENING OF THE JAPAN RED CROSS SOCIETY'S MUSEUM

stitutionál body that has agreed to sweeping democratic reforms.

Prince Tokugawa may be regarded as a symbol of that Japanese adaptability which has amazed and puzzled the modern world. How did such transformations come about? How could a feudal power remodel itself into a representative government so calmly and so rapidly? What native strength has reared and kept aloft that crimson canopy of State, under which plebeian Cabinet ministers answer the attacks on their policies? What force, blind or conscious, has driven those paper banners, demanding democracy, through the streets of the capital? Was it, as so many continue to preach, mere "imitation" of the West on the part of facile copyists?

Such a reply is far too glib. And the more one sees of Japanese politics, the more absurd it becomes. No, an explanation must be sought elsewhere, in the needs and nature of the people. Crimson canopy and paper banners may be borrowed paraphernalia, but the institutions represented by the first and the conflict of men and ideas betokened by the latter are very old and thoroughly native. They antedate Perry's trip to Japan and what is more—Columbus' visit to America.

The highly complex organization of Japan's feudal Government has been less generally emphasized than her refined art and martial ethics; however, it was equally characteristic. Too often the description of the nation has brought simple artisans or stern warriors to the foreground, while leaving in the shadow the capable and experienced men of civic affairs. They were not picturesque enough, perhaps, those canny merchants who conducted guild policies, developed their own banking system with its circulation of discount notes, and governed so well the city of Osaka that it could remain as free of meddling lords as independent burgher towns of Europe. Nor were those samurai deemed sufficiently heroic with their brushes and inkpots, in the place of swords, recording trials and deeds, keeping the thousands of volumes of legal documents that were handed down from ancestral ages, originating their own involved lawyers' jargon, and also supervising the handicraft industries— pottery, lacquer and cloth—that many lords were beginning to foster at the end of the eighteenth century, a growth which has been compared to the mercantile system in Europe. Unnoticed were those farmers and townsmen who were accustomed, centuries before they heard the word democracy, to elect their councillors, take charge of local fire-fighting, bridge-building, claim-settling or poor relief. It is perhaps hard to shed glamour over clerks, rice speculators, tax assessors, lawyers and brokers. But they were at their posts, whether we deem them "arty" or not, and a hard-headed, disciplined and experienced class of men they proved to be— life-givers to the nation.

Just as a hint of the real state of affairs in "simple, old Japan," it might be well to mention a quaint document from J. H. Wigmore's "Study of Private Law in Old Japan." This was the expense account of Gokurakuji Village in the Year of the Goat. Pen, ink and straw shoes had been bought for the headman; there had been costs for labor on a dam, for postal service, lodging for public guests, a law suit, repairing the storehouse roof, mending waterpipes. The whole amounted to several pennies and was signed by the farmers, Tarobei and Sajibei, and Kyemon's widow.

If villages were so painstaking, how much more complex was the management of towns! In Tokyo, in 1725, we find a conference body of some two hundred and sixty-five plebeian

headmen who kept watchful eyes on rice and wine importation, the morals of books and illustrated periodicals, and
issued passports, proclamations and certificates. In Osaka,
the burghers had elaborated their system. They had councillors, superintendents, censors, and special magistrates to
judge cases between citizens and outsiders. They paid no
taxes to the Shogun, only a New Year's gift, and they ran
their own business with the help of many bureaus for supervising temples, river-cleaning, registry of families, trade
guilds, castle supplies, account audits, fire patrol, port matters, weights and measures, licenses to ships and vehicles,
permits to individuals to own weapons, and prisons.

Does it destroy the poetic conception of jolly craftsmen to
know that their guilds issued shares and that, to the jealousy
of the rest, those of the sardine and saltfish dealers were
quoted highest? Is it shocking to suggest that samurai of
1297 A.D. were quite as concerned with forbidding interest
on bills of exchange as with vendettas? Is it *lèse majesté* to
intimate that many haughty dukes were less worried about
art than about the rice tickets and time bills they had issued
through their banks in Osaka? Or that, in old Tokyo, there
were not only tea houses filled with musical ladies but also
two exchanges to fix the market price of metals, and that the
prevailing level was reported promptly every morning to the
Finance Magistracy? I fear so, but how else are we to understand the ability of the Japanese to "modernize" themselves?

For men so loyal and well trained, it was not impossible
to renovate native institutions, bringing them up to date.
The ground work was laid. In truth, the most despotic Shogun had to operate through deliberative groups. Three such
were important in feudal Yedo: an all-powerful Council of
State, which "advised" and often controlled him; a Junior

Council of friendly chieftains, powerful and wealthy, without whose coöperation no large undertaking could be planned; and thirdly, a Board of Deliberation in which the noblemen of the city met as a Supreme Court. Another conference group convened in Osaka to consider judicial matters of local import. So it was relatively simple to transform the old gatherings into a Privy Council and Cabinet. The noblemen were easily assembled in the House of Peers and continued to hold as before the balance of power. The House of Representatives offered a channel of expression to bankers, lawyers, landowners and tax payers, such as for generations had been accustomed to the work of administration and had demonstrated the qualities of stability and decision. The Shogun was replaced by a Prime Minister but, in theory, that is what he had always been. The Emperor reigned, in theory supreme, but in practice isolated, as he had done since the fourteenth century. And the clerk-samurai went on about as they had done in feudal times, recording, assessing, supervising, conferring—only, they were now designated civil servants.

Westerners, of course, contributed something. Prince Tokugawa began to sit beneath a crimson canopy—in European monarchical style—instead of before a golden screen. The West marveled that he could do anything so "modern." Yet we may suspect that the chief jar was to his æsthetic susceptibilities.

It is not hard to see how Japan became Westernized. But how did it become democratized? What was in the feudal background that could lead to such an outgrowth? Chiefly, it seems, the fact that throughout the nation's history no ruling group has escaped challenge and conflict. At least three of the major contests of the twentieth century had precedents in the twelfth. Into a remote past may be traced the antagonisms beween nationalists and internationalists; between civilians and military men; and between aristocrats and plebeians.

The nationalist struggle is ancient and has engaged a much greater share of the thoughts and passions of the Japanese than of the Chinese. China was not so effectively challenged by India's civilization; her intellectuals were not compelled to spend so great a part of their force in puzzling out an attitude toward an invading culture; her scholar caste remained self-centered and was examined by the State on native, Confucian doctrines instead of foreign Buddhist philosophy. The Japanese, on the contrary, from the sixth century onward had had the problem of the foreigner uppermost in their minds. Numerous thinkers spent their lives planning ways to assimilate the alien cultures: by incorporating the Sun Goddess into Buddhism and the whole religion into the native State system, or by selecting themes from Chinese art to apply in Japanese circumstances. Another school, equally venerable, declaimed against all alien encroachments and valiantly strove to recover, or invent, some native ideal or quality to glorify in opposition. The two types of mentality clashed during the long period when Japan was isolated from the West. And when Western civilization succeeded Oriental cultures as a national peril, the Japanese were naturally better prepared than the Chinese to meet the challenge. The arguments and the methods of facing it had been developed during centuries.

Professors to-day in the Imperial University of Tokyo who debate theories of the monarchy, some declaring the Emperor should be an absolute ruler unbound by the Constitution, and others maintaining that he is like a Western sovereign, possessed of limited power, are treading accustomed paths. Their great-grandfathers in Tokugawa academies were quite as zealously arguing Confucian versus Shinto theories of the State and Society.

Similarly, the combat between civilians and the military forces goes back to ancient periods. The peaceful, luxury-loving courtiers and bureaucrats of old Kyoto in the South hated and feared the rude governors of outlying northern provinces, whose task it was to subdue forest outlaws or remnants of barbarian tribes. Each despised the other; and after the warriors, or samurai, conquered the country with their troops, their religious creed and ethics, the courtiers kept up the traditional hostility perceptible in the House of Peers to this day.

This quarrel appeared constantly during the early years of Parliament, though in a different form. Sometimes the army and navy men in the Cabinet succeeded in wrecking ministries; that of Saionji fell in 1912, because of a row over increased army divisions. They formed closed cliques, on the order of military circles in Western countries, demanding huge appropriations and encroaching on foreign affairs and education.

The struggle against them has been long. One blow was given to their prestige in 1914, when a navy scandal, akin in startling revelations to the Teapot Dome case in the United States, brought about the resignation of the Yamamoto Cabinet. But the real stroke was dealt over the Korean situation in 1919, when a change was made from the military government, which had provoked violent reaction among the Koreans, to a civil government. Sweeping reforms were instituted; the police became responsible to civilian heads; Koreans were admitted to the civil service; and a popular elective system was inaugurated gradually in native towns. Military men proved a failure in the work of colonization, and they surrendered to the civilians.

Presently the civilians began to win other victories. Under the Kato ministry, a wedge was driven into the Army and Navy Departments by the appointment of vice-ministers from ranks of civilian politicians. The military cohorts gave up their attitude of scornful independence of parties in 1925, when General Tanaka became President of the Seiyukai and, at a tea for foreign press correspondents, declared the "days of military domination are gone and the defense of the country is the people's business." Outspoken opposition has increased on the side of the civilians; the grave matter of policy toward China was threshed out on the Diet floor in 1923 when Viscount Kato, the "strong-arm" man, and Premier Kato, the more liberal statesman, carried on a remarkable verbal duel. Both business and labor, through their organizations, protested against the use of force in China in 1928, while Japanese newspaper editorials have clearly and frequently represented the public unrest over huge naval appropriations.

The real undoing of the military samurai type was, of course, the arrival of big business in politics. The old warrior clans, Satsuma and Choshu, tried vainly to keep business as well as politics within their grasp, but merchants turned away from them and financed parties in opposition to the bureaucrats—through which they have increasingly influenced foreign affairs. Business men were declared to be behind the withdrawal of troops from Siberia—a triumph over the military clique. Business men wanted the Russo-Japanese agreement for the resumption of trade. Business groups urged on the expenditures in Manchuria. Lately, in 1928, military men have themselves come out with statements favoring a peaceful attitude toward China and declaring: "Our primary interest is trade." Yet another sign of the times was the recent creation of a Business Man's Party, led

by a magnate of Osaka, which won several seats in the House
of Representatives.

The quarrel of plebeians against aristocrats is also of long
standing. Parliament itself was called into being by the lower
classes of samurai and the small clans, who demanded a hearing and created such a scandal over the Government's sale of
public lands to private interests that a national assembly
was granted to keep them quiet. Political parties were, true
enough, presided over by samurai, but the financial backing
was frequently provided by plebeian business men. In all
that Meiji period of agitation the slogans may have been
borrowed from Western inflammatory literature and the
forms suggested by Western example, but the Japanese easily
supplied their own animus and money.

So disdainful were the aristocrats toward lower ranks of
society that, owing to the fact his father was a farmer, they
conferred the title of "Prince" on Ito before making him
Premier. Later on, in 1918, no subterfuge could disguise the
fact that Premier Hara was a commoner and that in his
Cabinet were sitting experts in business and finance. The
aristocrats, entrenched in the House of Peers, have also
yielded before the growth of party government. Again and
again they brought about the fall of ministers who dallied
with the parties. But this fight is now over; the Peers met
a calamitous defeat in 1924 when they tried to govern alone
with the Kiyoura ministry; and now it is recognized that
every Cabinet must have the support of the parties in the
House of Representatives. More and more the young peers
are aligning themselves with political groups and, since the
reform of 1925, the aristocrats have lost the right to insist
on a majority in their own House.

Plebeian "bosses" at present practice the art of politics.
The older type of samurai statesman is rapidly becoming

a figurehead. Promoters and organizers do the work with increasing openness. Such is Mr. Oishi whom a lively countryman describes in this manner: "His bald head and his supposed habit of sinking into Zen contemplation have advertised his personality, and his roaring declamations about national danger . . . have made him an interesting subject for press interviews." Such bosses not only air their views to the journalists but frankly defy the peers and bureaucrats, as did Sennosuke Yokota shortly before he died in 1925. He was described, also by Dr. Washio, as "a brainy little man with forceful eyes, strong lips, an intensive forehead and a Napoleonic personality. Mr. Yokota has been recognized for years as the power and intelligence behind Mr. Takahaski whom he still uses as a blind." The portraits of such men now circulate among the public beside those of aristocratic amateurs.

The haughtiest statesmen to-day must make at least occasional gestures of recognition toward the masses. As Premier Tanaka stated in a speech on February 1, 1928, recorded for a gramophone company and given wide publicity: "The Government's social policies are based on the desire to increase the co-existence and co-prosperity of every class of people in Japan and all plans formed by the Government are for mutual coöperation and assistance among all classes of people. Whatever forms and shapes these plans may bear, they are all based on the traditional go-and-get-it policies of the Seiyukai." Politicians must lure the votes of villagers by offering road improvement programs, or by proclaiming popular if vague slogans like "retrenchment," and "industrialization." Radio instruction is given to new citizens; and the women must be remembered, too, for they are useful as campaign orators and party helpers nowadays. And there is always the possibility that, no matter how solidly seated the old parties may feel, a handful of independents may obstruct their moves. Yusuke Tsurumi, marshaling a group of six representatives under the slogan, "Give Liberalism to Japan," inaugurated new tactics in 1928 and for a moment held the balance of power.

The doomed "old order" was made vastly picturesque by the personalities of its great men and by their preoccupation, in idle moments, with the fine arts. Many of these figures might remind one of feudal dukes, surrounded by entourages of loyal bannermen, holding miniature courts for crowds of visitors, patronizing poetry and painting and, in a truly regal fashion, contracting marriage alliances with one another's political families. Into these circles of the elder chieftains, personal glimpses were obtainable. I saw the handsome abodes and the obsequious, silk-robed major-domos and servitors; the collections of art objects in their storehouses and the private altars laden with precious vessels; the deputations of formal callers; the banquets; the leisure hours beguiled by operatic arias from tuneful politicians accompanied on the harp by their wives; the disciplined children, at once proud and demure; the anxious conclaves of party men hurrying to leaders' homes to await news of a Cabinet collapse or the next campaign move. I saw this world in its intimate phases, when the family groups met in cosy privacy, and in the pomp of its public life, when avenues of wreaths led to the doorway and the garden was choked with rickshaws and limousines, while presents of gratitude or condolence, crested with chrysanthemums, were brought from the Imperial Household.

At its best, it was evident that the old order had many attractions: a grand manner, a generous gesture, a refined lavishness, a personal warmth. And without wishing to delay its departure, for it is an anachronism in modern times, I could yet grasp the complaint made by critics that something princely and romantic is departing from the world of Japanese politics.

The homes of the chief political leaders, in and around Tokyo, are still to a considerable extent more than headquarters; they are still courts. A leader is more than a figurehead; he is the personal friend, adviser, head of the clan; he is followed with the kind of devotion and loyalty which chieftains of a tribe exact; and, in the great manner, he is lavishly hospitable to the arts as well as his friends. If we could imagine the home of Coolidge as the resort of specialists in dragon-painting, that of Hoover the delight of experts in incense-burning, and the palace of Senator Norris as the chosen rendezvous of the Noh singers and the gardeners of dwarf trees, we might catch something of the atmospheric effect. If further, we could imagine a citizen flatly refusing to vote for Borah because his grandfather had been a *hatamoto,* or bannerbearer, under Senator La-Follette's grandmother, we might appreciate the complexities of the Japanese political situation. Ancestors have not yet been forgotten, nor *can* they so conveniently be ignored as in the New World.

Much intermarriage is practiced by political and commercial families. The clan spirit survives among those who are by no means connected by blood with any of the original hundreds of orders. Clan methods are employed, though the organizations themselves are rapidly breaking up and disappearing from the scene. The principles of a political party, for example, remain largely determined by the President and his inner circle; the President of a party is in effect a clan head. He prevents his party men from speaking as they will on the floor of Parliament; only a chosen spokesman, the "herald" of the chief, represents the party on major

issues. Finally, the President is above election by his group;
he chooses his own successor and inheritor, as Prince Katsura
dying in 1913 is said to have nominated in his will Viscount
Kato to take over his machine. The nearest American prototype is Theodore Roosevelt, who named Taft as his presi-
dential heir; he, too, attracted almost fanatical devotees and
his followers in large numbers remain loyal after death to
their chief; he, too, drew within his magic circle a variety
of admirers from out the great multitudes—notably hun-
ters, writers, and naturalists.

Prince Kimmochi Saionji, last of the Genro, or Elder Statesmen, is of course the supreme illustration of the institution of
the chief. Every detail related of him seems suited to the
political atmosphere of the Arabian Nights. That every important move must bear the approval of this revered sage,
long retired from office and dwelling remote from the center
of affairs in a country villa; that he should bear the name
"Great Eastern Temple" and have for his formal wife,
according to tradition, not a living woman but indeed the
White Serpent Goddess; that in leisure moods he should find
recreation in the singing of blind nightingales—all this belongs to another and romantic age.

Rather more mystery appears to envelop Prince Saionji
than the Imperial Household itself. The Emperor, Hirohito,
has been taking great pains to acquaint the people with his
Imperial life; he and his spouse have divested themselves of
several ancient formalities, discharging numbers of court
ladies, as an obsolete and extravagant group, and revealing
to the public many details of their habits, especially the
Empress' care of silkworms and the Emperor's hobby of a
biological laboratory. But no such intimate publicity sheds
light on Prince Saionji, the man far more responsible for

PRINCE SAIONJI, LAST OF THE GENRO

the conduct of the nation's business than a monarch whose dignity demands that he remain isolated from politics. The public has not known what goes on in Saionji's remote abode; it knows only that every day's reports include some such item as "Marquis Inouye called on Prince Saionji at his villa Sunday morning," or "Ex-Premier takes hasty trip South"; it knows that, continuously, a stream of visitors flows through his doors—cabinet officials, generals, diplomats, party bosses, courtiers from the Palace, "confidential messengers" of vested "interests"—and that these delegates, ceremonially attired, fans in hands, are ushered into the august presence and allowed to lay before it their problems and requests. On these visits hang important events, the downfall of a cabinet, the shifts of a foreign policy. But no outsider knows exactly what transpires within the sanctum or can guess which of these visits is merely for the sake of publicity, is a matter of formality, or is going to have extraordinary results.

That such streams of visitors should wait on the pleasure of an Elder Statesman is not especially odd; but, to our conceptions, it is curious that Saionji, more often than not, is said to sit perfectly silent throughout these interviews, speaking no word even at the close. Like many another Japanese statesman, he is proud of his impassivity, of his ability to hear startling news without "moving an eyebrow" and to give decisions abruptly. Thus, it is related of him that, when asked to choose the next premier, he "always gave his answer within twenty-four hours"; when Hamaguchi was chosen in 1928, Saionji was reported to have been consulted at 11 A.M. and to have answered at 11.30. The "silences of Saionji," followed by his quick decisions, are one of Japan's major mysteries.

However, in the case of Saionji, friends maintained that this "Oriental inscrutability" was but acquired with age. In his youth he had been a hot-headed Francophile and devotee of Rousseau's philosophy of naturalism; for a time, as an ardent liberal, he had joined in the demand for a Parliament; yea more, he had led the Imperial forces to battle for the Restoration. He had thus known enthusiasm and passion; he had waged campaigns of words and weapons. Then as years crept on, he had grown cool, cautious, ever more shrewd and skeptical. He had passed beyond excitement, beyond selfish ambition, beyond petty animosities or great emotions, beyond parties and personalities. All the haughty indolence, the mockery, of a disillusioned aristocrat—for Saionji belongs to one of the most ancient courtier families in Kyoto— seemed to rise uppermost in his character. At length like his French friend, the "Tiger" Clemenceau, he retired to a country dwelling with a garden. Here the whole political world, over which he had attained mastery during his active days as premier and as behind-the-scenes adviser, now is forced to pay him homage by making pilgrimage to his domicile. And it is his clever serving-maid, Ohana-*san,* whose favor is sought by the proudest visitor as a good omen.

Whatever may be thought of this secretive, indolent Sphinx and his position in Japanese affairs, one thing has long been clear—he is the last of his kind. The Japan that he represented, the political types he symbolized, are vanishing into a greater Beyond. No single man in a country villa can have such an awe-inspiring hold on newly enfranchised millions; the vague, looming shape of "the people" will dwarf the individual ghost. Here and there an enigmatic figure, like the American Colonel House, may continue to pull the wires in Japan, but the chance for a lone statesman to command the homage of all parties for a lifetime is over.

The old parties are shifting, changing, breaking up, while the new ones, forming among intellectuals, laborers, and farmers, are devoid of rites and ritual.

Already the aristocratic order of statecraft is rapidly dissolving. Of the elder bureaucratic statesmen, the main characters are dead. Count Goto was the last of the great chieftains who refused to ally themselves with the parties. The clan grip is weakening. Observers find the Choshu clan "almost entirely disrupted," while the Satsuma clan "barely keeps its last vestige of lingering influence." The House of Peers is decreasing in power and is assailed on every side; the Privy Council of statesmen lost ground in the death of Prince Yamagata and this last of the Genro, Prince Saionji, declines to name a successor.

No one indeed is more familiar with what is happening than Saionji himself. He knows that it would be useless to choose any person from the rising generation to replace himself, for in these times Elder Statesmen of the Arabian Nights design are no longer produced. Moreover, he permitted the passage of manhood suffrage and the coming of party government. And by bringing about the sudden overturn of General Tanaka's "strong policy" Cabinet in 1929, Saionji recognized the force of public opinion as a factor in political situations. So, imperturbable to the end, wrapped in the dignity that becomes a priest of the White Serpent of Shira-kumo, Saionji has as his final achievement made special abdication.

Nowhere was the meaning of transformation more vivid than in the home of the late Marquis Okuma, the orchid fancier, educator and politician, who led an early progressive party movement, fostered Waseda University, and who will be remembered in history as largely responsible, during the World War, for casting the weight of Japan on the side of the Allies—a move of profound importance to Europe as well as to all Asia. Chinese and Hindu delegates were in Tokyo at the time, prepared to make an offer if Japan thought the hour had come for a Pan-Asian uprising against the West. Should she unloose the turbulent forces of India and all the East and head a rebellion of races against races? It must have been an intoxicating draught offered to the statesman who presided as host to the conference. But with an ingenuity that suggests English character and perhaps the American McKinley's talent at the opening of the Spanish-American War, Okuma announced to the world that "Japan has no territorial ambition."

Kneeling on the matting of that plain, quiet room opening out upon the massed green foliage and pale statuary of a Japanese garden, my mind reverted to the stage play I had just witnessed, "The Seven Kinds of Laughter," and especially to the scene in which courtiers deliberated with the Shogun. Arrayed in a circle, hands concealed in sleeves, headdresses motionless, without the flicker of an eyelid, seemingly, they spoke one after the other in stately and sonorous language, arguing peace and war. Had the scene in this room been like that on the stage? Diplomatic dialogues? Scarcely perceptible smiles? Had the fate of the Occident and Orient been decided without the lifting of an eyebrow? Though he had been present on that momentous occasion, Count Goto, when questioned, simply sighed.

It is no mere coincidence that Okuma's garden has now been turned by the authorities of the University into an open park where thousands may foregather. Government in a garden is out of fashion. The statesman may no longer screen himself by shrubbery from the crowd; he must mount a platform and face that most modern of phenomena in the East: a voting public.

CHAPTER XXI

GENTLEMEN OF THE OPPOSITION

NOTWITHSTANDING the pull of modern interests, the spirit of antiquity in Jagan is vigorously, even fiercely animated; it is a force always to be reckoned with in affairs; and it is bodied forth in determined groups of men who form an "Opposition" movement to all the agencies of change. Thus antiquity is not confined to museum cases under the care of curators; nor is it merely revived from time to time by high-school amateurs draped in stenciled cheesecloth and brandishing cardboard swords.

One might suppose that tradition survives of its own accord, whereas the very reverse is true. Faith and organization—affection, scholarship and outlay—have worked hand in hand to preserve the racial heritage. If, for example, we may still see Noh dancing, it is because noblemen have dipped into their purses generously, and especially because the mother of an Emperor lent her prestige and enthusiasm to the cause. If we visit temples still in superb condition, we must remember that they were once in danger of being sacked and burned by mobs, if not sold by needy priests, and that only the timely combination of religious authority, Government aid, and private scholarship has kept them and their treasures intact. We too often think that the forces making for change are alone positive and virile, while the opposition is sheer inert, negative conservatism. The foolish rubber-stamp slogan of convention—the Orient is "awakened from a deep sleep"—is responsible for a wide and seri-

429

ous misunderstanding. Used as a catch-all phrase, it gives the impression, utterly false, that modern people are "awake" and alert, while old-fashioned folk are numbed with slumber. One must visit Japan to see how open and bright the eyes of the conservatives really are.

Indeed, the Opposition is perhaps more obstreperous than the Progressives in Japan. If deeds of violence are taken as a criterion, no less an authority than *The Japan Advertiser* insists that they are more frequent among groups of "superpatriots" upholding national virtues against alien ideas than among communists and radicals of all sorts. The Opposition, in fact, is a bundle of paradoxes; its ranks include scholars, artists, refined aristocrats, and religious mystics together with bullies, outlaws and assassins. It contains both the most charming and attractive elements, and the rowdiest and most lawless in Japanese public life to-day.

Who form the Opposition? Chiefly gentlemen of sufficient means, it seems. Farmers and workers remember too well the sufferings of the "good old days" to unite in active propaganda for their maintenance. And apparently it is men, rather than women, who form the bulk of aggressive conservatism. Of course they have the tacit support of many conservative women. The educator Miss Atomi, for example, tried to perpetuate tradition among her pupils and mingle art with athletics. But I met no rabid, widely known *anti*-suffragette in Japan. Surely I should have heard their names, at least, had there been stanch feminine *antis* as well known and active as the reformers. There were, curiously, some "*anti*-manhood suffrage" groups; one of these attempted to assassinate the Premier who seemed about to pass the Bill; and large numbers gathered in a Shinto temple to pray that the Bill might never pass. However, workers and women are not the organized obstructors of "progress."

BLIND MAN'S BUFF KNOWS NO EAST OR WEST

Is the Opposition a united body with a common goal? Evidently not. It seems to be composed of extremely dissimilar minds. No single type of "conservative" exists in Japan; nor is there any program or method characteristic of them all. Some of the Opposition are gentle, romantic dreamers who scarcely do more than lament, or collect fragments of the past; others hire gangsters to break up political meetings. Moreover, each group wishes to retain a different aspect of tradition: its art, morals, military virtues, or peasant simplicity. One faction upholds handicraft and agriculture against townsmen and traders, with the fervor of early American Jeffersonian Democrats; another wishes a return to the national isolation which marked the Tokugawa Age; others would rejuvenate a still earlier time of frank and free Pan-Asian intercourse. But perhaps no one really advocates a complete reversion to the past. Fencers, for instance, who wish to preserve the excellence of their art, would not go so far as to lead their pupils into prisons and let them get the practice by lopping off the heads of condemned criminals. Loyal "Sons of Yedo" still come together to sing firemen's songs, tell legends of the "volunteer companies," and compare their elaborately tattooed bodies designed with maple trees, dragons, and even processions of knights a-horseback; yet it is doubtful whether the most ardent firemen among them would abolish Tokyo's modern engines and equipment.

The sum total of Opposition ideals may be boiled down to a hope of salvaging some of the worth-while cargo from the wreck of the olden times, while letting the hulk itself sink into oblivion. Nevertheless, in doing that much, they raise questions of immense scope—questions, too, of worldwide pertinence. What are the worth-while qualities of the past? Can we make use of them to-day? Have we a place in the civilization of the machine for the cultures of ancient, localized, agricultural societies? And if we prefer, deliberately, to hold the best of antiquity as a living force in our hearts and homes, can we do so? Can any of us, in Orient or Occident, hold back Time?

Unquestionably, the Opposition has rendered mankind a service in preserving the treasures of the past from harm. It makes one smile to think how excited Westerners grow at the digging up of a buried civilization in Egypt or Chaldaea, while ignoring or disparaging this living antiquity in Japan. The heritage is magnificent. In her museums may be found wall-paintings comparable to those of Indian caves; dance-masks, said to have come from Gandhara, where they may have been modeled on the masks used by the Greeks; harps from Egypt; glass from Imperial Rome; and memorials of the ceaseless intercourse of West and East. And it all might so easily have perished! Impoverished knights sold their heirlooms, during the Restoration, and mobs menaced temples with destruction; we saw a pagoda at Nara that was once offered for sale by needy priests but is now a nationally guarded treasure. It took prompt action to feed the starving, disbanded troupes of Noh dancers who were left without a patron; to rescue artisans and encourage their work; to accumulate records patiently and set about the tremendous task of appraising the past according to modern standards of research.

So well has the Opposition done its work that Dr. Otto Kümmel of the Berlin Ethnological Museum, declared in 1927: "No country in the world has kept its art treasures—I avoid the terrible word 'curios' for Far Eastern art works as I would for a Rembrandt or a Michael Angelo—so jealously as Japan. . . . The result, at any rate, is that no art is worse represented abroad than the Japanese. Not even the Boston and Berlin museums—the only places outside of Japan where you can see at least a decent selection of Japanese art works—give anything like an adequate idea of the Japanese formative genius."

The result is a really amazing semblance of the contemporaneous about the most ancient parts of Japan. You do not see ruins, as in China, where wild grasses wave from broken pagoda balconies and gleaming tiles fall from the walls of the very Forbidden City beneath the grinding feet of camel trains. The Chinese have neglected their estate; in India, it has been left to the invading British to rescue many of the most important relics from decay and give them their due. But in Japan, the palaces are swept and clean as though used only yesterday; the temples are in repair and incense spirals above the altars.

More than in other Oriental countries, the Opposition is elaborately and consciously organized. We do not read of the Chinese bringing in their country folk to show the townspeople their agricultural dances. "Cultural preservation societies" are not general and large affairs. Chinese and Indians either take the past for granted, or else regard it as a hindrance. But in Japan, the past is considered a fountain to which thousands come with small pitchers, trying to scoop up a little of the bright abundance before the secret springs dry up forever.

Moral qualities of yesteryear appeal to many members of the Opposition as more important than objects of art. Admiring the social ethics of Asia's sages, those who can write try to keep them alive through popular magazine articles. Others prefer the demonstration method; such were the men, ancestral swords in their hands, who recently broke into a hotel ballroom, stopped the jazzing, and performed what they considered a more virile and artistic exhibition—a samurai dance. Such were the solemn protesters against the unveiling of France's gift to Japan—a statue—Rodin's "The Kiss." In speeches, moralists appeal to the people to maintain the strict discipline of tradition, especially to avoid luxury. But the most picturesque agency employed is the deification of those Japanese dead who best exemplify national virtues. In 1929, the eighth Tokugawa Shogun, a "reformer," who lived two hundred years ago, was deified in an ancient Shinto shrine of Ueno Park; he was honored by sacred dances all the night through and processions of tribute bearers came down the lane of stone lanterns to place cherry blossoms on his altar. Even more notable was the semi-deification of a woman of the fourteenth century, Lady Kusunoki. A group of noblemen explained that, as Christendom had exalted its womanhood by glorifying the Virgin Mary, so they wished to honor all Japanese femininity by paying homage to this supreme incarnation of its best qualities—a mediæval widow who educated her sons to uphold her Emperor, and who died a nun in the service of the Merciful Goddess. She guarded the "filial piety and loyalty which are the essence of our national life," and now her home and garden are to be restored as a national monument.

However, a moral aim is not always present in the Opposition groups. Many love the past for other reasons. Certain elderly citizens of Tokyo adopted a resolution in 1925 declaring themselves "against Western civilization" because "the spirit of gallantry is dying out before the onslaught of alien ideas." The Superb View Seekers' Society was formed to perpetuate as long as possible the memory of beautiful scenes; a group of its members, merchants of Osaka and their wives, dressed in olden costumes and with "ancient, square coins" in their money bags tramped on foot all the way from their city to Tokyo to have a last, fond glimpse of the Tokaido road, beloved of Hiroshige, before the motor car and billboard should destroy its charm.

Very general, indeed, is the prevalence of a purely artistic love of the past, unrelated to moral concepts. No country is fonder of exhibitions than Japan, and extraordinary ones are held to show the people at large what a patrimony has been left to them. The Imperial Family opened in 1927 its great library, with its thousands of volumes of early Buddhist writings and its long series of images of the emperors, some over a thousand years of age. And important, also, was the small but splendid exhibition given by the Imperial Household, the wealthiest temples, and the most distinguished families who lent their best treasures for a popular inspection. Nowhere else in Asia do the highest circles in the nation as readily bring out their prized heirlooms for the multitude to view. Here were "one of the three most perfect vases in the country"; the most precious folding screen; the oldest diary in Japan, of the Konoe family; the golden teakettle of the Todos; letters and diaries written by Nobunaga and other famous characters; and one of the finest and most celebrated swords, swung by many a ballad-renowned hero, yea by the mighty Hideyoshi himself.

Associations are formed of devotees of some single art, say Noh dancing, in order to hand down to posterity the technique and symbolism of the ancestors. And there are venerable masters who tell the public their secrets; the oldest tea dealer in Tokyo describes his method of brewing tea—which must be fresh and hand-picked, touched by no machine—in a century-old iron kettle, over a fire of charcoal, never of wood, and how he waits until it "sings a certain tune. According to a Buddhist priest who lived in the thirteenth century, the song of the kettle ready for tea should be like the sound of wind passing through pine trees."

Drama enthusiasts have gathered into the big library at Waseda tens of thousands of volumes on Oriental plays.

The fencers continue their skilled contests as of yore. The nation's greatest swordsmen meet, barefoot, unmasked, in full silk robes with their sleeves tied back, in a hall lighted only with candles, before a Shinto shrine. And women, still expert with the spear, exhibit "the womanly art of self-defense" practised in feudal times.

The samisen lovers, as well, grow sentimental, and hold services in honor of the discovery by a Japanese of a cat-skin substitute for snake-skin to cover the instrument. Perhaps the most curious of their celebrations was conducted by geisha and singers from all over Tokyo, who came with flowers and incense to invoke the memory of a deceased— The Honored Cat of the city's best samisen-maker.

Lovers of antique costumes gather at exhibits of robes, worn during the past three hundred years, showing the evolution of Japanese fashions from plain, warlike eras through gay eras when merchants' wives competed in the "beauty shows" of the race. Tokyo still is proud that the wife of a Yedo merchant, in a coral-embroidered robe, was successful over the wife of an Osaka merchant. Tokyo has always felt that its women were the best dressed.

So are the humblest factory workers encouraged to uphold tradition. They make pilgrimages, on their holidays, to shrines and famous mountains or to flower-viewing resorts. The soldiers, the children, and the machine operatives—the immense numbers of the barrack-dwelling Japanese—take pleasure in this scenic-historic sort of holiday. It has thus been said that the common people in Japan retain a stronger link with the past than Chinese factory workers who, coming in from the country to industrial settlements, lose all touch

Photo by *William Beard*

A SACRED DANCER IN THE TEMPLE GROUNDS

with the land, make no pilgrimages, have no feeling about the racial culture, no sense of continuity.

However, lawlessness no less than ethics, ferocity as well as politeness are heritages of Japan's bygone days. These, too, have their perpetuators in the *otokodate,* who still live on as a reckless element, in the *soshi,* or political bullies, and in the violent reactionary societies such as the Seven Births Society or the Black Dragons. While gentle-folk, painters, and lovers of the lute are holding elegant festivals in honor of the past, these "strong-arm men" are busy terrorizing the community by "demonstrations" such as throwing sand into newspaper presses, setting off fireworks in the gardens of radical politicians, and occasionally committing assault, blackmail, or, once in so often, a real political murder.

Such reactionaries are a genuine survival of another age— quite as much as aristocrats or tea masters. They descend in type from the denizens of the "underworld" of feudal Japan—an underworld which corresponded to that of Elizabethan England in its gang-organization and brawling, in its roystering temperament. Such strata were also to be found in any sort of society where government was loose and the subjects took the law into their own hands, forming "vigilantes." Especially was the Japanese brand found in Tokyo, the military headquarters of the nation, where hordes of idle soldiery collected. Accordingly, these modern violence makers are relics of the "Wild West" days of the people.

As far as my reading indicates there were several kinds of bullies in those dear, bad, olden times. First of all were the semi-knightly ruffians, below the samurai degree, yet not plebeian either, a species equally common to the whole European continent from Rome's "miles gloriosus" to the break-up of feudalism. Bold, idle fellows they were, apt for a bowl or a brawl, wearing kimono painted with blood-red or thunder-black and with monstrous, fierce swords and daggers stuck in their sashes, who liked to swagger along the roads and terrify honest citizens and goodwives. Rather more famous were the *ronin,* who were not merely swash-bucklers but veritable outlaws, living by wit or threat. Some-times they blackmailed merchants, and usually they had but to darken a doorway, hand on hilt, to receive hasty accom-modation. Often they curried favor with some lord, offering to do secret dagger work or run dangerous errands. But there was a third, less celebrated and quite different variety— the plebeian braves. The plain people in self-defense or-ganized gangs to fight off *ronin* and swashbucklers, while now and then a bold plebeian constituted himself a petty king of a district, demanding tribute in return for protection. The world of the common folk was ruled in this "boss" manner, when not controlled by groups and gangs—quite apart from the legal system. The battles fought between sol-diery and plebeian gangs have been interwoven with the folk legends, and the memory of great "bosses" is perpetuated, like our sagebrush badmen by the movies, in the popular melodramas. The people sang ballads and wrote plays about them, idealizing them for their bravery, for their defiance of tyranny. They developed romances about them, much as the English did about Robin Hood.

How these types are able to survive is a natural inquiry. Subsidies from political leaders take care of certain fellows and one society is said to have had the backing of a Cabinet minister. Independents live by blackmailing politicians, newspapermen, and public personages. The Kosuikai, espe-cially vigorous against socialists and communists, has been

described as an organization of "firemen, coolies, gamblers";
it was headed at one time by Count Oki who believed physical force was the main factor in human affairs, but who lost
control when the gamblers, disgusted because he would not
campaign to legalize their profession, pulled out of the
society. The Black Dragons has been directed by a university
professor, among others, and by the aged Toyama, known as
Japan's "Robin Hood." Thus they draw their funds from
all sorts of sources and have a wide assortment of sponsors.

They have many talents. Hardly a man in public life
may expect to escape their attentions. Count Goto, in his
last years, kept a *jiu-jitsu* expert to give *soshi* a hot welcome when they tried to molest him in his work, for several
times they attempted to break into his home or disrupt his
meetings. They have been responsible for a long series of
assassinations that have made public life a somewhat risky
career for the past twenty years. As late as 1921, a prime
minister was killed in Tokyo Station; and in 1925, a *ronin*
was sent to prison for an attempted plot on another premier,
to "prevent manhood suffrage." They have an accepted rôle,
not because they are violent, but because the development of
modern Japan has been closely connected with them for
many years; the *ronin* were among the first to rally around
the newly erected Government—naturally, for they saw more
hope of advancement through turmoil and the overthrow of
the ancient régime. For a generation, they hung around politicians, ready for action, as they had hovered around feudal
lords. But now Japan is making strenuous efforts to rid herself of these vestigial remains.

A leading newspaper, the *Asahi*, took a courageous stand
against them in 1928. It refused to print an advertisement
of a "patriot" society. Soon after, on a flimsy pretext, a
band of men rushed into the building, stopped the presses,

smashed furniture and shot stray bullets over the editorial heads. Weary of buying off such bands, the *Asahi* went to court about it. But other victims are not so courageous.

The tale of the strong-arm men is long and often fantastic. Where else would a fanatic "patriot," dressed in white kimono, with a letter of denunciation in his teeth, stab himself before a politician's doorway? A few of these patriots seem genuine in their convictions; others act for pay. Bullies have attacked proletarian members of the Diet, and have killed one; they rushed into the Soviet Embassy grounds and pinned a message with a dagger to a tree. They have furious altercations with labor: accusing a radical of throwing a can of sulphuric acid, they made a noisy "demonstration"; marching with banners condemning proletarian politicians as endangering the great principles of Nippon, they were captured and jailed for disorder. They made at least one very sacrificial display, in a town near Osaka, when they came at the bidding of some local boss and with daggers slew four political opponents, then walked to the police station and gave themselves up.

Where do they derive the principles which they so vehemently defend? They have not evolved these themselves. They have annexed the theories of the scholars, who form a third important element of the Opposition class. Scholars, it is true, do not participate in the struggle between old and new, forcibly, but their pronunciamentos on ethics, culture, religion, and the state form the theoretical groundwork of nationalism. They have constructed the ideals of "Japan's grand national virtues" which Robin Hood and his swarthy Dragons defend.

The revival of Nichirenism, a Buddhist sect of purely Japanese origin, with nationalist connotations, is a case in point. Forbidden by the Tokugawa Shogunate, it now claims millions of followers. Shinran, the other most famous Japanese Buddhist teacher, has also had an enthusiastic revival. However, this trend toward a racial or national Buddhism has been traced further in the chapter on Buddha's Modernists.

It is one of the neat ironies of history that Japan should have renewed many of her old customs to make a revolution palatable to the people. As a good example, the theories of Shinto "Emperor-worship," which is commonly taken to be characteristic of the Japanese mind, were indeed very little heeded in the days of the Tokugawas, when it was high treason for a lord to pay a respectful visit to his powerless sovereign; and if they were so vehemently preached during the past generation, it was to consolidate the rule of the Emperor after the usurping Shoguns were overthrown; it was to save the nation from civil wars by proclaiming a code of loyalty.

True therefore as it is that genuine lovers of tradition have been laboring to preserve the old culture—that is not the whole story. The shrewd statesmen long ago realized that an appeal to historic precedent was the surest way to dress up a radical change. They besought the scholars to hide, under the trappings of a glorious heritage, the real revolution that was being carried on to modernize Japan. Santaro, in an illuminating article, states the facts: "And it was a very clever and effective piece of statecraft that all the revolutionary changes and reforms were forced down the unwilling throats of the people under the awe-inspiring excuse that they were the revivals of long-neglected, august customs which had obtained at such and such a time under the reign of such and such Emperors." Several of the very strangest practices in Japan to-day are the forceful renewals, or even inventions, of politicians and scholars.

They do not spring from the "enigmatic soul" of the Oriental, but from the singularly calculating brain of the statesmen.

It is easy to find evidences. Take Shintoism. The very word Shinto is Chinese; the religion embraces some thirteen sects that differ widely in their tints of Buddhist thought and degree of "purity" from the original. Dr. D. C. Holton, one of the authorities on the subject declares: "The earliest records of Shinto were set down by Buddhist priests and at first it was a nameless set of beliefs and only became known when it was necessary to differentiate it from Buddhism." Contemporary scholars are struggling manfully to strain the native faith from the imported, but they seem to arrive at dissonant results. They agree neither on the interpretation of words in the Shinto liturgies nor on its principles. One faction says it is direct religious worship of the Emperor; another says it is only respect; a third calls it ancestor or nature worship and stresses the more primitive aspects of its early stages; a fourth names it the worship of a great Universal Principle and elaborates abstract and refined philosophy around it.

It is claimed that the cardinal virtue of Shinto goes beyond mere bodily purity in its philosophic characteristics of sincerity and uprightness. It is true that the chief ceremonies connected with it are those of physical purification, a complicated system ranging from the sprinkling of water with a leafy bough to the burning down of whole buildings "defiled." Ablution is everywhere performed, as I learned whenever I visited a Shinto spot; the trough of running water and bamboo dipper were conspicuous at the entrance. But Shintoism also involves mental purification, a scholar, Mr. T. Kuroda, explained to me, declaring that the reading of the Mannyo, ancient Shinto poetry, or the listening to the noble verses of the Noh dance exercises an uplifting and cleansing effect upon the thoughts. It has the power of confession and absolution.

If Shinto, which exalts the Emperor, has undergone such searching and reviving, it must not be supposed that the Imperial Household itself has remained unaffected. Outwardly, it appears to be the focus of ancient and picturesque services which have come down unbroken through the long line of the emperors—the longest of the world's reigning dynasties. The Emperor is the god-king; when he is born, white-clad archers twang their bows in salutation; innumerable rites make up the calendar of his years; his sword must be made by a certain iron-forger wearing ceremonial costume and dedicating his work by a Shinto priest's prayer. But things are more transient than they may appear. The Imperial Household has shown itself very progressive and extraordinarily ready to modify the habits of centuries.

The mere fact that the Emperor now dwells in Tokyo is in itself an innovation. When Emperor Meiji moved there in 1869 it was absolutely unprecedented in Japanese history, for no Mikado had ever lived so far north. And, more significant still, the supremely simple and genuinely Japanese ceremonies of his coronation were, in part, restorations. Santaro, in a concluding article on the Shinto religion, says that the Emperor Meiji deliberately discarded vestiges of the Chinese ritual for his coronation—laying aside the "red silk robe with patterns of tiger, dragon and fire" and bringing out an ancient Japanese robe patterned with clouds and cherry blossoms to "symbolize a monarch of peace and not of the sword." The rite, no less than the robe, was a reflection of the contemporary psychology. Instead of being carried out in the usual exuberant Buddhist style, with incense and liturgy, it was performed in renewed Shinto ritual—a native taste. "Simple evergreen branches, together with pink and white cloths, were offered at the altar of the gods. . . . We may rightly say that his coronation was absolutely unique in the history of Japan."

The very custom of giving large banquets to the people, observed by the present Emperor at his coronation, was an innovation of the wise Meiji and his followers. Formerly, an Emperor had not notified the people when he ascended the throne. He disregarded them. Nor were they supposed to pay much attention to him; only in very recent times was precedent so far broken as to allow plain citizens of Yokohama to present resolutions of welcome to their ruler. The splendid legend of the father-people relation, while undoubtedly hoary with age, is far more sedulously fostered in these times.

And there are other changes of late. The ladies-in-waiting used to form a most conservative group in Japan. They never married, but spent their lives within the castle compounds. They were always Kyoto ladies, speaking Kyoto dialect, and after all these years they still look down upon Tokyo as the rough North into which they were compelled to move. We are informed that they continue to order their textiles, cakes, and watermelons from Kyoto, for nothing Yedo produces is exactly to their taste. These ladies had two important orders to obey: always to rush to the Imperial apartments at the first intimation of earthquake, and second, never to venture into the Presence after having eaten an onion or while wearing maroon-colored garments. However, this picturesque force has now been reduced by the Imperial Family; some are allowed to marry; many have been discharged from attendance. So passes one definite nucleus of archaic Japan.

The great urge which unites the whole Opposition—

artists, roughnecks, and scholars alike—is to "preserve Japanese culture," for they all feel that the really precious racial wealth is more than a collection of objects, however beautiful; in fact, an unique spirit. About the old Japanese way of life there was a harmony of thought and action, a balance of dignity and simplicity, emotional warmth and yet a fine serenity; and they all believe that its loss would be irreparable.

On the qualities constituting this culture, they naturally divide. Some say the important thing is *Yamato-dashii,* the invincible temper of Nippon. Some call it *Odo,* the "sublime moral doctrine" of the East. Others, principally Black Dragons, are fond of a word meaning "profound national essence." And they define, as variously as they name, their interpretations ranging from chivalry, harmony, and unity to loyalty, æstheticism and sheer discrimination. That the important element is moral and political—the unity of the whole nation as a family under divine sovereignty—is an emphasis frequently heard. Count Yoshinori Futura, in the *Sun,* a Japanese magazine, says: "The monarch should form the center of spiritual life." And those extreme patriots, the Black Dragons, ascribe their hostility against Socialists to the idea that class conflict is comparable to fratricide, and is even sacrilegious in so divine a family.

Moderates find yet other moral phases worth praising: the warlike discipline of former times, the spiritual readiness to die at any moment for duty's sake, and the physical preparation to endure gruelling hardship. They commend the "cold practices" of earlier days when the Japanese used to exercise barefoot in the snow or run naked through the streets, dashing frigid water over themselves and praying for prowess at a shrine. They laud the corresponding mental attribute of self-sacrifice.

To persons less stern than either "Puritan" wing of the Opposition, the chief merit in their heritage is the artistic sense, manifesting itself in every department of life, from gardens to shoe patterns, from thought to gesture. And they especially like the exquisite sensitiveness to mood, in which their country has excelled. Writers devote themselves to naming the various moods, prevalent in old Japan, and to describing the dress patterns, garden arrangements, food and dishes, songs, poems, and philosophical thoughts that belonged to each. There was a light, cool, airy, elegant summer spirit known as *assari;* a dark, mysterious autumn one; and a stern, pale, winter mood. Each was endowed with a most elaborate system of symbolism, so that the whole year and the complete personality could merge together in sympathy. And whenever an individual had attained, by a splendid combination of effects, proper consciousness, he felt as happy as though he had created an epic, an oration, or any visible masterpiece.

A great number of Japanese really miss, most of all, the sense of security, of stability, lacking in the fluid modern world. In this temperament, they resemble the poignant Westerners who sigh for their own "golden age." Everybody once knew what was moral or immoral, it is said; what was æsthetic and what was boorish; just what to do in the case of bad luck—go to a Temma shrine and exchange carved wooden bullfinches with a fellow sufferer. One knew to whom loyalty was due and with how deep a bow to express it. Within a hair's breadth—far more exactly than among Europeans at the most stilted phases of their civilization—could be fixed the range of the gesture suitable for the reception of a guest at a tea party. The guest knew the position of the fingers on lifting the tea bowl—nay, more, the precise number of swallows (three and a half) in which the foaming liquid must be drained. A person could be as certain then of the survival of ancestral spirits as of the color of string to use in tying up a topknot. He could be as confident about his religious sect as his rank. With the same sublime exactitude, a father both knew what shape of cakes to serve at his daughter's wedding and what to do to be saved.

To become familiar with aspects of this Eastern culture is one of the deep emotional experiences offered by a sojourn in Japan. In three different ways, I grew acquainted with many of its manifestations: by meeting the grandparents, the elder generation of the Japanese, and hearing them discuss it; by going, week after week, as often as possible, to the theaters where the life of Old Japan is still faithfully mirrored; and finally, by a trip to the heart of the ancient world, Kyoto and Nara, where our host, Count Goto, in person guided us through many seldom opened and seldom described haunts enshrining the spirit of the past.

PART III

IN THE TWILIGHT OF THE GOOD OLD DAYS

CHAPTER XXII

THE GRANDPARENTS

OUR own grandfathers were sublimely confident that an eternal gulf of time, faith, and race separated them from their silk-robed, almond-eyed contemporaries of the East. The East and the West were, thank goodness, twain, each inscrutable and implacable to the other. A sword of hostility was placed between them by God and maintained by Rudyard Kipling. None of our grandparents looked forward to a day when Old East and Old West, become quaint and antiquated, should be lumped together by heedless youth, called "Mid-Victorian" and "Pre-Meiji," and the twain invited to meet at last—a common doom.

But as a matter of fact grandparents of two hemispheres were shocked, to nearly the same degree, by about the same things: the first horseless vehicle; the naughty young people who *would* waltz; Ibsen's Nora; women on bicycles; seaside community bathing. No Buddhist priest could have been more scornful of a woman attempting to lecture than the New England pastor of the nineteenth century who announced Susan B. Anthony by saying: "A hen will attempt to crow like a cock at 8 P.M. in the town hall." And our grandparents clung to the same kind of fancies as the Japanese; reluctantly they abandoned swords and side whiskers, hoops and bustles, as the samurai gave up swords and topknots, kimono and sashes. Nor has all vestige of the good old days disappeared. Here and there the high pompadour

451

of an elderly lady serves to remind us of the Old West just as the coiled headdress of a Japanese lady recalls the Old East. Our ancestors clung to the Latin and Greek classics, Shakespeare and Milton, handmade lace, solid silver, and the polite usages of formal visiting and New Year punch drinking, quite as the Japanese older generation clung to Chinese and Pali texts, Chikamatsu and the Mannyo, hand-painted silk, thick lacquer, and the polite usages of calling and New Year saké drinking. Both Mid-Victorian and Pre-Meijian were characterized by a puritanic obsession with moral doctrines, a distaste for the nude in art, a strong sense of family obligation, a condescension toward women, a sense of ownership in children, and a rigid propriety and formality which they released best in the company of chorus girls or geisha.

Neither the Japanese nor our own grandparents, however, were wholly conservative. They reacted to the encroachment of the modern world in varied ways. Many could only complain; the more articulate actively engaged in combats to defend their customs; others, aware of the inevitable, possibly enthusiastic about "progress," prepared a welcome for change. All these types are as common to Japan as the West. Indeed, nothing would be more unfair than to assume there is a universal cleavage between the old folks and the young on the question of novelty.

Even on the point of adventuresomeness the grandparents know no race. That was clear at a function in Tokyo, given to introduce young people to themselves by a progressive pair of elders. Youth of both sexes was shy and stiff. The girls, silent, with drooping shoulders and folded fingers, sat demurely in a flock at one end of the room, forming a picture especially striking for its high light—a beautiful noblewoman with eyebrows thin and arched as a moth's antennæ and a face like an ivory carving, who lifted no lid and rustled no sleeve the whole afternoon. At the other end of the room, crowded the young dandies in their black silks, arms tucked in their wide sleeves, hardly daring to look across the carpet at the girls. A pretty miss played the koto, or harp, and tremblingly retired to her corner; the young men, without looking up, discreetly applauded. Nobody spoke. But the grandparents! How they glided about, trying to "mix" their charges, create an atmosphere of sociability, and "make" conversation! The grandmother was so gracious, and the grandfather so jovial—and both so unavailing—that one guest's sympathies were wholly with the aged.

Elderly women have a bravery not excelled by the young; it is illustrated by persons such as the late Mrs. Imanishi who crossed the ocean in the days when Japan had only a sailing vessel that she might lecture to Americans on behalf of her people; and Mrs. Koto Kuroda, who conducted an American investigatory nurse through the Russo-Japanese war hospitals during a winter campaign—carrying with her a small samurai dagger for suicide should anything happen to her charge. These will do as examples; but the groups of their kind are large and forceful. Of such fiber were made the companions of the males of the Meiji era who threw overboard the ballast of centuries, in a crisis, to lighten the ship of state. They talked to me of the fire of their youth; how the words of Rousseau, of Whitman and of Tolstoi had come flaming into the Orient, and how they had prepared for a New Japan with such believing courage as youth hardly imagines to-day—for young people in Japan now share with the youth of the earth an after-war disillusionment. No young people confessed to me that they had passed through or were passing through a period of such enthusiasm, such joyous action as the old folks remembered and recounted.

So one discovered afresh on Japanese soil that it was the elders, not the youngsters, who have made the new society.

And yet the acme of conservatism is manifest among the grandparents at the Noh dances where æsthetes assemble. Foreigners are seldom present for the dances are not their sort of "show." Indeed even the Japanese public has until recently found itself shut out; only in late years have popular performances been given. Families of high station and means are asked to join the Noh societies as patrons—in fact membership may cost thousands of yen a year—and their lists, full of princes and magnates, read like those of Western opera-box holders. The audience moreover is exclusively composed of members and guests—aristocratic and artistic, or at any event very wealthy persons of the old régime. There is no cheap balcony.

Yet there is nothing "quaint" about these grandfathers who compose the bulk of an audience conspicuously lacking in youth. They are correct, severe, precise gentlemen of the ancient school. On their stiff black sleeves are blazoned the crests of distinguished families—crests that fluttered perhaps on *daimyo* banners or on a great general's iron war fan, ten centuries ago. Their crests are usually of flowers, *swastika,* or the new-risen moon rather than of the lions, boars, and unicorns Europeans used in such abundance. They carry in their thin, nervous, civilized hands the librettos of the Noh opera on which are traced in fluid script the musical notations and words they follow to refresh their memory, though the truth is they know their favorite arias by heart and are rendered irascible by the slightest variation in interpretation.

Also dignified and correct are the wives and sisters who accompany the gentlemen. They wear the plainest, darkest of robes, with very short sleeves, also crested, made of pure, heavy silk. Their backs droop, their eyes are downcast, and

their mouths "sucked in" after the fashion of modest womanhood in the age of romantic sentiment. Their coils of hair
glisten like the entwined tails of so many dolphins fresh
from the sea.

The audience kneels, four to a "box." Each party shares
the libretto, a brazier with a quilt to keep them all warm,
and a lacquer case of sweetmeats. They disdain applause or
other vulgar noises of approval. And what an array of faces
they present! Aristocrats in their serenity, they are nevertheless wrinkled with age and severe experience so that they
escape the appearance of smooth effeteness. They look wise
instead. These women are not attempting to seem young or
to "keep up" with adolescence; they are very well content
with their honorable years. These men attend no college
reunions to renew youth as if the quality were anything
desirable. They have left youth behind and found in maturity a peaceful recompense.

But hark! The clear scream of the flute is heard. The big
drum, freshly warmed over a brazier fire, gives out a hollow,
warning note. The player of the little drum interjects a few
oddly timed slaps. Then a chorus of kneeling men, wearing
brocade costumes that resemble "bungalow aprons" with
winged sleeves, their dark eyes downcast and fans in their
hands, begin a long, wailing, sonorous chant comparable to
a Gregorian, but interspersed with sudden, keen cries. In
this music the Japanese find a resemblance to old Buddhist
chants, but much of it even to them is not music so much as
impassioned recitation.

Down the rustic bridge toward the stage, decorated with
three fresh pine trees, come the dancers. No use to imagine
them human beings—these monstrous moving symbols!
Padded robes magnify their shapes; since all are made of
silk, chiefly by the patterns may one tell which denotes

armor and which a peasant's frock or an angel's wings.
Masks hide the faces of gods, demi-gods or demons. Pale
cameos, with dreaming eyes and mouths parted in charming
smiles, alternate with those contorted like the Greek tragedy
masks, which may possibly have inspired them, exhibiting
frozen grimaces, bulging eyes, and gilded noses, topped
by wild mops of red and black hair. The only human sign
betrayed by these ponderous, glistening effigies is the hand—
a wax-white hand, strangely small for the size of the image,
holding a wide fan, brilliantly painted.

About the dancing motions, also, there is little to suggest
humanity. For every lift of a foot or finger is slow beyond
belief—as patient, seemingly, as the budding of a flower, as
leisurely as a geological process. No action could be performed more tardily and yet be visible at all. To a Westerner, at first, it is appalling—positively agonizing. A
dancer takes many minutes to move a foot forward, to tilt
a fan; a complete turn may consume ten minutes of heroic
effort. The figures move like wraiths in a creeping night-
mare. A slowed-down motion picture resembles a race, compared to their progress. And the chorus moves on as dis-
passionately, wail on wail, cry after thud—a dark and dron-
ing background for an almost motionless dance! Very soon,
however, one begins to lose all sense of time; to forget how
many hours have passed since the first effigy appeared; to
abandon the counting of minutes. The mind becomes locked
in a trance, lulled by this soothing, magical calm. These are
gods—they cannot be hurried.

With a lofty disregard for the time element, the whole
program is arranged. In the old days, plays began with
sunrise, the first cry of the flute meeting the first red ray of
dawn. Now they begin later, but still continue through
most of the day. According to one of our hosts at such

plays, Mr. Ikenouchi, head of the Noh Preservation Society, the program opens with a religious or moral legend; then follows something warlike and gallant, to stir the pulses; then comes a play of graceful and quiet character, usually with a woman as heroine; something terrible succeeds, with demons and goblins; the whole concludes on a lofty note.

Two among the innumerable plays witnessed on various occasions stand out in memory as highly spectacular. One was the famous Spider Dance. A hideous demon casts through the air flying filaments of raw silk, soft as down, that settle about the head and shoulders of his antagonist, the warrior-emperor. Vainly the warrior whirls his blade— no edge could cut that horrible, white mesh. The sword is tangled; in his glinting armor he turns and turns like a bumblebee caught in a spider's snare. And the warrior realizes that this is no plain animal enemy, a dragon that any Saint George might slaughter with a well-wielded axe. This is incarnate Evil, beyond the reach of muscle or steel, standing so confidently quiet, sneering at human bravery. The Greek playwright never framed a more vivid drama of Fatality.

The other was the no less famous story of the Sun Goddess lured from the dark cave, where she had hidden, by the laughter and alluring dancing of the Immortals. The cave was represented on the stage by a tall, white-sheathed box like a coffin on end and the dance had ages ago been sublimated into an infinitely clever parade of symbols. Music and epic recitation with choral accompaniment mounted steadily in power and vehemence. A breathless suspense was built up, during all the tortuously slow progression, by the solemn weaving of gestures and the lifting of cadenced voices. And when at last, through the sheath as through a white cocoon, peeped the burnished image of the Sun—

crimson as flame—a kind of sigh went over the audience.
And I felt myself that I had participated in something akin
to creation. Mortal skill can portray no more subtly the
rebirth of a world.

The Grand Opera of the East is the Noh. It is patronized
by a leisured class which prides itself on possessing entertainment so slow and difficult as to raise it above the comprehension of the masses. And it makes artificial demands of its
audience; for if our opera postulates that singing is as
natural as speech, that a hero will whisper his love in high
C, that a fifty-year-old prima donna, impersonating a damsel
of fifteen, will coyly reply in a voice that sets steel girders
shaking—the Japanese Noh assumes that gesture is a substitute for sound: that a warrior, threatening an enemy, lifts a
fan; that an angel, in flight, raises her sleeve. However,
if Grand Opera has its lighter side in Comic Opera, so does
the Noh in the ludicrous mediæval farces called Kyogen.

But Noh is more moral than Grand Opera. It deals with
themes loftier than the jealousies of baritones. Religion has
had more influence on its development. For instance, an
angel-woman explains to a fisherman in dance forms the
glories of heaven; a god descends to aid a virtuous armorer
with an emperor's sword; loyalty of vassals is rewarded by
miracles. Rich skeins have been woven into what Mr. Ikenouchi calls the "brocade" of the Noh—nature worship,
native legends and Chinese maxims, Indian philosophy,
rhythms two thousand years old, cryptic oracular utterances,
poetry on eternal themes. Much of it is certainly Malaysian,
for the legend of the Sun Goddess and the cave has
been traced throughout the South Seas whence some of the
ancestors came; the decorations of pine trees remind us
that the earliest Noh were performed in the giant forests of
Nara; but there are startling points of similarity with Greek

drama, often observed, and some scholars are strongly inclined to emphasize the fact that an Indian king's emissaries
saw Greek dramas, mask and buskin and chorus complete, in
the courts of the Bactrian royalty. Certainly the mood is lofty
as the Greek and I used often to smile at the trick of the
Fates providing us in the pagan, and supposedly "immoral"
and "sensual" Orient, rather than in the West where it
might logically be looked for, with the loftiest and most
abstract of moral themes upon the stage.

Only in symbolism can such concepts find adequate treatment. Not in realism, but in cryptic utterance and formal
gesture is the highest faith disclosed. The West has never
fathomed the subtle meanings within the reach of the human hand. It uses feet and lungs for self-expression—high-
kicking ballet or full-throated singing. The East, on the
contrary, deeply impressed with the hands of Buddha that
bespeak so many things—meditation, "taking possession of
the world," or, most frequently, argumentation—has made
one of the most perfect of her arts out of gesture. The hands
of the East are slim and sensitive; they may be used to indicate the grace of butterflies or the accuracy of a whip-end.
And in each land of the East, the gestures conform, I believe,
to national genius; those of Hindu or Javanese dancers are
far more contorted and involved than the few, brief, very
plain gestures of the Japanese. There is nothing sinuous or
exaggerated in any pose of the Noh as there is in the god-
dances of Java. Now and then a Noh dancer kneels, but this
is a process requiring—so it seems to an impatient observer—
a quarter of an hour and naturally such an extreme is seldom
attempted. Usually the gods of the Noh converse in hand
motions, infinitely slow and solemn, revealing heaven and
hell at their finger tips.

Elemental is this approach to divinity. The abundant and

gorgeous elaboration of the more southern Orient in its pageantry of gods is wanting here. The Noh is archaic and as rude and formidable as the pre-Olympian gods, the Titans. The stage is utterly plain, of bare wood; the sole ornamentation is a giant pine tree painted on its wall. The bridge, or path, to the stage has three living pine trees tied to it. So are all the ingredients of the spectacle simple: low chanting of men, the thin scream of a flute, a half-folded fan extended in a poised hand stretching farther, farther, inch by minute, a white-shod foot lowered to the floor with infinite accuracy by miscroscopic degrees, the enigmatic smile of an ivory mask.

Beauty and color are concentrated in the textiles worn by the dancers. Their scarlet and green, gold and blue, fairly burn with clear brightness against the bareness of the wooden background. There is nothing "theatrical" or pretentious about them, for these costumes, in large part, are genuine apparel of great costliness, produced in the early days when Japanese craftsmen were so skilled they could sell some of their products to China herself.

I have seen many of these rare garments, handed down by the centuries, in private collections, one specially arranged by Mr. Ikenouchi and one owned by Marquis Hosokawa, an enthusiastic patron of the Noh. The latter display included a robe of beaten instead of woven gold; a thin film of sheer metal tissue was attached to the fabric—into which gleaming sheet was embedded, as in fine jewel work, half-open fans of rich embroidery in crimson, pearl, sky-blue. Of course Marco Polo had tales of the East to tell to the Venetians! Once one has seen and touched these golden robes, a positive shudder occurs at sight of the tinsel, makeshifts, and shoddy of overseas theatricalism. The most lavish decoration on the Western stage usually strikes wrong notes; it falls flat before the sublime beauty of genuine fabrics flashing, like flawless gems, against a soft-toned, bare wooden wall.

If restraint is the secret of Noh decoration, control is the secret of the dance. Motions so slow can be made only by a perfectly poised human machine, coördinated in every nerve and muscle. Though but the finger is moved, the whole body that supports that finger must be taut as a steel spring. The impression made by the Noh dance was of terrific power held in leash. And when I had opportunity to go "behind scenes" at a fine theater and talk with the actors, I found them united in saying they were under continual strain upon the stage where they must be tense and relaxed at once, somewhat like dancers on a tight rope. And as a young woman amateur of the Noh—for of course, women do not yet perform in a regular theater—Miss Tohmatsu, showed me the most elementary gesture, the proffer of a fan, I began to understand the muscular exertion behind that poise.

The audience, attuned to that tension and control, is one with the dance. An earthquake during a Noh performance convinced me of that. It was really a strong quake. The fragile structure rocked like a ship; timbers creaked and the wooden pillars, balanced lightly, swayed in odd rhythm. It seemed to me a strange wind was rushing through the building, like a gale before a storm. But no Japanese stirred. The audience ignored it; never moved a robe or shifted a folded foot. Throughout the tremors, the play went on. The chorus lost no note; not a single fastidious gesture of the dancers wavered. The lesson of the Noh, for both players and onlookers, is moral and physical control.

I have stayed so long by the Noh because I believe that its secrets are the secrets of Japanese inherited culture. This poise achieved by intensive training of the will and nerves and muscles, this integration of the body and mind, is the basis of all disciplined action, whether in tea cult, singing, dancing, fencing, etiquette, kneeling and bowing, writing, painting, chess, or meditation of the Zen School. The armor-maker and the painter often retire for a period of "mind-purification" before commencing a piece of work, the old craftsmen having been taught that by such effort the heart and hand will work harmoniously. It scarcely matters to a Japanese whether he studies tea serving or fencing—the control he learns from either art is the same. And hence appears the inseparable union of morals with skill in Japanese conventional training.

In so seemingly small a matter as writing a letter with a brush, all sorts of qualities and capacities are utilized. Mr. T. Kuroda expressed it this way: "All the vital strength of the student is brought into play. You may wonder, but it is true, nevertheless, when we would write with strength, this strength comes from the abdomen, from the center of the self. From this center flows strength to the arm and fingers, which must be obedient to the mind. The mental power is manifested through the extremities of the body; therefore, the extremities, or fingers, should be as flexible as the vital strength is powerful. . . . So a line, a stroke, a spot, must convey your full capacity, even your personality." If this is true of writing, it is still truer of painting, in which the Japanese have attained a muscular control that, authorities state, has never "even remotely been approached by the West."

Fencing, like writing, is allied in the Japanese mind with philosophy. The great teachers of former times were exponents of morality. Somewhat as American and English champions of sport justify them by concepts of "team play" and "honor," so the fencing-master of Japan hoped to develop will, control, and independence in his pupils, as well as agility. He taught the use of the sword and spear, the chivalric code involved, and the philosophic ideas appropriate to a warrior.

Warrior dances are accordingly masterpieces of boldly suggested power. Like the Indian brave's performances or the Pyrrhic dances of the Greeks, they are an art formed out of drill. The warrior in gilded mask and cumbrous armor leaps madly, yet in a second is frozen from furious motion to perfect calm. His heavy javelin is swung high, but its point is wielded as adroitly as a fan. So is the music, low, deep, and ardent, allied to the gestures. I have tried rapier work and known the icy thrill of watching an opponent's foil tip dart like a serpent's tongue—but no fencing match that I have watched elsewhere has had the terrible grandeur of Japanese sword play. Like the warrior dance, the duel is of almost sublime ferocity—an exercise in what the Elizabethans called "the honorable horror of war." And as one sits through it, he realizes what formed the character of those "grand old men" who turned Japan overnight into a modern nation; and of their wives, as well, who were drilled with the spear for "emergencies."

Apparently the complete contrast with the war dance is the tea ceremony, but its principles are much the same. Zen philosophy was especially adapted to the warrior, and yet it strongly emphasized the cult of tea. Both are exercises in the restraint which results in power. And both are surrounded by moral doctrines. There is much more to the tea ceremony than tourists at the Kyoto golden pavilion suspect.

The perfect ceremony is preceded by a special dinner, accompanied with special music. But this perfection grows prohibitory in cost. The dinner was formerly prepared by the host himself, but skilled cooks, trained in the art, are now patronized by wealthy connoisseurs. The tea banquet is elaborately formalized to the last detail. Chopsticks, for example, must be laid on the right side, never on the left where a prisoner's implements would be placed. As for the music accompaniment, when we heard it rendered by one known as the "Great Koto Player," it seemed severely archaic rather than opulently classical in form.

A disciplined humility is another phase of the Japanese control—brought to a zenith in the tea cult. A story illustrates it well: a rich man, coming into possession of a famous bowl, valued at thousands of yen, cut a slight imperfection into it which reduced its price, enabling him to serve his guests with less ostentation. Never, surely, was there a more imposing plainness, a more haughty self-effacement, than one finds in the atmosphere of the *chanoyu*.

As the host of Old Japan, whatever his rank, was expected to serve his guests in person, heat the kettle, sweep the garden path and sprinkle leaves upon it (the only comparison I know is our habit of punching sofa cushions to make them look "informal"), so his guests, leaving their swords outside, with their shoes, crept through a low opening and bowed themselves inside the cottage. But in these times, of course, daughters more and more take over the task; that proud humility no longer sits so easily on men.

Serving the guest was a cult in Japanese feudal life. There was always someone to serve and someone to be served. The woman, no matter how high born, must perform certain tasks for her husband and the Empress Dowager rose a half hour before her royal spouse to set the nation a housewifely example. The husband served his guests. Clan, court, church were ranges of hierarchies. Thus the tea ritual developed into an art what was at bottom a necessity.

Dancing, fencing, tea service, discipline and humility—how evanescent are these arts! And that is the chief impres-

sion I got of Old Japan: its perishable quality! Perhaps in
no other country does the past seem so real yet so frail. Its
ancestors have left behind chiefly living forms. Few monuments and no astounding pyramids, enormous baroque palaces, stern fortress walls like those of Chinese Soochow or
the French Midi, or the weird elaboration of Hindu stupas
attest to a ruined culture. The heritage of the past is alive—
in gesture, a tone, a mood. Let a single generation go heedless of these and the heavy cable that still binds the nation to
its mediæval anchorage will be snapped. That very fragility
seems to produce a wistfulness in the eyes of the grandparents, as, with trembling hands, they wrap up and put away
their tea bowls.

CHAPTER XXIII

WHERE PROBLEM PLAY YIELDS TO PAGEANTRY

THE past lives on in Japan at the Noh or in the tea ceremony and its witchery and realism also linger in the drama. The old-fashioned theaters of Tokyo stand just a few blocks away from the heart of the skyscraper district, but in spirit they are a thousand years removed, offering to the inhabitants of the modern city a surcease from the cares of the present. A brief rickshaw ride can transport one into a departed world, peopled with kings, dragons, ghosts, fox-women, dancing boys and feather-footed angels, as well as desperate outlaws, mendicant priests, courtesans, craftsmen and deities in disguise. Problem plays may be forgotten in such company, before such unexampled pageantry; and if a few dark anxieties still creep into this other, enchanted world, they meet the sure and superb solutions of wizardry and warfare.

It is an astounding offering that these old theaters still make. Nothing quite like some of their dramas is left, many people think, on the earth to-day. China, it is true, has her opera; Java her shadow shows; India her god epics; and the West its "revivals" of Shakespeare, Schiller and Euripides. But the Japanese theater, though not untouched by influences from Greece, perhaps from India, Java, China, Mongolia, and probably even Spain or Holland, is conspicuously indigenous and has a history of its own running far back into the ages. It is possible to witness in Japan stilted, archaic dramas of a very hoary antiquity; puppet-inspired shows; splendid tragedy resembling the Elizabethan in manner and guise; curious comedies and melodies once crooned in the primeval forest of Nara; and plays coming from the mediæval heart of the common people. The latter represent with marvelous accuracy and realism the everyday life of old Yedo, its slums and temples, shops and houses of pleasure, and they have been produced unchanged for generations by so much as the movement of a foot or the accent of a voice. It is the incomparable variety and the refinement of artistry as well as the splendor of fabrics and furnishings that make Tokyo so outstanding a theatrical capital.

Some persons may have to live with the electric signs of Broadway but I have a constant nostalgia for the banners, tall as those of a king's army, which rise rustling along the narrow lanes to mark the site of a Tokyo theater of the older sort. Breezes fresh from the waterfront lift and wave their green and crimson lengths in billowing rhythm. Piles of empty wine kegs guard the doorway to the playhouse, each inscribed with an actor's name, according to respected custom. Over the portal hang festoons of lanterns, low-swung, blazoned with the great names "Kichiemon," "Uzaemon," "Kikugoro," "Koshuro," "Baiko" and the other favorites—scions of Japan's actor royalty.

Within, the crowds are in native attire, for even the business man dons the flowing kimono for this type of theater. They throng past the garden with its actor shrine and lighted tapers; past the low-ceilinged restaurant where merrymakers kneel about lacquer tables, eating octopus and playing chess, the air rich with pungent odors; past the booths with their vivid mounds of toys, candy, paper flowers and mirrors for geisha to tuck in their hair. The crowd is full-skirted and flowing-sleeved, and its faces are wreathed with happy, irresponsible smiles; back and forth it presses, eating and shop-

ping and minding the babies, in intervals of a performance
that lasts from seven to eight hours and includes all sorts of
plays to suit every mood. A loud, wooden clapping is the
signal to hurry to the auditorium.

The great hall has festoons of lanterns hung about its low
balcony, while the stage is covered by curtains splashed with
the crane or bamboo or geometrical crests of actor families.
Japanese sound fills the space—not the harsh surf of an
Occidental throng, nor the uproarious pandemonium of a
Chinese theater, but a peculiarly soft, light, gay sound, better
suited to dwellers in paper houses, if punctuated by the wails
of stray babies or imperious clapping to summon more tea.

The audience settles down on the sloping floor like a huge
picnic party at an overcrowded beach, but even so into railed-
off compartments each just big enough for four cushions—
box seats in the most literal sense. One must learn how to
glide, with the skill of a tight-rope walker, along the narrow
partitions, sink into one's box and fold one's skeleton into
convenient compass without stealing too many inches from
one's neighbor. A pot of charcoal for chilly fingers is tucked
into the center for all four to share and a pink quilt is spread
over the knees; in such crevices as may remain are stowed
away a pot of tea, a bag of candies, a lacquer tray of cakes,
programs, souvenirs and a baby or two. Here, in sardine-
like but undeniably cozy sociability, one remains for hours,
rising only for occasional promenades and meals. First,
however, it is advisable to practice self-folding in the front
row of the balcony where, in case of a cramps attack, it is
possible to hang one's feet surreptitiously over the edge,
among the lanterns.

When one's feet are accustomed to subordination, there
comes a profound joy in this intimate atmosphere. A neighbor in heavy, crested silks, follows the play from an old

book containing Yedo actor-posters. There are incredibly ancient mothers-in-law with expressions full of wisdom and experience such as would make the fortune of any Dutch "old master." Attendants in gorgeously flowered pantaloons and butterfly sleeves trip along the railings, about the height of one's shoulder, handing teapots and refreshments above one's head in all directions. Geisha, with faces masked in white powder and tinsel confections in their hair, giggle conspicuously and cast coy, over-the-shoulder glances as they settle their perfumed robes. There are rollicking *ren-jyu* parties, or claquers, who are rewarded by the actor they favor with presents, especially towels marked with his crest. To such an audience, the plays are not "revivals" out of a dim past; it could not lose itself so completely if they were. They are familiar, absorbing drama and enthusiasm for them, so frankly displayed, carries one along in its currents.

Much of my own delight in the plays was, of course, due to exceptionally competent guides. Various friends, some of whom had been patrons of the theater since Meiji days, included me in their parties. Through the courtesy of the Imperial Theater management, moreover, I was not only offered seats at its own theater, which uses chairs, but at the older theaters, native style, such as the Meiji-za, the Ichimura-za, and the Shintomi-za where its actors often moved to perform classic plays. Mr. Ayukawa, the business manager, was an indefatigable translator and interpreter in front of the stage and a gracious go-between for curious foreigner and actors behind the scenes. Naturally the orientation was enormously aided by all such forms of coöperation. Otherwise I should have been blind to what anything meant in itself and to the significance of the whole in the national history.

The eight-hour fare—which is all the metropolitan police

have left of the former twelve-hour feasts—includes a variety of plays. There comes first, usually, a historical tragedy, dealing with the adventures of some noted hero, which instills a strong moral lesson of courage or loyalty. It is extremely old and symbolic in character and amazingly magnificent, grotesque and gory. Then follow dances, perhaps a Kyogen farce with its pristine slapstick humor or a later, merrier dance, a ballet with gorgeous settings, or a popularized version of a Noh dance, replete with legend. Finally arrives a melodrama of a more realistic, heart-rending character: a story of the underworld it may be, of tramps and burglars, or of peasants and bourgeoisie, or of noblemen, fine ladies and terrific battle scenes.

Thus, kneeling before the great stage, it is well to know that the productions are not indiscriminately "old Japanese." They belong to three quite different historic periods, representing Japan in different lights. To the mediæval belong *Kyogen* farces and many dances. To the seventeenth century belong the *Jidai Geki,* or historical plays, with their marionette technique. To the eighteenth and nineteenth centuries belong the romantic, sentimental tragedies and comedies, the so-called *Sewamono.* In a single performance therefore the theatergoer may live through hundreds of years of history and legend.

The effect these dramas have on the audience can be comprehended only by a knowledge of their origins. The classical drama, for instance, is the product of several streams: the ritual of the Buddhist Church, the recitations of troubadour poets, and the marionette theater. It is therefore highly artificial and suggestive rather than realistic in design.

One of the streams that shaped it was dancing, contributed by women in the beginning as one of their early acts of worship. Ever since the Sun Goddess was lured from her cave

By a female deity's pantomime, Japanese priestesses have performed sacred motions accredited to divine inspiration. The women of this race have danced before kings and gods like their sisters in other lands—in Burma, China, ancient Greece, modern Seville in honor of the Madonna, in Sicily to typify the joyous steps of Santa Venera in Paradise. In water boiled over a fire of sacred splinters from the temple of Ise, some of the first Japanese priestesses used to bathe before their performances. Women of the Ashikaga period employed two types of rhythm, the *odori* with the feet and the *mai* with the hands. And in 1592 a priestess trained in rituals, the famous Okuni of holy Idzumo, opened in Kyoto a traveling theater, the performers in which were also women who formed with her a company that developed religious dancing into a genuine drama accompanied by flute and samisen or biwa. But since the dances of those times were provocative as well as sacred, scandal arose in connection with the drama. Efforts were then made to substitute boys for the women performers but that did not improve the atmosphere of the theater noticeably. Finally *onnagata,* or men players, took over the female rôles and between 1664 and 1881 women were by edict forbidden the theatrical privilege, though there survive in Kyoto troupes of women who can perform the dances.

The second stream of influence was the *katari,* or recitation. In the days before Chinese writing was introduced, the emperor had his own bard who recited history in measured, solemn meter. Though the bard vanished in time, the recitation in this peculiarly grave, sonorous intonation continued. Women novelists of the Nara period had their works recited by poets in this measure, to the music of the plaintive biwa. Much later, in 1500, a woman composed the *Genji Juni-cho-dan,* or Twelve Stages of the Minamotos, which was recited

by a blind priest to the accompaniment of a koto. Gradually
these recitations became popular and were then supple-
mented by dolls as actors.

The first puppets came from Korea and the first puppet
theater was at Osaka, where Chikamatsu, Japan's "Shakespeare" as he is sometimes called, wrote for these marvelous
dolls long epics of love and war, such as Koxinga the Pirate.
While in Kyoto the plays were of tragedy and greed, in
Yedo they were of activity and gayety. But whether the note
was the one thing or the other, when men took the place of
dolls, they continued to act in the rigid, jointed, peculiar
way of the puppets. Human dolls these actors were.

Only about one hundred years ago did popular drama
begin to appear in written form. Though the acting remained an imitation of the ancient dolls, the plots now
concerned the plainer people and their sufferings, in the
main. Some were as frank and unashamed as Restoration
comedies in England. Others were morbid in their gory
displays, catering to the real or fancied tastes of the lower
classes by such means as crucifixion scenes and murders. So
degraded were popular plays considered that the samurai
were forbidden to attend the theater between 1634 and 1868
—either in the days of their unwritten or written concessions
to the masses. They were supposed to devote themselves
instead to the Noh dances and other aristocratic arts.

It has long been the custom for the actor families to own
specific plays, draw royalties from them, and hand down
their secrets of training in production to sons or adopted
children. Even the scene painting of certain plays has been
for eleven generations a monopoly of the Hasegawa family.
Epoch by epoch, however, the Japanese stage has developed
new drama in accordance with the changing popular life.
As in Yedo days, there were two types of theater: the ancient

dolls and the contemporary male actors, so to-day there exist, side by side, two kinds of performances: the old *Kabuki,* employing male actors solely, and the modern problem plays with female actors as well.

There is but one actor, Koshiro Matsumoto, who can impersonate the giant warrior, Benkei, hero of epic combats. And but one is equal to the "Seven Kinds of Laughter" in which all the furious emotions of a tricked and deserted Shogun are expressed by the wordless voice, now shaking with gusty rage, now sinking to a mere mumble, without losing at any time the mocking tinge of one who knows himself the victim of a sardonic jest. A man must live in mediæval moods who seeks to portray Herculean Benkei, cleaving twenty heads with a single scythe-like stroke, or the pitiably solitary figure of the Shogun, shaken with horror and humor. Let a single generation forget to hand down that tradition, long purely oral, and the plays will die too. All the research workers, learned doctors, and archæologists on earth will be ineffectual in restoring them to convincing life. The same thing applies to the conventions of the stage; only so long as audiences remember their origins will they be intelligible and appealing.

Ballets fill the intermezzo between dramas. These may be Noh stories in gaudier, more popular form; or they may be products solely of the folklore imagination. Perhaps courtesans whirl to the tune of staccato accents; or maidens with gleaming fans, representing butterflies, tease a sleepy lion; or a female demon lures a warrior through an enchanted forest to his death.

There is yet another kind of dramatic dance. And this, to me, was the most fascinating contribution of Japanese art. The dance of Baiko in "Wife of the Drum Player," is an example. Its story is brief: the widow of a murdered drum player comes to court to demand vengeance, bringing with her the crimson robe and gold-winged helmet of her husband. The court is a garden of cloudlike cherry blossoms, enriched by magnificence of courtier costumes. Here the wife pantomimes her story—and goes insane with the excitement and grief. Tall, gaunt, powerful as Lady Macbeth is she. Wearing the white robes of mourning, she clasps the crimson robe and gilded helmet of her dead lord and dances out her emotions. By the slow changing of her face, the eyes that widen and glitter, the voice, hoarse and strange, the frenzied chanting of the musicians, the blood-quickening pulse of the drums, her sad tale is forever imprinted on the mind. At last, she flings herself upon the gilded drum of her husband, standing on a high pedestal, and beats and beats and beats upon it until she sinks, lifeless, to the ground. It was an incident; a fragment of classic art.

Thus in Japan the dance is an intimate part of a story instead of an excuse for pleasant activity, arabesques, athletics, *les belles jambes,* and *pirouettes.* There is the perfect way to convey grief by the folded sleeve; to lament the departed by the outstretched arm; to indicate the falling of autumn leaves with the fan; to dance the spirits of children or demons. It is poised, measured, exact, even in its wildest frenzy. The expression is not that of an individual, of a Mordkin, or a Pavlowa, but of a type: the angered warrior, the happy maiden, the foolish clown.

The Western dance is an expression of freedom and athletics; of the desire to soar from the points of the toes, from the ball of the foot; to seize the air with the hands; to toss the head like a foal; to jump, to thrust, to whirl and click the heels. Musical comedies, with their strenuous antics by overworked, muscular chorus girls or the erratic, shaking and loose-jointed clog dancing of the American vaudeville, would be as queer in the East as the Noh would be in the West. The mellow East is, by contrast with the boisterous, gymnastic, grosser West, simply sensitive, discriminative, controlled, artistic.

The Japanese dance takes very little room. There is none of that bounding from one corner of the stage to another, finishing with a *pas de Basque* before the footlights. It is like revolving on a pivot—a quiet, inward, spiritual affair.

"Warriors" of the Russian ballet come leaping and flying on the scene, brandishing spears, displaying their swelling muscles in enormous bounds, spins, Cossack stamps. The Japanese warrior dances a strangely subdued, Pyrrhic dance, a crouching, light-spinning, almost dainty dance, the bright spear gyrating deftly and neatly as a surgeon's lancet over his head. It is delicate, precise, requiring as much nervous control as the other demands muscular prowess.

If the Japanese warriors are restrained, the women are infinitely more so. A minuet is more daring and flirtatious than the dance of the gayest beauty of the Shimabara. The men who take women's parts are exquisitely feminine; indeed they exaggerate timidity and refinement. The coy maiden, with a trailing branch of wisteria, with bright eyes peering over the top of a trembling sleeve, is a paragon of shyness. And some of the dancing is stately. Even the fingers of an Eastern dancer are invariably close together, so that the hand is like a long, thin leaf in the breeze! whereas the ideal Greek hand is one with fingers slightly parted, little finger slightly curled, index finger pointed upward—restraint versus expansion.

Each moment of the Japanese dance is a picture; so the whole dance is like a kaleidoscope of paintings. Now one recognizes the print of a lady with a fan; now that of a whirling sleeve; now that of a clumsy peasant in his straw hat; now the palanquin-bearer. All are clear-cut, with clockwork distinctiveness. The aim is not one of flowing and melting from one meaningless curve to another. All is sharp, angular, each moment set off from the next.

In similar ways, the music differs from ours by a world of psychology. The human voice accompanies the dance, making the song speech instead of abstract rhythm; it has a meaning; it tells a story; it is not merely lovely sound.

In no case does the song pour out, full-throated and strong from the lungs of some lusty tenor, a voice that shakes the last row of the Metropolitan Opera. An unthinkable thing in Japan! No place to develop that phenomenon in a paper-walled city! The fact is that Japanese song comes from curious gurglings in the throat and from hummings in the head; it is falsetto, of a pitch unfamiliar in any Western land. Strange cadences, unearthly notes! Yet in time, when an alien grows used to it, it awakens emotions of sorrow or suspense or stately dignity.

The voice is not that of a troubadour striving to reach a lady on a high balcony with a thrilling serenade. Nor of a roaring drinking song, battle pæan, or evangelical exhortatory hymn. It is melancholy and wistful in the mood of folk music in general; grave as befits a ritual; disciplined in the court manner.

One must cast off memories of Western music to appreciate it; become passive and receptive and sit for hours, listening and watching. Gradually the motions, solemn and slow, with fan and sleeve and sword, associate themselves with the song; with the cadenced, intense, fierce voice, lamenting; with the shattering cry of flutes, the minor keys of stringed instruments, plinking and plucking in the background. At last it all becomes a part of the heart; of vague sensations, sad and poignant and noble, floating like clouds in the mind.

Practically all the paraphernalia on the stage is valuable. Robes are genuine, rich and plain. So are the heavy amber ornaments. The swords are steel in the place of tin and rest in perfect scabbards; the helmets are not ordered from Eaves, but are straight steel and gold. Cherry blossoms on the trees are at least real paper blossoms, each fastened on its twig, in clouds and clouds. The houses, too, are true houses—small, light, open to view through doors—capable of being moved on the stage bodily, garden and roof and floor. By opening the walls of paper, the accustomed interior is revealed with its light decorations, a gleaming lantern, a single screen. The effect is neither "theatricalism" nor "realism." It can only be described as art.

The colors of the ancients were universally more keen and fresh than our own and the Japanese stage retains its ancient color sense. Scarlet and rose, purple and green and gold and silver are full-bodied, hot, fierce colors that speak directly and simply to the eye. The result is that, against a plain wood background, the brocades of a gentleman stand out like a golden bonfire. And a dancing girl in flamingo robes gives a comparable shock of color—for instead of being drowned out by a gaudy chorus or a rich backdrop, she is alone on the stage.

Finally it is in the treatment of line that the Japanese dramatic art is unique. Gestures are made a physical shorthand of the emotions. We too beat our breasts and wring our hands but not as condensation. Legend and sentiment expressed in the opening of a fan is that to the last degree.

After the classics follow the popular melodramas, created to please eighteenth- and nineteenth-century bourgeois, for whom no battles could be too gory—since they had never

worn swords themselves—and no scenery gorgeous enough
to satiate their covetous eyes. But though magnificence runs
riot, the moral end is ever kept in view. Instantly recognizable as types of noble or plebeian, good or evil, are the
characters: the knight errant, the injured peasant, the innocent village maiden and the merchant's wastrel son.

The romantic heroine played by such a master delineator
as Baiko Onoe is more than an individual; like her sisters,
the Greek and Elizabethan tragediennes, she sums up all
men's dreams of superb, doomed womankind. The romantic
hero, impersonated by Sojuro Sawamura, is incarnate gloom
—a Hamlet infinitely dejected. Very small and light, his
hands flutter gracefully as feathers in a breeze, his voice is
soft and pleasant and his manner courteous. But his face is
stern and cold; he wastes few words and, serener than
Western heroes, he surpasses them in deeds. In black brocade, leaning on his dead love's tomb, the moonlight glinting
on his two curved swords, he has other means than gestures
or long soliloquies to prove his melancholy. The Japanese
stage, child of feudalism, still tolerates a frankness appalling
even to a realistic modern; it allows him to commit
suicide in full view with utter *sangfroid* and the most devastating regard for detail.

Sometimes horror is carried almost to unendurable lengths
on the boards but then so was it in actual life. In "The
Trial of the Sword," Kichiemon revives the former practice
of testing the new blade on a living being. In this case it is
tried out on a criminal. The tableau is lurid: a body
stretched on the ground; the warrior, ferocious but typical
of his age; the vast sword uplifted in hideous suspense;
courtiers in splendid robes; cherry blossoms; weeping peasants; cries for mercy. And the sword descends. At that
point, in a regular Western play of the present time, some-

body would dash in with a reprieve. But, as in a *Grand Guignol* thriller, the happy ending is absent in this case. No detail of the unspeakable carnage is omitted. Yet let us remember how Sir Philip Sydney of the Elizabethan day, incarnation of the ideal English gentleman, in his novel, "Arcadia," describes the hero, a Greek, slaying rebellious peasants and townspeople—cracking open their heads with fierce, majestic joy, upholding the pride of his nobility. Kichiemon and Sir Philip Sydney could have chummed together, just as Benkei and Beowulf.

The climax is always an unforgetable picture, as for instance in the tale of the destruction of the Heike clan. First the great court ladies, tragic and proud, follow their husbands dead on the battlefield to death in the sea, saving their own "honor" by casting themselves from the cliff. Yoshitsune alone stands like Horatio at the bridge fighting, fighting until his white silks are red with his blood and his hair is disordered like that of a specter, his face a picture of determined but hopeless woe. At last with the ultimate sweep of his sword he thrusts back the enemy and climbs the cliff. There he ties himself with his crimson sash to a huge anchor which he raises in his arms—a many-pronged anchor raised in his arms! The enemy warriors draw back in awe. The orchestra reaches its crescendo, as Yoshitsune in his turn leaps into the sea, anchor and all. The Heike Clan has come to an end.

Terrible grandeur like this makes the modern treatment of Shakespeare plays seem puny indeed. We are willing enough to have the villain murdered, but we like to have it done with a shot behind the scene. Though we accept the idea of murder, we shrink from the actuality of the deed. Now the Hollywood movies are tutoring us, again, in mediæval violence, in murders with axes and guns, in the revolting aspect of violent death. Just as the Japanese ban the most gruesome of Pre-Meiji plays, Hollywood brings sadism back to the stage.

Yet, it must be said, if the East still faces the realism of death, it shrinks from that of love. No Easterner could bear to gaze on Western love scenes without the same spasm of horror that we have in the climax of his Sword Trial. There are amatory scenes in the old Japanese plays, but so decorous, so restrained, so like our stage murders! Take the dance pantomimes for illustration. Here the meek maiden, in the wisteria-broidered costume, dances daintily, now hiding her bright eyes behind her embroidered sleeve, now stamping a white-shod foot or twirling and twinkling a small silver fan. The hero, grave, impassive of countenance, without a glance in her direction, dances a profoundly solemn dance all by himself on the other side of the stage. A most iron-hearted lover, one would say, a most heedless Romeo—until one sees him, in the next act, commit suicide for her sake.

It is not always easy to distinguish recent plays from the inherited drama, but the general distinction lies in the social emphasis. Thus the modern work bears much the same relation to the classic drama that the Ukiyo prints bear to the early silk paintings of the court. In the field of modern playwriting on classical lines, women are rapidly winning acclaim.

Perhaps the most famous and the finest of such work is the play, *Kakiemon*, which the great Nizaemon, one of the oldest actors in Japan, holds as his property. In this play he is one of the most appealing of characters, an aged pottery-maker, who, with his family on the verge of starvation, at last discovers the secret of making a rare vase—of a peculiar and lovely red which to-day bears his name—and accordingly gives happiness to all. The dancing of the old

man, his sorrows, his wistfulness, his overwhelming joy at
the discovery are a sweet and gracious thing. The aged, wise
man of the people! One meets such in the countrysides of
Japan, constantly, and recognizes their tenderness and their
pride amid their poverty.

In this type of play there is dance pantomime of the
marionette mode and prolonged conversation. Two characters squat on cushions, pipes in hands, and talk for hours, it
seems, in unhurried, low, polite speech growing minute by
minute in feeling and intensity but never reaching gesture.
The voices do not rise in anger or grief; they express suffering and helplessness in the presence of Fate. Nor do the
faces change a muscle; yet the emotion is there—in the eye,
in the mouth. Nor is the audience restless; it will have its
dinner in the theater by and by. Meanwhile the slow working of Destiny may pursue its irrevocable course. There is
time to bow, to fold hands in sleeves, to reply. Then, when
the climax does come, it is genuine and powerful and
convincing.

There are no local models for the Bowery Bum, the flashy
horse thief, the daring speculator, the tough girl of the
frontier, the wax-mustachioed villain, the bulldog detective
—ever-recurring favorites of the United States. Instead the
popular models are usually poor old peasants, gentle courtesans who sacrifice themselves for love, and thieves quick
and nervous who, possessing the inevitable heart of gold,
have also a softer exterior than their kind in the West. And
there is one decidedly unique model for melodrama in the
East, namely the Buddhist priest who is frequently presented
in scandalous guise. However impoverished the people's
hero may be, he is above a sodden boor. He leaves his muddy
shoes on the step without the hut; he kneels in a proper
manner on the bare ground; he pours his tea, lights his pipe,

bows to his visitors and friends as gravely as a fine gentleman, though rain and snow be falling through his leaky
roof. No rogue but has a certain polish; no dancing woman
but has a kind of modesty and grace; no villain but does his
dastardly deeds with a rigid etiquette.

Japanese popular taste enjoys melancholia. It dwells with
sympathetic relish on suicide, disappointed lovers, bad men
or fallen women who deny themselves for others. Rarely is
it gratified with the happy ending, the miraculous good fortune—the coach and four, the patrimony of a duke. It
would seem next to blasphemy, wholly unconvincing, to
have a hero discovered to be the long-lost heir to a kingdom,
or a poor dancing girl awakened to be the *daimyo's* bride.
Since the golden surprise is rare enough to be incredible
in Japanese social life, it forms no part of drama. Poor
young men and maidens are unable to ride off in a grand
equipage or in a great motor car. They consider themselves
lucky in a Japanese play if they get to marry at all.

Some of these plays, of course, deal with "high society"
and feudal codes rather than with industrial and sex struggle
in spite of their modern date of authorship. In such cases
the classical formula is apt to be adhered to with considerable fidelity, portraying peasants contented with rusticity;
queens who face death bravely; fairies turned by malicious
demons into monstrosities; warriors called upon to suffer
rather than to think out disarmament proposals. On such
material is built the play *Muromachi Gosho,* written by a
modern writer, Kido Okamoto. Those who go to Kyoto do
so with a new feeling after seeing it performed. It closes
with a note from a flute—a sweet cry from the ancient bamboo instrument—sole friend of a blind and rejected warrior-
lover, about to seek oblivion in a river.

Many questions arise as one muses in this Eastern theater

of the earlier mode. How long can the Japanese remain divided between their life and their dreams? How long can they retain love of the old society and yet enjoy the new? Ten years ago they were wholly content to watch plays of feudal life; Ibsen's "Ghosts" was a failure. To-day, it is a real success. Slowly they are becoming conscious of another drama, the revolt of feminists, of children against parents, men against overlords, overlords against destiny— themes untouched in the lantern theater streets. What compromise can be made?

There are students of Japanese drama, notably Professor Miyamori, who believe that another generation will no more behold, in all its glory, the glittering mediæval pageantry of the *Kabuki* plays. Times are altering. New drama, new life, the movies, the younger audience with its strange demands surge to the front. The actors are turning away from tradition themselves, to innovations. The precious masks of the puppet dolls of the Osaka Theater, on which living actors modeled themselves, were destroyed in a recent fire. They can be copied but never so well. Is the *Kabuki* therefore doomed?

No one can foretell with certainty. But there is still time to enjoy the classics and to learn from them the lessons they have to unfold. It is still the privilege of the modern world to witness this cultural survival in its midst—a treasure house of art that has escaped exploitation by the foreigner; a kingdom of make-believe that has evaded the American press agent. It is incredible that the *Kabuki* should be thriving at all at this hour; it is an anachronism, like a mastodon on Main Street.

But our own "classic" drama, equally anachronistic, is in the hands of high-school amateurs or little-theater enthusiasts in cheesecloth drapes. Greek masks are in museums and "educational exhibits"; the plays are studied by savants, who argue over interpretation. Energies are devoted to "reconstructing" Greek or Shakespearian drama and to lamenting the passing of such antiquities; yet little attention is paid to the *Kabuki* stage, still alive with the vigor of direct use and wont. When it, too, is no more and only fragments and documents lie buried in museums, perhaps its value may also be realized, if too late. Future generations may envy the twentieth century its privilege of seeing actually in working condition this product of the East and of all antiquity.

It is hard to tell which is the greater miracle: the survival of these dramas, that have come down unchanged by so much as a sigh or a flutter of a fan from father to son through the centuries, or the audience that enjoys them. Music that delighted the ears of Japanese contemporaries of Charlemagne, farces that raised their first chuckles in mediæval warrior circles, dances whose symbolism was evolved by white-robed priestesses in primeval forests unquestionably are romantic. But so are the people who feel romance.

The citizens of Greater Tokyo—millions of theatergoers —for the most part find the *Kabuki* nearer to their hearts than the modern problem play or custard pie comedy. Though they live in modernity and earn their daily rice in industry, they are still attuned to the rhythm and imagery of outmoded times. To discover a parallel case, one must imagine the present population of London mainly applauding Will Shakespeare, at the Old Globe Theater, produced by men and boys, actual descendants of Burbadge and his fellow actors, while a small minority secedes to sample Ibsen. Or one might fancy a modern audience in Athens crowding to the amphitheater to applaud the tragedies of Æschylus produced in the exact, ancient manner with masks, cothurnus, and tragic chorus, while some "Acropolis Cinema

Hall" just across the way competed for favor with a high-powered salesmanship skit.

That is the miracle. The past in Tokyo is alive and it actually competes with the present. Ibsen, Shaw and Charlie Chaplin fail to supersede the kings and fairies, ogres and distressed maidens of early times. On one side of the Senda-gaya, contemporary life is presented with its conflicts and realities; across the river, exists one of the most amazing refuges from life ever created by mortals. There is no such theater capital elsewhere in the world to-day.

CHAPTER XXIV

FROM "FORGETTING WINDOWS"

ONE might think Japan had a dearth of buildings of cultural significance if advertisements alone were relied upon, for these emphasize human or purely natural curiosities—blossom festivals, dancing girls, rickshaw pullers, and the sacred shape of a mountain. It is true that the country is comparatively poor in historic piles of stone—pyramids, a Borobudor, a walled Soochow or Carcassonne, a Versailles or a Potsdam. Nevertheless it possesses royal and religious edifices of wood that rank among the wonders of the earth. Some are frescoed with what has been described as a "decorative richness unrivaled in any country of the world," while one of the temples is declared by the critic, Louis Ledoux, "unspeakably sublime and matched, if matched at all, only by St. Mark's in Venice" and possibly another church in Palermo. The glow of Byzance is equalled by the gold-walled palace apartments in Kyoto; while the European rococo or the extravagant excesses of the Portuguese churrigueresque style are paralleled by the scarlet lacquer carvings of Nikko. Not even in China are interiors more gorgeous.

For several reasons however these treasures of Japan have received less popular attention than her flowers and her dances. Many of the finest are accessible only by special favor and permission must be sought from Lord Abbots or the Imperial Household—a course out of the question for the hurried or unitiated newcomer to the Empire. But the real cause lies deeper: in the fact that the value of any relic of the past depends on the sentiments associated with it. That is, if the love of the Italian Florence prevails throughout the West, it is born of a steeping in the atmosphere of the Renaissance when Dante, Boccaccio and Savonarola moved in the grim shadows of its crenellated walls. So too in the case of Kyoto, the fine southern capital built like Florence by a river in a cup of blue hills. There also every inch of dust is rendered sacred by the imprint of dead heroes' feet. By yonder bridge, the warrior-monk, Benkei, joined in historic combat; in this ravine the gentle saint, Honen, preached his gospel of faith and meekness to a war-distraught generation; in that rustic cottage high on a terrace overlooking a majestic view in the setting of Fiesole, an exiled, unhappy monarch found such consolation in the vista that he named the moon-shaped aperture in the wall his "Forgetting Window"; the small room in nearby Nara, thirteen centuries old, called the Hall of Dreams, was chosen for his hours of meditation by the wise and peaceable Prince Shotoku, a convert to the revelation of Buddha's Way. But to feel the same reaction to the ancient capital of Japan as to Florence, one must be equally familiar with the fierce contests between church and state in the Island Empire. Then the splendor of the Manto sect's shrine, so ornately carved with phœnixes, elephant heads, demons and flowers of gold turned by the sun's morning rays into fantasies of yellow fire, will assume its dramatic place as a factor in the war of extermination waged by the Shogun against a militant, pompous church, in another Reformation, in a clime of corresponding mentality.

Yet a third reason may be advanced for the failure to appreciate the old buildings in Japan. The merit of most of these structures lies in their unity with nature and their decorativeness. This quality is something far more difficult to photograph than the attributes of the well-known buildings of Europe. For example there is a temple near Kyoto where some of the choicest paintings in the Orient are preserved. Every paper-walled apartment is frescoed by a master hand. A room, decorated seemingly with millions of trembling, flying, gray-green bamboo leaves, opens on others painted with flower carts and monkeys, cats dozing under peonies, a brown waterfowl mournfully standing on a dead tree stump in autumnal mist, dancing noblemen with resplendent pantaloons and whirling scarves and fans. Each room folds out upon a garden as carefully designed as the interior, with two monster sequoias of California height at the center and about their base small red maple trees, clipped firs, stone bridges and still pools for the reflection of the foliage. But how can this be reproduced in pictures? It is a warm, living thing instead of an inanimate monument. It depends upon sunlight, the range of color from fresco to garden, spaciousness and calm for the total effect. A camera can handle a Westminster Abbey. Kyoto's superlative achievements must await a new agency of communication.

The outstanding characteristic of Japan's wonderful buildings is their division into the ultra-simple and the ultra-ornate. And this distinction is particularly impressive owing to the circumstance that the more spectacular were built by the humbler personages.

The simplest tombs in Japan are those of her greatest Emperor, the wise Meiji, and his wife, illustrating the extreme restraint that distinguishes the possessors of spiritual power in Nippon—the sons of Heaven ruling by divine right —from those of the temporal arm—men of worldly origin who seized the power from priest-kings. High above Kyoto

AN OLD FEUDAL CASTLE

and approached by a long drive through a forest, these tombs are set. Countless gently rounded hills loom on the horizon, clothed in pine and at the season of my visit in autumn-burned bamboo. Only the curved top segments of the hills were visible for the bases were sunk in a sea of white fog. Nowhere stood a sign of house or road. Not a sound was heard. Silence, fog, and files of hills were the composition for a painting of the old Sung school.

But facing the panorama was an enclosure with a plain Shinto gate, in the center, of unpainted and uncarved wood. According to Shinto custom, we paused at a brimming stone well to wash our hands before passing through the gate. We then stepped upon a broad terrace. Before us rose two giant mounds, in contour suggesting the mountain silhouettes all around. Their dazzling purity was unmarred by statuary, carving or flowers. That was all there was to see at Momoyama. Nothing but mountains raising curved summits of bronze and umber foliage out of fog and, high among them, two round tombs. Yet a stark, classic majesty had been secured.

On the contrary, the most gorgeous resting place, one of the most pompous in the world, stands farther north among the temples of Nikko which seem carved from giant blocks of solid scarlet lacquer. It was built to honor an ex-village headman, Ieyasu the Viceroy. Nor is this the only anomaly in the Japanese realm. The quiet garden at Mount Hiei was the retreat of an Emperor, a son of the Sun Goddess, but the vast masonry of the castle at Osaka was designed to pamper the luxurious tastes of warrior Hideyoshi, the son of a farmer mortal. As for the imposing fortress palace in the heart of Tokyo, that too was planned by a lord and inhabited by the farmer boy's successors, the Shoguns. Only in modern times has an Emperor dwelt there.

Consequently, if Nikko is the incarnation of the lavishness we are inclined to expect of the East, it is also the expression of power. Set in a forest of cryptomeria trees it recalls the California redwood groves. Everywhere the green defiles of enormous trunks, overgrown with moss and mold, make perspectives which dwarf the human forms of pilgrims to the size of puppets. Down these damp, still vistas, the temples glow like magically petrified bonfires whose flames of gold, white, and crimson are caught and held at the utmost twist and leap. One approaches along the aisles by a series of climaxes; now, far off, a scarlet gate stands forth; then, under the tree boughs, two grimacing Kings of Hell brandish their weapons; or, in a vast semicircle of the forest, a priestess in dangling headdress is dancing; again, pompous terraces lead up from court to court, gate to gate, until it seems that beams could bear no more burdens of carved and painted monkeys and peonies, elephants, lotus and gilded waves, that roofs could curl in no more curious ways, and that any edifice more ornamental would cease to be an edifice and become a heap of brilliant deposits. The elaborate scheme is only held in leash by the fact that the towering forest shuts in with cool green upon it all. Nikko is the farthest toward the baroque that Japan has ventured.

A similar contrast between the classic expression of divine right and the pomp of physical might is revealed by two palaces in Kyoto. In the one, the Gosho, generations of the Imperial Family lived in monastic simplicity and sometimes indeed close to actual impoverishment. As remote as possible from the baroque is this regal residence surrounded by severe walls of white plaster and black beams. The grounds contain no color, no gaudy pavilion, no carving. Neither grass nor flowers grace the ground. Moss alone carpets the entire area with a truly royal thickness, here billowing over a mound, there flooding a level space or creeping up the trunk of an immense tree. I had never imagined moss could be so voluminous. The paths are of gravel, edged like seashores with pebbles but carefully placed, smooth and oval. The trees of great age and size have roots either developed or trained to grow largely above ground where they coil and writhe like bundles of huge pythons. Around their trunks have been cultivated gray, incredibly wrinkled wisteria vines of equally unusual girth; they wind their tentacles up and up the trees to a great height from which they drip their long, strange hair. A stream of sluggish, greenish water moves through the garden and across it is flung an old bridge with the hump not in the center, as the symmetry-mad Occident would place it, but on one side; it is partially covered with wisteria and near it stands a crumbling lantern. This is an eerie, gray retreat befitting the political drama represented in that change from the pomp of the Shogunate to the modest refuge of the Imperial Household.

Nijo Castle, built by the Viceroy, or Shogun, nearby, is so magnificent as to appear a direct affront to royal sensibilities. And this was precisely what Hideyoshi intended. He erected it in the sixteenth century, pouring immense sums into its decoration "as an unmistakable indication that the might and wealth of Japan were represented here and not in the Gosho—where the Emperor dwelt." Nijo was surrounded with a mighty wall of gray stones, smoothly cut and fitted without mortar, that rose from a green moat in a long inward curve, upholding another layer of white plastered stones set with great beams of dark wood retained in position by handwrought nails; on these huge timbers were laid the crowning roof of dark tile shaped like swallows' wings. We rolled under an imposing gateway, between heavily studded doors, into the courtyard where sentries stood on guard.

One feels so safe and small within these great feudal fortresses of Japan, for they awe with their protective strength. The race has built its tea cottages tiny and doted on dwarfed trees but, when it came to erecting defenses against a foe, neither stone nor timber was spared. No suggestion of the "quaint" or the "wee" creeps into the mind as one stands behind such soaring bulwarks, gazing at the stone steps that lead, twisting, to the blue sky where men-at-arms pace to and fro. Huge pines strain upward, seeming to stretch starved claws toward the wall edge and crows scream and laugh on their topmost boughs. The Shogun's palace lacks that menacing aspect of some of the European strongholds, so grim with their heavy buttresses, loopholed for cannon and recessed with dungeon-depths. Nijo's walls are white and trim and imply discipline more than danger, but they are very impressive.

A second large gateway, built of solid timber, the beams ending in a swirl of painted carvings depicting phœnixes in flight, its roof loaded with weathered thatch, leads into the inner court where the palace still stands. This structure seems especially huge, perhaps because of the tendency to consider everything in Japan in miniature. Here are vistas of high, dim rooms, some with heavily coffered ceilings and all paneled and screened in paper covered with gold. Gold appears in every possible design: in mist-like clouds, in plain, heavy coats, or inscribed with flowing strokes. Gold gleams through a painted bamboo forest amid which life-size tigers stalk, radiant pheasants peep, or enameled butter-flies wing their way. Down long verandahs beyond countless rooms open landscapes of flat sheen. The enormous palace seems a mass of gold.

TO JAPANESE EYES, A VERY ELABORATE INTERIOR ARRANGEMENT

Each chamber is decorated in a different mood. One is a leopard room where fierce cats leap or crouch within a green-stemmed glade. Cats with gnashing teeth, protruding eyes and amusingly pillow-like shapes betray the fact that their native creator had never seen such jungle apparitions and thought them merely playful, overgrown tabbies. One hall is adorned with eagles; another has a ceiling on which fourscore golden peacocks were embossed, each in a different attitude; a third, planned for ministers of state, displays wild geese in flight. There is a rooster room, a fog room, a cloud room, a spring-flowers antichamber, an autumn-melancholy salon, and I never figured how many more. All the floors about these rooms were especially constructed to squeak musically—they were called "nightingale floors"— since the Shogun liked to know who was moving about and particularly whether anyone was stepping stealthily behind him.

Within these apartments lived the ladies of state. Upon these low balconies they leaned, quoting verse; here harps were plucked with ivory nail guards and chubby baby dancers shook their sleeves and spun around; here fans were painted and eyebrows plucked, plots were hatched and elegant hearts were broken. I could see the shadowy figures move about me. Had I not learned from the old dramas on the Tokyo stage how they behaved and spoke, knelt and sang?

Through a multiplicity of golden-walled boxes we came at last to the grand Hall of State. It was quite large enough to have served in a European baronial castle, but it was far from a replica of its distant contemporary. No fireplace roared with flame fit for roasting whole swans and a boar; no rough stones were hung with thick tapestry; huge goblets, the clank of armor, guttered torches and oaken settles seating a battalion were wanting. This hall was more delicately planned and equipped. The acreage of the floor was covered with fine matting bound with brocade. Two walls were paper on frames of lacquer; the others were painted wood. At one end was a raised dais where once had rested the cushion throne of the mighty Shogun himself. On the wooden wall behind was painted an enormous pine tree, life-size, whose slanting trunk and gnarled boughs, veiled in a gray mist of needles, loomed against a background of shimmering gold. A mere canopy over a chair has never made so appropriate a setting for a high potentate.

As I knelt in that empty audience chamber, I could well imagine the living Shogun above me, in his wide brocade trousers and exaggeratedly puffed sleeves—just as I had observed him in the plays. He would be leaning an elbow on a tasseled cushion and his face would be solemn and weary but I rather suspected all the same that he would be on the alert for any sound from the nightingale floors and corridors. And right beside him, sunk into the wall behind a sliding panel, was a handsomely decorated "safety chamber" which was opened for us to peer into. So long as he took no chance, he was still the mighty Shogun.

One could fancy this hall below him filled with kneeling courtiers costumed in puffed layers and starched billows of gauze and with little black topknot-protectors on their heads. The soldiers, in bamboo armor, would be leaning on their tasseled spears. Ministers would be reading their reports in that sonorous, courtly speech of past centuries, punctuated from time to time by genteel bows. How human everyone seemed—no more incomprehensible or alien than the Western noble folk whose ghosts haunt the castle corridors of Europe.

And what scenes, significant in history, have been enacted on this spot! This hall is as dramatic a place as the Tennis Court of the Paris Revolution for here in 1867 the last of the

Shoguns, Keiki, humbly handed in his resignation to the
Emperor, accepting for an overweeningly proud line of Tokugawas the humiliation they had imposed on royalty. Here
the Emperor Meiji met the Council of State and pledged
himself to establish a deliberative assembly for the nation.
Thus an act was performed as an import as profound for
Asia as Napoleon's abdication signified for Europe.

If Nijo Castle is the Versailles of Japan, the Katsura
Palace is its Petit Trianon where courtiers once played at
elegant rusticity. It was also built by Hideyoshi who engaged the greatest of his people's garden-geniuses to design
the perfect setting. The glory of the place is accordingly its
garden, an original which inspired many tinier imitations
in various parts of the Empire. In order not to look too artificial it was partially enclosed by a dense forest; again,
as in other famous Japanese gardens, I was struck by the
boldness with which artists set off their dwarf trees against
the majestic cryptomeria or natural maple groves. They
seemed to feel that the gnomish spirit of the stunted trees
belongs best to the forest and that the finest gardens are
those hinting of a dark wilderness from which they have
been wrested. Thus, like Japanese civilization as a whole,
the garden is inseparable from the mystery of trees. Pines
form the adornment of the Noh dance, the background for
the shogun's throne, the environment of the tea cult, and the
emblems of the Shinto faith. It is this very kinship with
Nature which saves the nation from being so unbearably
cute as some writers would represent it. Its finesse finds so
complete a foil in arboreal majesty.

The peculiar excellence of the Katsura garden lay in the
large number of different views embraced within its compass. From each stepping stone, some fresh impression
could be gained. Now it was an island with storm-tossed

pines hinting at the real islands of the typhoon-swept Inland
Sea; again it was a peaceful pool artfully framed in a vine;
the next moment it might be a wonderful bridge of rhythmic
form. Vignettes were endlessly composed and recomposed as
we promenaded round about. Matching the garden was the
palace building of an obviously royal rusticity. It was perfect
in the smallest detail, even the doorlatches, for instance, being
cunningly wrought in shapes of the crescent moon to harmon-
ize with the moon-shaped windows. Balconies overlooked the
choicest views and from one of these, the Moon-gazing
Platform, could be seen a distant lantern in which fireflies
used to be imprisoned to give the proper twilight mood and
a waterfall whose tone was subdued to sound just the right
faint murmur to noble exquisites. The Palace was charming—but oh, how chilly!

In this pavilion, where no heat could be introduced to
spoil the dainty wood-joinery, the frail walls, one saw hol-
lowed-out stone bathtubs, furnishing rather more evidence
of personal cleanliness amid the discomfort than in
Potsdam, Fontainebleau or Versailles. This royalty humped
over charcoal embers, nursing frigid feet, bravely bearing pain, made a species of poetry out of the terrors of
autumn and winter. It went into ecstasies over the shape of
snow mounded over the limb of a tree, the fall of distant
water, the flicker of a bird's wing, the splash of crimson
leaves on a sandy path. Verses were written on such things.
Wonderful textiles were chosen to symbolize the seasons.
The very doorlatches, window shapes, picture tassels expressed
the æsthete's refinement. No royal contemporaries in the
courts of Europe could have been sensitive to such a degree.
It is impossible to picture the early Burgundians, for example—those bold, rude, lusty fellows of the epics—clustered
about a stream, dropping gilded fans to watch the fine shapes

they made as they floated away. Cultured, exquisite were these folk of Japanese legend—and doubtless more stoical too than many a doughty Frank or Saxon blowing foam from a full drinking-horn and toasting his toes before a burning tree.

In other shells, in European castles and palaces or on the nobly beautiful marble terraces of China's Forbidden City, I had not felt more than the natural sadness evoked by all places where life was once abundant and now has fled. But there seemed something more wistful about the melancholy of Japan. Perhaps this was partly due to the fact that her old palaces were so close to Nature, and hence so near to high mystery, and partly due to the character of her political drama. If much of the regal temper was very conventional in an Eastern fashion—finding stilted images in autumn rain, sleeves wet with tears, the cry of lonely cranes in the marsh—yet the feeling had a substantial basis, for Japanese emperors more than other rulers have been at the mercy of fighting men. So their courtiers had other reasons for being convinced of the insecurity of life than Buddhist doctrine—they were reduced to sackcloth and ashes by warring clansmen time and time again.

Fujiwara, Heian, Hojo, Minamoto and Ashikaga were more powerful and often more luxurious than the Divine Family itself with which they intermarried by force and which they ordered to withdraw into monasteries at their will. Did not the Shogun send away a Son of Heaven to hide from men in a small, rustic cottage far up the mountainside? But his refuge was different from a barren island hovel. The Japanese Elba, a thing of beauty, could be a joy forever!

One of the walls of his cottage the Emperor pierced with a crescent-shaped aperture framing in its gentle curves a scene of the most perfect and tranquil loveliness. By this opening when oppressed by cares of State, he would often retire to dream. So it became known as his "Forgetting Window." I too have looked through that small window upon that selfsame scene and felt that its beauty was rare enough to cause a lapse in the most imperial memory. Nature and genius in collusion had planned an arrangement of watercurves and sky, stone and pine needles in which hardly an inch was left disregarded in the huge picture. Every foot of sand in the paths had been swept by long strokes of a broom into gentle tidal markings; every twig on the dwarfed trees had been twisted to a predestined shape; the very moss had been trained on the stones and the stones selected, pebble by pebble, for form and size. It had been the lifework of a great mediæval artist and is to be rated, I believe, with a very few choicest spots on earth. It is a supreme heirloom. As splendid a reason is thus presented for visiting Japan as the Altar of Heaven offers for a trip to Peking. Nowhere may one more utterly shed thoughts of the present than by this truly named Forgetting Window looking out, as through a magic casement, on the past.

Unluckily the garden, like many of the rare sights of this country, is not so open to the public as many other shrines. This exclusion however is almost imperative. Versailles and Potsdam may be visited in crowds, for life and animation suit admirably their halls and terraces. But the old gardens of Japanese emperors, though also large and nobly proportioned, would be spoiled by hurried footfalls and strident ejaculations. Their charm is the mood of dreamy solitude they induce, heightened by the circumstance in the case of the Hiei garden that it belonged to a monarch during fifty years of enforced retirement from the world. These were not show places on the order of European palaces. They were hermitages for æsthetically inclined and closely secluded royalty.

At the highest spot in the Hiei garden stands a tea house three centuries old but still in such good condition that its verandah is as polished as when an emperor was reflected in its surface. On one corner of this verandah, we were told, he was wont to sit meditating under a bough. A tree stood beside the tea house, its arm made to imitate the sweep of its predecessors centuries ago and create a frame for the view. The scene remains the same beloved of the ruler: a far-off spacious vista of Kyoto, the curving flash of the river spanned by bridges and bordered by willows—the whole softened, in the autumn, by misty clouds. From this site the deposed monarch could watch the city and the palace he had been compelled to resign to the Shogun; they lay before him framed by the arms of the guardian tree.

But if the Emperor grew too restless at the sight he had only to turn a corner of the verandah and find peace within the forest. A path had been planned for him, in part cunningly embedded in casual patterns with ruby and gray stones suggesting fallen leaves and in part made of the finest white sand. On the morning of our visit, it was freshly swept, still showing the strokes of the broom so that we could observe what art this implied, sweeping the paths of an emperor, each stroke curved as perfectly as with a brush. The sand was as tempting to the foot as new-fallen snow.

Forest clothed the entire height in which the garden was set with huge mountain shoulders that folded protectingly on either side of the terrace. The whole hillside in autumn was turned into what the Japanese aptly call a "brocade," in which pine trees form the rough background while the chief design is red maple splashes and powdery gold bamboo feathers. We too entered this forest, following the Emperor's course which twisted along through the hushed, dark, cool depths. Little steps were formed in the most fanciful irregularity, one of a satin-gray stone, another just below of a tree root, as if the ladder had been fashioned by nature instead of persistent man. The path wound under the lichen-crusted stems of old trees, past a wonderful lantern pierced with moon-shaped openings and topped with a roof resembling a thick toadstool crust. The trees stood steeped in thin fog and their cloudy foliage of green, of gold, of crimson, was motionless. No birds sang above. Enormous spiderwebs, jeweled with moisture, bound the trunks together in a texture so large and yet delicate that one imagined they had been in the weaving for hundreds of years by the great many-limbed monsters that sprawled in their hearts. The spiders were so big and so conspicuous that apparently it would be a foolish fly indeed that ignored the enemy. But perhaps the spiders cared more about assisting the gardener, by hanging so quietly under the foliage in a dew-beaded web. No doubt these were poetic spiders, "spiritually" above flies.

At one point in the long descent we came to a rustic bridge spanning an inlet to the lake. From the top of its curve we could look down a shadowy ravine filled with quiet, dark water named the "Autumn Color Ravine." One of the grand sights of the land, where the best spots for viewing cherry or maple blossoms have been catalogued and compared, is this scene. Possibly because the water was so dark and clear, it reflected with such startling warmth the scarlet clouds of leaves that hung over it. Japanese maples are a true sensation; their leaves are small thin-pointed stars, in autumn painted with the deepest, strongest scarlet than can be conceived. A few of the stars had fallen on the surface of the water, the rest were mirrored, and the whole lake looked like a sheet of fine, warm-toned, mediæval stained glass.

But it was from the porch of a distant cottage that we suddenly encountered the "Pond Where Dragons Bathe," a shining, islanded expanse, guarded by a pair of miniature castles which rose, white as swans and curved as swords, from the water. Beyond the farthest shore opened a wild immensity of mountain prospect; and viewed through drifting mist the scene was that of another world in which any magic thing might happen. I half expected a silver-scaled dragon to emerge from the pond, flicking the moisture from his rough sides, and trundle up the bank. And I so lost myself in fancy that when a hoarse scream broke upon the air, instinctively came the thought—the voice of the Dragon!

Deafeningly it rose; then subsided completely. The trees stood immobile; not a ripple stirred the lake; no monster had raised his crest. And then I realized that it was a modern Dragon I had heard—a factory whistle from new Kyoto—whose bellow had shattered the enchantment.

CHAPTER XXV

THE LOTUS AND THE DYNAMO

Noh and the tea cult, classic drama, or landscaped gardens, altars and halls of state display phases of that culture so valiantly defended by champions of the "good old days." But to realize fully what an emotional factor the past is in the life of present-day Japan, one should do what the natives themselves do when they wish to escape the depression of modern surroundings and refresh their spirits with Nature and great memories—namely, go to Nara.

Nara still keeps an astonishingly strong hold on the Japanese minds. Plainly successful, "hustling" city youths admit to day-dreams in which they run away from Tokyo or Osaka turmoil and hide for the remainder of their lives in one of the monasteries that abound in the hills of the South. Many adults, having spent a quiet year or two there between college and a career and finding themselves unable to shake off the spell of that holy place, return to it for vacations or to meditate when they are confronted with a crisis in their lives. Some persons are willing to make real sacrifices to attain the peace of Nara; an acquaintance broke off promising relations with a business concern and with his bride moved to Nara in search of contemplative release.

This rôle of Nara is a feature unique to Japan. In other nations, the modified monastic tradition cares for the gilded youth in universities such as splendid Oxford or Heidelberg, where adolescents may enjoy romantic and dreamy, but well-supervised leisure. Japan has preserved the older ideal as well as accepted the new. Her refuge for youth invites also the mature and the aged; it is a region devoted to forests and philosophy, watched over not by proctors but by the ghosts of mediæval hermits.

Of course one may visit Nara as a sightseer. Curios for the curious are there in plenty. The left eyeball of Buddha, the gold-leaf prayerbook of a ninth-century statesman, or the divinity that once guarded the pillow of an empress are visible among countless objects, beautiful or merely odd. But chiefly one goes, not so much to see as to feel, to relax tension, to yield before a mood created in one of the most tranquil, history-hallowed landscapes, practically unmarred by modern invasion, left in the world.

What is this mood? What is the spirit that lingers in this secluded valley? The Japanese have difficulty in formulating to a foreigner what they experience. They approach their holy places with awe and humility, scarcely giving articulate expression to the peculiar emotions stirred in their presence. Often they can tell us no more about the meaning of Nara than a famous poem communicates on the Great Shrine of Ise:

> "What it is
> That dwelleth here
> I know not;
> But my heart is full of gratitude
> And the tears steal down."

But if we try to analyze "what it is that dwelleth here," at Nara, we find some definite clues. A certain feeling of simplicity and strength is evoked for us by dark and mighty forests and by sacred animals wandering in their depths like enchanted beasts of mediæval fable. This primeval and religious atmosphere is deepened by the fact that so many heirlooms are still displayed in settings such as, East or West, are far older and more poetic than museums: temple reliquaries and kingly treasure chambers. In such backgrounds relics have more power to summon sentiment in the beholder. Moreover in Nara we are face to face with a legendary past for some of its buildings are among the oldest in Asia. The Horiuji Monastery in the neighborhood is the world's most aged wooden building; the Todaiji is the largest wooden structure; and the Shoso-in is one of the very few places on the earth where valuables so ancient have been obtained without excavating and in their original position. Some idea of the antiquity of the place may be formed by remembering that the Hall of Dreams at Horiuji is many centuries older than the Temple of Heaven at Peking or the Forbidden City; that it antedates the Ming tombs at Nanking and India's Taj Mahal by about eight hundred years.

But it is not because Nara is so hoary with age that we pay our respects; rather are we drawn to her by the bright youth of her sculptures. In the city's prime, Buddhism had just brought the revelation of divine mercy to the forest-dwelling, tribal Japanese; thus enveloping the oldest of its art in the incomparable freshness of a dawning faith. Not yet had art degenerated into overladen ornament and appeal to a superstitious populace nor were idols turned out by the gross from factories. Even the sublime great Buddha at Kamakura, he of world fame, is more modern, mature, sophisticated; whereas the Nara treasures are rather adolescent divinities, thin as certain Gothic carvings. Their lotus pedestals await formalization. In some of the early examples we see a long stem that lifts the blossom swaying high in the air and holding barefoot, soft-robed figures with joyous faces, making gestures of gentleness and mercy.

Admirers of this period of Buddhist art are an increasing international band. One of the first was the American, Fen-

A CARVING OF KWANNON, GODDESS OF MERCY, AT NARA

ellosa, who besought the priests at Horiuji to unwrap the figure of their Kwannon swathed for a thousand years. When they consented there was revealed a severely simple yet gracious masterpiece—one of the highest achievements of Asiatic art. More and more, art students are turning to such relics to study the early glory of Buddhist sculpture instead of relying solely on those surviving in war-harrowed China or in her plundered stores scattered throughout the world.

What has kept such an atmosphere at Nara is the fact that life departed from this isolated capital in the ninth century after Christ. Since then, it has been abandoned behind high mountain ranges, left to decay and to the encroachment of forests on its broad plain. There is a slumbering town called Nara now, subsisting on woodcarving, goldfish-growing and pilgrims, but it lies far off from the sites of the old capital and Imperial tombs or shrines. Some of these, untouched by excavators, still are hidden by soft mounds, covered with grass and sacred groves. Worn old roads and paths lead across the valley and through the woods to cloisters for men and for women, to a temple where rice paddles are heaped as votive offerings by pious peasants, or to some tiny shrine commemorating the love suicide of a famous beauty and the willow tree upon which, so legend relates, she hung her embroidered cloak.

The streets of Nara are populated largely by the tame, sacred deer, who wander down the silent, shuttered lanes, or in wide avenues mix with the ordinary traffic of bicycles, rickshaws and bullock carts. Some come singly, hunting pilgrims whom they waylay and tease for rice cakes. Often, on lifting the eyes to a distant hill some proud, little head is noticed, raising spiky horns against the sky. Frequently the deer descend in droves, gamboling over the mossy park spaces, running tilt against a tourist who displays his cakes too openly. They will leap upon him like overgrown dogs, their forefeet against his breast, battle among themselves for booty and then, capriciously, run away in long leaps over hedges and low walls, and escape under the great stone gate that guards the entrance to their home, the forest.

If one follows these beautiful guides, one may wander for hours up the rocky path that leads to a shrine concealed in the wooded hills. Stone lanterns, lighted but once a year during a midnight festival, line the path; there are thousands of these memorials, built in all sizes and shapes, some like spreading umbrellas and others beside them tiny as toadstools, with brims crumbled by age and water-drip. If it is a feast day, throngs of men, women and babies from neighboring villages will be clambering up and down, buying cakes from gayly kimonoed vendors, not talking much but smiling constantly and turning to watch the pilgrims from afar, recognizable by white coats and straw hats.

The trees shut the path closely in—huge oaks and cryptomerias—and the dark ground between their columnar aisles is covered with tall ferns, plumed grasses and dripping moss. Deer trip and bound through the glade. Does peep from behind lanterns; rude old bucks clamor for food; fawns rustle in the ferns or nest between great roots. The forest, like others of Nara, is far too neatly tended to seem rough or forbidding; but, if not primitive, it makes a primeval appearance and overawes by sheer extent—more than a thousand acres are included in this single shrine-park—and by the girth of individual tree-giants. And as one penetrates farther into its recesses, fancying oneself in Sherwood Forest, perhaps, one is reminded that, after all, Robin Hood's was a mere modern compared to this park. The shrine in its heart was founded a century before King Alfred ruled over a Britain yet covered with oak tangle and thicket.

The deer inhabitants at Nara belong, also, to another world than that of Sherwood Forest. Instead of being targets for noble or outlaw, they were protected by religious rulers. In the eighth century, the Empress Koken, a zealous convert, forbade the destruction of any living creature in her domain. Buddhists have regarded animals as more than the servants or even friends of man—as manifestations of the Universal. Saigyo, the Japanese poet and lover of animal life, antedated the Christian Saint Francis by two centuries. The East was many generations before the West in obtaining vision of the oneness of man and nature. The Japanese, in particular, have appreciated the mysterious qualities of animals. Though they had been meat-eating, hunt-loving people before they fell under the mild sway of Buddha, they became more vegetarian than the Chinese. They hymned the animal in poems; they captured the very essence of cat, monkey, or tossing-maned horse in painting and carving. It was indeed a serious clash of racial attitudes when, in the early days of foreign intercourse, several Western intruders insisted on hunting deer and got themselves inconveniently shot by outraged natives.

This early communion between man and animal is most enchantingly indicated by the so-called "deer-calling ceremony," which is one of the chief entertainments offered to visitors by the mayor and governor of the prefecture. One is roused in the early, foggy morning to hurry toward a place in the park where tables are spread with platters of ceremonial rice cakes, each imprinted with a likeness of the Nara Buddha, recalling the legend that Buddha, the merciful, in one of his incarnations, gave himself for food to hungry animals. For a considerable space of time, nothing happens. No sign of life is to be seen in the still fog-bound, forested hills.

Then, from far away, floats a pale cry. Nearer and nearer the call comes. And at last, up the mountainside, through the mist and between the tree stems, may be seen a leaping shadow playing on a flute—startlingly like the shape of a dancing Pan. The figure runs and leaps, goat-fashion, and after him scamper other gray shadows, all growing larger and ever more distinct as they race downward. Finally, like images on a tapestry that come to life and leave their flat, two-dimensional world, the shadow troupe dashes out of the misty curtain, becomes warm and actual. It proves to consist of a keeper, with a wooden flute, and his hungry charges, the deer, who dash out madly, shaking the fog from their flanks, as though frantic to escape their unreal world and be alive again. They leap and snatch at cakes. Big bucks stage battles with locked horns; fawns run around in circles, crying dismally; and wild confusion reigns in the stamping herd.

With a prolonged stay in Nara, a deep peace descends over the spirit. Time glides softly away as one wanders through the still woods, in pursuit of nimble phantoms, or down half-deserted lanes, pausing to watch the shadow of a horned head against a wall or stare at the curiously similar reflections of a tall pagoda and a giant pine tree that stand together by the lake brim. Often one may join bands of quiet pilgrims in search of some celebrated relic, perhaps a grotesque image of a King of Hell, or the likeness of some tragic saint, such as the statue of a shaven-headed nun, preserved in the Hokkeji Nunnery, whose sad fate so resembled the lot of countless European women in mediæval times. A twelfth-century court beauty, she was immured in a cloister and her lover in a monastery, by their families, and from the letters they wrote each other during long imprisoned lives her personality was revealed. At night, there is

THE SACRED DEER AT NARA

Photo by *William Beard*

almost nothing to do in Nara but ramble in the semi-lit parks, listening to the unhappy cries from the forested hills, which sound as though children were lost and frightened there, but which really are voices of the deer.

The healing power of nature to Buddhist minds is made clear to a sojourner in this valley. Here the divinities created by early artists show most evidently the close affinity of nature and religion; they wear coronets of metal vines, and the nimbus-shields behind their heads unite petals and pointed flames. Throned and crowned with flowers, the Goddess Kwannon also carries in her hands, instead of the more usual flaming ball, lotus stalks. Before the bronze Buddha of Nara, that gigantic image made by Japan as if to confute those who call her "land of the miniature," one sees, in autumn, harvest offerings of bright grain and crimson persimmons laid in bundles. And the monks and sages who once dwelled here, if the wooden carvings represent them truly, must have developed expressions on their wrinkled old faces of the most gentle radiance, as though they had drawn very near to the sublime realization of a single spirit behind the most various symbols—tree, bud, fawn, frog, man.

At length, by such an atmosphere, one is prepared for the Shoso-in, one of the strangest sights in existence. Opened for two weeks in the entire year, in autumn, and then not at all if it rains, this may be seen by guests of the Imperial Household. It is much more than a museum; it is a treasure house to suit a sultan and a sanctuary as well. The magic name of the Imperial House, written upon the sealed doors, has alone protected it for more than a thousand years against the most lawless hands. Civil war might rage around and other buildings go up in flames, but in all these centuries, the fiercest soldiers refrained from breaking the seal, so profound was their reverence for this written word. As old inventories show, most of the things put in there centuries ago still remain, preserved by sheer "moral influence." More holy than Egypt's often-looted pyramids is this repository of the Japanese emperors.

In a park of old trees, the Shoso-in has stood intact for eleven hundred years and more. It looks like a log cabin. A log cabin, did I say? No, a tree cabin, for it is composed of enormous, age-blackened timbers from primeval forests. Their girth and the stretch of the whole high structure, reared above ground on stilts, carry us back in fancy to an age when giants, gods and heroes walked the earth. Within its dark recesses, where we were guided by flashlights, are kept the original treasures of the Imperial Family, chiefly belongings of the Emperor Shomu, put here, after his death, by his consort who tells us in a touching missive how she and her court sorrowingly laid away the objects he had touched. Bronze mirrors of phœnix pattern have a grace fit to reflect the courtliest of faces. Swords rest here of classic shape; flowered carpet fragments that suggest an Indian origin; curious thin-necked samisen; drinking-horns; heavy lacquerware; fans, canopies and flags; harps so old that Chinese no longer know them and one is actually thought to be of Egyptian origin; glass cups that may have come from crumbling Rome, via China, in the seventh or eighth century.

In the depths of this silent forest, within this huge timber cabin, where one might expect to see only rude and clumsy implements, the life of a thousand years ago gives evidence of an astonishingly sophisticated quality. These are far from primitive things—scrolls of paintings, religious utensils, carved masks of dancers, shelves of herb and animal medicine, chess and backgammon boards, brass spoons and silken sandals, ivory scepters, chests and harps, incense wood and brocade sheets, and the crown of Shomu's Empress. They are products of the civilization that had invaded Japan, generations before Roman culture had done much to polish wild Britons on another island at the other side of the globe.

Before European Charlemagne was trying to learn how to write, a Japanese emperor, already taught the fine arts by missionaries from China and converted to the new religion, was drinking from a Roman goblet, listening to music from an Egyptian harp, playing Indian chess, and watching the dancing of a semi-Greek masked player. A generation or so before Charlemagne made himself protector of Christianity and assumed the crown of the Holy Roman Empire, an equally solemn scene was held in Nara, when Shomu appeared before the Great Buddha "with all his Court and declared himself the servant of the Buddha, the Law and the Church." Both Charlemagne and Shomu were forest kings, whose people had long been hunting and warring in the tall timber; both cast longing eyes upon distant citadels of foreign culture. Both achieved the exotic learning, in part by conquest and in part had it thrust upon them; so eager were the Japanese to discover the secret of the Chinese calendar that, so the story goes, they sent an envoy to inveigle a minister of State into a chess game, in which the secret was the stake. Both kings, as befitted their rude origins, built of timber and with peaked roofs, Gothic and Japanese alike, it is maintained, patterned after the nomad's tent-pole. Thus, however vast the differences between Japan and Europe, a Western guest need not feel alien and uncomprehending here, in this resin-fragrant air of the Shoso-in. He may share the awe of his hosts, and marvel at this reminder of the strong, bold and vigorous past that belongs not merely to the Japanese but to humanity.

A more mellow sight is the temple compound of Horiuji,

most ancient of wooden Buddhist structures, whose contemporaries in China were long ago devoured by time or flame. It, too, is a strange survival, standing alone on the wide plain outside Nara. The great city of which it was an ornament has left nothing but a few mounds and stones as reminders of the palaces and broad avenues, once gay with bright-tiled gates and banners. Horiuji, however, even in its loneliness, wears a very cheerful aspect of sunny simplicity. Its old age does not seem very grim; the beams, though tobacco brown, uphold their weight of thatch as sturdily as ever; gargoyle-like demons have withstood the pressure of thirteen centuries. The giant bronze bell continues to give out a deep-throated call to acolytes. And within, though many objects have been removed to the Nara Museum, remain rich stores of images, properly served with altars and flowers. Religious devotions are still paid before the glittering, enthroned divinities and, in one hall, Count Goto uttered a short invocation on behalf of his guests, as though to emphasize the truth that this is, like the Shoso-in, more than a museum collection—namely a shrine where a living spirit hovers.

In one building, I saw the famous wall paintings that have so often startled observers by their close resemblance to Greek-based frescoes in caves of India, or to similarly inspired Byzantine art of early Italy. Though they are about as old as Horiuji, the colors are strong and the lines clear; large, lustrous, East Indian eyes, so different from those of later Chinese and Japanese paintings, betray their exotic origin. Here, as in other chambers of the Horiuji, the thing that most strikes an observer is the common traits and the common background of East and West.

Thus we see how human were the noble patrons of religion in either hemisphere. Just as many a merchant and his wife are presented in Christian art—as for instance in Dürer's work—among the adorers of a Madonna, so here we find, in a superb group, the likeness of Prince Shotoku and his small, cherub-like children, pictured with the Goddess of Mercy, Kwannon. And in another temple, the Hokkeji Nunnery, a statue of Kwannon is kept for which, so it is said, the Empress Komyo herself was the living model— the sculptor, according to legend, fashioning it from her image reflected in a pond.

How the similarities crowd thick and fast! Here are the haloes which have in common with those of Western saints an origin in the sun rays of the Alexandrian Apollo and still clearly betray the flame shape; rosaries; and altar utensils. And how amazing the suggestions of Greek influence in the statues themselves. Ordinary Buddhas give one no preparation for these early figures, so simple and so sublime. They are tall, gracious, lithe, in contrast with the eccentric, heavy, sometimes sullen forms of a later time. Some of the most precious are to be seen in tiny tryptiches, quite like the private shrines of noble families in Europe; these infinitely delicate miniatures of haloed saints, set against inlaid or filigreed screens, were the house shrines of royalty in Japan.

Among them all, I discovered the ideal Buddha. Others seen in Tokyo shops had never satisfied; they were too fat and gross, or too pinched and ascetic; some were more graceful than thoughtful; others were not meditating but taking a sound nap. But here the perfect image appeared. Not more than a foot high—an ivory-toned miniature among neighboring colossi—he was seated on a lotus, his finely carved fingers in the pose of meditation, thumb to thumb. The scroll-like scarves about his shoulders seemed to find the flawless contour as easily as his mind attained the ultimate repose. His face expressed imperishable peace.

The Lord Abbot of Horiuji, a grave man in deep-toned,

flowing robes looked as though he too had discovered the secret of contentment, living in this sun-drenched quiet among these noble lineaments. He invited us to drink tea in his garden within which was a small pond, a few patiently trained fir trees, a small maple as red as a flame. According to monastic rule his male visitors alone were asked to come indoors. In our banishment we were nevertheless served by an acolyte with lacquer bowls containing pink and green cakes in the form of fishes, brown bean jelly and tea in porcelain cups. After a long stay in the sun and the silence, we left the great orange-painted gate of Horiuji with the benign host framed in the portal and turned to witness scenes as old in derivation as the carvings we had just seen within the temple.

A short space away from the temple on the banks of a river stood some of the most celebrated groups of young maple trees in all Japan and then in full autumnal splendor. Under each a rug was spread and upon it a picnic party was making merry. Men were kneeling and quaffing cups of warm, honey-colored wine. Waitresses were scurrying about with trays of tinted cakes. Samisen were strummed and under one tree a droll coquette of a baby, in the florid costume of a geisha apprentice, turned and stamped and waved a flowered parasol while spectators kept time for her tiny feet by clapping hands. Another little girl, in the same kind of robe, with a white-painted face and strange, staring eyes, was dancing solemnly all by herself near the water's edge. Some family parties had brought flocks of children to tumble and romp. A reeling old man, catching sight of us, started in our direction to toast us in his cup of wine and shout what appeared to be bacchanalian jests of a non-translatable order. Standing there under the maple trees, by the rapid river, watching the sylvan mirth, it seemed to me that I was transported even further back in time than by the crowned images of Horiuji. They represented the Apollonian spirit; this the Dionysian. They were patterned after the sun god; this evoked the memory of Pan.

Such was the careless joviality of the Age of the Gods, of which Japanese legends, preceding the arrival of Buddhism, inform us. Then in Japan, as in the pagan West, men danced in honor of their divinities—beautiful dances for the noblest and vulgar dances for the demi-gods. Then immortals were not too proud to stoop and make love to mortals. Hell was near as Heaven to the earth, and the Japanese fishergod, like Orpheus, could descend to claim his dead spouse. In those days, too, animals and men were gigantic and valorous beyond any of a later time; plentiful were the dragons that lay, greedy as Minotaurs, in dank caves of Japan waiting for tribute of maidens; and doughty as a Perseus or a Saint George was the Susanoo-no-Mikoto who could slay any scaled and fire-breathing creature with his enchanted sword. Those were the good, great days when the gods laughed. Buddhist divinities only smile ineffably, but the early Japanese gods were prank-playing and fun-loving; a throng of eight hundred joined in one glorious chorus of merriment at the dancing of the Funny-Faced Maiden, who lured the Sun Goddess from her cave. Did not Plato reprove Homer for letting the gods laugh so uproariously on Olympus? The Homeric Age of Japan was as reckless with its gayety.

There was a dark, as well as a merry, side to this early life before the coming of the world religions, Buddhism and Christianity. And the Japanese, like the Germans, were unable to accept a new religious art without some reservation; they loved to carve queer, contorted gargoyles and gnomish figures, through which their baffled, repressed pagan spirit could find some outlet. It seemed to me that the East

has on the whole wrought more artistically with this demo-
niacal nature. Christendom had its gargoyles and its horned
and hoofed Satan, but where will you find so magnificently
represented in a statue, as in Nara's Mio Kings, all the
fierce, devilish elements in humanity? The Japanese sculptor,
Unkei, immortalized them in the giant King of Hell, with
bulging eyes, arms gnarled as old trees, and menacing scowl.
Buddhism, it seems, did not have a Prince of Darkness
opposed to the powers of light, and so the Mio Kings are
rather helpers than enemies of Buddha. One of the four
Mio Kings is sometimes shown, according to the Ko-ji
Ho-ten, with "his left foot crushing Mahesvara, who had
all the passions, while his right foot annihilates Uma, wife
of Mahesvara, who had all the curiosities; these two unhappy
creatures were accused of having had the taste for learning
and knowledge other than those of Buddhism." Other
strange images may be found in temples scattered throughout Japan, and sometimes their devotees honor them with a
wild, carnival frolic.

The sunny laughter and the frenzied ecstasy are passing
from modern Japan. They belonged to the "golden age"
that is doomed. Perhaps when it is entirely vanished, we
can begin to appreciate it. We may develop nostalgia for
the songs the folk used to chant under the maple leaves to
the rhythm of fluttering fans and clapped hands. We may
yearn in a cold water era for the warm wine and the
pagan epicureanism that asked for no more than a rug
spread by a swift river, under a beautiful young tree, and a
few fair hours in which to achieve happiness. And senti-
mentalists will mourn over that irrecoverable rapture.

One is reminded of an old legend from Europe, belonging
to a time when Christianity was slowly conquering and destroying the pagan gods along the shores of the Mediter-

ranean. Some sailors on a wind-blown skiff, so the story tells, passed near an island, densely forested, and from a dark grove they heard a voice crying: "Woe! Great Pan is dead!"

In the East there was no single deity such as Pan to incorporate the wildness of animals, forests, pagan laughter, dark ecstasy. Nor did Buddhism seek so abruptly to uproot those deep emotions which Christianity attacked. Something primeval and gripping still lingers in Nara. Only gradually, imperceptibly for the most part, has the quality which the West knows by the name of Pan been vanishing from Japan. That is why, in the presence of the giant oaks, the sacred deer, the archaic divinities and the revelers under the trees, the Japanese, instead of indulging in any tragic wail, merely whisper: "What it is that dwelleth here . . ."

Perhaps that inevitably is the reason however that some persons cannot live in Nara in spite of the temptations. It is possible to fancy one's self resigning from the world and retiring to this lovely spot behind the green-blue mountain range, among rivers, shrines, deer shadows and crumbling lanterns, walls painted with Indian houris and reverberating bell-voices. A lifetime would pass tranquilly, perhaps in studying the "Way" with nuns whose doctrines have been unaltered since the days of their royal patron, Empress Komyo; or in singing, or sipping tea, or merely in wandering with an escort of animals along mountain trails. One understands the desire of the Japanese to bury themselves here in an atmosphere of early joy and simplicity. And one knows, too, how they must shudder at the return from Nara to a domicile, say in Osaka.

The modern world lies just the other side of the mountain range, Ikeyama. A train shoots along the Nara plain, across the shimmering rice paddies, past the crooked roads lined with goldfish ponds in which hereditary skill breeds, from age to age, such incredible, gaudy monsters as flourish in their midst. It runs beside hummocks, betokening some relic of the city once covering so mighty an extent with swallow-roofs and labyrinths of walls. And it disappears into a tunnel. After a roaring darkness of eighteen minutes, it comes out high on the other side of the mountain. Below, far away, is spread another great plain—a black, rather than a golden one. One may see industrial Osaka, a swarm of dark tile roofs, a network of telephone lines spun over these, and a noisome cloud of smoke hovering above all. Swiftly, the train descends the mountainside, approaching this great, dismal space, where once Hideyoshi fought to unify Japan, and where now rises the noise of another historic conflict—that between Eastern and Western civilizations.

A foreigner who witnesses this transition from Nara to Osaka—a passage of a thousand years in eighteen minutes—must look upon industrialization with dismay, if not loathing. He must feel apologetic as he looks at the sensitive faces of fellow passengers, young Japanese. What a mental struggle for them to make this change! To leave the other side of the mountain, the yellow plain, heaped with the tumuli of a dead civilization, shadowed by forests, peopled with ghosts and deer—to exchange the lotus for the dynamo, and face the blackened arena of the New Japan!

And yet, what choice has any of us? This is an unreal past that Nara shows us. Nara is a never-never-land, as Japanese will tell you, if you require meed of consolation. The evil that the past contained has perished; only beautiful things, angels and trees, have survived. But how much suffering the golden plain has also known! The reason Nara was abandoned was in itself no idyllic one: the Court moved to escape a grasping Buddhist hierarchy. Civil war has ravaged the forests. Not far away, on Mount Hiei, thousands of idle and vicious monks, corrupt as were so many in Europe before the Reformation, were burned to death, along with their temples, by command of the Shogun who condemned them because they left the sacred book unrolled and gave themselves up to varied and outrageous sins.

When one thinks, indeed, about that lamented past, its unhappiness must be remembered as well as its beauty. The music of koto recitals may charm our ears with its quaintness; but the old songs, like European ballads, are concerned with cruel deeds and lost loves. They relate the terrible necessity of the warrior Naozane, forced by martial ethics to kill a young lad, the age of his own son, and send the head, together with the boy's favorite flute, to the enemy camp; how, hating himself, Naozane fled to a monastery and donned ascetic robes. They relate the lamentation of a general ordered to an unnecessary battle by stupid, silk-clad courtiers; or the wail of an exiled concubine, so melancholy that her lover mistook it to be the sighing of wind through the pine boughs.

The pageantry of the classic stage need not blind us, either, to the tragedy of the plots. Now the story may concern Hironobu, the print-maker, who committed suicide rather than yield to a patron on a point of art, and, dying, exhorted his favorite pupil to paint for the populace, never the nobility. Or it may be the amazing dance of a nobleman who pretended to be a fool, crazy about the Noh, that the Shogun might not suspect him of dangerous brains; with marvelous skill, the actor portrays the silly simper and childish gestures and the occasional flicker of bitter intelligence that betrays itself. These do not show us an entrancing, happy past!

One remembers, too, that the seemingly gentle and even tedious tea ceremony once was an opportunity for wild excesses, when gallants with dancing girls performed it with revelry in surroundings of extravagance. In the fifteenth century it had to be "reformed," and the modern, decorous ceremony was the work of an official censor of the Shogun.

If the lifted eyes meet a temple or shrine on every hill, the mind recalls with a sigh that these do not all owe their building to an especially fine quality of Eastern soul. Many were erected because a marauding knight in civil war would be prevented from firing the forest if he saw the grove made sacred.

And there were always grumblers in the East as in the West. Moralists were complaining of degeneracy before jazz emerged from Africa. The critic, Dazai, in the 1700s in Japan, detested that new fangled instrument, the samisen, and insisted that "its slightest tone . . . sets the evil heart in motion." That music we now consider so classic, he condemned as "vulgar music," saying it "pleased the ears and eyes of the people and they, seeing that it represented the vulgar heart of their own times, were amused and thought it funny, and thinking the classical music not so funny, finally would have it no more." So our ancestors lamented in the waltz age! Really noble music, one gathers, in any zone, died long before the saxophone appeared.

The past is so irrecoverable by modern man, Japanese or Western, and probably so undesirable in its totality that one need not take leave of Nara in a mood of vain regret. Nara has a positive impression to make as well as a negative. She offers the final realization of the unity of two hemispheres. If Tokyo and Osaka show the Twain meeting amid the smoke of factory chimneys, confronting common problems of industry, imperialism, feminism or democracy, so Nara invites us also to remember that East and West are by no means new acquaintances but were introduced to each other in a remote antiquity. On her golden plain, in the treasure house of Shomu, Rome left a visiting card twelve centuries ago; at Horiuji, the spirit of Athens finds its incarnation. In their art, religion, philosophy, and in the actions and ideology of their aristocrats, peasants, warriors, and priests, Orient and Occident exhibited, if not always mutual influence, at least universal behavior traits. One feels more confident that, with such a common background, they can face a future increasingly coöperative.

Nara, in short, but enriches the gift that Japan makes to her guests—a globular sense. Wishing to cultivate this feeling among his own people, the Emperor Meiji, when he was crowned in 1868, commanded to be placed in his throne room, as a conspicuous object among the courtly robes and altar ornaments, a school globe of the world. It was a characteristic racial performance which one scarcely knows how to greet—whether with a smile or a sigh. But the longer the sojourn in the country the more profound the interpretation one chooses to read into this royal gesture of universal awareness.

European travel simply pushes back the curtain of an American's horizon, while leaving beyond Vienna or the Balkans or Constantinople a "jumping-off place" on the other side of which stretches a realm either of nothingness or of vague terrors. In Japan, convinced that there exists no such realm of fearful shapes, he comes at last to a recognition of the spinning world on which he rides—a world that defies the bookish division into hemispheres. The abiding delight of an explorer to the Far East is thus more than a feeling of fellowship with Balboa discovering a new expanse of the earth. Rather it is the reflection, however pallid, of the elation in a Galileo to whom the revolving sphere is revealed.